THE YELLOWSTONE STORY

THE YELLOW

A HISTORY OF OUR

Revised

BY AUBREY L. HAINES

The Yellowstone Association for Natural
in cooperation
University Press

STONE STORY

FIRST NATIONAL PARK

Edition

VOLUME ONE

Science, History & Education, Inc.
with
of Colorado

Published by the University Press of Colorado
P.O. Box 849
Niwot, Colorado 80544
(303) 530-5337

Printed in the United States of America.

The University Press of Colorado is a cooperative publishing enterprise supported, in part, by Adams State College, Colorado State University, Fort Lewis College, Mesa State College, Metropolitan State College of Denver, University of Colorado, University of Northern Colorado, University of Southern Colorado, and Western State College of Colorado.

The paper used in this publication meets the minimum requirements of the American National Standard for Information Sciences – Permanence of Paper for Printed Library Materials. ANSI Z39.48-1984

Cover illustrations: Volume I, Old Faithful Geyser in eruption (1940); Volume II, Lower Falls of Yellowstone River, viewed from Artist's Point (1945).

ISBN: 0-87081-391-9

10   9   8   7   6   5   4   3   2

To Jack Ellis Haynes,
known to his friends as "Mr. Yellowstone"
from his long and helpful association
with our first National Park.

ILLUSTRATIONS

MAPS AND CHARTS

By Kenneth A. Erickson unless otherwise credited.

CONTENTS

"That it has been given to one to see the beauty,
the grandeur, and terror of this region . . .
before the tourists troop through it in unbroken
procession, *laus Deo*."

— Thomas Henry Thomas, 1888.

PREFACE

The Yellowstone Story is an outgrowth of a work begun with
Jack Ellis Haynes shortly before his death in 1962. Those
who knew "Mr. Yellowstone," as Jack was often called
from his long association with the Park, also know of his deep and
abiding interest in its history, but even they are not always aware that
he lived in the area part of each year except two of his seventy-seven.
It was there that he summered in his boyhood, worked in his father's
business enterprises as a young man, and became an outstanding
concessioner in his own right. During those years he met many
characters of the Yellowstone past, saw much of its history made and
had a hand in some of the making—sometimes by helping shape
events and sometimes by recording them.

Jack's interest in an accurate re-creation of the Yellowstone of
yesterday progressed from furnishing historical comments, which
were always a feature of his Yellowstone Park guide book, to writing
those scholarly accounts that provide a charming coverage of such
outstanding events as President Arthur's visit in 1883, the Haynes
Winter Expedition of 1887, and the five stagecoach holdups. It was
his desire to do even more, by turning his former guidebook feature,
"Tid-bits of History," into a "Yellowstone Story" (his title), and it was
there our collaboration began.

With Jack's passing, just as the work was fairly launched, I was
at once deprived of an old friend and a co-author who has been sorely
missed. There are places where the story could have been better told
by him, for Jack was a delightful storyteller; but, if his style is missing,

much of what he knew survives in secondhand form. Thus, though he was not spared to have a hand in the writing, Jack's influence is here and he is truly an authority for this book.

Of course, a book is always the end product of much encouragement and assistance. In this case, Superintendent Lemuel A. Garrison—who was aware of the need for a centennial history a decade ago—gave the project a push by arranging for my transfer from an engineering assignment into a newly created position of Park historian. That moved the Yellowstone Story from a private hobby to an official basis, probably saving it from oblivion after Jack's death.

Others of the Park staff who have had more than a little influence on this work are the four chief Park naturalists, Robert N. McIntyre, John M. Good, William W. Dunmire, and R. Alan Mebane; Dr. Mary Meagher, whose services as curator and pro tem librarian were constantly requisitioned to dig something out of museum storage or sleuth the library for a hard-to-find reference; Bill Keller, whose camera and darkroom were always as available as his technical know-how, and the succession of typists who copied reams of notes and labored over rough drafts and final manuscript pages (among them, Ann Martin, Jean Swearingen, Cathy McPherson, and my wife, Wilma, stand out prominently).

Outside the Park, helping hands were extended by historians Ray H. Mattison and Roy E. Appleman, of the regional and Washington offices of the National Park Service. Others whose assistance deserves special notice are Dr. Merrill G. Burlingame, Montana State University (Bozeman); Dr. Duane V. Hampton, University of Montana (Missoula); Dr. Richard A. Bartlett, Florida State University (Tallahassee); Miss Mary K. Dempsey and Miss Leslie B. Heathcote, former librarians, respectively, of the Montana State Historical Society, Helena, and the Montana State University Library here at Bozeman. Lastly, those persons too numerous for particular mention—the sons and grandsons of early explorers, the stagecoach drivers, old soldiers, former employees and early visitors—who stopped at Park headquarters to share their knowledge of other days, and thus put flesh upon the bare bones of history.

If this work has succeeded in what was proposed—re-creation of enough of Yellowstone's past to typify the whole of it—it is because the author has had the assistance of so many people, as well as the help of others, now gone, who wrote about our first and largest national park. In this regard, the reader should not expect an exhaustive treatment of any phase of Yellowstone's complex and extensive history; rather the intent has been to do only as much as is necessary to an understanding of the flow of events. There *are* occasional drier-than-dust factual treatments—for they could not always be avoided —but these are leavened with interludes intended to show the drama and comedy, also, as typical of life in Wonderland as elsewhere.

Should it seem to some that this work has been a long time in the writing, I take refuge in not being the first to struggle with the problem of how to present adequately a subject so large in a compass as small as the covers of two volumes. Another Yellowstone historian, Hiram M. Chittenden, was troubled by this problem, in a day when the Park's history was not nearly so long or so involved. In a letter to Acting Superintendent Anderson on March 28, 1895, he remarked: "I am afraid that you think I have been a good while at this work, but I came to the conclusion that I might better not do it at all than to do it poorly." As the truth of his statement bore upon me through familiarity with the Park's vast literature, I came to understand that strange supplication of an unknown newspaper correspondent of nearly a century ago, who wrote in his "Cactus Canticle,"

> Come, gentle Muse, my furnace fill with coal,
> Oil-up the heavy journals of my soul,
> File sharp my tongue, and belt-up my jaw bone,
> I sing an idyl of the Yellowstone.
>
> *Bozeman Avant Courier*
> February 18, 1876

May you enjoy the Yellowstone Story, finding something of the spirit of a great Park in it—despite the fact that you have every right to exclaim with the Queen of Sheba, "the half was not told me!"

Bozeman, Montana   Aubrey L. Haines
February 15, 1977

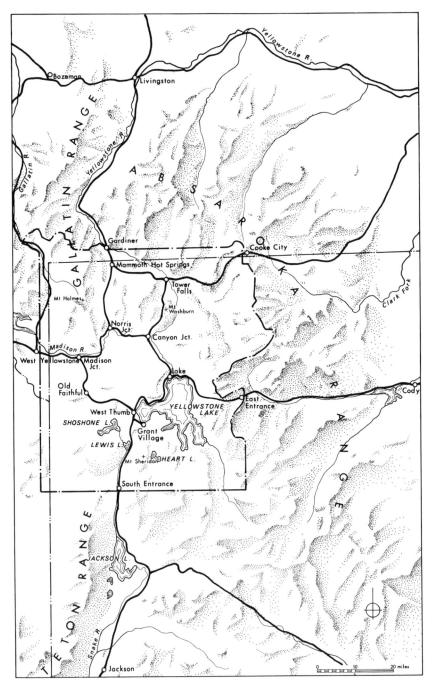

Yellowstone National Park and vicinity.

INTRODUCTION

The Yellowstone is that high, mountain-girt plateau lying astride the crest of the Rocky Mountains in the northwest corner of Wyoming—an area of such natural beauty and unusual features that "Wonderland" has long been its fitting sobriquet. There, within an area larger than the states of Delaware and Rhode Island combined, are superlatives of scenery, geology, and wildlife in a grandly primeval setting; a very appropriate locale for our first, largest, and most influential national park.

For those who have not seen this great plateau—really a series of volcanic plateaus with an average elevation of eight thousand feet—it is best described as having the general appearance of a forested plain more than fifty miles across, incised in varying degree by the drainages of three major rivers and partially enclosed by a rim of rugged mountains rising two to three thousand feet above the general level.

A closer look at this fabulous region should begin with the mountains that tend to isolate it from surrounding areas. Extending entirely along the eastern verge of the plateau, and westward to the Yellowstone River on the north, is the Absaroka Range, while the southern extremity of the Gallatin Range protrudes into the northwestern corner to complete the northern rim and some of the western. This fishhook-shaped barrier of lofty snow-capped summits is effectively breached in only three places: at Sylvan Pass, east of Yellowstone Lake; at Colter Pass, near Cooke City in the northeastern angle, and by the defile of the northward-flowing Yellowstone River. From that prominent skyline, which includes the highest point in the Park

—Eagle Peak, with an elevation of 11,358 feet—the southern and western rims sag toward a jumble of lower, forested ridges which give a particularly open aspect to the southwest corner of the plateau.

Within that mountainous rim stand two isolated groups of peaks: the Washburn Range, which is centrally positioned in the northern half of the plateau, and the Red Mountains, which are similarly situated in the southern half. An indistinguishable feature of the topography is the Continental Divide, meandering in unlikely fashion among the rolling ridges west and south of Yellowstone Lake. Taken as a whole, the Yellowstone Plateau has a distinctive charm which Henry Gannett recognized when he wrote, "In one essential respect the scenery of the Yellowstone Park differs from that of nearly all other parts of the Cordilleras, in possessing the element of beauty, in presenting to the eye rounded forms, and soft, bright, gay coloring."*

Cradled on the Yellowstone Plateau, and in its surrounding mountains, are the headwaters of three great rivers: the Snake, which breaks through the southern rim on its way to the westward-flowing Columbia; the Madison, which slips out through a low gap upon the western flank in its course to the Three Forks of the Missouri, and the Yellowstone, which passes the mountainous northern verge by deep and forbidding canyons, also destined to pour its clear waters into the turbid Missouri.

The master stream of the area, the Yellowstone, has its ultimate source in a jumble of peaks beyond the southeast corner of the Park and it descends through a broad, willow-covered valley to sparkling, blue Lake Yellowstone lying ensconced in a 100-mile shoreline arranged like the print of a great, maimed hand. From those 300-foot depths, the river continues lazily northward through meadows that were once lake bottom. But this idling ends abruptly at the Falls of the Yellowstone, where a drop of 115 feet is followed shortly by another of 308 feet. Thereafter, the river foams along the bottom of the Grand Canyon, in a deep trench that arcs around the eastern base of Mount Washburn. Below this canyon, the Yellowstone is joined by the Lamar River, an important tributary entering from the east; then the combined flow pours down through the Black Canyon to the mouth of the Gardner River and the north boundary of the Park.

The two streams completing the major drainage pattern of the

---

*F. V. Hayden, *Twelfth Annual Report of the United States Geological and Geographical Survey of the Terrtories... 1878* (Washington, D.C.: Govt. Printing Office, 1883), part 2, p.473.

plateau—the Snake and Madison rivers—are less spectacular, but important, because the former is associated with three beautiful lakes (Heart, Lewis, and Shoshone), while the two branches of the Madison nourish the principal geyser basins. Two streams originating outside the mountainous perimeter of the Yellowstone Plateau complete the hydrography of the Park. They are the West Gallatin River, in the northwest corner, and the Falls River (with its tributary, the Bechler) in the southwest. The latter drainage system has many beautiful waterfalls where its headwaters break over the escarpment facing upon the plains of Idaho.

Yellowstone's thermal features, of which there are an estimated 150 geysers and more than 5,000 hot springs, hot pools, and steam vents, are as dependent upon the plentiful water supply as they are upon the internal heat of the earth. Thus, all the important geyser basins are found along streams and on lake shores, and of the six areas which are so classed, three on Firehole River and one on the Gibbon River contain all the great geysers of the Park. These great geysers are without peers anywhere in the world, while the Mammoth Hot Springs have been likewise preeminent since their New Zealand rivals were destroyed by volcanic eruptions in 1886. Such superlatives, backed by the minor features found in numerous "hot spots" scattered throughout the area, have made the name Yellowstone synonymous with thermal activity, perhaps even creating a false impression that the Park is only a colossal, steam-operated freak show.

Indeed, to look upon Yellowstone as a mere hot-water extravaganza would be to overlook its obvious beauty and the less obvious fact that this area is also an unusual wildlife habitat, a great outdoor zoo preserving a more representative sample of the primeval fauna of the American West than is now found anywhere else. Here, living under conditions very nearly those existing when white men first entered the area, are elk, buffalo, mule deer, moose, antelope, bighorn sheep, black and grizzly bear, cougar, coyotes, wolves, beaver and a number of smaller animals, as well as many species of resident and migratory birds. Only one species of the original fauna has been lost—the white-tailed deer, which was a marginal occupant of the Yellowstone Valley. A faunal assemblage of the size and character of the Park's could not be maintained naturally in a smaller or less varied habitat.

A long time ago a Chinese was asked, "How do you like this country, John?", and he replied, "Hellee countly—'leven months winter, other month alle same."*   While that is a deliberate exaggeration, it does express a widely held belief that the Yellowstone winters are of arctic severity. The climate *is* characterized by short, cool summers and lingering winters, but the latter are far from unendurable. This reputation for severe winters is not based so much on extremely low temperatures—for cold spells seldom last more than two or three days—as upon the persistence of moderately low temperatures, accompanied by cloudiness and frequent light snow. While it can be depressing, such weather is rarely a hindrance to a warmly dressed man or woman in a region where the chill factor is seldom great because of the low humidity and infrequency of strong winds.

On the other hand, a Yellowstone summer is delightfully similar to early May at lower elevations in the northern United States, except that a touch of frost is a possibility any night. Add to that a glorious, open fall, with crisp, invigorating days and frosty nights, and you have a climate that balances out.

Should this introduction seem too brief, we hasten to assure the reader it is but the bare boards of a stage on which to marshal actors who, by help of sights and sounds and smells embalmed with more or less perfection on the printed page, should bring you once again that "world apart"—THE YELLOWSTONE.

---

*Item in *Bozeman* (Mont.) *Avant Courier*, Apr. 12, 1883, p. 3, c. 4.

I

OF PRELIMINARY THINGS

In the beginning God created the heaven and earth.
—Genesis 1:1

CHAPTER 1

WHAT'S IN A NAME?

Towers decay
But a great name shall never pass away.
— *Benjamin Hood*

Through association with our first and largest national park, the name Yellowstone has assumed a significance that goes far beyond its importance as a place name. Originating in an Indian designation for one of the major tributaries of the Missouri River, the name has become synonymous, both here and abroad, with much that is basic to the national park idea; it conjures up images of superlative geology, scenery, and wildlife, combined with unusual recreational opportunities. It is a famous name with a very interesting background.

Earlier maps of that portion of New France known as Louisiana hold no hint of the existence of the great southern tributary to the Missouri River which we know as the Yellowstone. The explorations of the de la Verendryes did not greatly increase the geographical knowledge of the upper Missouri region, but they did have the effect of opening a route from Canada to the Mandan towns on the Missouri in what is now North Dakota. Peter Pond's diary shows that a regular trade had been opened by French Canadians prior to 1763,[1] and one of them, Old Menard, settled among the Mandan Indians as early as 1776. He was known to David Thompson, geographer of the North West Company, who considered him "in every respect as a Native . . . an intelligent man . . . brave, gay, and boastfull" and he was still living there with his Indian wife when the Lewis and Clark Expedition passed westward.[2]

Through such habitués, early explorers obtained from Indian sources much information concerning the country higher up the Missouri. Menard is credited with giving Jean Baptiste Truteau accurate information concerning the Yellowstone River "some 300 miles beyond Fort Mandan" in the year 1796, and he may have been the source of the notation "Rock or Crow River" by which that stream made its debut, cartographically speaking, on Collet's map. A map of unknown authorship which appeared in 1797 used the designation "R. des Roches Jaunes,"[3] and it was that form which was translated into English as "Yellow Stone" by Rene Jessaune for David Thompson in 1798.[4]

Historian Hiram Chittenden thought the French forms of Yellowstone—Roche Jaune and Pierre Jaune—were literal translations of the Minnetaree Indian expression, *Mi tse a-da-zi*, but he was uncertain what had prompted the Indians to use such a name. He indicates it could refer to the yellowish sandstone bluffs which are prominent along much of the river's lower course, or to a very colorful feature within Yellowstone Park—the Grand Canyon.[5] Actually, the facts at hand indicate the former as the probable inspiration for the aboriginal name.

The Indians once known as Minnetarees (their separate identity was lost during nineteenth-century tribal consolidations) were a branch of the Siouan Hidatsas. At some time prior to their first contact with white traders, these Indians were forced from an earlier homeland, in the vicinity of Devils Lake, North Dakota, by the unrelenting pressure of other Siouan people. Moving to the Missouri near the mouth of Heart River, they allied themselves with the Mandans and adopted the semi-sedentary life of those agriculturists. Thus, there was nothing in the background of the Minnetarees that would have resulted in a traditional knowledge of the upper Yellowstone River.

Prior to the time when they obtained horses, about 1750, the hunting excursions of the river Indians were very limited, and, even after they were mounted, the mouth of the Yellowstone River—three hundred or more miles distant—was undoubtedly on the periphery of their activities. The mountainous headwater region, an equal distance farther westward, was certainly beyond their reach. In this connection, the broadest territorial claims advanced by the river Indians in later treaty negotiations with the U.S. government extended westward only to the mouth of Powder River; which probably represented the limit of their geographical knowledge.

On the other hand, the Crow Indians who lived along the lower Yellowstone River had an entirely different name for the stream. To them it was the *E-chee-dick-karsh-ah-shay* (there is some difference of opinion regarding the spelling),[6] which means Elk River, a name derived from the fact that it provided a migration route for those animals while passing between their summer range on the Yellowstone Plateau and their wintering grounds at lower elevations. In 1883, the editor of Livingston's first newspaper reminded readers that it was mere chance that had bestowed the name of Yellowstone upon the noble stream flowing past their doors. In his opinion "had Lewis and Clarke first reached the head of our valley instead of its furthest extremity doubtless they would have entered the name in their journal as Elk river and that might have been the name till the present." To that correct assessment it is only necessary to add that the editor was probably not fully aware how much a product of chance the name Yellowstone was. Only the chance acquisition of the whole Louisiana Territory by purchase from a hard-pressed Napoleon Bonaparte made it possible, and also politic, for us to promote the Anglicized form, Yellow Stone, over its French antecedents. Even so, Roche Jaune died hard, for the name was well established with map makers and remained in use through the first quarter of the nineteenth century.

The Yellowstone River did not come to the attention of many Americans east of the Mississippi until Nicolas Biddle published Captain William Clark's map in 1814. Of course President Jefferson had information much earlier from two sources: a map showing the "River Yellow Rock," dispatched to him on April 7, 1805, by Lewis and Clark as they prepared to leave the Mandan towns and continue up the Missouri; and a letter sent by that master of intrigue, General James Wilkinson, governor of Louisiana Territory. On October 22, 1805, he wrote to the president as follows:

> The Bearer hereof Capt. Amos Stoddard who conducts the Indian deputation on their visit to you, has charge of a few natural productions of this Territory, to amuse a liesure moment, also a Savage delineation on a Buffaloe Pelt, of the Missouri & its South Western Branches . . . it exposes the location of several important Objects, & may point the way to a useful enquiry—among other things a little incredible, a volcano is distinctly described on Yellow Stone River.[7]

General Wilkinson had already undertaken that "useful enquiry" of which he spoke by fitting out a small private expedition to explore the Yellowstone River,[8] but no more is known of the venture; possibly it aborted, which was the fate of the next Yellowstone Expedition.

The war of 1812 put an end to the activities of those American trappers and traders who had penetrated to the Rocky Mountains in the wake of the Lewis and Clark Expedition, and further official exploration was out of the question. This hiatus was filled by British traders who developed a very lucrative commerce with the Indians of the upper Missouri River and embarked upon what amounted to a policy of trapping-out the northern Rocky Mountains while they could. That, and a general feeling the British were arming Indians against our frontier, led to a strong postwar sentiment for "showing the flag" on the Missouri River, which was to be accomplished mainly through the establishment of a military post at the mouth of the Yellowstone River.

An editorial appearing in the *St. Louis Enquirer* in October 1818 gives some idea of the purpose to be served by the Yellowstone Expedition:

> The establishment of this post at the mouth of the Yellowstone will be an epochal event in the history of the West. It will go to the source and root of the fatal British influence which has for so many years armed the Indian nations against our western frontier. It carries the arms and power of the United States to the ground which has hitherto been exclusively occupied by the British Northwest and Hudson's Bay Companies. Now American arms and American policy will be displayed upon the same theater. The Northwest and Hudson's Bay Companies will be shut out from commerce of the Missouri and Mississippi river Indians; American traders will penetrate with safety the recesses of the Rocky Mountains in search of furs; a commerce yielding a million per annum will descend the Missouri River. The name of the Yellowstone river will hereafter be familiar to the American ear.

Of course, a plan so grandly conceived could only be executed by the power of steam, for the American of 1818 was as dazzled by the promise of Fulton's darling, the steamboat, as we are today by the promise of the harnessed atom. A contract was given Colonel James Johnson to build a fleet of five steamboats, at a cost of $256,000, in his Pittsburgh yards. The vessels were to be used to transport a garrison commanded by Colonel Henry Atkinson and a scientific corps of geologists, naturalists, artists and topographers under Brevet Major Stephen H. Long, as well as the armament, equipment, and supplies for hundreds of men.[9]

The completed vessels proved to be less satisfactory than anticipated. Three were unable to enter the Missouri River because of their deep draft, and the other two, after spending an entire summer struggling against the current of the lower river, barely got beyond the present state of Missouri—to the Council Bluffs—and only one-third of the distance to the mouth of the Yellowstone.

All that was accomplished in 1819 was establishment of a military cantonment at the Council Buffs, later to be known as Fort Leavenworth. There, the improperly supplied garrison spent a terrible winter, losing over one hundred men to scurvy, which debilitated several hundred more. The American people were horrified, for they had expected so much—they had even been led to believe that the steamboat *Western Engineer* could be taken across the Rocky Mountains to the Columbia River to sweep that stream free of the British, in keeping with the terms of the Treaty of Ghent—and it was the magnitude of their expectations that generated their revulsion. Congress began an investigation that uncovered such gross mismanagement that the Yellowstone Expedition was broken up in the spring of 1820.

This ill-fated venture would be without significance to the Yellowstone story except for a subsequent happening. Major Long, with two junior officers, seven enlisted men and seven civilians, was ordered to explore the sources of the Platte, Arkansas, and Red rivers, which he did. In the official report of the expedition, Long characterized much of the west as almost entirely unfit for cultivation and certainly uninhabitable by people depending upon agriculture for their livelihood. He thought the area between the Platte River and Canada, from Iowa to the Rocky Mountains, was fit only for a buffalo range and as a barrier against hostile incursion from the far west. This Great American Desert thesis, which had originated with Zebulon M. Pike a decade earlier,[10] found such acceptance that it became the official policy of the United States not to promote penetration of the headwaters region of the Missouri River. That decision, and the status quo established by it, prevented an early discovery of the Yellowstone and inhibited the settlement of the Louisiana Territory's hinterland; thus, it may well have been instrumental in preserving the unique features of the Yellowstone wilderness until a time when the American people were prepared to undertake the stewardship of such a novel area.

Colonel Atkinson succeeded in reaching the mouth of the Yellowstone in 1825, where he and Indian Agent Benjamin O'Fallon concluded treaties with fifteen tribes; but it was a decade after the failure of the Yellowstone Expedition—which was to have made the name of the river "familiar to the American ear"—before a substantial fort was built on the Missouri River opposite the mouth of the Yellowstone. This Fort Union, constructed in 1829 by Kenneth McKenzie, was not a military post but an estalishment of the American Fur Company, and was initially supplied in the manner typical of Missouri River commerce in that day—by keel boats laboriously propelled upstream by means of sail, oars, poles, or the cordel, a line with which men on shore or in shallow water towed the boat. But Pierre Chouteau thought the job could be done better with steamboats, and he argued for them until he was at last allowed to contract for a vessel, to be built to his own specifications, for supplying Fort Union and other fur-trade posts along the Missouri River.

His boat, named *Yellowstone*, was launched in the spring of 1831 at a cost of $8,000.[11] It was a side-wheeler drawing 5½ feet of water when loaded with 75 tons of freight—twice the draft and only one-fourth the capacity of later boats—and was really not a good boat for the upper Missouri River. However, the *Yellowstone* proved Chouteau's point by reaching Fort Pierre in 1831 and Fort Union in 1832. Artist George Catlin was a passenger on this voyage and it was his experience in the Indian country that later led him to make the first, though unproductive, suggestion for the establishment of "a nation's park, containing man and beast, in all the wild and freshness of their nature's beauty."[12] After a second season in the service of the American Fur Company, the *Yellowstone* was sold into the New Orleans sugar trade.

The Yellowstone River attached its name to other features. The great lake shown on William Clark's Map of the West as Lake Eustis—so called after the secretary of war in President Jefferson's cabinet—was briefly known also as Sublette's Lake, before popular usage settled the matter by identifying the lake with the river.[13] During the mining era of the 1860s the two great waterfalls below the lake were frequently referred to in the newspapers of Montana Territory by the name of their nourishing stream; the popular usage thus reflected was given an official recognition in 1868, when the map prepared by Captain W. F. Raynolds to accompany his *Report on the Exploration of the Yellowstone River* was at last published.[14]

Captain Raynolds also supplied that region of ill-defined "wonders" with its sobriquet. He called it the Valley of the Upper Yellowstone, which, for a time, carried an appropriate connotation of mystery. It was used in that sense by the local press and by the explorers of 1869—David E. Folsom and Charles W. Cook—as a title for the magazine article describing their trip.[15]

These men, and their contemporaries on the mining frontier, knew the mountain barrier lying east of Yellowstone Lake as the Yellowstone Range, but that name has not fared as well as most derived from the root word. As Chittenden has pointed out in an unpublished study, the name had "not only the right of priority, it had become indisolubly wedded to the literature and history of the Park."[16] Yet, Captain W. A. Jones, of the U.S. Army Corps of Engineers, undertook to change the well-established name of those mountains to Sierra Shoshone as a result of his fortunate crossing of the range in 1873. That euphonious but not very appropriate designation was so galling to certain members of the U.S. Geological Survey that they successfully promoted another change to Absaroka Range—a name that is neither euphonious nor appropriate, and is also nearly unpronounceable (say it *Ab-sar-kee*, which is the Indian name for the Crow nation—the "children of the large beaked bird"). Although Chittenden thought it entirely without justification and argued for a return to the earliest usage, Absaroka has stood,

The mining era generated another Yellowstone expedition. In the spring of 1863, James Stuart led a party of miners out of the town of Bannack (then in Idaho Territory) toward the lower Yellowstone Valley to prospect for gold and look for townsites. Misfortune dogged them, and they were unsuccessful in both objectives, but some stragglers did well enough. William Fairweather and five men were hurrying to catch up with the expeditioners when they met Crow Indians along the Yellowstone River. The Crows often took advantage of such weak groups and did so in this case by robbing the Fairweather party and sending the would-be prospectors back whence they had come. On the return they worked the gravels of Alder Gulch and made the strike that became the Fairweather mining district (Virginia City and vicinity). The influx of gold seekers and others who came to share the wealth of the new El Dorado provided a population sufficient for organization of Montana Territory on May 26, 1864.[17]

During the decade that followed discovery of the Montana gold fields, so-called Yellowstone expeditions became monotonously common—or at least the usage did. Six ventures designated in that manner were products of the mining era: one led by James Stuart in 1864, one attempted by James Fisk in 1865, one captained by Jeff Standifer in 1866, two that aborted in 1867 and 1869, and one under the more elaborate title, Yellowstone Wagon Road and Prospecting Expedition, in 1874. Two other ventures known as Yellowstone expeditions were more directly concerned with the exploration of the area now included in the Park: the Washburn party in 1870 and a winter junket in 1872-73 by Al Jessup, a thrill-happy world traveler of that day.

Over the years, the name Yellowstone has been associated with a variety of places and ventures. Its use in designating our first and largest national park has made it a familiar word here and abroad, yet, strange as it may seem, the new park remained without a name for some time. The men who wrote the organic act of March 1, 1872, were satisfied to refer to "The tract of land in the Territories of Montana and Wyoming, lying near the headwaters of the Yellowstone River,"[18] and it was in the course of early correspondence between the secretary of the interior and his newly appointed superintendent for the "public park" that the area finally became Yellowstone National Park.[19]

Other civil divisions that have used the name were the Yellowstone National Park Timberland Reserve, set aside from the public domain by presidential order on September 10, 1891; the Yellowstone Forest Reserve, created from the aforementioned area in 1902, and Yellowstone County, Montana, created out of Gallatin and Custer counties on February 26, 1883.

Two towns have been identified with Yellowstone: Yellowstone City, established at the mouth of Emigrant Gulch in 1864, and Yellowstone, Montana—previously Riverside and now West Yellowstone. The name has also served as a handle for a coal deposit (the Yellowstone Coal Field), a newspaper (the *Miles City Yellowstone Journal*), and a beverage (Yellowstone whiskey). A number of personalities have become identified with Yellowstone, most prominently Yellowstone Kelly, an early scout and guide; Yellowstone Jack, the nickname for Jack Baronett; and Jack Haynes, familiarly known as Mister Yellowstone.

In the realm of transportation this burgeoning name has made a large place for itself. A keelboat named *Yellowstone Packet* carried such fur-trade notables as Jim Bridger, Hugh Glass, and Jedediah Strong Smith up the Missouri River in 1823; and a flatboat called simply *Yellowstone* returned Montana miners to the States via its namesake river and the Missouri in October 1864. In addition to the steamer *Yellowstone*, which voyaged on the Missouri River in 1831 and 1832, at least two other river steamers carried that name. A *Yellowstone* was listed as reaching Cow Island on the upper Missouri River in 1864,[20] and the Yellowstone Transportation Company—an enterprise of two Bozeman residents, Nelson Story and Dr. A. Lamme—had a light-draught steamer of that name built at Jeffersonville, Indiana, in 1876 for service on its namesake river.[21] Adver-

Luther S. "Yellowstone" Kelly, an army scout who served under Gen. Nelson A. Miles. From Kelly, *Yellowstone Kelly* (1926).

tisements prior to the steamer's departure from St. Louis on May 9 announced its intention to ascend the Yellowstone River to "the head of navigation," but a lack of patronage along the river caused Captain John M. Bryan to change the destination to Fort Benton on the Missouri.

Apparently the *Yellowstone* did not handle well on that trip, and it was decided to lengthen the hull before engaging in the traffic for which the vessel was intended. Thus, it was not taken up the Yellowstone River until the summer of 1877, being then engaged with many other boats in the movement of military supplies for the continuing campaign against the Sioux Indians (a service that wrecked two steamers that summer, the *James G. Rankin* and the *Osceola*).

In 1878, the *Yellowstone* made an early start for the ephemeral head-of-navigation on the Yellowstone River. After a slow voyage during which the vessel was troubled by low water and damage to its boilers and wheel, Pompeys Pillar was reached by mid-June. There, while trying to stem the rapid current, the rudder carried away and it was necessary to drop the boat back eight miles and discharge its cargo. The difficulties encountered on that trip should have demonstrated that steamboating was impractical above the mouth of the Big Horn River; however, the desire to land freight as near Bozeman as possible was such a powerful lure that the Yellowstone Transportation Company made another attempt to reach Benson's landing.

But the voyage of 1879 was disastrous. Leaving St. Louis on April 29, the steamer again made a slow passage up the Missouri and into the Yellowstone River, where it was wrecked on June 4 while attempting to pass the Buffalo Rapid eight miles below Fort Keogh. Unable to stem the rapid current, the boat swung against a submerged rock and was lost with much of its 180 tons of freight.

This disaster, which put an end to the Yellowstone Transportation Company, could have crippled work in the new Yellowstone National Park. Superintendent P. W. Norris had intended to ship his equipment and supplies for that season by the *Yellowstone*, but his freight arrived at the Bismarck railhead too late for loading. Thus, he was forced to ship his outfit by the conventional Missouri River packet and ox-freight route, and was spared a loss that would have seriously impaired his effort to open the Park.

There was also a Yellowstone ferry, which utilized a succession of locally built scows operated after 1865 on a cable strung across the river a few miles below present Livingston, Montana. In that day, before wire rope, cable failure was frequent and the crossing claimed a number of lives.[22]

In the present century, the name Yellowstone has appeared on the high seas, carried by two vessels commissioned by the United States Navy. The first was built by the Moore & Scott Iron Works at Oakland, California, in 1918. Following its commissioning as a Naval Overseas Transportation vessel on September 21, 1918, the first *U.S.S. Yellowstone* hauled cargo from the United States to European ports until May 24, 1919, when it was decommissioned and returned to the shipping board.

The second *U.S.S. Yellowstone* is a destroyer-tender (AD-27), built by the Todd Pacific Shipyards at Seattle, Washington, in 1945. The vessel was named "in honor of the great American National Park," and was commissioned January 16, 1946. During more than twenty years of service with the Atlantic and Pacific fleets, this ship has received nine annual awards for battle efficiency, as well as many other commendations.[23]

The name Yellowstone has had some special and interesting land transportation applications. In the heyday of staging in the Park, most visitors were carried in horse-drawn coaches designed especially for sightseeing. These four-horse, nine-passenger rigs had forward-facing seats and open sides and were known as Yellowstone wagons.

Yellowstone was a word that appealed to several railroads. It appeared in the chartered names of two branch lines (the Yellowstone Park Railway and the White Sulphur Springs & Yellowstone Park Railway), and in the naming of a series of distinguished special cars. The Northern Pacific Railroad has so named at least four business cars. The original car was created by altering the sleeping car *Mandan* and renaming it *Yellowstone*.[24] Called the director's car, it frequently accomodated important guests, among them ex-President Ulysses S. Grant. As guest of honor at the "last spike" celebration which concluded construction of the Northern Pacific Railroad, General Grant, who had signed Yellowstone National Park into existence while president, appropriately travelled to and from that gala event in the Director's car.

In 1885, the Yellowstone car was sold to Frank J. Haynes and remodeled for him into the Haynes Palace Studio. An article contributed to the *Photographic Times* states that the cost of the remodeled car was $13,000 plus $2,000 for furnishings and equipment. Within its 66-foot shell was living and working space, which allowed photographer Haynes to carry on a peripatetic business along the main line and branches of the Northern Pacific Railroad for twenty years.[25]

The records of the railroad's mechanical division show that at least two other business cars successively bore the name *Yellowstone*.

Car no. 8, built in the Como shops in 1898, was so named and used until 1921, when it became a superintendent's car, at which time the name was re-used for a new director's car. It was supplanted, in its turn, by a car known as the *Yellowstone River*, which has served the president of the road since 1955.[26]

Other uses of the name Yellowstone associated with transportation came out of the beginnings of the automobile era. The efforts to promote automobile tourism to and through the Park led to organization of a Yellowstone Trail Association, which laid out a route from St. Paul. This Yellowstone Trail was one of the first marked, cross-country routes in the nation.

Of course, the word Yellowstone has been used extensively in the naming of business enterprises within the Park. Among them are the Yellowstone Park Improvement Company (certainly a flagrant misnomer), the Yellowstone Park Association, the Yellowstone Park Hotel Company, the Yellowstone Park Transportation Company, the Yellowstone National Park Stage Line, the Yellowstone National Park Transportation Company, the Yellowstone-Western Stage Company, the Yellowstone Park Camping Company, the Yellowstone Park Camps Company, the Yellowstone Park Lodge and Camping Company, the Yellowstone Lake Boat Company, the Yellowstone Park Boat Company, and the present Yellowstone Park Company, which is, in a way, the legatee of all the foregoing concerns.

Outside the Park, present commercial use of the name Yellowstone has been made by such diverse enterprises as a dairy, a pipeline company, a Bible-study encampment, a floral shop, a flight service, a taxi service, a service station, a boys' ranch, a travel agency, an insurance agency, several trailer parks and motels, and a lumber mill.

The whole story behind the name Yellowstone has not been given here, only enough to show how an Indian name for a great river has proliferated. It is a strong name with a favorable connotation; certainly, Roche Jaune or Elk River would not have served so well. Yellowstone was just right and even petty commercialism does not dim its luster; it is a name that conjures up something of geysers and bears, canyons and great waterfalls, and it carries with it a romantic aura that cannot quite be defined. Perhaps that is because The Yellowstone is, in part, a product of our daydreaming.

CHAPTER 2

OUT OF THE MISTS OF TIME

The Creator made the World—come and see it.
—From a Pima Indian Prayer

The first visitors to the area that is now Yellowstone National Park probably were prehistoric hunters who followed Ice Age mammals into the drainage of the Yellowstone River near the end of the Pleistocene glaciation, and after them came other Stone Age people who have used the area into modern times. Recent evidence suggests that use was continuous, and that neither prehistoric nor modern Indian inhabitants feared the hot springs and geysers.

The people who appeared in the Yellowstone at least as early as the tenth millenium before Christ are now thought of as descendents of primitive family groups that began moving up the Pacific coast of Asia about 40,000 years ago.[1] This migration, possibly reinforced from the interior of Siberia, continued over what is now Bering Strait into Alaska on a land bridge left by the withdrawal of ocean water tied up in the continental ice sheet. Where the icy, fog shrouded waters of the strait now roll, there was a grassy plain—a doorway to the Americas, standing open for thousands of years.[2] From Alaska, which was then ice-free, the progenitors of our first visitors drifted down the northwest coast and through the interior valleys of Canada, during interglacial periods, to populate both continents.

Today's limited knowledge of prehistoric peoples allows only broad groupings on the basis of adherence to a common way of life, as deduced from artifacts and refuse found at campsites and hunting kills.[3] First, there were the Early Hunters, who roamed in small groups, following and slaying such large beasts as the mammoth and the ancient bison. Their principal weapon was a short spear propelled by an *atl-atl*, or throwing stick, which served as an extension of the arm to increase the range and thrust of the spear. These nomads used fire and dressed hides, but their manner of sheltering from the elements is yet unknown. Nor do we know anything of their customs or ceremonies. A further identification of certain of these people has been made on the basis of their distinctive stone work, leading to such designations as Clovis Man for the makers of the stone projectile points first found at a mammoth kill site near the town of Clovis, New Mexico, and Folsom Man for the makers of another type found in association with the bones of extinct bison near Folsom, New Mexico. Both types of stone points have since been found widely distributed and invariably used in hunting those animals.[4]

The first visitors' presence in the Yellowstone area at least 11,000 years ago was suggested by discovery of the heel portion of an obsidian projectile point at Gardiner, Montana, near the north entrance to the Park, in 1959. Mr. Otho Mack found the fragment in the excavation for the post office building then under construction. Recognizing it as of a very early type, he contacted the University of Colorado Museum, where the curator of anthropology, Joe Ben Wheat, expressed his opinion that it was "undoubtedly a Clovis Point"—an identification later confirmed by Dr. Marie H. Wormington.[5] From what is known about the use of Clovis points and the habitat preference of the mammoth, the Gardiner locality of 11,000 years ago can be pictured as a wrack of postglacial debris, the silt and boulders thinly veiled by transitional vegetation consisting mainly of grass and willows. There our Early Hunter probably camped, sitting by his fire to replace a projectile point broken in an unsuccessful cast. But this is merely logical conjecture.[6]

Interest generated by the find at Gardiner led to recognition of other evidences of Early Hunters in the area immediately north of the Park. Among available artifacts were two lanceolate projectile points known to have been found on the summit of Ash Mountain in 1900. They proved to be variants of the Agate Basin type, but the probable significance of their location (upon an exposed summit at an elevation of 10,240 feet) was not apparent at once. In July 1963 the author talked with the U.S. Forest Service fire lookout on Lookout Mountain, a prominent summit on the divide between Slough Creek and Buffalo Fork about four and one-half miles north of the Park boundary. This man's interest in Indian things had led him to make excursions to neighboring peaks and ridges in search of arrow heads. He had made many surface finds, which he had carefully recorded. His information indicated that people had hunted and camped on the ridge tops and "hanging valleys" (carved out by glacial action above an elevation of 9,000 feet) as early as 8000 B.C.[7]

All the projectile points that could be attributed to Early Hunters—fourteen, consisting mainly of Hell Gap, Agate Basin, and Eden Valley types—were found quite high. Possibly the animals hunted then lived on the ridges, as the bighorn sheep now do through much of the year and deer and elk do in fly-time; or, the lower and now very desirable areas could have been unavailable because of lingering remnants of glacial ice or postglacial lakes. For whatever reason, it is evident that some Early Hunters lived as mountaineers on the heights immediately north of the Park.

The only evidence yet found of the presence of Early Hunters within what is now Yellowstone Park is a Hell Gap point picked up in 1955 at Nez Perce Creek within the Lower Geyser Basin.[8] A recent investigation by the U.S. Geological Survey indicates the level of Lake Yellowstone was once much higher than it is now—perhaps by as much as 90 feet—and that it covered a larger area.[9] Otherwise, for Early Hunters the Park was much as now—a forested land interspersed with hot springs and geysers.

A gradual change from the cool, moist anathermal climate of the glaciers to warm, dry altithermal was paralleled by the disappearance of much of the Ice Age fauna on which the Early Hunters subsisted. This "great extinction," which was virtually complete by 6000 B.C., has been variously attributed to cataclysmic geological events, to disease, and to the activities of man—the fire-user and hunter—as well as to climatic change; and, while the overkill theory is now considered best, it remains to be proved what eliminated some species entirely, while sparing others. During this period, the Great Plains suffered severely; streams and ponds dried up, soil was blown about in great dust storms, and vegetation was impoverished, so that the area was largely uninhabitable for man. But in favorable locations, and particularly in the mountains, the effect was not nearly so great.

The nomadic Early Hunters disappeared with the Ice Age fauna, and their place was taken by others whose way of life has suggested the name Foragers. Theirs was a roving existence within a limited area, a constant search for food by family groups who used all the edible products of the land—insects, reptiles, fish, roots, seeds, berries, and such birds and animals as they were able to obtain. Hunting was done mainly with the *atl-atl*-propelled throwing spear during this Middle Prehistoric period, though several innovations that appeared toward the end, such as the operation of bison traps and jumps, and the grinding of vegetable foods, may have eased the stringency of the Forager economy.

The marginal nature of their subsistence tended to limit the movement of these people to a locality where the meager food resource was relatively dependable. Thus, their peregrinations took on the character of seasonal visitations to favorable localities, relatively short, repetitive journeys instead of the long, aimless wanderings in the wake of animal herds, which was characteristic of their predecessors.

As should be expected under the circumstances, evidences of Forager occupation are few or entirely absent from plains areas during the periods of greatest climatic severity (the drought-plagued altithermals), but in the mountains Foragers appear to have maintained themselves.[10] This is particularly true of the Yellowstone Plateau, which they appear to have continuously occupied. There, the seasons dictated a pendulum-like movement: from wintering grounds in those protected valleys that enter deeply into the plateau to summer hunting grounds at higher elevations, and back to the wintering grounds in the fall—perhaps no more than fifty to one hundred miles in each direction. Areas that were definitely used as wintering grounds were the Lower Basin on the West Gallatin River, the Yellowstone Valley between Yankee Jim Canyon and the mouth of the Gardner River, the Clarks Fork Valley in the vicinity of Red Lodge and along the North Fork of the Shoshone River below its junction with Middle Creek. Evidences of transitory summer occupation are found throughout the mountains and on the Yellowstone Plateau, and the concentration of Forager artifacts around Lake Yellowstone has led Dr. Carling Malouf to presume a relatively large population.[11]

Such a population would be indicative of a more favorable environment than is generally credited to altithermal times. Archaeological investigations at the Rigler Bluffs site (a complex of prehistoric hearths or fireplaces near Corwin Springs in the Yellowstone

Valley[12]) hint that the local climate of the fourth millenium before Christ was moister than at present, perhaps at least equivalent to the climate now enjoyed in Montana's western valleys. Large charcoal granules found between the stones of a rock-lined fire pit provide the means for fixing the era of use *and* the species of wood burned (it was western yew, a species not found east of the Bitterroot Valley at present).

During the later part of the Middle Prehistoric period, the climate progressed toward the mediothermal condition typical of our time. This amelioration appears to have been accompanied by a faunal increase, which allowed the Foragers to place greater dependence upon hunting. Thus, another and better life style emerged by degrees from the older foraging existence.

The transition from the Middle to the Late Prehistoric period was marked by development of communal hunting of bison in the areas adjacent to the Yellowstone Plateau and by the grinding of vegetable foods. The people of the final period—the Late Hunters—began to use the bow and arrow and cooking vessels after the time of Christ. The change in weaponry is evidenced by a change in projectile point styles: from the large lanceolate and corner-notched types of the Foragers to small corner-notched and side-notched types better suited to use on the smaller arrow shafts. Because the small side-notched points are most numerous, there is a tendency to consider them *the* typical arrow heads; actually they are only the final modification in the sequential development of stone projectile points.

The Late Hunters had a powerful though short-ranged weapon in the bow and arrow,[13] and its peculiarities dictated hunting methods that anchored them to particular localities and prevented a return to the nomadism of the Early Hunters. In the vicinity of their wintering grounds, these people built driveways consisting of stone piles and brush arranged along natural routes followed by the hooved animals; and they built hunting blinds overlooking springs and passes in the surrounding hills. Such coverts put them within arrow range of their prey, particularly when footmen were employed to drive the animals in. That these new hunting techniques were supplemented by gathering activities is evident from the grinding stones and the fragments of fresh-water mussel shells found at their numerous campsites along the Yellowstone River.

The abundance of campsites in the wintering places hints that the Late Hunters were better off economically than their precursors. The favorite sites on the banks of the Yellowstone between Yankee Jim Canyon and the Gardner River were used so heavily that large areas remain nearly sterile from the accumulation of carbon and bone lime. But evidences of these people are not limited to the climatically mild valleys; their summer camps, which were usually smaller because they scattered out in family groups, are everywhere evident on the Yellowstone Plateau and in its surrounding mountains.

The connection of some widely separated events makes it possible today to sort these faceless Late Hunters into recognizable groups. A significant aspect of the Late Prehistoric period was a general restlessness manifested in extensive movement of aboriginal groups—movements that led to the tribal distribution of modern times. The following sequence of events has been postulated.[14]

As the Caddoan people spread westward from the Mississippi Valley into the area now included in Oklahoma, Kansas, Nebraska, and southern South Dakota, three Athabascan groups began a southward drift from their homeland near the Arctic Circle. One of the latter halted in southern Canada to become the Sarsis, while the others continued southward straddling the Rocky Mountains. The western prong eventually penetrated to the Southwest where they attacked the Pueblo people and made a place for themselves as the Navajos, while the eastern prong fought their way past the Caddoans to the Southern Plains where they became the Apaches.

Toward the end of the Late Prehistoric period, the Apaches acquired horses and iron weapons, using them to gain control of the Great Plains; with the Navajos, they befriended two groups of Uto-Aztecans (the Utes and the Comanches), while another group of Uto-Aztecans from the Great Basin, the Shoshonis, began moving northward into the plains of the Snake River and eventually spilled over the Continental Divide into present Montana and Wyoming.

Dr. Malouf believes that this movement was initially a peaceful, disconnected spreading of small groups into adjacent territory.[15] By the end of the seventeenth century, the Shoshonis had established a frontier that roughly approximated the Continental Divide through present Wyoming; there were Kiowas to their east in the Wyoming Basin and Flatheads northward from Yellowstone Lake; to the west they had bulged into Montana via the passes opening upon the headwaters of the Missouri River. Meanwhile, the Crows and the Hidatsas, who once occupied lands immediately west of the Great Lakes, were being pushed toward the Missouri River by other Siouian Indians who had obtained guns through their contacts with whites; farther north the Assiniboins were similarly displacing the Blackfoot people westward from the Red River.

The Spanish horses and iron weapons that fell into Indian hands during the Pueblo revolt in New Mexico increased the turmoil created by earlier migrations and white contacts. As the historic period opened—it is arbitrarily considered to have begun in A.D. 1700 in the trans-Mississippi West—the Comanches abandoned alliances with the Navajos and Apaches, plundering the one and driving the other from all but the least habitable portion of the Southern Plains. They also turned upon their kinsmen, the Utes, driving them into the mountains of Colorado and Utah. Some of the plunder thus obtained by Comanches was passed along to their northern relations, the Shoshonis. Well mounted, armed with iron weapons, and equipped with leather armor and stout shields covered with bull-hide, the Shoshoni warriors drove eastward into the Wyoming Basin and northward through Montana to Canada. Their rapid advance thrust the Kiowas eastward toward the Black Hills, and the Salishan people (Flatheads and the Plains Pend d'Oreilles and Kutenais) eastward into the valleys of western Montana and northern Idaho.

But the Shoshoni triumph was short-lived. By A.D. 1740 they were pitted against Piegans who had obtained guns through Assiniboin and Cree middlemen. With their terrible new weapons, the northern Indians drove the Shoshonis out of most of Montana, while the continuing migration of the Crows drove them deep within the Wyoming Basin.

As the nineteenth century opened, the Indian tribes in and around the Yellowstone Plateau were at last distributed in a now familiar pattern. The Piegans, a band of the Blackfoot people,[16] held Montana north of the Yellowstone River from the Musselshell River to the Divide. The term Blackfoot, applied to them and their allies, is believed to have been given because their moccasins were discolored from walking through the ashes of prairie fires. They boastfully called themselves "the best legs in the mountains," and usually preferred to travel afoot when on raiding expeditions in order to better engage in the ambush tactics which were their special mode of warfare. Predatory forays took them hundreds of miles into the country of their neighbors, where they fought both Indian and white with skulking persistence. The ravages of smallpox finally put an end to Blackfoot aggressiveness.

The Crows occupied the country from the Yellowstone River southward into Wyoming between the Powder River and the Absaroka-Wind River mountain chain. They called themselves *Absarokas*, "people of the large beaked bird,"[17] and, while the origin of their common appellation is not definitely known, it appears to be a too-literal translation of the French, *gens de corbeaux*. It is said that the sign-language pantomime used by these Indians to identify themselves—hand motions resembling the flapping of wings—was presumed by French Canadian interpreters to represent the labored flight of the large raven so conspicuous in the northern Rocky Mountains.

As a people the Crows were proud, vain, and cleanly, but also overbearing and quick to press an advantage. They were a graceful people, known for their horsemanship and thievery, with the general reputation of rascals. Though ordinarily friendly to the whites, they occasionally plundered them if it could be done with impunity, and they were notoriously unreliable in their alliances with other Indians.

The Shoshonis occupied the country from the Wind River and the Absaroka Mountains westward to the Blue Mountains of Oregon, and from the mountains that cradle the headwaters of the northern branches of the Snake River southward into northwestern Utah and northeastern Nevada. They shared their "homeland," the Snake River Plains, with a related group, the Bannocks, with whom they intermarried and acted in concert on most matters. The name Snakes, by which the Shoshonis are generally known, is believed to have originated in another of those misinterpretations of Indian sign language. The Shoshonis designated themselves by making a sinuous motion of the hand with the index finger extended, which was intended to mean that they were the grass-weaver people (from their former use of grass mats in erecting habitations). However, the sign was misconstrued as the track of a snake. As for the origin of the word *Shoshoni*, the best surmise is that it represents an uncomplimentary Siouian expression applied to them by their Crow neighbors.

The wide variance in physiographic and climatic conditions in the country of the Shoshonis—from semidesert to alpine regions— was matched by equally great differences in life styles. Subgroups were recognized and designated on a dietary basis, as "buffalo eaters," "deer eaters," "salmon eaters," "sheep eaters" and "root diggers." The result was a structured society, with the buffalo hunters at the top, socially and economically, and the sheep hunters and root diggers at the bottom as have-nots. The distinction was not tribal but economic.

A particular group of the Shoshonis, the Sheepeaters, were the only Indian residents of the Yellowstone Plateau and are generally poorly understood.[18] These *Tukudikas* were a mixture of Shoshoni "walkers" and Bannock mountain dwellers. They were not outcasts so much as people who could not compete in the Indian society

This engraving of an Indian identified by E. S. Topping as a Sheepeater in *Chronicles of the Yellowstone* (1883): p. 12 is one of several posed photographs made of this man on the Qu' Appelle River in Canada. A different pose can be seen in the F. J. Haynes photograph reproduced by Freeman Tilden in *Following the Frontier* (1964): p. 320; there, in an illustration titled "Sitting Bull's 'last hostile tepee' . . . ," the Indian is shown standing and holding a brass-frame Winchester instead of a trade gun. The engraver took the liberty of reversing the photographic image and adding clouds, but similarity of details on the brush shelter establish the engraving as based on F. J. Haynes' work. Thus, it is a virtual certainty that the Indian portrayed here is not a Sheepeater, and similar doubt shadows two other photographs frequently used as representations of Sheepeaters.

established by introduction of the horse and the gun. Lacking both, there was nothing left for them but to eke out an existence in the less desirable portions of the Shoshoni domain—along that mountainous frontier extending from the Wind River Mountains of Wyoming along the Absaroka and Gallatin ranges, which partially rim the Yellowstone Plateau, and westward in the rough country along the Continental Divide between Montana and Idaho.

Ake Hultkrantz, in his excellent study, "The Shoshones in the Rocky Mountains,"[19] considers the Sheepeaters essentially Shoshonis who had "retained the old way of living from the time before horses were introduced and who established a specialized mountain culture." He describes them as living in very small groups, often of family size; traveling on foot, accompanied by large dogs which were used for hunting and as beasts of burden (they were sometimes packed, and sometimes pulled V-shaped dog travois); and living on berries, herbs, fish, small animals, elk, deer, and bighorn sheep. He adds:

> They hunted particularly the latter, which were very important as food and clothing. Since these animals appeared in very small herds, the individual method of hunting was the most suitable. This situation and the fact that the forested areas were hard to travel through are probably the main reasons that these Indians' socio-political organization in olden times was so elementary."[20]

Only at the winter encampments did the Sheepeaters come together in numbers requiring something more than familial guidance; even there, there was no definite chieftainship, but only the limited authority of some old man whose wisdom and experience was recognized. As a people, they were timid but not unfriendly, and their philosophical outlook was animistic. Altogether, their life style was a holdover from the Late Prehistoric period.

There remain, in Yellowstone Park, some curious conical structures of dried poles, which are often called Sheepeater wickiups. Actually, such temporary dwellings are not in the Shoshoni tradition, for the typical shelter of those Indians (where they had not adopted the pole-and-hide tipi from neighboring tribes) was a low brush structure often covered with grass mats. (The mountain-dwelling Sheepeaters varied this by building the shelter against the face of a cliff or overhanging rock in order to utilize the heat reflected from a fire at its base.) But the tribes of the Northern Plains, including the Crows and Piegans, habitually used a conical lodge of dried poles— perhaps ancestral to the tipi in design—when making short, dangerous expeditions in small groups. A few men on a hunting trip away from the tribe could provide themselves with an overnight shelter in a few hours, and, covered with grass, brush, bark, hides, or blankets, it was reasonably wind- and rain-tight; but, most important, it screened their fire from hostile view.

George Bird Grinnell long ago identified the Yellowstone wickiups as Crow hunting lodges, and Dr. Malouf recently came to the same conclusion as the result of his archaeological investigations, which showed only a very transient use and none of the household debris that would have remained from even a seasonal use by Sheepeaters.[21] A third type of shelter found in Yellowstone Park is an open-topped pen made by piling up logs and rocks to form a shoulder-high barricade. Such structures were used by Salishan people and are probably relics of that ancient time when the Yellowstone Plateau was Flathead country.

The Bannocks have already been noted as co-existing with the Shoshonis, from whom they differed in being more warlike and self-reliant. The name is not Scotch in origin but comes from their own word *Panaiti*, which can no longer be translated accurately. However, it is thought to refer to the characteristic upswept hairdo of the warriors or to an earlier residence farther west. Of more importance here is the fact that the majority of the Bannocks, like the Shoshonis they sojourned with, had a typical plains culture when white men first met them; that is, they owned horses, lived in skin tipis, and subsisted on buffalo taken in great communal hunts.

Living at some distance from the Yellowstone Plateau were the Flatheads and Nez Perce Indians. The Bitterroot Valley was occupied by Flatheads who did *not* deform the heads of infants,[22] as was the high fashion among their Salish relations along the Pacific Coast. Application of such a name to them has been accounted for in two ways: as a result of early voyageurs observing among them some visitors with deformed heads; or again, as a misunderstanding of the universal sign language. Their identifying sign consisted of placing the flat of the hand beside the temple, intending to show that they were the Salish with the flat or normal heads, not those who deformed heads by making them peaked (a much-desired beauty treatment on the Coast).

Across the Bitterroot Mountains from the Flatheads lived the Nez Perce Indians, whose homeland was in western Idaho and adjoining portions of Oregon and Washington. The French name by which they were known means "pierced noses," referring to the practice of perforating the septum of the nose to receive a *Dentalium* shell after the manner of certain coastal Indians.[23] However, it was a custom that seems to have fallen into disfavor early in the nineteenth century. Both the Flatheads and the Nez Perces were honest, brave, and sincerely religious. They were also consistently friendly to the whites, and the war into which some bands of the latter tribe were ultimately driven is the most tragic struggle recorded in western history because it was so unnecessary.

Such were the Indians who lived upon or made use of the Yellowstone Plateau and its environs in the historic period. From the time the Shoshonis were driven back into the mountains by the Piegans on the north and the Crows on the east, the mountain dwellers who occupied the Yellowstone bastion were harried by roving bands of enemies. Thus, they became understandably timid, occupying hidden retreats in summer and fall when the danger was greatest and descending into the sheltered river valleys to winter when it was safe to do so.

The first contact between the Sheepeaters and the whites within the limits of the present Park appears to have been with unknown trappers in the Lamar Valley. Osborne Russell, who met a group there in 1835, describes them:

> Here we found a few Snake Indians comprising 6 men 7 women and 8 or 10 children who were the only Inhabitants of this lonely and secluded spot. They were all neatly clothed in dressed deer and Sheep skins of the best quality and seemed to be perfectly contented and happy. They were rather surprised at our approach and retreated to the heights where they might have a view of us without apprehending any danger, but having persuaded them of our pacific intentions we then succeeded in getting them to encamp with us. Their personal property consisted of one old butcher Knife nearly worn to the back two old shattered fusees which had long since become useless for want of ammunition a small stone pot and about 30 dogs on which they carried their skins, clothing provisions, etc on their hunting excursions. They were well armed with bows and arrows pointed with obsidian. The bows were beautifully wrought from Sheep, Buffaloe and Elk horns secured with Deer and Elk sinews and ornamented with porcupine quills and generally about 3 feet long. We obtained a large number of Elk Deer and Sheep skins from them of the finest quality and three large neatly dressed Panther skins in return for awls axes kettles tobacco ammunition etc. They would throw the skins at our feet and say "give us whatever you please for them and we are satisfied We can get plenty of Skins but we do not often see the Tibuboes" (or People of the Sun).[24]

Russell's party contacted Snake Indians on four separate occasions, to their mutual benefit, but chance meetings with Piegans were another matter. Early in the winter of 1829-30, a party of trappers on a fall hunt were attacked near Cinnabar Mountain, losing two men and all their equipment. One of the men who escaped to wander alone through the Yellowstone country was young Joseph L. Meek, then a novice with but one season's experience trapping.[25] Osborne Russell and three companions had a bitter experience with a band of that hated tribe while encamped on Pelican Creek, near Yellowstone Lake, in 1839. They escaped with their lives but lost all else; even so, they fared better than a party of forty trappers who blundered onto the scene a little later. Though they defeated the Piegans, that victory cost the trappers five lives and many wounded.[26]

The forays of the Blackfoot people into the Yellowstone country continued for another three decades and were even given some justification in a treaty concluded at Fort Laramie on September 17, 1851, between the United States and several Indian tribes. Among the provisions was recognition of Crow rights to all the lands east of the Yellowstone and the Continental Divide. The allocation of most of the Yellowstone Plateau to Crow and Piegan Indians was unfair to the resident Sheepeaters (who were never consulted), but they could take some consolation—if, indeed they had any awareness of the whole business—from the fact that the high-handed doings of Indian commissioners were as readily and as arbitrarily undone. In this case, the Crows lost all their lands in the drainage of the Yellowstone River south of the forty-fifth degree of north latitude in a treaty of May 7, 1868, and the Piegans were entirely dispossessed by a cession of their Yellowstone lands ten days later.[27]

The Crow and Piegan Indians were not the only outsiders to invade the Yellowstone Plateau during the nineteenth century. Events on the Snake River plains during the days of the fur trade gave rise to an invasion of a different sort. There the Shoshonis and Bannocks had developed a typical plains culture based on the buffalo, which were once found as far west as the Blue Mountains of Oregon. But the combined profligacy of Indian and trapper brought the buffalo to extinction west of the Continental Divide by 1840. With the buffalo went the Indian's principal support—his source of food, clothing, and shelter. It was soon apparent to those buffalo eaters that they must either "go to buffalo" or lower their standard of living to the brush wickiup level of their less fortunate relations.

The Bannocks and many Shoshonis preferred to make hunting migrations to the buffalo country across the mountains, and they worked out a route that became known as the Bannock Trail.[28] Beginning at the Camas Meadows in Idaho, this Indian thoroughfare crossed Targhee Pass and traversed the broad basin of the Madison River; then it climbed over the Gallatin Mountains near Mount

Bannock Indians whose fathers regularly crossed the Yellowstone on hunting excursions. From Brower, *The Missouri River* (1897).

Bannock Indians living in a typical brush wickiup on the Fort Hall reservation in 1872. From W.H. Jackson's photograph no. 632.

Holmes and descended Indian Creek to the Gardner River. After traversing Snow Pass to Mammoth Hot Springs, the route continued up Lava Creek and through the Blacktail Deer Creek meadows to a crossing of the Yellowstone River near Tower Fall (the Bannock Ford); it then followed the Lamar Valley and went over the Absaroka Range into the Clarks Fork Valley, from which the Indians could debouch upon the buffalo ranges of the Yellowstone Valley or the Wyoming Basin.

As rugged as this route might appear to be, it had advantages. The country traversed was the nominal possession of friends and relatives—the Sheepeaters—so that the unwieldy caravans, encumbered by women and children, horse-drawn travois and numerous pack animals, were relatively secure from hostile attack. Also, the route was developed upon what a military man would recognize as internal lines: a short arc giving access via connecting trailways down prominent drainages (such as the Madison, Gallatin, Yellowstone, Stillwater, Clarks Fork, and Shoshone valleys) to buffalo ranges lying in a larger, peripheral arc. Indians using the Bannock Trail could halt within the shelter of the mountains while scouts slipped down to a buffalo range checking for game and enemies.

Trips to the buffalo ranges of Montana and Wyoming often were made in concert with Flatheads and Nez Perces, and the larger parties sometimes wintered on the lower Yellowstone or on the Wyoming plains, returning to their homeland the following summer. Use of the Bannock Trail was confined to a forty-year period that ended in 1878, when General Nelson A. Miles defeated the dissident Bannocks who attempted to emulate the Nez Perces' retreat of the previous year. At some places in the northern part of Yellowstone Park, the deeply indented track of the Indian thoroughfare can still be seen in the line of sagebrush that has grown where pony hooves once trod.

The Sheepeater Indians, who were the only residents of the Yellowstone Plateau in the historic period, were never recognized by our government as having a valid claim to the area. Instead, an unratified treaty of September 24, 1868, was used as justification for placing all the Shoshonean groups on small reservations. Chief Washakie's band of Shoshonis went to Fort Washakie on the Wind River, while the remainder of the Shoshonis and some Bannocks went to Fort Hall on the Snake River. The remaining Bannocks and most of the Idaho Sheepeaters went to the Lemhi Reservation. The Sheepeaters thus isolated in the Yellowstone region were placed in an increasingly difficult position, and Chief Washakie finally extended them an invitation to join his people on the Wind River Reservation, which they did in 1871.[29]

   The decade following the opening of the Sioux War in 1867 was a time of widespread Indian unrest. The brief use of John Bozeman's road to the Montana Territory was the principal irritant that precipitated the conflict; but it was the Northern Pacific Railway surveyors, and others seeking advantages along the proposed route, who kept the trouble simmering. As a result, the northern approach to Yellowstone Park was the scene of many brutal incidents and was not really free of raiding parties until the hostiles were rounded up following the Custer fight in 1876. No small party was safe; travel to the new park and activities to develop it were equally inhibited.[30] At the close of this period two Indian wars—Nez Perce (1877) and Bannock (1878)—swirled briefly across Yellowstone Park. Except for the anticlimactic purchase of the narrow strip of Crow Indian Reservation lying between the forty-fifth parallel and the north boundary of the Park on April 11, 1882, the role of the Indian in the Yellowstone story closed with those two "tempest in a teapot" wars.

   The small parcel of land obtained from the Crow Indians is the only part of Yellowstone for which we can show a bill of sale. Our title to the remainder of the Yellowstone National Park was not obtained directly from its aboriginal occupants but is, instead, based on a sequence of events that began two centuries before the first white visit. In fact, our present possession of any part of the Park is due entirely to a fortuitous series of happenings. That we, a young nation, should have gained any foothold in the trans-Mississippi West is remarkable, for we were not populous or rich, and we were certainly naive in matters of diplomacy; yet these events did give our nation continental stature.

   The succession of territorial claims and counterclaims through which our title descends began in 1603, when King Henry IV of France granted the charter of Acadia to Pierre Du Gast. Through that instrument, Du Gast was given the whole of North America between the fortieth and forty-sixth degrees of north latitude, which, of course, included the Yellowstone region. In 1606 a permanent French settlement was founded at Port Royal, now Annapolis, Nova Scotia. In that same year, the English established a counterclaim when King James I granted the first charter of Virginia. Through it, the lands lying along the coast of North America between the thirty-fourth and forty-fifth degrees of north latitude were given to two companies, and George Popham, representing the most northerly—the Plymouth Company—planted a colony at the mouth of the Kennebeck River in the present state of Maine on August 19, 1607.[31]

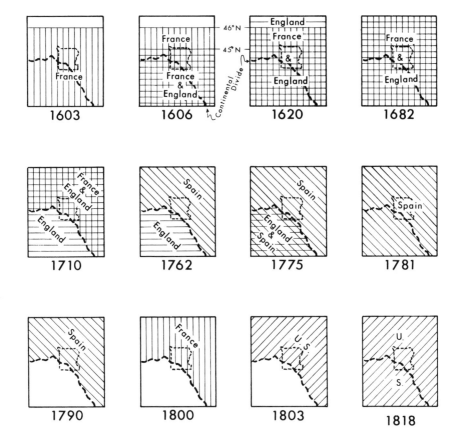

1603   1606   1620   1682

1710   1762   1775   1781

1790   1800   1803   1818

1819

DERIVATION
OF
AMERICAN
SOVEREIGNTY

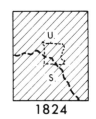

1824

In 1620, the Plymouth Company received a separate charter, which reads:

> Wee, therefore . . . do grant . . . [lands] lying and being in Breadth from Forty degrees of Northerly latitude from the Equinoctial Line, to Forty Eight Degrees of the said Northerly Latitude, and in length by all the Breadth aforesaid throughout the Maine Land, from Sea to Sea . . . termed and called by the name of "New England in America."[32]

Thus, there was a French and an English claim to the Yellowstone region, although neither knew anything of its existence. In this territorial rivalry, France gained a distinct advantage when Robert de LaSalle claimed the lands drained by the Mississippi River for King Louis XIV in 1682, naming the area Lousiana. His claim was countered in 1710 when English and Colonial forces captured Acadia in Queen Anne's War, thereby extinguishing the French claim to that portion of the present Park lying on the Pacific slope. Thus, the Continental Divide became the boundary between relatively unclouded claims—French to the east and English to the west.

France suffered another military disaster in the French and Indian War. As the inevitable defeat became apparent, France ceded her province of Lousiana to Spain on November 3, 1762, ostensibly as compensation for losses suffered by her ally on behalf of France in the worldwide Seven Years' War. However, the transfer was only partially effective, for England insisted on having the eastern part of Louisiana when a treaty was arranged with France and Spain on February 10, 1763. In that manner, the part of the present Park draining to the Mississippi River fell under Spanish sovereignty.

In 1775, the Spanish became alarmed over Russian activity on the Alaskan Coast and sent several expeditions northward from California. These became the basis for a vague Spanish claim to the Pacific Northwest coast; so that whatever claim to the western portion of the Yellowstone region the English may have had by virtue of their earlier conquest of Acadia was checkmated by the Spanish, and then destroyed entirely by the Treaty of Paris which ended the struggle of the American colonies for independence in 1781. Spain was left dominant in the trans-Mississippi West.

That situation did not last long. The brief Spanish claim to the Pacific Northwest was destroyed by the Nootka Convention of 1790 between Spain and England. Fortunately, the English lacked the interest to advance a claim of their own, leaving the Pacific slope portion of the Yellowstone region entirely free of claimants.

Following his conquest of Spain in the year 1800, Napoleon forced that nation to return Louisiana to France, but relations with England were soon in such a state that the Emperor anticipated a renewal of war, and, since there was no possibility that France could prevent its remote American possession from falling into the hands of her old enemy, Napoleon decided to sell the province before it was taken from him. In November 1802, an offer was made to President Thomas Jefferson: France would sell the entire province of Lousiana to the United States for 60 million francs, and we would assume the so-called French-spoliation claims, estimated at $3.75 million. This offer was accepted, and we obtained the Louisiana Territory for $27,267,621.28 by a treaty of cession dated April 11, 1803.

At this point we had most of the Yellowstone region; the bases of our title to the remainder are far from sound. In later negotiations with England over the establishment of our northern boundary west of the Rocky Mountains, we claimed the Oregon country on three grounds. First, by discovery and occupation, through Captain Gray's finding of the Columbia River in 1790 and John Jacob Astor's fur trade settlements along its course in 1809. Second, through the pretension that the Louisiana Purchase included lands extending to the Pacific Ocean—which it never did; and third, by alleging a cession from Spain. In regard to the latter, the United States did claim the coast above Spanish California in 1818, but in 1819 this claim was countered by Spain upon the royal order of King Ferdinand VII.

In the course of the boundary negotiations that began in 1824, the British government took the position that our boundary with Canada should follow the forty-ninth parallel westward to the point where it strikes the northward-flowing branch of the Columbia River, then follow down the center of that stream to its mouth. While it would not have allowed us all the territory we subsequently obtained, it was a tacit admission that our claim to most of the Oregon country was a satisfactory one.[33] From that time on our sovereignty in the Yellowstone region has never been in question.

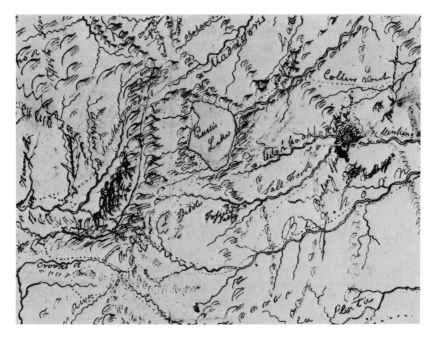

Manuscript map compiled by William Clark from informants during the period 1806-11. Original in the Coe Collection, Yale University.

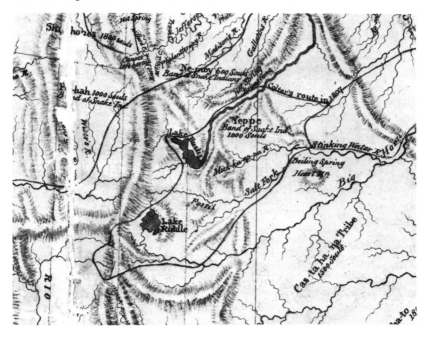

Engraving made by Samuel Lewis from Clark's manuscript map, printed in the *History of the Expedition under the Command of Captains Lewis and Clark,* 1814.

CHAPTER 3

IN PURSUIT OF PELTRY

*He [Manuel Lisa] shortly after dispatched
Coulter, the hunter before mentioned, to bring some
of the Indian nations to trade. This man, with a pack
of thirty pounds weight, his gun and some ammunition, went upwards of five hundred miles to the
Crow nation; gave them information and proceeded
from them to several other tribes.[1]*

That brief statement, with the mute testimony of William
Clark's Map of the West,[2] is nearly all the record there is
concerning the solitary journey that John Colter took
into the Yellowstone wilderness in the winter of 1807-08. Indeed, it is
only because of the notation Hot Spring Brimstone, shown where the
track of his wandering crossed the Yellowstone River, that there can
be any certainty he saw some of those thermal features for which the
present park is renowned; he is, therefore, entitled to be called the
area's white discoverer. With Colter began an intermittent commercial exploration that lasted until fur trading ended in the northern
Rocky Mountains.

John Colter was a Virginian frontiersman who had been a
member of the Lewis and Clark Expedition from October 15, 1803, to
August 5, 1806, when he was given his discharge at the Mandan towns
on the Missouri River. He had served the expedition well, and was

John Colter. From a painting by Paul Rossi (1963). Used with permission.

allowed to join two American trappers, Forrest Hancock and Joseph Dixon, who were among the vanguard of those taking advantage of our acquisition of the Louisiana Territory to ply their trade at the sources of the Missouri River. After a winter spent along the middle course of the Yellowstone River, the partnership dissolved, and Colter was descending the Missouri, bound again for the settlements, when he met the flotilla of Manuel Lisa near the mouth of the Platte River. It appears that Colter was easily persuaded to return to the mountains in the service of the Missouri Fur Trading Company, and the information he had gathered while trapping along the Yellow-stone undoubtedly influenced Lisa's decision to build Fort Raymond at the mouth of the Big Horn River in October 1807.[3]

Lisa proposed to draw in customers by sending out experienced men to advise neighboring tribes of the location of his trading post. Among the men who did so, John Colter accomplished most; indeed, his 500-mile tour, much of which was performed in winter through mountainous terrain, testifies to uncommon woodsmanship and endurance. According to Thomas James, who knew him in 1809, Colter was then thirty-five years old, "five feet ten inches in height and wore an open, ingenious, and pleasant countenance of the Daniel Boone stamp." He noted that Colter had been formed "for hardy indurance of fatigue, privation and perils."[4] Such was the man who launched into the wilderness in the fall of 1807 from Lisa's unfinished fort at the mouth of the Big Horn River.

The inherent defects of Clark's map make it impossible to fix Colter's route accurately from that source alone; but it is now the general opinion of historians that he went up the Yellowstone River to Pryor Creek and by the Indian trail over Pryor Gap to the Shoshone River in the vicinity of Cody, Wyoming—the "Colter's Hell" of the trappers; then he advanced up the Big Horn and its headwater, the Wind River, and crossed Union Pass into Jackson Hole. From there he may have crossed Teton Pass, returning to the Snake River, above Jackson Hole, by way of Conant Pass; he then circled the west shore of Yellowstone Lake and went down the Yellowstone River to the Indian trail-crossing near Tower Fall, continuing on that trailway up the Lamar River and Soda Butte Creek to the headwater of Clarks Fork, from which he was able to regain his outward-bound route at Pryor Gap.[5]

Of course Brackenridge's statement that Colter went to "the head of the Gallatin Fork and the Grosse Corne of the Yellowstone" could be interpreted to mean the journey was made in the reverse order.[6] This would have greatly reduced the puzzling duplication of effort that is so apparent when Colter's route is compared with that of George

Drouillard at nearly the same time;[7] it would also have taken Colter across the Yellowstone Plateau before the onset of winter. However that may be, some points along the route can be identified with reasonable certainty, among them the crossing of the Yellowstone River at Tower Fall. It is the only place where the river can be forded by a man traveling afoot, and then only during the low water of late fall and winter. Just below the crossing, at the mouth of Tower Creek, is a group of tepid springs, while the east bank of the river for several hundred yards above and below the crossing is an odiferous area known locally as the sulphur beds; those evidences of volcanism at the only practicable crossing of the Yellowstone River for many miles in either direction account for the notation Hot Spring Brimstone on Clark's map and leave little doubt that John Colter passed that way on his solitary journey. He was undoubtedly the first white visitor to see some of the Yellowstone wonders.

Because of the lapse of American enterprise in the Rocky Mountains during and after the War of 1812, the next trappers to reach the Yellowstone Plateau were men of the Canadian North West Company. Alexander Ross recorded the wanderings of a brigade led by Donald McKenzie in 1818, noting "boiling fountains, having different degrees of temperature,"[8] but his failure to mention landmarks makes it impossible to identify the particular features seen.

The following year there was another visitor known only by the initials "J.O.R." and the date "Aug. 19, 1819," which he carved on a tree in a ravine about one-quarter mile above the upper falls of the Yellowstone River. When discovered by P. W. Norris in 1880 the markings showed plainly, but in 1895 Hiram Chittenden found them "now practically illegible from overgrowth."[9]

Alexander Ross returned to the Yellowstone country in 1824 as a brigade leader in the service of the Hudson's Bay Company (which had absorbed the North West Company three years earlier). He crossed from Fort Oakinogan, in what is now northcentral Washington, to the headwaters of the Missouri River. The foolscap folios that made up his official report to the Hudson's Bay Company contain the earliest written description of a Yellowstone geyser: "Saturday 24th [April]—we crossed beyond the Boiling Fountains. The snow is knee deep half the people are snow-blind from sun glare."[10] Apparently the brigade worked back and forth between Idaho and Montana but did not go eastward beyond sight of the mountains. An interesting confirmation of the presence of Hudson's Bay Company trappers in the Yellowstone region was reported many years ago by Superintendent Norris. While constructing a wagon road along the shore of Beaver Lake, near Obsidian Cliff, his crew found a cache of iron traps resembling those used by the Hudson's Bay Company in former years.[11]

American interest in the wealth of furs available in the Rocky Mountains developed rapidly after General William H. Ashley issued his call, in 1822, for "one-hundred young men to ascend the Missouri River to its source." Among the men who enlisted in his enterprise were some who would later see the Yellowstone country, including James Bridger, Thomas Fitzpatrick, Jedediah S. Smith, and Daniel T. Potts. The first contingent, led by Major Andrew Henry, was to ascend at once to the mouth of the Yellowstone River and over-winter there, to be joined by a reinforcement under Ashley in 1823. Harassment by Blackfoot Indians took a toll of the lives and property of the wintering party, however, and because of the hostility of the Missouri River Indians, the expected reinforcement was prevented from reaching them. Consequently, Major Henry moved up the Yellowstone to the mouth of the Big Horn River for the winter of 1823-24, and, in the spring of that year, launched his trappers south and west through Wyoming and across the mountains into the Great Basin, where they were at last successful.

While it has been said that American trappers reached the Yellowstone Plateau in the summer of 1824,[12] it appears more likely that they did not go that far. According to Mattes,[13] Jedediah S. Smith and six unidentified trappers (perhaps including Jim Bridger and Baptiste Ducharme) explored the country northward from Green River by way of the Hoback into Jackson Hole, from which they crossed Conant Pass to the Teton Valley. Thus, they turned west just a few miles short of the present south boundary of Yellowstone Park.

The extended explorations of 1824 were made possible through an arrangement for supplying the men of the Ashley-Henry enterprise with merchandise brought overland to them at a prearranged time and place. This rendezvous system was a drastic change from the former use of fixed posts (which were better suited to trade with the Indians), and it allowed groups of white trappers to spend most of their time on the beaver streams, free of the necessity of making long journeys to deliver furs and receive supplies. However advantageous the new system may have appeared to the trapper, it was the company that prospered through the reduction of stock on hand and operating overhead (by eliminating unproductive trading posts and often-idle employees); for the trapper, it was but a tyranny of "mountain prices," which kept him more or less in debt for his outfit, for the foofaraw for his Indian squaw, and for the riotous binges celebrating the annual get-together. It was a system that insured a rapid and thorough ransacking of every nook and corner of the Rocky Mountain wilderness—the Yellowstone Plateau included.

French Canadian Trapper. From a painting by E.S. Paxon (1902). From Yellowstone Park Museum collection.

Trapper in High Country. From a painting by C.M. Russell (1911). From the Mackey Collection, Montana Historical Society, Helena.

Just when the first of this new breed of trappers began to take fur in what is now Yellowstone Park is not known but they were definitely there in 1826. An account by one of them appeared in the *Philadelphia Gazette and Daily Advertiser,* September 27, 1827,[14] to become the first published description of Yellowstone features. Because the letter was known for years only in its anonymous and carefully edited form, there were many attempts to credit it to various literate trappers known to have been in the Rocky Mountains about that time, but, through one of those fortunate happenings, its authorship was finally established.

In 1947, two elderly ladies, Mrs. Kate Nixon and Miss Anne G. Rittenhouse, approached the National Park Service with an offer to sell three letters written 120 years earlier by members of their family. The letters were concerned with the western experiences of Daniel T. Potts, a young man from Montgomery County, Pennsylvania, who was one of the original members of the Ashley-Henry enterprise, and they illuminated some shadowy phases of the fur trade. Most important of all, they included the original letter from which the Philadelphia editor had drawn his material. The letters were purchased by the Yellowstone Library and Museum Association, which has since made them available to scholars.[15]

The following is the text of the letter Potts wrote to his brother, Robert T. Potts, July 8, 1827, from Sweet Lake (now Bear Lake), Utah:

Respected Brother

A few dass since our trader arived by whom I received two letters one from Dr. Lukens the other from yourself under date of January 1827 which gives me great congratulations to hear that you are both happy wilst I am unhappy also to hear from my friends shortly after writing to you last year I took my departure for the Black-foot Country much against my will as I could not make a party for any other rout. We took a northerly direction about fifty miles where we crossed Snake river or the South fork of Columbia at the forks of Henrys & Lewis's forks at this place we was dayly harrased by the Black-feet from thence up Henrys or North fork which bears North of East thirty miles and crossed a large ruged Mountain which sepparates the two forks from thence East up the other fork to its source which heads on the top of the great chain of Rocky Mountains which sepparates the water of the Atlantic from that of the Pacific. At or near this place heads the Luchkadee or Calliforn [Green River] Stinking fork [Shoshone River] Yellow-stone South fork of Masuri and Henry's fork all those head at an angular point that of the Yellow-stone has a large fresh water Lake near its head on the verry top of the Mountain which is about one hundred by forty Miles in diameter and as clear as crystal on the south borders of this lake is a number of hot and boiling springs some of water and others of most beautiful fine clay and resembles that of a mush pot and throws its particles to the immense height of from twenty to thirty feet in height The clay is white and of a pink and water appears fathomless as it appears to be entirely hollow under neath. There is also a number of places where the pure suphor [sulfur] is sent forth in abundance one of our men Visited one of those wilst taking his recreation there at an instan the earth began a tremendious trembling and he with dificulty made his escape when an explosion took place resembling that of thunder. During our stay in that quarter I heard it every day. From this place by a circutous rout to the Nourth west we returned two others and myself pushed on in the advance for the purpose of accumalating a few more Bever and in the act of passing through a narrow confine in the Mountain we where met plumb in the face by a large party of Black-feet Indians who not knowing our number fled into the mountain in confusion and we to a small grove of willows here we made every preppar-ation for battle after which finding our enemy as much allarmed as ourselves we mounted our Hourses which where heavyly loaded we took the back retreat. The Indian raised a tremendious Yell and showered down from the Mountain top who had almost cut off our retreat we here put whip to our Horses and they pursued us in close quarters until we reached the plains when we left them behind on this trip one man was closely fired on by a party Black-feet several others where closely pursued. On this trip I have lost one Horse by accident and the last spring two by the Utaws who killed them for the purpose of eatting one of which was favourite Buffaloe Horse this loss cannot be computed at less than four hundred and fifty Dollars by this you may conclude keeps my nose close to the grind stone A few Days previous to my arival at this place a party of about 120 Black feet approached the camp and killed a Snake [Indian] and his squaw the alarm was immediately given and the Snakes Etaws and whites sallied forth for battle the enemy fled to the Mountain to a small concavity thickly groon with small timber sur-rounded by open ground in this engagement the squaws where busily engaged in throwing up batterys an draging off the dead there was only six whites engaged in this battle who immediately advanced within pistol shot and you may be assured that almost every shot counted one the loss of the Snakes was three killed and the same wounded that of the Whites one wounded and two narrowly made their escape that of the Utaws was none though who gained great applause for their bravery the loss of the enemy is not known six where found dead on the ground besides a great number where carried off on Horses. Tomorrow I depart for the west we are all in good health and hope that this letter will find you in the same situation I wish you to remember my best respects to all enquiring friends particularly your wife

Remain yours most afffectionately etc
Danl. T Potts

Potts soon abandoned his not very profitable life as a trapper, but he is remembered by the attachment of his name to a small hot spring basin one mile north of West Thumb junction in Yellowstone Park.

It seems probable that the Yellowstone Plateau was visited by American trappers every year after 1826. Robert Meldrum claimed he visited the geysers in 1827, and the irrepressible Joe Meek was harried into the northern part of the present Park in 1829. Young Joe had signed on as a trapper at St. Louis, Missouri, that spring, accompanying the annual supply train to the mountains. From the rendezvous at Pierre's Hole (now the Teton Valley, Idaho), he traveled northward with a band of trappers up Henrys Fork, through the Madison Basin to the Gallatin River and down that stream to the Indian trail that passed over the Gallatin Range into the Yellowstone Valley at the mouth of Tom Miner Creek. Moving up the Yellowstone River to the vicinity of the Devils Slide, the party was attacked by Piegan Indians who killed two of the trappers and scattered the remainder, who lost most of their horses and equipment. The lucky novice, whose career could as easily have ended there, escaped alone into the Yellowstone wilderness and was sufficiently impressed by what he saw to provide Mrs. Francis Fuller Victor with lurid details forty years later.

Escaping across the river with only his mule, blanket, and gun, the nineteen-year-old moved southward for four days, then "ascended a low mountain in the neighborhood of his camp—and behold! the whole country beyond was smoking with the vapor from boiling springs, and burning with gasses, issuing from small craters, each of which was emitting a sharp whistling sound."[16] There is nothing in that statement to identify the hot spring basin he had reached, and his further description of the region as "immense, reaching far out of sight," and having "larger craters, some of them four to six miles across," from which "issued blue flames and molten brimstone," so little resembles any particular locality that Chittenden felt the necessity for "making some allowance for the trapper's tendency to exaggeration."[17]

Undoubtedly, the experience was a traumatic one, and the lad who had already lost his mount in wild flight can be excused if he saw the Norris Geyser Basin (probably the area he reached) as considerably larger than it is. Also, the Norris basin is one of those odiferous areas with enough of a hint of brimstone to have raised half-forgotten imaginings of the infernal regions out of Joe's Methodist past. Fortunately for Joe, two of the older trappers—sent out by Captain

Sublette to round up such fugitives—found him and brought him back to camp, which was moved, with great difficulty and privation, up the Lamar River and across the Absaroka Range to the Stinkingwater.

In 1829, Fort Floyd (soon to be called Fort Union) was built at the mouth of the Yellowstone River by the American Fur Company, a concern that had begun muscling into the Rocky Mountain fur trade two years earlier. The fur trade had been developing steadily since 1822. The original Ashley-Henry enterprise was managed by General William Ashley after Major Andrew Henry retired from the business in 1824. Ashley managed to make a quick fortune and retired two years later, leaving the enterprise in the hands of a partnership composed of Jedediah S. Smith, David E. Jackson, and William Sublette. This company (known as Smith, Jackson, and Sublette) sold out, in 1830, to a group of "partisans," or brigade leaders, who continued the business under the name of the Rocky Mountain Fur Company. By this date, the heyday of the fur trade was over, and the new concern found itself involved in ruinous competition with the American Fur Company, which had rapidly extended its operations from Fort Union into the mountains. In the next four years, every trick was employed to discomfort a competitor: brigades were led on wild-goose chases, streams were deliberately trapped out, small parties were led into Indian ambushes, prices paid for furs were rigged to gain control of the output, and loyalties were subverted.

One of the trappers who transferred his loyalty to the American Fur Company was Johnson Gardner, originally an Ashley-Henry man who had become the ruthless leader of a band of American "free trappers." It was Gardner who managed the thinly veiled robbery through which the Hudson's Bay Company brigade leader, Peter Skene Ogden, was relieved of a small fortune in furs in 1825 (to the great advantage of William Ashley), and he remained a satellite of the Smith-Jackson-Sublette partnership until it was dissolved. But Gardner seems not to have cared much for the Rocky Mountain Fur Company and transferred his operations to the headwaters of the Missouri River.

The books kept by the American Fur Company at Fort Union in 1832 show that Johnson Gardner entered into an agreement with Kenneth McKenzie for sales of furs then "en cache on the Yellowstone River,"[18] from which it seems probable that it was in the fall of 1831 or the spring of 1832 that he first trapped that beautiful mountain valley to become known as Gardner's Hole. It was for this illerate, often brutal, trapper that Gardner River was named, ranking it second to the Yellowstone River as the oldest place name in Yellowstone Park.[19]

Joe Meek as a trapper. From Victor, *River of the West* (1870), engraved from a photograph by Jos. Bucktel.

Joe Meek came back to the Yellowstone country with his brother Stephen in 1831, and it is said that Thomas Fitzpatrick and Jim Bridger trapped there in 1832. Information provided by Warren Angus Ferris, a clerk of the American Fur Company, indicates that Manuel Alvarez led a brigade of its trappers across the Yellowstone Plateau in 1833, discovering the great geysers of the Firehole River basins in the process.[20]

Stories told at the rendezvous by the men who had accompanied Alvarez led Ferris to visit the great geysers the following year in order to satisfy his curiosity about them. He says:

the accounts they gave were so very astonishing, that I determined to examine them myself, before recording their descriptions, though I had the united testimony of more than twenty men on the subject, who all declared they saw them, and that they really *were* as extensive and remarkable as they had been described. Having now the opportunity of paying them a visit, and as another or better might not soon occur, I parted with the company after supper, and, taking with me two Pend d'Orielles [Indians], set out at a round pace, the night being clear and comfortable. We proceeded over the plain about twenty miles, and halted until daylight on a fine spring, flowing into Camas Creek. Refreshed by a few hours sleep, we started again after a hasty breakfast, and entered a very extensive forest called the Piny Woods, which we passed through, and reached the vicinity of the springs about dark [May 19, 1834], having seen several small lakes or ponds, on the sources of the Madison; and rode about forty miles; which was a hard day's ride, taking into consideration the rough irregularity of the country through which we had travelled.

We regaled ourselves with a cup of coffee, and immediately after supper lay down to rest, sleepy, and much fatigued. The continual roaring of the springs, however, for some time prevented my going to sleep, and excited an impatient curiosity to examine them; which I was obliged to defer the gratification of, until morning; and filled my slumbers with visions of water spouts, cataracts, fountains, jets d'eau of immense dimensions, etc.etc.

When I arose in the morning [May 20], clouds of vapor seemed like a dense fog to overhang the springs, from which frequent reports or explosions of different loudness, constantly assailed our ears. I immediately proceeded to inspect them, and might have exclaimed with the Queen of Sheba, when their full reality of dimensions and novelty burst upon my view, "The half was not told me."

From the surface of a rocky plain or table, burst forth columns of water of various dimensions, projected high in the air, accompanied by loud explosions, and sulphurous vapors, which were highly disagreeable to the smell. The rock from which these springs burst forth was calcareous.[21] and probably extends some distance from them, beneath the soil. The largest of these wonderful fountains, projects a column of boiling water several feet in diameter, to the height of more than one hundred and fifty feet—in my opinion; but the party of Alvarez, who discovered it, persist in declaring that it could not be less than four times that distance in height—accompanied with a tremendous noise. These explosions and discharge occur at intervals of about two hours. After having witnessed three of them, I ventured near enough to put my hand into the water of its basin, but withdrew it instantly, for the heat of the water in this immense couldron, was altogether to great for comfort, and the agitation of the water, disagreeable effluvium continually exuding, and the hollow unearthly rumbling under the rock on which I stood, so ill accorded with my notions of personal safety, that I retreated back precipitately to a respectful distance. The Indians who were with me, were quite appalled, and could not by any means be induced to approach them. They seemed astonished at my presumption in advancing up to the large one, and when I safely returned, congratulated me on my "narrow escape"—They believed them to be supernatural, and supposed them to be the productions of the Evil Spirit. One of them remarked that hell, of which he had heard from the whites, must be in the vicinity. The diameter of the basin into which the water of the largest jet principally falls, and from the center of which, through a hole in the rock of about nine or ten feet in diameter, the water spouts up as above related, may be about thirty feet—There are many other smaller fountains, that did not throw their waters up so high, but occurred at shorter intervals. In some instances the volumes were projected obliquely upwards, and fell into the neighboring fountains or on the rock or prairie. But their ascent was generally perpendicular, falling in and about their own basins or apertures. These wonderful productions of nature, are situated near the centre of a small valley, surrounded by pine covered hills, through which a small fork of the Madison flows.[22]

Warren Angus Ferris has the triple distinction of being the first tourist to visit the Yellowstone wonders, for he went there out of curiosity rather than for commercial reasons as his contemporaries had; the first to provide an adequate description of a geyser, and the first to apply the word "geyser" to Yellowstone thermal features.[23] By virtue of his earlier training as a surveyor, he was the best-educated white man of his period to enter the area, and it is regrettable that he had only a few hours to explore and observe. His is the first factual report; it has neither the inadequacies nor the exaggerations of earlier accounts.

As Ferris was leaving the Rocky Mountains and the fur trade, another man was entering that business, and he, too, was a good observer and a competent diarist, recording much of interest about the Yellowstone region during several trapping ventures in it. He was

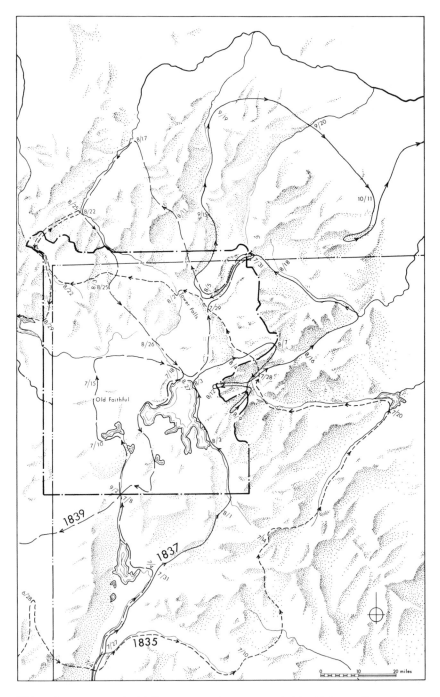

Visits of trappers to the Yellowstone region as recorded by Osborne Russell, 1835, 1837, and 1839.

Osborne Russell, a Maine farmboy who sought an adventurous life by engaging to serve the Columbia River Fishing and Trading Company organized by Nathaniel Wyeth in 1834. Russell first entered the present park area July 28, 1835, while on a fall hunt out of Fort Hall on the Snake River. On this first of his five visits, Russell and the trappers crossed the Absaroka Range into the drainage of the Lamar River, following that stream down to the beautiful, open valley below the mouth of Soda Butte Creek—Russell's "Secluded Valley," of which he later wrote:

> There is something in the wild romantic scenery of this valley which I cannot . . . describe; but the impressions made upon my mind while gazing from a high eminence on the surrounding landscape one evening as the sun was gently gliding behind the western mountain and casting its gigantic shadows across the vale were such as time can never efface from my memory.[24]

The Lamar Valley has retained, to a remarkable extent, that idyllic character which led Russell to note, "For my own part I almost wished I could spend the remainder of my days in a place like this where happiness and contentment seemed to reign in wild romantic splendor."[25]

One of the band of Sheepeater Indians living in the valley drew a map with charcoal on a white elk skin, and from it the trappers learned that the outlet of Yellowstone Lake was southwest, a day's travel over very rough country and that the river they were on united with the Yellowstone a half day's travel to the west; from there, he knew it ran westward through a deep gorge (the Black Canyon) before reaching the open valley below present Gardiner, Montana, but that was the extent of his geographical knowledge. Deciding not to go on to Yellowstone Lake, their original objective, Russell and his party continued down the Lamar River, forded the Yellowstone where the Indian trailway crossed opposite Tower Fall, and moved westward across the meadow at the head of Blacktail Deer Creek, and through the pine forest beyond, to Gardners Hole, which was described, trapper fashion, as forty miles in circumference. After two weeks of trapping beaver there, they crossed the Gallatin Range and left the Yellowstone area on August 22.

Russell was back on the Yellowstone Plateau on August 10, 1836, as a trapper in a brigade led by Jim Bridger. Working ahead of the slow-moving camp, he and two others entered from the south at the "Dividing spring" (Two Ocean Pass), which he described twenty-three years before Captain W. F. Raynolds admitted such a phenomenon *might* exist. Russell wrote:

On the South side about midway of the prarie stands a high snowy peak
from whence issues a Stream of water which, after entering the plain it
divides equally, one half running West and the other East, thus bidding
adieu to each other; one bound for the Pacific and the other for the
Atlantic ocean. Here a trout of 12 inches length may cross the Mountains in safety. Poets have sung of the "meeting of the waters" and fish
climbing cataracts but the "parting of the waters" and fish crossing
mountains I believe remains unsung as yet by all except the solitary
Trapper who sits under the shade of a spreading pine whistling blank-
verse and beating time to the tune with a whip on his trap sack.[26]

Passing down Atlantic Creek into the valley of the upper Yellowstone River, Russell and his companions trapped that marshy stream
to the inlet of Yellowstone Lake, where the camp came up with them
on August 16. From there, the brigade passed along the east shore of
the lake to a "beautiful plain which extends along the Northern
extremity of the Lake." Near their encampment, Russell had his first
view of the thermal wonders of the area, and he was particularly
impressed by a roaring steam vent he thought capable of working "an
engine of 30 horse power."

From that place, Russell and six companions veered off to trap
the mountains that parallel the north boundary of the present Park.
Rejoining the camp in Gardners Hole, the reunited brigade moved
cautiously down to the Yellowstone River and was out of the mountains on August 29.

The hunt during the summer of 1837 differed from that of the
previous year in that Russell and his five companions were not
supported by a brigade, but were left to move independently until
mid-October, when they were to meet Lucien Fontenelle's party on
the Yellowstone near the mouth of Clarks Fork. Again entering the
Yellowstone area by Two Ocean Pass on August 1, the party retraced
the route of the previous year to the Lamar Valley, then proceeded to
trap the mountains to the north and east. There was enough of the
poet in Osborne Russell that he could not help daydreaming over
"those stupendous rocks whose surface is formed into irregular
benches rising one above another from the vale to the snow," but his
companions were indifferent to the magnificent scenery around them.
He says:

My comrades were men who never troubled themselves about vain and
frivolous notions as they called them; with them every country was
pretty when there was weather and as to beauty of nature or arts, it was
all a "humbug" as one of them (an Englishman) often expressed it. "Talk
of a fine country," said he, "and beautiful places in these mountains, if
you want to see a beautiful place," said he, "go to Hingland and see the

Duke of Rutlands Castle!" "Aye," says a son of Erin who sat opposite with an Elk rib in one hand and a butcher knife in the other while the sweat rolling from his face mingled in the channels of grease which ran from the corners of his mouth, "Aye an ye would see a pretty place gow to old Ireland and take a walk in Lord Farnhams domain; that is the place where ye can see *plisure*. Arrah an I were upon that same ground this day Id fill my body wid good ould whiskey!" "Yes," said the backwoods hunter on my left, as he cast away his bone and smoothed down his long auburn hair with his greasy hand, "Yes, you English and Irish are always talking about your fine countries but if they are so mighty fine," (said he with an oath) "why do so many of you run off and leave them and come to America to get a living!"[27]

Russell trapped on the Yellowstone Plateau twice in the summer of 1839. On the first visit, from July 7 to 28, he entered the area by way of the Snake and Lewis rivers and proceeded to Shoshone Lake where he found "about 50 springs of boiling hot water" at the western extremity. There, another trapper showed him a geyser they called the Hour Spring. As he described it,

at this spring the first thing that attracts the attention is a hole about 15 inches in diameter in which the water is boiling slowly about 4 inches below the surface; at length it begins to boil and bubble violently and the water commences raising and shooting upwards until the column arises to the hight of sixty feet, from whence it falls to the ground in drops on a circle of about 30 feet in diameter, being perfectly cold when it strikes the ground. It continues shooting up in this manner five or 6 minutes and then sinks back to its former state of slowly boiling for an hour and then shoots forth as before. My Comrade Said he had watched the motions of this Spring for one whole day and part of the night the year previous and found no irregularity whatever in its movements.[28]

Continuing northward, Russell's party passed through the geyser basins along the Firehole River, taking particular notice of a large boiling lake where the rising steam was of three distinct colors— "from the west side for one third of the diameter it was white, in the middle it was pale red, and the remaining third on the east light sky blue"—which accurately identifies the Grand Prismatic Spring at Midway Basin. From Madison Junction, Russell's party moved eastward through Hayden Valley to the outlet of Yellowstone Lake and then to the Secluded Valley and on toward the Clarks Fork, beyond the present Park.

Russell would have been better off if he had not returned that summer, but he was back, encamped at Pelican Creek near the outlet of Yellowstone Lake, on August 27. The following afternoon while he and another trapper named White were lounging about camp (which was on the prominent bench where the present road to the east entrance rises out of the Pelican Creek swamp on the east side), they were attacked by Piegan Indians and were fortunate enough to escape, wounded, into the adjacent forest. There they spent a miserable night while the Indians ransacked their camp.

The two wounded trappers, with another who had been hunting at the time of the attack, "left the place heaping curses on the Blackfoot nation," though Russell admitted such expressions "neither injured them or alleviated our distress."[29] They managed to make their way afoot around the shore of Yellowstone Lake, down the Snake River and over the Teton Mountains to Fort Hall, and Russell, at least, never returned to the Yellowstone country.

Harsh as that experience was, Russell's party fared better than another which met the Piegans a short time later. That group of forty men, including Baptiste Ducharme, Louis Anderson, Jim and John Baker, Joe Power, and L'Humphrie, had entered the Yellowstone region by way of Two Ocean Pass and moved up the east shore of Yellowstone Lake. Near Squaw Lake (which should be called Indian Pond), they collided with the Piegans in a battle that cost five trappers' lives and many wounded before the Indians were driven off on the second day of fighting.[30]

In 1840, fur trading as an organized business ended in the northern Rocky Mountains. Those trappers who remained had to turn to other ways of earning a living. Typical of them, Jim Bridger built a way station on the Oregon Trail (Fort Bridger), from which he guided emigrants and such notables as Sir William Drummond Stewart, who hunted through the Yellowstone country in 1843. Later, Jim served as an incomparable scout for the United States Army. While performing such prosaic services, those trappers-turned-guide passed along much of the considerable geographical knowledge of the fur-trade era to later explorers of the West.

Such men as Captain W. F. Raynolds, Lieutenant J. W. Gunnison, and the Jesuit explorer-priest, Father Pierre Jean DeSmet acknowledged their debt to Jim Bridger in print and through the place names used on their maps.[31] Indeed, some of the earliest names to appear as the Yellowstone region was delineated were such trapper designations as Gardner River, Elephant Back, Alum Creek, Sulphur Mountain, and Burnt Hole. The word-of-mouth knowledge handed down from the trappers was also influential in stimulating later exploration of the Yellowstone and its wonders. Such information served to spur the curiosity of a number of Yellowstone explorers, from Captain Raynolds, who failed to reach the plateau, to the Washburn party, whose examination of the area in 1870 has become famous. In the preface to his published account, N. P. Langford says:

> I first became acquainted with Bridger in the year 1866. . . . He told me in
> Virginia City, Mont., at that time, of the existence of hot spouting
> springs in the vicinity of the source of the Yellowstone and Madison
> Rivers, and said that he had seen a column of water as large as his body,
> spout as high as the flag pole in Virginia City, which was about sixty (60)
> feet high. The more I pondered upon this statement, the more I was
> impressed with the probability of its truth.[32]

Unfortunately, the trappers as a group are most often remembered for their storytelling rather than for their very real contributions to the geographical knowledge of the West. Jim Bridger has
been particularly maligned in our time as a colossal liar—a sort of
Munchausen of the American West. This is unfair, not only because it
obscures the man and his accomplishment, but also because it fails to
comprehend the true nature of the trapper's tall tale. Among the
trappers, as with other illiterates and semiliterate groups, storytelling
was a form of entertainment.

Osborne Russell showed the true nature of this folkway:

> The repast being over the jovial tale goes round the circle; the peals of
> loud laughter break upon the stillness of the night which after being
> mimicked in the echo from rock to rock it dies away in the solitary
> [gloom]. Every tale puts an auditor in mind of something similar to it
> but under different circumstances, which, being told, the "laughing
> part" gives rise to increasing merriment and furnishes more subjects for
> good jokes and witty sayings such as Swift never dreamed of. Thus the
> evening passed with eating drinking and stories enlivened with witty
> humor until near Midnight all being wrapped in their blankets, lying
> around the fire, gradually falling to sleep one by one, until the last tale is
> "encored" by the snoring of the drowsy audience.[33]

Thus, storytelling was just entertainment among the trappers, and in
no way a part of the serious affairs of their rough life; yet they were as
quick to guy a tenderfoot as many a westerner since their time.
Undoubtedly, it was from that proclivity toward "stuffin' dudes" that
Jim Bridger's reputation suffered.

Several "Bridger stories" have become firmly rooted in the literature of Yellowstone Park, forming the principal legacy from the
trapper past. There are seven stories that are commonly attributed to
Bridger; they are concerned with the petrified forest, Obsidian Cliff,
and Alum Creek, and with less specific locales such as the stream-
heated-by-friction,   the   echo-used-as-an-alarm-clock,   the   fish-
cooked-in-hot-water, and Hell-close-below. Of those, three were certainly told by Jim, while the others appear to be literary accretions of
a later time.

Jim Bridger, circa 1866. From a photograph in collection of Kansas State Historical Society, Topeka. Used with permission.

Foremost among the genuine tales—those known to have been told by Bridger—is the one about the petrified forest. According to J. Cecil Alter,[34] a trapper by the name of Moses "Black" Harris first told it for the record in a St. Louis tavern in 1823, when Jim Bridger was yet a rattle-brained youngster. A quarter-century later, George Frederic Ruxton picked up the story and recorded it in a delightful manner,but still attributed it to Harris through a fictional character called Kilbuck, who says:

... and the darndest liar was Black Harris—for lies tumbled out of his mouth like boudins out of a bufler's stomach. He was a child as saw the putrefied forest in the Black Hills. Black Harris come in from Laramie; he'd been trapping three year an' more on the Platte and the "other side"; and, when he got into Liberty [Missouri], he fixed himself right off like a Saint Louiy dandy. Well, he sat to dinner one day in the tavern, and a lady says to him:

"Well, Mister Harris, I hear you're a great traveler."

"Traveler, marm," says Black Harris. "This niggur's no traveler; I ar' a trapper, marm, a mountain-man, waugh!"

"Well, Mister Harris, trappers are great travelers, and you goes over a sight of ground in your perishinations, I'll be bound to say."

"A sight, marm, this coon's gone over, if that's the way your *stick floats.* I've trapped beaver on Platte and Arkansa, and away up on Missoura and Yaller Stone; I've trapped on Columbia, on Lewis Fork, and Green River, I've trapped, Marm, on Grand River, and the Heely [Gila]. I've fout the *Blackfoot* (and d____d bad Injuns they are); I've *raised the hair* of more *than one* Apach, and made a Rapaho come afore now; I've trapped in Heav'n, in airth, and h____l; and scalp my old head, marm, but I've seen a putrefied forest."

"La, Mister Harris; a what?"

"A putrefied forest, marm, as sure as my rifle's got hindsights, and *she* shoots center. It was out on the Black Hills, Bill Sublette knows the time—the year it rained fire—and everybody knows when that was. If that wasn't cold doin's about that time, this child wouldn't say so. The snow was about fifty foot deep, and the bufler lay dead on the ground like bees after a beein'; not whar we was tho', for *thar* was no bufler, and no meat, and me and my band had been livin' on our moccasins (leastwise the parflesh) for six weeks; and poor doin's that feedin' is, marm, as you'll never know. One day we crossed a *canon* and over a *divide* and got into a peraira, whar was green grass, and green trees, and green leaves on the trees, and birds singing in the green leaves, and this in February, wagh! Our animals was like to die when they see the green grass, and we all sung out hurraw for summer doin's."

"Hyar goes for meat," says I, and I jest ups old Ginger [his rifle] at one of them singing birds, and down comes the crittur elegant; its darned head spinning away from the body, but never stops singing, and when I takes up the meat, I finds it stone, wagh! "Hyar's damp powder and no fire to dry it," I says quite skeared.

"Fire be dogged," says old Rube, "Hyar's a hos as'll make fire come"; and with that he takes his axe and lets drive at a cottonwood. Schr-u-k, goes the axe agin the tree, and out comes a bit of the blade as big as my hand. We looks at the animals, and thar they stood shaking over the grass, which I'm dog-gone if it wasn't stone, too. Young Sublette comes up, and he'd been clerking down to the fort on Platte, so he know'd something. He looks and looks, and scraps the trees with his butcher knife, and snaps the grass like pipe stems, and breaks the leave a-snappin' like Californy shells.

"What's all this boy?" I asks.

"Putrifactions," says he, looking smart, "putrifactions, or I'm a niggur."

"La, Mister Harris"; says the lady, "putrifactions! Why, did the leaves, and the trees, and grass smell badly?"

"Smell badly, marm!" says Black Harris, "would a skunk stink if he was froze to stone? No, marm this child didn't know what putrefactions was, and young Sublette's varsion wouldn't *shine* nohow, so I chips a piece out of a tree and puts it in my trap-sack, and carries it safe to Laramie. Well, old Captain Stewart (a clever man was that, though he was an Englishman), he comes along next spring, and a Dutch doctor chap was along too. I show him the piece I chipped out of the tree and he called it putrefaction, too; and so, marm, if that wasn't a putrefied peraria, what was it? For this hos doesn't know, and *he* knows *fat cow* from *poor bull*, anyhow.[35]

Captain W. F. Raynolds had Jim Bridger for a guide in 1859-60, and he thought it not at all remarkable that men cut off from civilization "should beguile the monotony of camp life by 'spinning yarns' in which each tried to excell all others." As he says, "some of these Munchausen tales struck me as altogether too good to be lost." One was to the effect:

In many parts of the country putrifactions and fossils are very numerous; and, as a consequence, it was claimed that in some locality (I was not able to fix it definitely) a large tract of sage is perfectly petrified, with all the leaves and branches in perfect condition, the general appearance of the plain being unlike that of the rest of the country, *but all is stone,* while the rabbits, sage hens, and other animals usually found in such localities are still there, perfectly petrified, and as natural as when they were living; and more wonderful still, these petrified bushes bear the most wonderful fruit—diamonds, rubies, sapphires, emeralds, etc.etc. as large as black walnuts, are found in abundance. "I tell you, sir," said one narrator [note that he does *not* say it was Bridger], "it is true, for I gathered a quart myself, and sent them down the country."[36]

Thus, Raynolds shows that the petrified prairie story of Harris had become generalized, and indefinite as to locality, and may have become a part of Bridger's repertoire by that time.

Definite attachment of this tale to the Yellowstone fossil forests did not appear until 1874, when R. C. Wallace heard it from three miners living in Jack Baronett's cabin at the mouth of the Lamar River. As Wallace tells it, after directing his party to "Specimen Mountain where we would find many petrified stumps and logs," they also mentioned "that many miles to the east there was a petrified forest still standing with petrified birds in the branches singing petrified songs."[37]

Perhaps it was such a localizing of the hoary old trapper tale that led Hiram Chittenden, in his original edition of *The Yellowstone National Park* (1895), to offer his opinion that

> the visitor to the region of petrifactions on Specimen Ridge in the north-east corner of the Park, and to various points in the hot springs district, will have no difficulty in discovering the base material out of which Bridger contrived the following picturesque yarn. According to his account there exists in the Park country a mountain which was once cursed by a great medicine man of the Crow nation. Every thing upon the mountain at the time of this dire event became instantly petrified and has remained so ever since. All forms of life are standing about in stone where they were suddenly caught by the petrifying influences, even as the inhabitants of ancient Pompeii were suprised by the ashes of Vesuvius. Sage brush, grass, prairie fowl, antelope, elk and bears may there be seen as perfect as in actual life. Even flowers are blooming in colors of crystal, and birds soar with wings spread in motionless flight, while the air floats with music and perfumes siliceous, and the sun and the moon shine with petrified light![38]

In that manner, a Yellowstone myth was created from a vague oral tradition of the trapping fraternity, and it was done in a way that has led several generations of readers to believe that Yellowstone's Specimen Ridge provided inspiration for the petrified forest story, and that Jim Bridger was its author, although neither belief finds support in available accounts. The nearest thing to an authentic Bridger version is a secondhand story told by General Nelson A. Miles in 1897. According to him,

> One night after a supper, a comrade who in his travels and explorations had gone as far south as the Zuni Village, New Mexico, and had discovered the famous petrified forest of Arizona, inquired of Bridger:
> "Jim, were you ever down to Zuni?"
> "No, thar ain't any beaver down thar."

Trappers storytelling. From *The American West* (Nov.-Dec. 1976). Used with permission.

A standing petrified tree of the "forest" on Specimen Ridge. From the author's collection.

"But Jim, there are some things in this world besides beaver. I was down there last winter and saw great trees with limbs and bark all turned into stone."

"O," returned Jim, "that's peetrifaction. Come with me to the Yellowstone next summer, and I'll show you peetrified trees a-growing, with peetrified birds on 'em a-singing peetrified songs."[39]

General Miles' story suggests that Bridger did have a stock petrified tree story based on Yellowstone features, but the details provided indicate it was not a bit more elaborate than the version Wallace had from the three miners in 1874. There seems to be no valid basis for the elaborate details Chittenden has read into his version (the Crow medicine man's curse, and the petrifaction of flight, odors, and light), and even less excuse for the coat of personalized varnish added by a later scholar.[40] If lying was one of Bridger's sins—as some have hinted—it was seldom *original sin*; he has had willing collaborators.

Those who wish to savor some genuine Bridger stories are referred to Raynolds and to Ware.[41] The latter states that Bridger's stories always followed the same formula, and he thought they had been told so many times he had each one memorized. Ware adds, "He had probably told them so often that he got to believing them himself."

As for those other purported Bridger stories concerning Obsidian Cliff, Alum Creek, the echo-used-as-an-alarm-clock, and the fish-cooked-in-hot-water: all that can now be said for them is that they appear to be latterday fabrications. According to James Stevenson, who knew Bridger well during the period 1857-60, Bridger's stories "as he acted and told them would not be the best and most refined bits of language . . . one could conceive of; but rather the reverse."[42] However, he did consider the old frontiersman one of the most remarkable among all those trappers who came into the Yellowstone in the pursuit of peltry; perhaps it is fitting that what have been unfairly called old Bridger's lies remain the area's most vibrant link with its trapper past.

CHAPTER 4

PICK AND SHOVEL PILGRIMS

They say there is a land
Where crystal waters flow
O'er beds of quartz and purest gold
Way out in Idaho!

CHORUS
O Wait, Idaho, we're coming
Our four-horse team will soon be seen
Way out in Idaho.[1]

W hen that song was written, Idaho was the El Dorado—
the latest and most promising of a succession of
mineral "strikes" which spread from the Mother Lode
country of California like a ripple on a pond. Argonauts overflowing
the southern placers found some gold on the coast of Oregon Territory in 1851. From there, gold was traced northward, through Washington Territory and into British Columbia during the 1850s, but
those strikes were neither rich nor extensive. After the end of the
Indian wars of 1855-59, miners were able to move eastward into a
country known as Idaho, and there they found good diggings on Oro
Fino Creek, a tributary of the Clearwater River.

That rich strike, with others in the drainages of the Salmon,
Boise, and Owyhee rivers in the years 1861 to 1863, was the magnet

that drew a rough and active population into the northern Rocky Mountains. But not all of the miners and would-be miners came from the West; there were unlucky Pike's Peakers from Colorado, and both the war-weary and the adventurous flocked from the East. Many of the latter, like the young man who scribbled on the flyleaf of his diary the doggerel at the opening of this chapter, never reached the Idaho of their dreams, for the elusive mineral frontier advanced to meet their slow-moving wagon trains and they were lured to newer strikes in what would later be Montana Territory.

How the Montana, Wyoming and Idaho areas became so designated is briefly as follows. The country east of the Continental Divide came under United States sovereignty through the Louisiana Purchase of 1803, as mentioned, while that westward was obtained through the Webster-Ashburton Treaty with Great Britain in 1846. The eastern portion was organized at once as Louisiana Territory: a vast wilderness that was divided into two territories in 1804—with the northernmost retaining the name of Louisiana until 1812, when it became Missouri Territory. Across the mountains, Oregon Territory was organized in 1848 in the domain of the Provisional Government of Oregon, an autonomy which preceeded the assumption of United States sovereignty in the area that now includes Oregon, Washington, Idaho, and those portions of Wyoming and Montana west of the Continental Divide. As Oregon Territory began to be settled, its unwieldy extent became obvious and a new territory—called Washington—was created in 1853 from the portion of the parent territory lying north of the Columbia River and the parallel of forty-six degrees north latitude.

The following year (1854), Missouri Territory was reduced in size by the organization of Nebraska Territory, which included everything north of the fortieth parallel from the White Earth River to the Continental Divide. Thus, the east slope portions of present Montana and Wyoming passed from the jurisdiction of Missouri Territory to the new Nebraska. In 1857, when Oregon became a state with its present boundaries, the portion excluded was attached to Washington Territory, so that all of present Idaho, with the west slope portions of Montana and Wyoming, was temporarily under the jurisdiction of Washington.

Dakota Territory was organized out of Nebraska in 1861, including the two Dakotas and present Montana and Wyoming to the Continental Divide. A rapid growth in population in the "Idaho mines"—that part of Washington Territory that is now central Idaho and southwestern Montana—during the early 1860s soon created local problems which led to the organization of Idaho Territory in

1863. As originally constituted, the new territory included all of present Montana and Wyoming, as well as Idaho; but that was a transitory situation. The population of the newest mining region in the territory—the area around Bannack, on a headwater of the Jefferson River—grew so rapidly during the following year that Montana Territory was organized in 1864, and construction of the Union Pacific Railway after the Civil War contributed sufficient population to the area for the organization of Wyoming Territory in 1868.

At that stage of their development, the territories of Idaho, Montana, and Wyoming had the boundaries with which they later passed into statehood—except for an oversight in delineating Montana. When that territory was organized out of Idaho in 1864, the area to be transferred was temporarily returned to the jurisdiction of Dakota Territory. But the boundaries established for Montana failed to include all the intended area, leaving a little triangle known as the Dakota splinter isolated upon the western flank of the Yellowstone region. The detached fragment—a small wedge between the Continental Divide and the parallel of forty-four degrees, thirty minutes north latitude—became evident with organization of Wyoming Territory in 1868, and it was added to Montana Territory in 1873 by the Congress through "An Act to readjust the western boundary of Dakota Territory."[2]

The accompanying outline maps show, step by step, the jurisdictional changes resulting from readjustment of territorial boundaries in the Yellowstone area prior to the establishment of Yellowstone National Park.

The prospectors and miners of the 1860s formed a transient population, forever on the go. Converging upon each new discovery in great numbers, they overtaxed both the source of mineral wealth and the available supplies, so that lack of income and ruinous prices soon forced the majority to move on.

The effect was an ever-widening search that ultimately reached every part of the northern Rocky Mountains.[3] Even the Yellowstone Plateau (which had been the exclusive haunt of Indians during the two decades following the effective end of the fur trade about 1840) was visited repeatedly by parties of prospectors. Though they found little in the way of riches, like their trapper precursors they brought back tales of the wonders they had seen; and their information, or misinformation—for such it often proved to be—excited the interest of many Montana citizens in the wonders of the Yellowstone region. Thus, the miners and the prospectors share honors with the fur trappers in influencing the definitive exploration of the area.

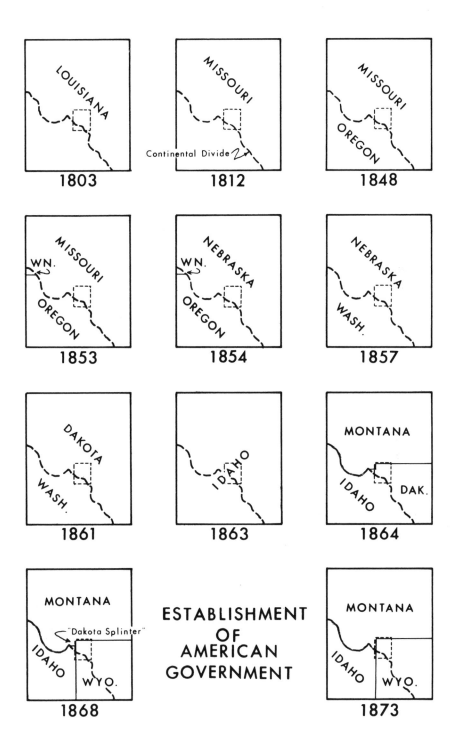

1803 — LOUISIANA

1812 — MISSOURI — Continental Divide

1848 — MISSOURI / OREGON

1853 — WN. / MISSOURI / OREGON

1854 — WN. / NEBRASKA / OREGON

1857 — NEBRASKA / WASH.

1861 — DAKOTA / WASH.

1863 — IDAHO

1864 — MONTANA / IDAHO / DAK.

1868 — MONTANA / "Dakota Splinter" / IDAHO / WYO.

ESTABLISHMENT
OF
AMERICAN
GOVERNMENT

1873 — MONTANA / IDAHO / WYO.

The first prospectors to reach the Yellowstone Plateau were an overflow from the excitement that brought the town of Bannack into existence. A man by the name of John White made the initial strike at Grasshopper Creek on July 28, 1862, and he was soon joined by miners working some indifferent placers along Gold Creek, at the north end of Deer Lodge Valley, while others arrived that fall with the Idaho-bound wagon train which James L. Fisk conducted from Minnesota by a northern route. As a result, Bannack had a population of 500 the first winter and several thousand the following year. But even before the tide of gold-seekers reached flood proportions, the disappointed began to look elsewhere for their fortunes.

Among the latter were some prospectors who banded together late in the summer of 1863 to explore the Snake River to its source. These men chose as their leader "Colonel" Walter Washington deLacy, a capable, forty-four-year-old civil engineer who had almost nothing in common with the "forty thieves"—as he called his comrades—except an adventurous spirit.[4] In addition to a thorough professional background, deLacy had profited from hard soldiering in Mexico and the far West; yet, his was a modest, self-effacing nature, so that his leadership was not military but only a loose fellowship from which individual prospectors could, and did, depart as they saw fit.

Several groups split off before September 5, when the party reached the forks of the Snake River, just within the southern boundary of present Yellowstone Park, where they found "hot springs with cones four or five feet high."[5] From there they turned westward and climbed onto the Pitchstone Plateau; but that route did not suit all the men and some split off, under Charles Ream, to continue up that fork of the Snake now called Lewis River. DeLacy, with the thirteen men who preferred his leadership, struck northward to Shoshone Lake, which they reached at the mouth of Moose Creek, then passed around the eastern end and ascended the little stream that bears his name.[6] From the head of DeLacy Creek, they were able to cross the Continental Divide into the Lower Geyser Basin.

Meanwhile, Ream's group pushed up the Lewis River to the Lewis and Shoshone lakes, passing along the south side of the latter to the geyser basin at the western extremity. From there they crossed to the Firehole River and followed down it, through the geyser basins. Below the Lower Geyser Basin both groups followed the same route to the point where the Madison River breaks free of the Yellowstone Plateau, seven miles east of the present town of West Yellowstone. From there, Ream's party continued down the Madison River, while deLacy's turned northward along the foot of the Gallatin Range and down the West Gallatin River as far as Spanish Creek before continuing westward.

Neither deLacy's nor Ream's men found gold in paying quantities, but they did bring back a wealth of geographic information. Undoubtedly, word of their findings—the absence of valuable minerals and the presence of hot springs in the Yellowstone region—was spread to every camp in the Montana gold fields by returning prospectors; but, if it wasn't, deLacy made both facts readily available in 1865. In that year he published his *Map of the Territory of Montana with portions of the Adjoining Territories,*[7] which showed a "Hot Spring Valley" (the Firehole geyser basins) at the head of the "Madison Fork," with other hot springs at the head of an unnamed lake draining southward into "Jackson's Lake." In 1867, Surveyor General Meredith of Montana Territory identified the unnamed lake as deLacy's Lake, and it was so known until changed to Shoshone Lake by Professor Frank H. Bradley, of Hayden's Geological Survey of the Territories.

In discussing the name change in his report to Dr. Hayden, Bradley commented on deLacy's work in the following unkind terms:

> The numerous and outrageous errors of the map show that neither as discoverer nor as mapper of this lake has Mr. DeLacy any claim to a perpetuation of his name; and, since the Lake occupies a position entirely different from that assigned to DeLacy's Lake, we have decided to drop that title, and to call this, in our maps and reports, Shoshone Lake, as being the head of one of the principal forks of the Shoshone or Snake River.[8]

Of course, even such a mild-mannered man as deLacy could not overlook that criticism of his professional competence, and, since he thought Dr. Hayden was the author of the blunt opinion, he addressed a letter to Major Martin Maginnis, then representing Montana Territory in Washington, stating, "Profr. Hayden in his published report of 1872 speaks of me in connection with this Lake in a very unhandsome & very undeserved terms. He seems on many occasions to have been actuated by unworthy feelings of jealousy." In his own defense, deLacy stated that he had never claimed that his map was correct in all particulars, or that he had been entirely over the region in question: "I do claim, however," he added, "that I was the first to publish the fact that South Snake river took its rise in a large lake, north of Lake Jackson, and flowed into it—a fact confirmed by Dr. Hayden's own surveys."[9]

Although friends of deLacy interceded with Hayden, he did not disavow Bradley's decision beyond a belated statement that "properly

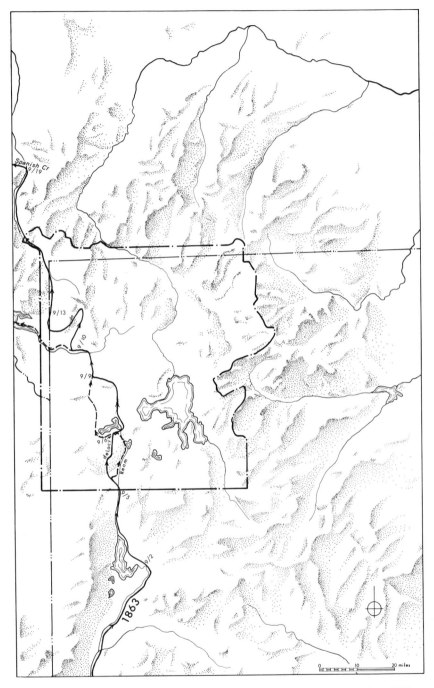

Prospecting trip of the deLacy and Ream parties in the Yellowstone region, 1863.

the lake should probably be known as DeLacy's Lake, but, as in the case of Yellowstone Lake, the name that has the right of priority has not been retained."[10] DeLacy lost his lake, but his map has fared better. Recognizing the limitations imposed upon his work by the sources he was obliged to use, a scholar has given deLacy the accolade of having "wrought a memorable map of a new Territory and had he never done anything else, he would have given us sufficient reason to honor his memory."[11]

Chittenden believed that deLacy might have passed into history as the real discoverer of the Yellowstone wonderland "but for the fact that he failed to appreciate the true importance of what he saw";[12] but that is not a valid reason for denying deLacy the status of a discoverer—for he did understand the unusual character of the thermal phenomena he had seen.[13] Instead, the problem remains the impossible one of determining a real discoverer among so many worthy candidates; deLacy must share honors with some who preceded him and with others who followed him in the extended drama of Yellowstone discovery.

In 1863 there was another Yellowstone Expedition, this one proposing to explore the lower reaches of the river rather than its headwaters. Led by James Stuart, the expedition was indirectly responsible for the discovery of gold in Alder Gulch, as noted in Chapter 1, and served to introduce two important characters to the Yellowstone scene (though, for one, the experience was vicarious).

Among the men who narrowly escaped with their lives when Indians (probably Sioux) shot into their camp on the night of May 12 was Samuel Thomas Hauser, a thirty-three-year-old civil engineer who had given up a good job on the Missouri-Pacific Railroad to go hunting gold in Idaho in 1862. During the attack a ball struck him in the left breast, penetrating a thick memorandum book and lodging over a rib; without that fortunate intervention he would probably not have lived to become a Montana banker, a millionaire businessman, governor of the Territory, and one of the Yellowstone explorers of 1870.[14]

Hauser's adventures on the Yellowstone River made quite an impression on another young gold-seeker—a sickly St. Paul bank clerk named Nathaniel Pitt Langford, who escaped the failure of a family-run bank by leaving Minnesota with the Fisk wagon train in July 1862.[15] In fact, Langford was so enthralled by Hauser's adventure that he cut himself in on the action in letters to his family in Utica, New York. His indiscretion later created a touchy situation when Hauser came to know the relatives:

Hauser, you remember that I told you of *"blowing"* to my nephews and nieces in Utica about *our* Yellowstone trip. Now don't you for the world say a word about it, as if I wasn't there, for I would not have them know that I was *gassing*, for anything. It was a piece of foolishness that I'll never repeat, but not a word from you. So be careful: and don't let this letter be seen. Burn it up.[16]

There was much activity by prospectors in the Yellowstone region in 1864. James Stuart took another expedition of seventy men down the Yellowstone River for the purpose of avenging the attack made upon his party of the previous year; but they found no Indians and turned to prospecting the drainages of the Big Horn and Stinkingwater (Shoshone) rivers. Finding no gold, Stuart returned to Virginia City with half the party, while the others worked southward under the leadership of Adam "Horn" Miller.

These men crossed the mountains into the valley of the Wind River, from which they moved to the Sweetwater and on over South Pass, shedding small parties as they moved; only fourteen of the original expeditioners remained by the time they reached the Green River. From there, six men—the Phelps-Davis party—moved northward into Jackson Hole to prospect and split again. George W. Phelps, with two comrades, crossed Two Ocean Pass to the upper Yellowstone River, passed around the east side of the lake and continued downriver on the same side to the mouth of the Lamar, from which they followed a trail made by white men down to a recent "strike" at Emigrant Gulch.[17] John C. Davis and his partners followed the same route except that they crossed the Yellowstone River above its falls, thus passing along the west edge of the Grand Canyon instead of the east.

Davis, who had also been a member of deLacy's expedition of the previous year, has provided an account which shows that he differed from the usual preoccupied gold-seeker in being somewhat aware of the Yellowstone's wonders. He also explains the origin of a prominent place name, Pelican Creek:

We camped on this creek, and noticed several large birds which appeared to be wild geese. I shot one, which managed to fly out some distance in the lake before it fell. I swam out after it, and became very much exhausted before I reached it. It looked as if it might be good to eat so I skinned it, and then the boys concluded it would hardly do. I hung the pelican—for that was what it was—on a tree, and it was found, afterward by Miller, who came by with his party.[18]

Miller, who also continued downriver to Emigrant Gulch, turned the Pelican incident into a place name during his many years of residence in the upper Yellowstone country.

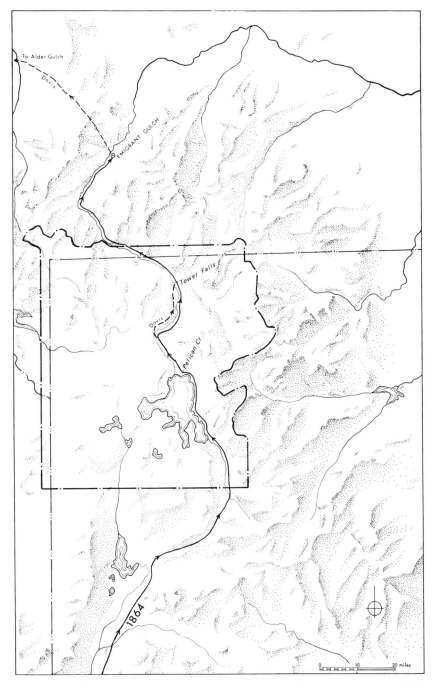

To Alder Gulch

Davis

EMIGRANT GULCH

Tower Falls

Davis

Pelican Cr.

1864

0   10   20 miles

Prospecting trips of the Phelps and Davis parties in the Yellowstone region, 1864.

Before we follow the party of white men whose trail up the Yellowstone River was traveled in the reverse direction by Phelps and his comrades, it should be noted that significant route explorations had been made. At the opening of its mining era, Montana could be reached from the west by the Mullan Road (really little more than a good packhorse trail across a mountain wilderness); from the east by Missouri River steamboats (the stage of water and other factors being favorable); and from the south by a prairie track that left the old Oregon Trail on the plains of the Snake River and passed northward over the Camas Meadows, through Beaver Canyon to a low pass over the Continental Divide, and then down Red Rock Creek and the Jefferson River. All three were long and tedious, and there were several attempts to find alternate wagon-road routes, particularly through Wyoming from the Oregon Trail. When James Stuart's 1863 expedition was fifty miles above the mouth of the Big Horn River—the day before they were shot at by Sioux Indians—three hard-riding strangers approached from a distance. They proved to be John M. Bozeman, John Jacobs, an old trapper, and the latter's half-breed daughter. They were scouting out a wagon route, to be known as the Bozeman Trail. This route left the emigrant road at Deer Creek, one hundred miles west of Fort Laramie on the North Platte River, passed northwest to a crossing of Powder River east of Salt Creek and skirted the eastern flank of the Big Horn Mountains to a crossing of the Big Horn River below its lower canyon; continuing from there, it crossed to the Yellowstone Valley somewhat above the mouth of Clarks Fork, from which the route followed up the south side of the Yellowstone to a crossing near present Springdale, Montana, and into the Gallatin Valley by what is now called Bozeman Pass.[19] An attempt to bring a wagon train over the new route that summer was thwarted by Indian hostility, though Bozeman did get through with a small party of mounted men. The route was opened in earnest the following spring when both Bozeman and Jacobs brought wagon trains through; however, they were preceded by Jim Bridger who conducted a wagon train to the Gallatin Valley by a somewhat different route.

Bridger's "Pilgrims," as emigrants were then called, were met at the mouth of Shields River early in July by prospectors who told them gold had been found a short distance up the Yellowstone River, at a place they called Curry's Gulch. The strike had been made late in the fall of 1863 by Thomas Curry, who found pay dirt at the mouth of a narrow gorge that opened out of rugged mountains on the east side of the Yellowstone between its first and second canyons.[20] Before he and his two companions could develop their prospect, they were robbed by Crow Indians and forced to retreat to Alder Gulch for the winter. They appear to have returned in the spring with a large party, intending to work claims, but most of the reinforcement went up-river looking for something better, and Curry was left with too few men for safety; hence the effort to recruit emigrants from the Bridger wagon train.

How successful they were at first is not clear. William Emory Atchinson wrote in his diary at the camp on the north bank of the Yellowstone east of Shields River:

> Tuesday July 19, 1864. Laid over for the purpose of prospecting. About 30 men went out. In fording the Yellow Stone three men were nearly drowned having missed the ford and struck the channel. They were, however, finally rescued. Prospecting party in ascending a deep gulch were met by a party of six hundred Indians and driven back. Thus ends, for the present, prospecting on the Yellow Stone.[21]

Emigrants from several wagon trains did reach Curry's diggings by August and established themselves in a town called Yellowstone City—a huddle of forty cabins and three hundred persons one-half mile below the mouth of the cleft that was becoming known as Emigrant Gulch.[22] The fondness of wayfarers for the locality is remembered in the name of the stream flowing from the gulch and the great peak towering over it, but Yellowstone City was transitory—fated to disappear from current maps as its traces have disappeared from the ground; while it thrived, it furthered exploration of the Yellowstone region by providing a base for prospectors.

The first such party to follow the Yellowstone River into its nurturing mountains consisted of the thirty or forty well-equipped men under George A. Huston who had accompanied Curry back to his strike from Alder Gulch.[23] Thinking they could do better, most of them continued up the Yellowstone and its East Fork, now the Lamar River. From the mouth of Soda Butte Creek they crossed the southern spur of Mount Norris and were encamped on a stream flowing from the northeast when Indians ran off their saddle horses and pack-horses. Left with only two donkeys for transportation, the party broke up.

Most of the men decided to backtrack with Huston,[24] so they took what they could carry on their backs and on one donkey, and made their way down to Emigrant Gulch, finding traces of gold en route at Bear Creek (named for a hairless cub seen there).[25] It was the trail of this party that was followed downriver by the Phelps-Davis and Miller groups of the fragmented Stuart expedition. The remaining twelve men who ascended the Yellowstone with Huston loaded what they could on the other donkey, cached the remainder of

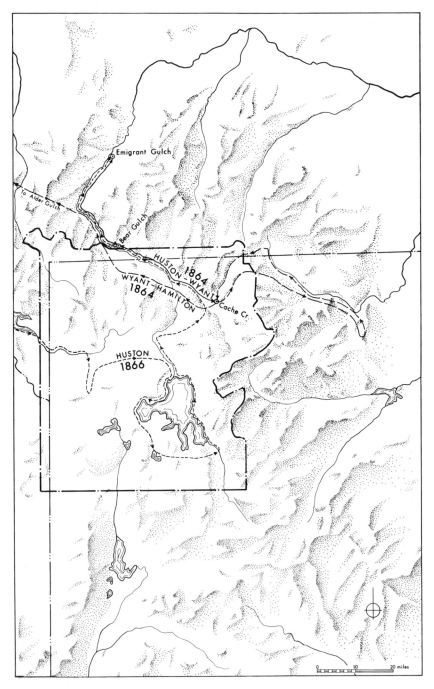

Prospecting trips of Huston, Wyant and Hamilton, 1864, and of Huston, 1866.

the equipment and supplies, and continued up that stream, which has ever since been known as Cache Creek.[26]

The little party, which included H. W. Wyant and William Hamilton, crossed over to Crandall Creek and went as far east as Heart Mountain before returning up Clarks Fork and around by Soda Butte Creek to the place where they had been set afoot. Resupplying from the cache left there, they prospected the escarpment that forms the southern rim of the Lamar Valley, then left the Yellowstone Plateau by way of the Bannock Indian trail and its connecting trail-way down the Yellowstone River from the mouth of the Gardner.

Most of the prospectors who came out of the Yellowstone region in the summer and fall of 1864 returned to Alder Gulch by way of the Gallatin Valley, where they found the beginnings of settlement: six log cabins along a creek within the limits of present Bozeman, Montana.[27] On his arrival in Virginia City, George Huston organized another party that ascended the Madison and Firehole rivers to the geyser basins, but his comrades were reputedly so appalled by the great geysers that they left the vicinity in haste.[28] Their experience in that area in late fall, when the cold air was vapor-laden (and thought by them to be suffocatingly noxious), developed a persistent myth of "death valley"—a fiction appearing occasionally in later writings.

The population of Yellowstone City declined rapidly in the spring of 1865, as many emigrants moved on to other camps, and those who retained claims rebuilt in a less exposed location at the mouth of Emigrant Gulch, where the post office of Chico was established January 15, 1865.[29] Prospecting was temporarily discontinued in the upper Yellowstone country as interest veered to such new strikes as Last Chance and Confederate gulches; in fact, the available record indicates the only activity on the Yellowstone Plateau was the visit of a prospector by the name of George Harvey Bacon to the Upper Geyser Basin with a party of Indians. But there was activity of another sort in the Yellowstone Valley.

The first session of the Territorial Legislature, which convened at Bannack in December 1864, gave a charter to a company organized by bank clerk Nathaniel P. Langford for the purpose of building and operating a stage road and telegraph line between Virginia City and the "head of navigation" on the Yellowstone River. This enterprise, which had gotten control of the privileges of another company formed to build a toll road between Bozeman, Montana, and Laramie, Wyoming, was incorporated January 20, 1865, as the Bozeman City and Fort Laramie Wagon Road and Telegraph Company (facetiously called the Broad Gauge Company). In a letter written from Virginia

City to cousin Will Doolittle, April 22, 1865, Langford has this to say
of his road project:

> I enclose a slip from the *Montana Post*, which will show you that we do
> not mean to be idle here. This road is a large scheme, being some 1,500
> miles in length, and two-thirds of it running through hostile Indian
> country. But the route is bound to be opened sometime by some one,—
> and why not by us? With this and my collections, I have my hands full.

To that he added on November 14, "Our large road Co. of which I am
President takes much of my time. . . . *My prospects were never better,*
and I believe that I shall make something handsome the coming
year."[30] The company got no further than placing ferry boats at
crossings of the Yellowstone, Clarks Fork, and Big Horn rivers before
the hostility of the Sioux Indians to the use of the Bozeman Trail
reduced traffic over that route to an insignificant trickle and obliged
the ferrymen to retreat to the safety of the Montana settlements. This
Indian trouble was immediately fatal to Langford's enterprise, and
eventually to the Bozeman Trail.

Short-lived though it was, the Broad Gauge Company did leave
a mark. The lumber for its ferryboats had been sawed at the mouth of
the first creek below Emigrant Gulch by John J. Tomlinson, who had
hauled machinery across the plains for his little water-powered mill,
for which Mill Creek was named.[31] His mill also produced much of
the lumber used in the construction of the Mackinaw boats in which
miners—successful and otherwise—returned to the States.

The pivotal event of 1866 was an effort to reopen the Bozeman
Trail by establishing forts along the route. Three were built: Fort
Reno at the crossing of Powder River, Fort Phil Kearny on Big Piney
Fork, and Fort C. F. Smith at the crossing of Big Horn River; but
they were so inadequately garrisoned and supplied as to be unequal to
the purpose, while their very presence stirred the Sioux to greater
ferocity. Their ineffectiveness was not yet apparent in July, when Jeff
Standifer led a hundred miners eastward on another of those periodic
forays into the Wyoming Basin. His gold-seekers were no more
successful than those who accompanied James Stuart in 1863 and
1864. They found pay dirt scarce and Sioux Indians plentiful; in fact,
the Indians were so numerous that some of the prospectors were
unable to get back to Montana and had to spend the winter at Fort C.
F. Smith.[32] The remainder escaped from the "Land of Massacre" by
way of its southern door, where they came under the influence of
agents then busily recruiting former Confederates (as a considerable
proportion of the Montana miners were) for service with the French
in Mexico; it is apparent from the diary of A. Bart Henderson that
many took the bait.[33]

Thus, the Standifer Expedition was effective in drawing the attention of Montana prospectors away from the Yellowstone region. So much so, in fact, that only one visit by prospectors is recorded for 1866. Toward the end of spring, George Huston led another small party up the Madison River to the geyser basins, where they spent several days before crossing over to the Mud Volcano by way of the east fork (present Nez Perce Creek). The trail of Idaho-bound horse thieves was found along the Yellowstone River (the earliest mention of that interesting traffic which persisted for nearly a half-century between Montana and Idaho),[34] and Huston's party followed it around the west side of Yellowstone Lake to Heart Lake, where they struck out eastward to the upper Yellowstone River. Crossing the river, they followed the east shore of Yellowstone Lake, completely circled the lake, then descended the river to its falls, crossed Mirror Plateau to the East Fork of the Yellowstone (now Lamar) River, and followed it and the Yellowstone down to Emigrant Gulch.[35]

Huston and his five companions had much to say about the wonders they had seen on their remarkable junket, and one Pilgrim with journalistic tendencies was duly impressed. He was Legh R. Freeman, who ceased his toiling among the innumerable boulders of the gulch to record some details—exaggerated, but recognizable—which he later made use of as editor of the *Frontier Index,* a peripatetic newspaper which followed the construction of the Union Pacific Railroad in 1868.[36] It is also probable that Freeman communicated enough of what he heard to James Hamilton Mills, who had briefly tried his luck at Emigrant Gulch before joining the staff of Montana's first newspaper, the *Montana Post*, at Virginia City, to enable him to make that earliest of all comparisons of the Yellowstone scenery with the better-known Yosemite Valley.

In the issue of July 14, 1866, the editor remarks:

> The Scenery of the Yosemite Valley as described by Bowles in his new book, "Across the Continent," though very grand and peculiar, is not more remarkable than the scenery at the passage of the Yellowstone through the Snowy Range one-hundred miles northeast [southeast] of this city. The rocks on either side, for a great distance, are equal in height to those of the Yosemite, and the river steals through them with the swiftness and stillness of an immense serpent, leaping into joyous rapids at the point of its release. We should like to have Bierstadt visit this portion of our Territory. He could make a picture from this piece of scenery surpassing either of his other views of the Rocky Mountains.

In the spring of 1867, John Bozeman and Tom Cover left the Gallatin Valley on a trip to the Bozeman Trail forts, where they hoped to get contracts for supplying the soldiers with flour. While camped about thirteen miles east of present Livingston, Montana, on April 18, they were caught off guard by Indians who managed to kill Bozeman. Undoubtedly, this was an isolated act by renegades, and unrelated to the warfare the Sioux were waging against the trail forts; but the Gallatin Valley settlers chose to read into that killing a great peril to themselves. They called for help, which the acting governor of Montana Territory supplied by raising and arming Territorial Volunteers.

This Meagher War, as it is termed (for the volatile, Irish liberal politician and ex-Civil War general who launched it), resulted in the establishment of fortifications for the protection of the Gallatin Valley: Fort Elizabeth Meagher, east of Bozeman, and Camp Ida Thoroughman at the mouth of Shields River.[37] The latter, also known as Camp Green Clay Smith after Meagher's death that summer, effectively screened the upper Yellowstone country from Indian attack, allowing a resurgence of prospecting up-river from Emigrant Gulch.

Interest had been sparked by a haul of $8,000 in gold dust and nuggets, which "Uncle" Joe Brown and three others took from a river bar at the mouth of Bear Creek in 1866.[38] Their luck, and the increased security, tempted Lou Anderson to go higher up the Yellowstone River with a small party. They found gold in a rocky crevice at the mouth of the first stream above Bear Creek, naming the place Crevice Gulch (the name survives in Crevice Creek, Crevice Mountain, Crevice Lake, and Crevice ranger station). The following day A. H. Hubble went hunting up the river and, when questioned that evening as to the nature of the next side-stream, he said, "It's a hell roarer." His remark provided the name for Hellroaring Creek, and later for a conical, rocky peak at its mouth. On another day, Hubble was again in advance and was again questioned about the next side-stream ahead of the party. According to him, "Twas but a slough." Although they afterward found a rushing torrent, which cost them a loaded packhorse in crossing, the name Slough Creek stuck. This party ascended the East Fork, crossed over to Pelican Creek, which they followed to its outlet into Lake Yellowstone, went down the river to the crossing later called the Nez Perce ford, and took the Mary Mountain route to the Lower Geyser Basin. From there they followed the Madison River to the settlements and Virginia City.[39]

Another prospecting venture is of interest here. Our knowledge of this visit to the area which is now Yellowstone Park—and many other facets of its history from 1867 to 1873—comes from the diary of A. Bart Henderson, whose compulsive record provides the only satisfying view of the activity of prospectors in the area.[40] Henderson was Jeff Standifer's lieutenant in 1866, which speaks for his experience as a prospector; he was as hard-fisted and hard-drinking as any of his kind, yet sensitive to his surroundings and literate too, as his "Journal" testifies. Whence he came and where he went are unknown, but we may conclude, from his involvement in the Mexican adventure, that he was one of those southerners so numerous in Montana during the post-Civil War era.

The diary of Henderson's 1867 prospecting trip opens August 12, when he left Deer Lodge, Montana, accompanied by John W. Powell, William Allen, and a Captain Bracey; all of them "two sheets in the wind and the third fluttering with 2 bottles of whiskey in our cantinas." Their route was southward along the stage route to the Camas Meadows, then over the Snake River plain to a crossing of Henrys Fork near its junction with the Snake River, after which they traveled up the Snake into Jackson Hole and crossed Two Ocean Pass into the valley of the upper Yellowstone River. From their camp near Bridger Lake, on the evening of August 29, they saw the waters of Yellowstone Lake fifteen miles to the north, but, as they "were at a very great loss to know what it was," Captain Bracey, according to Henderson's diary, proceeded to solve the problem.

> He soon had Capt. DeLacy's map spread on the grass, tracing out the different rivers that he found marked on the map.
> The Yellowstone Lake he soon found to be 15 miles long & 5 miles wide. This was all contrary to what we could see with our own eyes. . . . After examining the map & scratching his head several times John remarked that the body of water that we could see was nothing more nor less than the Pacific Ocean & that neither Capt. Bracey or Capt. DeLacy knew anything about the country. . . . However, we all concluded that we was on the Yellow Stone, & in sight of the famous lake.

Henderson's party had no particular difficulty following the Yellowstone River and the east shore of the lake until they came to Lake Butte, which descends steeply to the water. In attempting a detour eastward, they "soon became so entangled in the fallen timbers that it became necessary to chop them out," and several hours were consumed in log-hopping before they regained the beach. Their camp that night (August 31) was near the thermal feature called the Butte Springs, and, since it was raining the following day, they laid over there. While Powell fished in the lake for trout, finding "a few of them quite wormy," Henderson took a stroll along the beach, past Beach Springs, to that peculiar place later called Curiosity Point (probably Storm Point). There, according to his diary, he found

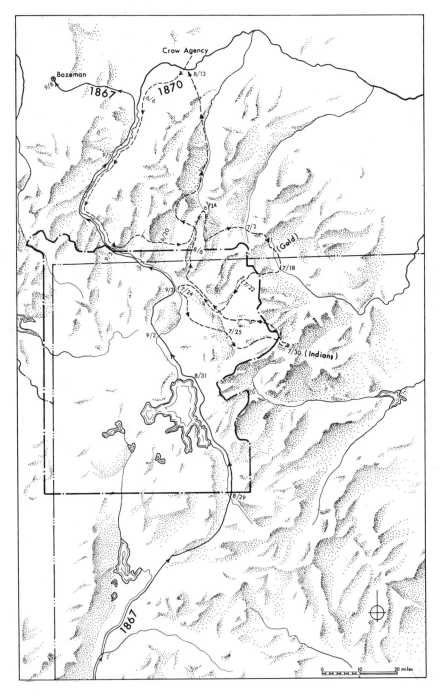

Prospecting trips of A. Bart Henderson in the Yellowstone region, 1867 and 1870.

several very singular formations, some being in the shape of the lid of a jar, or paint, or shaving box . . . formed as true as if turned in a turning lathe, in fact very much as if they was. I returned to camp with several very strange specimens, which I packed away very carefully. I consider these the most wonderful specimens that ever was found & would like very much to spend one summer here.

Continuing on to the outlet and down the west bank of the Yellowstone River on September 2, the Henderson party, which now included a wandering Englishman by the name of Jack Jones, came upon a "trail of about 80 barefooted tracks," which were "smoking" fresh. Certain that Blackfoot Indians had made them, and knowing of no good that could come from meeting those people, the prospectors abruptly changed their course so as to put the Yellowstone River between them and the red men. Where they crossed (probably near the mouth of Otter Creek) the river was rapid and deep, and the horses were soon swimming.

John [Powell] waited until we all landed safe, he then took charge of John Bull, or Jack Jones . . . who swore he would drown as he could not swim. However, Powell told him to dry up, & take his horse by the tail, & he would land him safe. After everything being ready John started in, John Bull & all. They landed all right.

After they unpacked their outfits and spread them to dry, Henderson shouldered his rifle and strolled downriver a few hundred yards and was

very much surprised to see the water disappear from my sight. I walked out on a rock & made two steps at the same time, one forward, the other backward, for I had unawares as it were, looked down into the depth or bowels of the earth, into which the Yellow plunged as if to cool the infernal region that lay under all this wonderful country of lava & boiling springs. The water fell several feet, struck a reef of rock that projected further than the main rock above. This reef caused the water to fall the remainder of the way in spray. We judged the falls to be 80 or 90 feet high, perhaps higher.

Apparently they did not see the lower fall, although their route on September 3 paralleled the Grand Canyon for several miles. Opposite the Washburn Springs, which Henderson thought would "be a very great wonder in the course of time," they were able to stand on the rim of the canyon and observe the Yellowstone River looking like a white ribbon laid in the bottom of its great chasm—a view to "cause anyone to shudder." A dim trail zigzagged up the mountainside to the west of the Washburn Springs and led them into the basin of Tower Creek and down to a campsite at the foot of Tower Fall.

As the party continued down the Yellowstone, Henderson noted "a large stream coming in on the east side" (Lamar River), and with it the first indications of mineralization since leaving the Snake River. On September 5, from their camp at the mouth of Gardner River, they saw steam arising from a cluster of white hills several miles to the south. Assuming the vapor came from more hot springs, they passed on without investigating and were soon out of the land of wonders.

While prospectors were abroad in the Yellowstone, other events were taking place. Early in May, C. J. Baronett and four other prospectors, marooned at Fort C. F. Smith after the breakup of the Standifer Expedition, reached Bozeman by skirting the foothills on trails unknown to the Sioux. They reported the garrison in dire straits. Cut off from their base of supplies (Fort Laramie) by the Indians who controlled the Bozeman Trail, they had been without flour since after Christmas and were destitute of coffee, sugar, and tobacco, and were, in fact, subsisting on corn, bacon, and "hardtack."[41] Colonel deLacy, acting as engineer officer for the Montana Volunteers, was then engaged in fortifying the Bozeman and Bridger passes. When he heard of the state of affairs at Fort C. F. Smith, he loaded eight wagons with Gallatin Valley flour and potatoes and started to the relief of the garrison. Although there were many gloomy predictions, the supply train with its escort of forty-two militiamen got through.[42]

The usefulness of the Montana Volunteers ended that summer with establishment of Fort Ellis three miles west of Bozeman, on the site now occupied by the agricultural experiment station. It was named for Colonel Augustus Van Horn Ellis, 124th New York Infantry, who was killed at the battle of Gettysburg July 2, 1863. During the nineteen years of its existence as a military post, Fort Ellis was the staging point for numerous official and unofficial explorations of the Yellowstone region; troops stationed there were involved in the Sioux, Nez Perce, and Bannock wars, and though not always appreciated locally, the fort exerted a stabilizing influence that was necessary in the pre-railroad days.[43]

On the Idaho side of the Yellowstone Plateau civilization encroached somewhat upon the wilderness when Gilman Sawtell located a "ranch" at what are now known as Staley's Springs, on Henrys Lake.[44] His principal occupation was the spearing of large lake trout which he packed in ice and hauled to Virginia City over a rude wagon trail across Raynolds Pass and down the Madison River. His route, known as the Virginia City Road, became very important in the early years of the Park.

It is said that the area now included in Yellowstone Park gained its first white resident in the fall of 1867, when George Huston located opposite the mouth of Bear Creek,[45] while three miners—Arch Graham, Jack Crandall, and a man variously called Dougherty or Finley—soon afterward began working a claim at the mouth of Crevice Creek, continuing operations there in 1868.

During the summer of 1868, two brothers, Frederick and Phillip Bottler, took land in the Yellowstone Valley opposite Emigrant Gulch to become the first settlers between Bozeman and the present Park. (This statement excludes the previous locations by miners because they were both temporary and illegal, being on what were then Indian lands.) The Bottler ranch[46] was at first more of a base for hunting and prospecting than a ranch, and it was on one of his periodic trips into the upriver country that Frederick came upon the evidences of a grisly tragedy.

In August 1869, the three miners at Crevice Creek decided they weren't doing too well and joined two other prospectors in a trip to the head of Boulder and Stillwater rivers and then to Clarks Fork. There Crandall and Dougherty remained to prospect, while the others returned to the Yellowstone drainage. That fall a party of twenty men, including Frederick Bottler and Adam "Horn" Miller, went over to Clarks Fork expecting to meet Crandall and Dougherty there; instead, they found a despoiled camp, and the heads of the two men stuck on the points of picks and tin cups on the ground before them, signifying that Indians had surprised them at their meal. From that event, the stream upon which the camp was made took its present name, Crandall Creek.[47]

A. Bart Henderson went back into the Yellowstone in 1870. He left the Crow Agency on June 6, in the company of James Gourley, Adam "Horn" Miller, Ed Hibbard, and a man known only as Dad. At Emigrant Gulch they found twenty-five men working for a very small return, and, while tarrying there, "got on a spree & run all night." There were only two miners working at Bear Gulch, "making from three to five dollars a day." Continuing up what Henderson called the South Fork of Bear Gulch, his party crossed the divide and descended Horse Creek onto Hellroaring Creek about three miles north of the present Park boundary.

Above Hellroaring Creek, on June 21, they found a beautiful flat, "which we gave the name of Buffalo Flat [now Buffalo Plateau], as we found thousands of buffalo quietly grazing." Dropping into the valley of Buffalo Fork, they followed that stream nearly to Boulder Pass, where Henderson noted on June 28: "Buffalo bull ran thro the tent, while all hands were in bed." Turning back toward the present

Park, they encountered another old bull while crossing the divide toward Slough Creek; he charged the packtrain so suddenly that Henderson had time for only one shot before the bull ran over him and attacked the horses. What a melee that must have been, with loaded packhorses scattering every way from the enraged buffalo. Fortunately, the bull was soon killed.

Gold was first found in the vicinity of Lake Abundance, but prospecting was complicated by grizzly bears. On July 9, Henderson and Dad "met an old she bear & three cubs. After a severe fight killed the whole outfit, while a short distance further on we was attacked by an old boar bear. We soon killed him. He proved to be the largest ever killed in the mountains, weighing 960 pounds." On the tenth, "killed six bear today," and on the eleventh, "I was chased by an old she bear today. Clime[d] a tree & killed her under the tree."

Finding that the late-lying snow had kept the groundwater too high for placer mining in that area, the prospectors abandoned the field to *Ursus horribilis* and moved on to the Clarks Fork Valley, where they made the strike that developed into the Cooke City mines. However, instead of settling to work there, they decided to prospect some more and return in the fall; so, they crossed the mountain to Cache Creek, traveled down it and the Lamar River, naming the Soda Butte and Soda Butte Creek as they passed by; then, doubling back along the top of Specimen Ridge and the rim of the Mirror Plateau, they ascended the Little Lamar River to the divide between Sunlight Creek and the North Fork of the Shoshone River.

While the party camped there, Henderson and Ed Hibbard went to look for a route into the Shoshone drainage; they soon heard shots from the direction of camp, and returning, they "saw at a single glance that the camp was surrounded by Indians who already had our horses in their possession." Adding their fire power to that of the three men who had barricaded themselves in camp, they drove the Indians off; yet the party was still in quite a predicament. Without horses to move their food, tools, blasting powder and twenty-seven bear skins, they could only cache what could not be carried and set out afoot. Thirteen days later they were back at the Crow Agency, having covered something like 110 miles, mostly mountainous, by way of the Lamar River, Slough Creek, and Boulder River. So ended the brief but hectic era of the prospector.

The Yellowstone region was thus explored quite thoroughly by the prospecting fraternity by midsummer of 1870. Indeed, had their knowledge of the area been assembled at that time, there would have been no need for the definitive exploration described in the next chapter. But the prospector, like the trapper, suffered from a credibility gap, though with less excuse.

Storytelling as a form of campfire entertainment may have served the prospector as it had the trapper; but the prospector told his stories to the newspapers, which sprang up wherever a stampede matured into a town of some permanence. On the printed page the prospector became an unmitigated exhibitionist more often than a serious reporter, which led to a rather low opinion of his public statements. Of course, the frontier editor was no paragon of truthful reporting, and perhaps should carry some of the blame.

The following is a sample of the coverage the Yellowstone country had in the public press during the mining era:

> Good story. We clip from an eastern paper. Mr. Edward Parson, just returned from Montana, tells the editor of the Leavenworth *Commercial* a marvelous story. Last July, himself and four companions, while exploring the headwaters of the Yellowstone, came upon an Indian mound, surmounted by a huge stone. Dislodging this stone and several others, they found themselves in a Indian catacomb, containing the skeletons of thirty warriors. Lying beside the bones were numerous ornaments, among them many twisted circlets of gold. Some of these were of unusual size, weighing one and a half to two pounds. What chiefly attracted attention was a massive basin or kettle that occupied the centre of the apartment. This massive article proved to be pure gold, and was so heavy that the party had great difficulty in removing it from its resting place and bringing it into the upper air. The adventurers were enabled, by means of their axes, to sever the mass into portable pieces, laden with which the party turned their steps homeward.[48]

He who would have a further draught, prospector style, at the fountain of fantasy, should consult Legh Freeman or Charles Sunderlee.[49]

CHAPTER 5

BEYOND THE RANGES

Something hidden. Go and find it. Go
and look behind the Ranges—
Something lost behind the Ranges.
Lost and waiting for you. Go!
　　　　　　　—The Explorer

I n those lines Rudyard Kipling has expressed the spirit of the true
explorer: the driving curiosity that sets him apart from the fur
trapper and the prospector, whose interests are instinctively
commercial. This breed, the explorer, being less preoccupied is more
discerning and more inclined to adequately record his observations.
And so, in the Yellowstone region, as generally throughout the West,
the burden of definitive exploration has rested upon men whose
purpose was simply to find out what lay behind the ranges.

While the definitive exploration of the area we are concerned
with was essentially the accomplishment of a triad of parties (Folsom,
1869; Washburn, 1870; and Hayden, 1871), each of which made
particular and important contributions to the emerging popular
image of the Yellowstone Wonderland, there was an earlier beginning.
General James Wilkinson (mentioned in Chapter 1) was sufficiently
intrigued with the idea of exploring the upper reaches of the Yellowstone River to send out a small party in 1805, but with what result we
do not know. One of the purposes of the vaunted Yellowstone Expedition of 1819 was exploration, which was to be accomplished by a
scientific corps under Major Stephen H. Long, but his efforts proved
essentially negative through giving undeserved support to the Great

American Desert thesis. The result was a slackening of official interest in western exploration during the following two decades. It required those catalytic events of the 1840s—the opening of the Oregon Trail, adjustment of the Oregon question with Great Britain, and our territorial aggrandizement through the war with Mexico—to revive the flagging interest in western exploration per se.

At long last there was a revival of scientific curiosity about the West and with it came renewed interest in the Yellowstone region. It was a renaissance which at first leaned heavily on the geographical knowledge of the fur trappers. Some gleanings from that source appear on a Map of the Rocky Mountains prepared by Washington Hood, of the U.S. Army Corps of Topographical Engineers, from information provided by William Sublette. On it he was able to show a large "Burnt Hole" on the headwaters of Madison River, to the west of a sweet potato-shaped Yellowstone Lake and separated from it by a narrow mountain ridge. Also shown is a "Gardner's Fork," which enters the Yellowstone River from the west well below the lake, and a knowledge of Mammoth Hot Springs is indicated by the notation "Boiling Spring White Sulphur Banks."

A decade later, Jim Bridger's familiarity with the Yellowstone region was utilized by another officer of the Corps of Topographical Engineers. While guiding Captain Stansbury's Utah expedition in 1849-50, Jim described the headwaters of the Yellowstone to Lieutenant John W. Gunnison in terms "most romantic and enticing"; yet, the impressions recorded by the young engineer in his history of the Mormons[1] is also reasonably accurate and quite comprehensive. In it is a Yellowstone Lake sixty miles long (the only exaggeration in Bridger's information); geysers conservatively described as spouting seventy feet "with a terrific, hissing noise, at regular intervals"; the falls and Grand Canyon of the Yellowstone River, and what Bridger called the Great Springs, presumed to be Mammoth Hot Springs from his mention of the delightful baths available in the terraced pools.

Additional insight into Bridger's geographical knowledge of the Yellowstone region is provided by the map drawn by Father Pierre Jean DeSmet in 1851.[2] The far-ranging Jesuit priest got his information from Jim at the Indian council held near Fort Laramie that year, and in several particulars its accuracy is remarkable. DeSmet's map shows a "Two Ocean Riv." flowing into a mountain pass, from whence it is divided into two streams, one marked "Pacific," descending to Snake River, while the other, or "Atlantic" branch, feeds into the upper Yellowstone River. Improbable as that presentation of the hydrography of Two Ocean Pass may seem, it is essentially correct.

The condition exists because a South Two Ocean Creek and a North Two Ocean Creek flow into the pass from opposite sides to merge their waters in swamps from which Pacific Creek flows southwest into Jackson Hole and Atlantic Creek flows northeast into the Yellowstone Valley.

Other entries on DeSmet's map indicate more interest in the thermal activity of the Yellowstone region than appears in Gunnison's brief account. The Mammoth Hot Springs, shown as "Sulphur Mountain," are correctly placed on the left bank of "Gardener's Riv." (a remarkable rendering of Bridger's Virginian drawl). A "volcano" (more about this later) is noted along the Yellowstone River north of its lake, which is again given a length of sixty miles and has "hot springs" on its eastern shore. While there is no indication of the hot springs or geysers on the headwaters of Madison River, a "Fire Hole Riv." makes its appearance as a prominent eastern branch, with the area between it and Yellowstone Lake designated as a "Great Volcanic Region about 100 miles in extent now in state of eruption."[3] DeSmet's presentation of Yellowstone geography included a southern branch of the Madison River, with two lakes strung on it like beads, the whole drainage labeled "DeSmet's L. and Riv." This obvious misconception of the Shoshone-Lewis Lake system was later repeated by members of the Hayden Survey, who also thought those lakes drained northward to the Madison instead of southward to the Snake.

The foregoing review of *reliable* fur-trade knowledge of the Yellowstone region gives some idea of the tantalizing information that was probably available to Lieutenant Gouverneur K. Warren when that able officer of the Corps of Topographical Engineers began the mapping of the Yellowstone River in 1856. His efforts got no farther than the mouth of Powder River, but the project was continued three years later under Captain William F. Raynolds, whose lot it was to attempt the first organized exploration of what is now Yellowstone National Park.

Raynolds' failure to penetrate the mountain barrier surrounding what he considered "the most interesting unexplored district in our widely expanded country"[4] was not due to a lack of interest in its wonders, nor to any lack of ability or perseverance as an explorer; rather, an unfortunate combination of schedule and weather balked his efforts. The expedition was operating under orders that specified its several objectives and the sequence in which they were to be accomplished. Thus, he moved out of winter quarters at Deer Creek on the upper Platte River on May 10, 1860, committed to a determination of the most direct and feasible route "from the Yellowstone to the South Pass, and to ascertaining the practicability of a route from the sources of Wind River to those of the Missouri"; furthermore, it was an assignment that had to be accomplished in time to allow simultaneous descents of the Missouri and Yellowstone rivers as the expedition returned to the settlements.

At the junction of the Popo Agie and Wind rivers, Raynolds divided his expedition into two parties: one, under Lieutenant H. E. Maynadier, with Lieutenant John Mullan commanding the escort, was to descend the Big Horn River and then skirt westward around the base of the Yellowstone mountains to the Three Forks of the Missouri. The other party, under Raynolds' personal direction and guided by Jim Bridger, was to follow the valley of Wind River into the mountains, hoping to cross over to some stream leading to the Three Forks and a juncture with Maynadier's party on the last day of June. For that uncertain traverse, which Raynolds hoped would bring him to the head of the Yellowstone River,[5] there were but six weeks available.

Upon reaching the head of the Wind River, Raynolds saw there was no pass northward to the Yellowstone, and Bridger was able to say, as they contemplated those forbidding mountains: "I told you you could not go through. A bird can't fly over that without taking a supply of grub along." To that, Raynolds "had no reply to offer and mentally conceded the accuracy of the information of 'the old man of the mountains.' "

Unable to reach the upper Yellowstone drainage from the east side of the Continental Divide, the party continued their westward march, crossing by Union Pass (named by Raynolds) into the drainage of the Gros Ventre River. They descended to that stream by way of Fish Creek, losing a precious week in the struggle with late-lying snowdrifts; but a point was finally gained from which Bridger thought they could cross back to the upper Yellowstone. And so, on June 7, Raynolds, accompanied by Bridger, Dr. Ferdinand V. Hayden (naturalist), Antoine Schoenborn (artist), J. D. Hutton (topographer), and four men followed a little valley up to the "dividing crest of the Rocky Mountains." From there, "It did not require long to decide that further progress was impracticable. From the southward we had already passed over ten or fifteen miles of snow . . . nothing was in sight but pines and snow. . . . A venture into that country would result in the certain loss of our animals, if not the whole party."[6]

Remarking that they were compelled to content themselves with listening to marvelous tales of burning plains, immense lakes, and boiling springs, without being able to verify those wonders, Raynolds

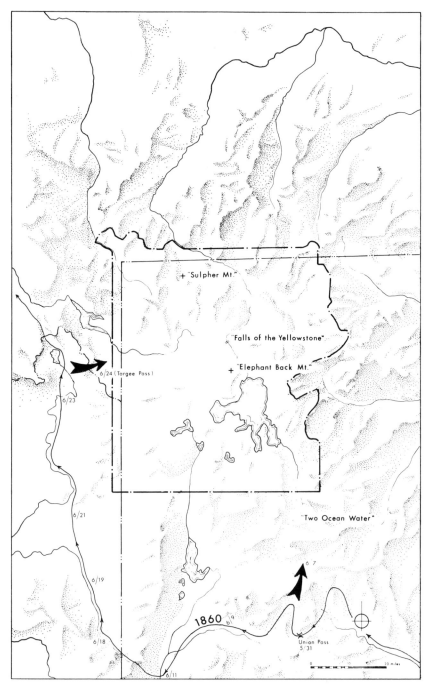

Attempted exploration of the Yellowstone region by the Raynolds expedition, 1860.

turned away from that mysterious land, continuing the march to the Three Forks of the Missouri by a more roundabout route that took them over Teton Pass, up Henrys Fork of the Snake River to the Low Pass now named for Raynolds, and down the Madison River. Meticulous adherence to an exacting schedule left little opportunity for side excursions, but there was one worth noting. After crossing the outlet of Henrys Lake,

> Mr. Hutton, Dr. Hayden, and two attendants turned to the east and visited the [Targhee] pass over the mountains, leading into the Burnt Hole [Madison] Valley. They found the summit distant only about five miles from our route, and report the pass as in all respects equal to that through which the train had gone. From it they could see a second pass upon the other side of the valley, which Bridger states to lead to the Gallatin. He also says that between that point and the Yellowstone there are no mountains to be crossed.[7]

Yet they were unable to take advantage of that open door for there remained but five days to reach the rendezvous with Lieutenant Maynadier's party at the Three Forks of the Missouri.

Raynolds' expedition put an end to the work of the old Corps of Topographical Engineers, which soon disappeared in the chaos of the Civil War, and even his long delayed report was a casualty of that conflict insofar as the Yellowstone region was concerned. When finally printed in 1868, the account was largely stale news; having failed to add materially to the scientific knowledge of the terra incognita, what he had to report might have served the purpose of drawing attention to the vagary of popular knowledge, but Raynolds was too late—definitive exploration was already developing from another direction.

In the spring of 1865, Father Francis Xavier Kuppens, a young Jesuit priest attached to the old St. Peter's Mission on Sun River near present Great Falls, Montana, had an opportunity to accompany a group of Piegan Indians on a buffalo hunt in the country between the Missouri and Yellowstone rivers. In the course of that practical evangelism, this Belgian (he was one of a number recruited by Father DeSmet in 1857) heard about the Yellowstone region. He says, "many an evening in the tent of Baptiste Champagne or Chief Big Lake the conversation, what little there was of it, turned on the beauties of that wonderful spot. . . . There was sufficient in the tale to excite my curiosity."[8]

Father Kuppens was able to induce some of the young men to take him into the area he had heard so much about, and there he saw what he termed the "chief attraction," including the Grand Canyon and the geysers of the Firehole basins. Upon his return to St. Peter's Mission, Kuppens described his unusual excursion to Fathers Ravalli and Imoda, and then his experience was relegated to the anecdotal limbo.

Late in October of that same year, while the sights of the Yellowstone trip were yet fresh in Kuppens' mind, a party of horsemen going from Helena to Fort Benton was caught in a sudden, savage blizzard from which they took shelter at the mission. The nearly frozen riders included Acting Territorial Governor Thomas Francis Meagher, Territorial Judges Hezekiah L. Hosmer and Lyman E. Munson, two deputy United States marshals, X. Beidler and Neil Howie, and Cornelius Hedges. The latter wrote, "We were received with a warm welcome and all our wants were abundantly supplied and we were in condition to appreciate our royal entertainment."[9]

Their entertainment, during several storm-bound days at the mission, included much about the Yellowstone trip of Father Kuppens, who says:

> On that occasion I spoke to him [Meagher] about the wonders of the Yellowstone. His interest was greatly aroused by my recital and perhaps even more so, by that of a certain Mr. Viell—an old Canadian married to a Blackfoot squaw—who during a lull in a storm had come over to see the distinguished visitors. When he was questioned about the Yellowstone he described everything in a most graphic manner. None of the visitors had ever heard of the wonderful place. Gen. Meagher said if things were as described the government ought to reserve the territory for a national park. All the visitors agreed that efforts should be made to explore the region and that a report of it should be sent to the government.[10]

There was no opportunity to make the proposed exploration until 1867, when the Montana Volunteers erected those forts—Elizabeth Meagher and Ida Thoroughman—that served to shield the Gallatin and Yellowstone valleys from the raiding Sioux. With a Yellowstone expedition at last feasible, the *Virginia City Montana Post* of June 29, 1867, carried this announcement:

> The Expedition to the Yellowstone country mentioned a short time since is now organized, and it is the purpose of the party to start from the camp on Shields River [Ida Thoroughman] in about two weeks. The expedition will be gone some three weeks and will go up the river as far as Yellowstone Lake. A number of gentlemen have expressed a desire to join the party. We refer those in Helena to General Thoroughman, who will be at that city on Monday, and will give all desired information. Parties who have leisure to make this fascinating jaunt can ascertain particulars from Judge Hosmer or T. C. Everts.

The expedition was crippled at the last moment by Meagher's death in the waters of the Missouri River at Fort Benton. None of the territory's influential men cared to absent themselves in the Yellowstone wilderness during the period of readjustment which followed, and the projected exploration degenerated to a scout by a company of Montana Territorial Volunteers under "dashing" Captain Charley Curtiss, accompanied by Surgeon James Dunlevy. Though the newspaper coverage describes the expedition as proceeding to "within a few miles of the lake near the head of this great valley," it evidently was terminated at the Mammoth Hot Springs, where the field correspondent became enamored with the possibility of developing a borax mine.[11] As an exploration, the Curtiss-Dunlevy expedition was somewhat of a dud, its only value being in the encouragement it gave to a further effort by "some select party, well prepared and equipped."

The available information on the Yellowstone region at the close of 1867 allowed a correspondent of the *Frontier Index* to provide a reasonable description of the area's main features, including the lake, falls, and geysers, to which he added this prophecy: "A few years more and the U. P. Railroad will bring thousands of pleasure seekers, sightseers and invalids from every part of the globe, to see this land of surpassing wonders."[12]

A number of the interested gentlemen who failed to go up the Yellowstone River with the Curtiss-Dunlevy expedition in 1867 made feeble attempts to organize parties to explore the Yellowstone in 1868 and 1869. Regarding the latter, the *Helena Herald* for July 29, 1869, announced:

> A letter from Fort Ellis, dated the 19th, says that an expedition is organizing, composed of soldiers and citizens, and will start for the upper waters of the Yellowstone the latter part of August, and will hunt and explore a month or so. Among the places of note which they will visit, are the Falls, Coulter's Hell and Lake, and the Mysterious Mounds. The expedition is regarded as a very important one, and the result of their explorations will be looked forward to with unusual interest.

A shortage of troops due to the Indian unrest deprived the expedition of an escort, however, and all but three of the citizens refused to go without such protection. The bold ones were David E. Folsom, Charles W. Cook, and William Peterson, and, according to the latter, their decision to go regardless was somewhat impetuous. They had returned, disappointed, from Helena to Diamond City, where all three were employed by the Boulder Ditch Company, which

David E. Folsom.   From Langford,   *The Discovery of Yellowstone Park, 1870* (1905).

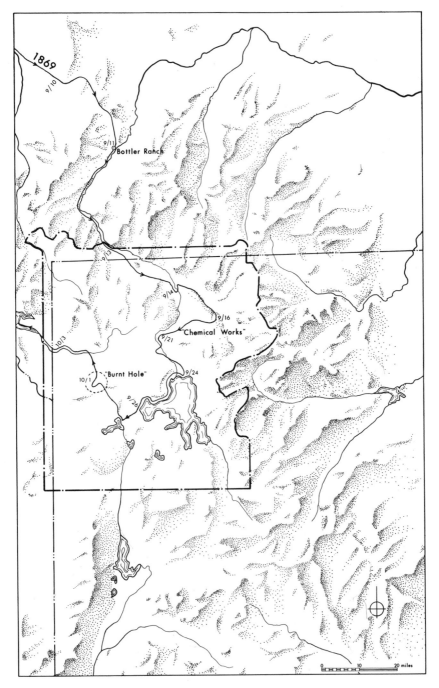

Route of the Cook-Folsom party, 1869.

supplied water for hydraulic mining in Confederate Gulch. Cook said, "If I could get one man to go with me, I'd go anyway." Peterson spoke up, "Well, Charley, I guess I can go as far as you can," and Folsom added, "Well, I can go as far as both of ye's,"[13] so they started the next day.

Cook and Folsom were rather untypical Quakers, while Peterson was a former deep-water sailor, but long residence in the mining camps of the northern Rocky Mountains had prepared them for such an expedition. All were good shots, well versed in woodcraft, and self-reliant; Folsom was trained in surveying and Peterson was a packer with practical experience gained in freighting to the Idaho mines. Yet, their own confidence in their ability was not shared by the friends who saw them off with such parting remarks as, "good-bye, boys, look out for your hair"; "if you get into a scrap, remember I warned you"; "if you get back at all you will come on foot," and "it's the next thing to suicide."

In addition to their five horses (three for riding and two for packing) the "outfit" included a repeating rifle, Colt revolver, and sheath knife for each, one double-barreled shotgun, ammunition, fishing tackle, five pairs of blankets, two buffalo robes, an axe, a small camp kettle, coffee pot, two frying pans, three tin cups, four tin plates, three knives, forks and spoons, to which they added (at Bozeman, the last place where supplies could be purchased) 175 pounds of flour, 25 of bacon, a ham, 30 pounds of sugar, 15 of ground coffee, 10 of salt, 10 of dried fruit, 50 of potatoes, and a dozen boxes of yeast powder. In addition to those essentials, they had a pick, shovel, and pan with which to improve any "prospects" they might chance upon, and some items dictated by individual wisdom (Cook brought a pair of French field glasses; Folsom a pocket compass and thermometer, and Peterson had two balls of stout cord). The prospecting tools were the only useless things they took along.

The route followed by these adventurers between Bozeman and the mouth of the Gardner River is an important way into the Yellowstone wilderness. From Fort Ellis, two and a half miles east of town,[14] they followed the old emigrant road toward Bozeman Pass for five miles (to Meadow Creek), then a former Indian trail up that stream six miles to the divide between the Gallatin and Yellowstone drainages. From there, the way led down Trail Creek eleven miles, to the point where it debouched into the Yellowstone Valley,[15] then crossed a dry bench, through sagebrush and prickly pear cactus, for seven more miles to a ford over the Yellowstone River opposite Emigrant Gulch.[16] The track was well used and plain enough that far; it was the way the miners had gone since 1864.

A faint trace that held to the right before the ford was reached continued up the west bank of the river for several miles to the ranch established by the two Bottler brothers, Frederick and Phillip, in 1868. Beyond that rude homestead,[17] generally considered to be thirty-nine miles from Bozeman, there were only the occasional hoofprints of unshod Indian ponies and the drag-marks of travois poles to mark the aboriginal trailway up the Yellowstone. Eleven miles from Bottlers', another stream called Trail Creek (because it provided access to the West Gallatin River), now known as Tom Miner Creek,[18] entered the river from the west. This tributary marked the end of the open valley between the "first" and "second" canyons; and there the direction of travel changed from southwest to southeast, while the valley narrowed to a rocky slash (present Yankee Jim Canyon) crowded with slide-rock intermixed with stunted trees.

Above the three-mile-long confusion of this second canyon, the valley widened again and the Indian trail led easily across a succession of sagebrush-covered flats for the remaining thirteen miles to the mouth of the Gardner River. Midway, an isolated ridge, crowding against the river on the west side of the valley, provided a landmark called Cinnabar Mountain, or sometimes Red Streak Mountain, from the picturesque feature later known as the Devils Slide.[19] The small streams that reach the Yellowstone River below and above Cinnabar Mountain—Mol Heron and Reese creeks—did not gain accepted names until another decade had passed.

On the first evening after leaving the Gallatin Valley, Cook, Folsom, and Peterson camped on the bank of the Yellowstone near the ford by which the miners crossed to Emigrant Gulch. Since the party intended to visit the diggings the following morning (September 11), they made a late start, but they somehow missed the ford and arrived at the Bottler ranch. Folsom was not impressed by the un-chinked cabin "with a roof through which every passing shower would filter for hours," nor by the improvidence of allowing cattle to feed from unthreshed wheat, yet those first settlers to lodge permanently in that part of the Yellowstone Valley had probably accomplished all that could be expected in one brief year. At the time, the brothers were out hunting in order to add to the stack of antelope and elk hides which was their "cash" crop.

As a result of the late start, the day's journey ended only three miles beyond the ranch when a chilling afternoon rainstorm forced the party to camp early under a tent improvised from blankets. It was a place of blue noses and chattering teeth, from which they were glad to depart promptly the next morning.[20]

A little more than eight miles from that camp they came upon a solitary wickiup on the bank of Tom Miner Creek. It was a barely adequate structure of poles thatched with grass, occupied by two old Indian women who were busy gathering and drying chokecherries. By the repeated use of the word *Tonkey*, the elder of the two crones made it clear that they were Sheepeaters. The three adventurers rode on without discovering what message the Indians tried to communicate by pointing up the river and counting to thirty by opening and closing both hands three times.

While they scrambled over and around the jumble of slide-rock in Yankee Jim Canyon a band of antelope dashed by so close that Cook was able to bag one with the shotgun. Soon after that fortunate encounter, they "camped close to the river on a narrow bottom and fared sumptuously on antelope steak and trout from the water."[21]

On September 13 the journey continued up the Yellowstone River past Devils Slide to the mouth of the Gardner. There, the ancient Indian trailway forked, one branch ascending Gardner River and the other paralleling the Yellowstone while climbing onto the Blacktail Deer Creek Plateau to pass around Black Canyon.[22] They took the latter route to a pleasant campsite in an open meadow near the head of Rescue Creek (an inappropriate name that developed from the exploration of 1870).

The Indian trail they had followed to that point trends southward from the meadow, crossing a low ridge to a junction with the east-west thoroughfare known as the Bannock Indian Trail. By continuing on the Indian route, the Folsom party could have passed easily up the Yellowstone Valley; but they mistrusted the southward jog and struck off eastward through the rough country closer to the river which was their guide. The day's journey produced only a chance meeting with more Sheepeater Indians (of whom they were unnecessarily alarmed, for these Indians had no more sinister objective than to cadge a little ammunition or some matches). From them the party learned what the old women had tried to tell them: simply that there were thirty lodges of their people on the trail ahead. A mile farther on, about where Tower Junction now is, they reached the Bannock Indian Trail, leading to a good campsite near the ford by which that route crosses to the east bank of the Yellowstone.

The presence of hot springs and other features in the vicinity induced the party to lay over a day to explore their first Yellowstone wonders. Scrambling over the Overhanging Cliff, with its fine view of the outcropping columnar basalt arrayed along the opposite wall of the canyon, they descended to the Calcite Springs and proceeded to poke about the springs and vents that are undoubtedly the source of John Colter's tantalizing note on the Clark Map of 1812.[23] While collecting specimens there, Cook nearly ended up in a steam vent later found to have a temperature of 194 degrees. Folsom thought he took his narrow escape rather coolly, considering the temperature. The ramble was concluded with a visit to the foot of Tower Fall (though they did not name it) on the return to camp.

From information obtained from prospectors who had been in the area at an earlier date, it was understood that the canyon beginning a short distance above their camp was continuous to the Falls of the Yellowstone, an obstacle "through which no one had been able to pass."[24] The Folsom party therefore decided to cross the river at the ford opposite their camp, follow the valley of the East Fork (Lamar River) for a day's travel, and then cross over the Mirror Plateau in a direction calculated to bring them out near the falls. The route was successful but tedious.

That first night after crossing the Yellowstone River they camped in a forest-rimmed glade just below Calfee Creek. There, they were oppressed by a feeling of loneliness as they listened to the voices of the night. Folsom says,

> The wolf scents us afar and the mournful cadence of his howl adds to our sense of solitude. The roar of the mountain lion awakens the sleeping echoes of the adjacent cliffs and we hear the elk whistling in every direction. . . . Even the horses seem filled with a feeling of dread, they stop grazing and raise their heads to listen, and then hover around our campfire as if their safety lay in our companionship.

The trek across the Mirror Plateau toward the Falls of the Yellowstone began with a steep ascent up Flint Creek. The weather, which was dismal at the outset, turned increasingly stormy, and they sought shelter early in a grove of spruce trees below the summit. In that refuge they were comfortable enough in the blanket tent throughout the storm, although the six inches of snow it put down on the following day worked a hardship on the picketed horses.

The morning of September 19 dawned clear and cold, with the snow-covered landscape glistening in the bright sunshine which presaged a better day. Progress was slow after the plateau was reached: they traveled five miles to an overnight camp west of Wrong Creek on the first day; an equal distance on the second brought them to the vicinity of Josephs Coat Springs, where they spent the afternoon investigating the very active thermal features and killing an elk to replenish their meat supply.

The way was easier on the twenty-first with no underbrush or fallen timber, and Cook was riding ahead, followed by the two packhorses to which he was momentarily giving his attention, when his saddle horse stopped abruptly. The animal had halted on the brink of the Grand Canyon in the notch between Artist and Sublime points. Cook Says, "I sat there in amazement, while my companions came up, and after that, it seemed to me it was five minutes before anyone spoke." After that first awe-inspiring view, the Folsom party made their way along the rim of the canyon, past the two falls, to a grassy bench on the east bank of the Yellowstone above the present Chittenden Memorial Bridge, and there they camped.

The following day they spent at the falls: "a day that has been a succession of surprises," according to Folsom, who thought, "language is inadequate to convey a just conception of the awful grandeur and sublimity of this masterpiece of nature's handiwork." While there they measured the height of both falls with Peterson's ball of twine and a forked stick. This was accomplished by Cook lying prone upon the rock at the lip of the fall and paying out the twine over the stick in accordance with signals from Peterson, who stood below where he could observe the descending weight. The result obtained for the Upper Fall (115 feet) was remarkably close to the accepted figure of 109 for that drop; at the Lower Fall, where mist and turbulence interfered with the work, they did not do so well.[25]

On September 23, the Folsom party left that "beautiful, picturesque, magnificent, grand, sublime, awful, terrible" Grand Canyon of the Yellowstone and continued on the east side of the river to a crossing opposite Crater Hills. Much of the day went into exploring the many thermal features there and at Mud Volcano, near which they camped for the night. The Mud Volcano was particularly impressive. Then, as now, it was a mud-filled cave opening upon a hillside, but the power of its frequent and regular activity was so great the three explorers could hear every explosion at their camp a half-mile away and imagined they could feel the ground tremble beneath them (as it did in the immediate vicinity of that awe-inspiring grotto.)

Soon after breaking camp the following morning, the Folsom party recrossed the Yellowstone River at what would later be known as the Nez Perce ford and followed the east bank to the outlet of the great, blue lake that extended into mountain-girt "arms" nearly twenty miles to the south.[26] Turning east along the lake shore, they found a pleasant campsite on the grassy bench west of Mary Bay. At that place they were able to take their choice of ducks, geese, and trout to augment their dwindling supplies; indeed, it was the condition of the larder which decided them to turn homeward after marking their *ultima Thule* with a piece of rock on which Folsom inscribed their names and the date, and then inserted in a mortise in a pine tree.[27]

Returning to the outlet of the lake, the Folsom party forded the Yellowstone at a riffle in the vicinity of the present Fishing Bridge and continued along the north shore of the lake, intending to cross in a westerly direction into the drainage of the Madison River, which they knew would lead them back to the settlements of Montana Territory. About noon they came to Bridge Bay, the present site of a crowded campground and bustling marina. Folsom's description of that little Paradise Lost is nostalgic now:

> We came to a small grassy opening upon the opposite side of which was a beautiful little lake, separated from the main lake only by a sandbar, which the surf had thrown up across the narrow neck which formerly connected them. . . . This was about one thousand yards across and was nearly reefed. Large flocks of geese and ducks were feeding near the shore or floating gracefully on its smooth surface. Beyond the lake the timber was tall and straight and to appearances as thick as cane in a southern swamp. This was one of the beautiful places we had found fashioned by the practised hand of nature, that man had not desecrated.

He added that it looked so inviting, with cool shades and a "vision of a supper upon fat ducks," they decided to camp there.

On the twenty-sixth, the journey continued along the lake shore to the hot spring area now known as West Thumb, where they found so much to see that they laid over two days before pushing directly west, across the pine-covered ridges lying between Lake Yellowstone and the Firehole River headwaters of the Madison. As they were ascending the ridge west of Thumb Bay, Folsom took a final look at Yellowstone Lake in its mountain setting:

> . . . this inland sea, its crystal waves dancing and sparkling in the sunlight as if laughing with joy for their wild freedom. It is a scene of transcendent beauty which has been viewed by few white men, and we felt glad to have looked upon it before its primeval solitude should be broken by the crowds of pleasure seekers which at no distant day will throng its shores.

A due west course on the twenty-ninth led the Folsom party to Shoshone Lake near its northernmost bulge. They escaped from those geographically confusing environs as deLacy's prospectors had six years earlier by ascending the stream now known as DeLacy Creek and crossing over the Continental Divide onto White Creek, which led them into the Lower Geyser Basin after three days of rugged, cross-country traveling.

Thus, it was evening of October 1 when they rode out of the timber opposite the Great Fountain Geyser just as it began to play. Cook says, "The setting sun shining into the spray and steam drifting towards the mountains gave it the appearance of burnished gold, a wonderful sight." Their reaction was to take off their hats and yell with all their might! They camped on White Creek, just above the geyser.

Having previously obtained some information from prospectors, they were able to identify the locality as the Burnt Hole or Death Valley.[28] The latter designation seems to have created some apprehension, for Folsom says: "Although we experienced no bad effects from passing through the 'Valley of Death,' yet we were not disposed to dispute the propriety of giving it that name." Indeed, the absence of faunal life gave support to such a misinterpretation; but how were they to know that the ungulates, and their predators, preferred greener pastures among the mountains at that season, or that the Firehole River was barren because the native fish of the Madison drainage were blocked-out by waterfalls?

A layover of a day allowed the Folsom party to visit the Middle Geyser Basin—the "Hell's Half Acre" of Victorian tourists—where they noted that the stream of hot water discharged was sufficient to warm the Firehole River to blood heat a quarter of a mile below. Their observation that one spring about 250 feet in diameter "had every indication of spouting powerfully at times" is probably the first recognition of the eruptive nature of Excelsior Geyser.[29]

The homeward journey was completed on October 11, making the elapsed time longer than anticipated and causing friends some concern. Of the immediate flurry of interest in this exploration, N.P. Langford says:

> On his return to Helena he [Folsom] related to a few of his intimate friends many of the incidents of his journey, and Mr. Samuel T. Hauser and I invited him to meet a number of the citizens of Helena at the director's room of the First National Bank in Helena; but on assembling there were so many present who were unknown to Mr. Folsom that he was unwilling to risk his reputation for veracity, by a full recital, in the presence of strangers, of the wonders he had seen. He said that he did not wish to be regarded as a liar by those who were unacquainted with his reputation. But the accounts which he gave to Hauser, Gillette and myself renewed in us our determination to visit that region during the following year.[30]

A published account of the experiences of the Folsom party was given limited circulation quite by chance. In September 1868 Cook had met a Mr. Clark who had come to Diamond City on some mining business, and in the course of conversation told him some of the rumors concerning the Yellowstone region. The easterner's interest was so aroused that he proposed they explore the area; a proposal which got as far as a visit to Helena to discuss the project with "Judge" H. N. McGuire (who later published the first newspaper at Bozeman and was well acquainted with the area immediately north of the present Park). His advice was that it was too late in the season for such a venture, and Mr. Clark returned to his eastern home without the experience of a Yellowstone trip.

Soon after returning from the 1869 exploration, Cook received a letter from Clark, who had somehow heard of the earlier plans for a general exploration of the headwaters of the Yellowstone (see page 91) and had correctly assumed Cook would be a member of such an expedition. He wanted to know what had been found. By return mail he was given information on the exploration from which the Folsom party had just returned, which so intrigued Clark he offered his services in finding a publisher for an article covering their adventures. Cook and Folsom collaborated in preparing a manuscript from their personal diaries; it was sent to Mr. Clark, who had some knowledge of how to proceed, having contributed articles of his own to magazines.

Both the *New York Tribune* and *Scribner's* (or *Harper's*) magazine[31] refused the manuscript because "they had a reputation that they could not risk with such unreliable material." A less exacting publication, the *Western Monthly Magazine* of Chicago, finally accepted the account and published it in the issue of July 1870 under Cook's name (probably because he was the one known to Clark). It has been inferred that this publication was not distributed because the offices of the magazine were destroyed in the great Chicago fire of October 8 to 11, 1871, but that is not so. Nor did the loss of the printing plant in the fire which burned out the Drake and Farwell Building on September 4, 1870, interfere with distribution of the July number. The subscribers had received their copies prior to the fire and only a small reserve stock was lost.[32]

During the winter following the Folsom party's return from the Yellowstone wilderness, David Folsom went to work in the Helena office of the newly appointed and just-arrived surveyor general of Montana Territory, Henry D. Washburn. There, Folsom met that other civil engineer and Yellowstone explorer, Walter W. deLacy, and together they revised deLacy's "Map of the Territory of Montana . . . ," which had first appeared in 1865, with a view to presenting the Yellowstone region with greater accuracy. This 1870 edition, which came off the press in time to serve the Washburn party of that year, was a tolerably good map, portraying the Yellowstone Lake correctly for the first time as well as relating the various drainages and features with reasonable accuracy.

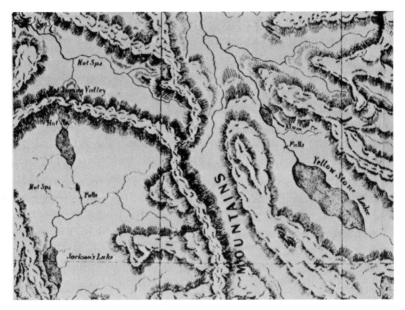

Section of W. W. deLacy's "Map of the Territory of Montana. . . ," 1865 edition, showing his limited knowledge of hydrography and thermal features.

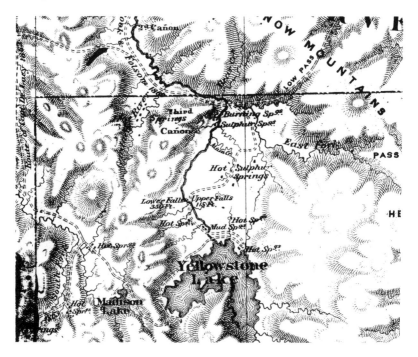

Section of W. W. deLacy's "Map of the Territory of Montana. . . ," 1870 edition, showing information obtained by Cook and Folsom in 1869.

Folsom gave General Washburn much detailed information on the Yellowstone region and its wonders, and he is credited with a similar suggestion to that made by Thomas Meagher in 1865—that the area should be reserved for public use as a park.[33] The basis for Folsom's suggestion is apparent in certain remarks made years later by his old comrade, C. W. Cook, at the Park's Golden Anniversary celebration at Madison Junction in 1922.

> The night before we came to this junction we camped a little way up the Firehole River. We had decided to make that the last camp on our exploration and to follow the Firehole down to the Madison River and home.
>
> In the camp that night we were talking over the great array of natural marvels we had seen and the scenic beauty of the area we had traversed.
>
> Peterson remarked that probably it would not be long before settlers and prospectors began coming into the district and taking up land around the canyons and the geysers, and that it would soon be all in private hands.
>
> I said that I thought the place was too big to be all taken up, but that, anyway, something ought to be done to keep the settlers out, so that everyone who wanted to, in future years, could travel through as freely and enjoy the region as we had.
>
> Then Folsom said "The Government ought not to allow anyone to locate here at all."
>
> "That's right," I said, "It ought to be kept for the public some way."
>
> None of us definitely suggested the idea of a national park. National parks were unknown then. But we knew that as soon as the wonderful character of the country was generally known outside, there would be plenty of people hurrying in to get possession, unless something was done.[34]

These then, were the contributions of the Folsom party of 1869: a descriptive magazine article, a greatly improved map, a suggestion for reservation in the public interest, and the encouragement of the Washburn party which followed their footsteps in 1870.

That compulsive wanderer in the West, Philetus W. Norris, came up the Missouri River as the summer of 1870 was opening, and at Helena found his old friends, Governor William Ashley, Truman C. Everts, and Henry D. Washburn, still excited by the reports of Cook and Folsom, who had returned from the Yellowstone region the previous fall. There was talk of making up a party to go back by way of the Madison River in the autumn, but Norris found the plans vague, and being "firm in the opinion the Yellowstone route was the true one," he set out to learn what he could about that approach to the land of geysers.

With such an objective, he went with Everts to Bozeman where they located an old, decrepit trapper named Dunn, from whose statements Norris was able to make a rough map of the route used by Jim Bridger in passing from the Gallatin Valley to Green River, via Yellowstone Lake, in 1865.[35] That information appears to have encouraged Norris to go farther, so he parted with Everts at Fort Ellis (where the latter was seeking to obtain the privilege of running a post trader's store) and crossed the divide into the valley of the Yellowstone River. There he found the Bottler brothers, Frederick, Phillip, and Henry,[36] who were keeping bachelor hall at their ranch opposite Emigrant Gulch. With those "moral, temperate, and industrious mountaineers," he spent several days.

Since the object of Norris' visit was to "ascertain the possibility of an exploring party going through the upper cañon and the Lava, or ancient volcanic country beyond, so as to reach the wonders said to be around Yellowstone Lake," he arranged to make a reconnaissance with Frederick. Actually, the timing was poor; the streams were in flood and the guide had not entirely recovered from a mauling received six months earlier while disputing the possession of a berry patch with a family of grizzly bears. Regardless, all went well for a time.

They passed through the second canyon, climbed Electric Peak and obtained a fine field-glass view deep into what is now Yellowstone National Park. The essential purpose of the trip was satisfied and they should have taken the back-track to the Bottler ranch; but they were elated, thinking they "could be the first white men to reach the Sulphur Mountains and Mud Volcanoes, and possibly the great falls and Yellowstone Lake,"[37] and so they rashly pushed on.

Descending from Electric Peak—probably by the north ridge between Mol Heron and Reese creeks—they were attempting to cross the swollen Reese torrent when the guide was swept off his feet, washed downstream, and nearly drowned. His painful bruises, and the loss of their only rifle, left them no choice but to retreat to the Bottler ranch. So, there went Norris' opportunity to steal a march on the Washburn party.

On his return to Helena, Norris found the plans of his friends less firm than he had hoped, which led him to write home,

Shall soon decide whether General Washburn, Surveyor General from this Territory, friend Everts and Judge Hosmer, once of Toledo, Major Squier, the Bottlers, and our humble self join in another expedition to the unexplored region of the Yellowstone Lake. If so, shall go no farther this season; if not, shall try to cross the mountains to Oregon, down to Columbia, then to California, and return in autumn.[38]

Apparently his conclusion regarding the possibility of a Yellowstone expedition that season was negative, for he hied himself off to the Pacific Coast.

At about the same time, Nathaniel P. Langford (who was unemployed after losing his position as collector of internal revenue for Montana *and* an appointment to the governorship of that territory, as the result of an imbroglio between President Johnson and the United States Senate) found a job that took him back to Montana and probably had much to do with getting the Yellowstone exploration off dead-center. A visit with Jay Cooke in Philadelphia, where he was entertained on June 4 and 5 at the financier's suburban estate "Ogontz,"[39] evidently led to some understanding between them concerning the usefulness of Yellowstone exploration in the grand scheme of Northern Pacific Railroad publicity.

The need of the moment was for promotional material useful to Jay Cooke & Company's task of financing the Northern Pacific Railroad. Part of the money for that enterprise was to be advanced by the financial house, on the security of a mortgage against railway properties, and the remainder was to come from the sale of bonds. Thus, it was necessary for Cooke's firm to engage in some potent advertising, and a man with a broad knowledge of Montana Territory, and the ability to present it in a light that would promote the railway, was a valuable asset. From Langford's viewpoint, how could he attract more attention to Montana Territory, and incidentally to the railway, than through an exploration of the land of wonders that lay in such close proximity to it?

Langford's personal diary records his return, following that meeting, to Montana via St. Paul, where he interviewed Major General Winfield S. Hancock, who commanded the military department of Dakota (of which Montana was then a part), with the result that Hancock

> showed great interest in the plan of exploration which I outlined to him, and expressed a desire to obtain additional information concerning the Yellowstone country . . . and he assured me that, unless some unforseen exigency prevented, he would, when the time arrived, give a favorable response to our application for a military escort, if one were needed.[40]

Langford arrived at Helena on July 27. He indicates that the previously vague proposal to explore the Yellowstone region in the autumn of 1870 "took definite shape" about the first of August, when twenty men were enrolled for the enterprise. That sudden resolution, so nearly coincident with his arrival, hints that Langford was the "spark plug"; subsequent events suggest it was his relationship with Jay Cooke & Company that placed him in that role.

The Yellowstone expedition was barely organized when word was received that the Crow Indians were uneasy, and the old fear of raids on the upper Yellowstone River and into the Gallatin Valley swept away the faint-hearted, leaving only eight stalwarts. At that ebb-point, Langford and Samuel T. Hauser wrote a letter to James Stuart, of Deer Lodge, seeking to enlist the hardy frontiersman in their venture. His reply was encouraging:

> I am just d____d fool enough to go anywhere that anybody else is willing to go, only I want it understood that very likely some of us will lose our hair. I will be on hand Sunday evening, unless I hear that the trip is postponed. Fraternally yours, Jas. Stuart.
>
> Since writing the above, I have received a telegram, saying "twelve of us going certain." Glad to hear it—the more the better. Will bring two pack horses and one pack saddle.[41]

Meanwhile, General H. D. Washburn was making arrangements for a military escort, as the following letter indicates:

Genl H. D. Washburn   Fort Ellis, M.T.
Surveyor General Montana   August 12th, 1870
Dear Sir

Your kind favor of the 9th ult—came yesterday—and I reply—at the first opportunity for transmittal Judge Hosmer was correct as regards my *earnest desire* to go on the trip proposed—but mistaken in relation to my *free agency* in the premise. To obtain permission for an escort will require an order from Genl Hancock—authorizing Col. Baker—to make the detail.

If Hauser and yourself will telegraph at once on rec't to Genl Hancock at Saint Paul, Minn—stating the object of the expedition &c and requesting that an order be sent to the Comdg officer at Fort Ellis, M.T. to furnish an escort of an officer and five men—it will doubtless be favorably considered—and you can bring the reply from the office when you come down or send it before—if answer comes in time. Col. Baker has promised me the detail if authority be furnished. And by your telegraphing instead of him—the circumlocution at Dist Hdqrs will be obviated I will reimburse you the expense of the messages which should be *paid both ways* to insure prompt attention.

I will be able to furnish Tents and camp equipage better than you can get in Helena—and I can furnish them without trouble to your whole party.

Hoping that we can make the trip in Company I have the honor to be

                                                  Your Obdt Servant
                                                  G. C. Doane
                                                  Lt.2nd Calvary, U.S.A.

Please let me know what steps you take in the matter as soon as convenient.[42]

General Henry D. Washburn. From an original photograph by Mathew Brady, 1869. Used with permission of R.H. Washburn, Phoenix, Arizona.

The suggested telegram was sent, and General Hancock, true to his earlier promise, authorized the escort. The *Helena Herald* of August 13 noted that the "long talked of Yellowstone Expedition" was to depart at 8 o'clock Monday morning (the fifteenth), but, before the issue went to press, a postscript was added: "Since the above was in type, we learn the time for departure has been postponed until Wednesday, next, one of the party—Mr. Stuart of Deer Lodge, having business that will detain him until then." But the business was more onerous than that: James had been selected for jury duty, from which the judge declined to excuse him, and he had to be dropped from the roll.

General Washburn was prevailed upon to take command in Stuart's place and the expedition was able to move out on the seventeenth. But it was an inauspicious, halting start. The members were to assemble at 9 A.M. in front of Washburn's office (on Main Street, at the foot of Broadway), yet it was afternoon before the party was ready to move. According to Hauser's diary,[43] three packs fell off the horses after 300 yards, and a second packer had to be found to manage the uncooperative animals. By the time that problem was solved, it was 4 P.M., so the pack train was left with the packers, Elwyn Bean and Charles Reynolds, and the two black cooks, "Nute" and "Johnny". Most of the gentlemen-adventurers then rode on to Nick Greenish's Half-way House for the night. In reporting the departure, the *Helena Herald* noted that "several of the party, we are informed, were 'under the weather' and tarried in the gay Metropolis until 'night drew her sable curtain down,' when they started off in search of the expedition."[44]

All in all, the expedition cannot be considered as fully operational until the morning of August 22, when it stood ready to depart from Fort Ellis, the final preparations completed, a last flurry of celebrations and entertainments in Bozeman over, and only the Yellowstone wilderness ahead. The party gathered there consisted of nineteen persons: in addition to the packers and cooks, there was the leader, Henry D. Washburn, a former major general in the Union army who used his influence to obtain the post of surveyor general for Montana Territory in the hope that a western residence would restore his war-ravaged health; Nathaniel P. Langford, then enjoying some notice as the "late Governor of Montana" (though that was never official); Samuel T. Hauser, president of the First National Bank of Helena and a civil engineer by training; Warren C. Gillette, a merchant of the firm King & Gillette; Benjamin F. Stickney of the mining and freighting firm of Plant, Stickney & Ellis; Truman C. Everts, former assessor of internal revenue for Montana Territory, and Walter Trumbull, his assistant (they had just been ousted from their federal positions in the patronage scramble that accompanied General Grant's assumption of the presidency); Cornelius Hedges, a struggling young partner of the law firm of Lawrence & Hedges and a correspondent for the *Helena Herald*; and Jacob W. Smith, "late of the Montana Hide & Fur Co.," whose particular fate it would be to excite the animus of friend Langford.

The party was completed by a military escort from the Second Cavalry under Second Lieutenant Gustavus C. Doane, who entered the Civil War in the California Hundred and afterward joined the postwar regular army to become a frontier officer par excellence. His detail consisted of Sergeant William Baker and privates John Williamson, George W. McConnell, William Leipler, and Charles Moore, the latter having some ability as an artist.

Give the assembled expeditioners forty horses and mules (mostly horses), a dog with the unpromising name of Booby (which he did not wholly deserve), rations for thirty days, and a "pavilion" tent obtained with arms and ammunition from Fort Ellis; add a few luxuries, like a box of cigars a Bozeman friend gave to Hedges on the eve of departure, and the explorers are ready to go.

The route followed was the same the Folsom party had used the previous year; the first night camp was on Trail Creek. There, some of the boys settled down to a session with the cards, as they were to do frequently throughout the trip. It had been Jake Smith's misfortune to go broke in an earlier game while in camp near Fort Ellis,[45] so he put up his hat to be shot at for twenty-five cents a shot. The hat was riddled, but Jake raised enough cash to open another game of twenty-one about which Gillette says, "Fortune however favored him not, for he soon arose from his blankets without a cent; he stood his loss & the jests of the party with the greatest good humor."[46] Except for his reluctance to stand guard duty, which he felt was a needless burden, Jake fitted into that boisterous company right well.

The departure from Trail Creek was delayed by a miscalculation on the part of the herders. At daybreak they freed the animals from their picket ropes to allow them better grazing. But the troop horses didn't take breakfast; instead, they started for Fort Ellis, and the soldiers had to borrow horses to bring back their mounts.

During the second day, while the party was passing from Trail Creek to the Bottler ranch, they saw Indians. Apparently a few Crows from the reservation across the Yellowstone River spied on the party, creating reactions that varied from Langford's fearful estimate of "one hundred or more of them watching us from behind a high butte,"

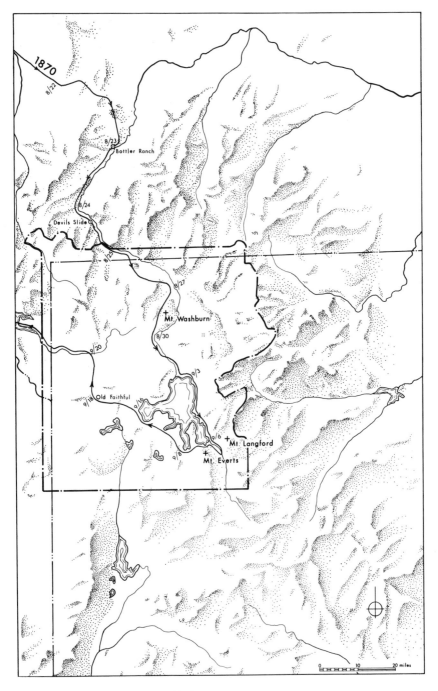

Route of the Washburn party, 1870.

to Lieutenant Doane's matter-of-fact "we met several Indians belonging to the Crow agency, 30 miles below."[47] Despite the apprehension of some members of the party, this was their only meeting with Indians, who proved much less of a problem than James Stuart had expected.

Everts, who had gorged himself on wayside berries on the first day, became ill before the Bottler ranch was reached, and it was decided to leave him there where he would have better shelter should his condition take a serious turn. His comrades made an uncomfortable camp nearby, where they passed a rainy night lying "heads and tails" in Doane's large tent. By noon of the following day the weather was clearing and, since Everts was showing signs of improvement, it was decided to move the camp up the valley a few miles and await him there.

This third camp, below present Yankee Jim Canyon, was such a pleasant place they named it Camp Euphemia;[48] there, in contrast to the wet and dismal encampment of the previous night, they were able to "spread out on the prickly-pears" and spend the long twilight bringing their notes up to date, smoking, and exchanging reminiscences, while several even climbed a nearby height which they then designated "Washburne's Peak."[49] The pleasant breezes of that evening turned to an Icelandic gale before morning, and breakfast had to be eaten under the shelter of the river bank on what Trumbull called "a two-foot beach."

The recovered Mr. Everts came into camp at ten in the morning and the expedition was soon in motion toward the mouth of Yankee Jim Canyon, which began a short distance above camp. The Indian trailway winding through the slide-rock was so rough they had to dismount and lead their horses, but even that was hard on the animals. Above the canyon the trail was better, with the "marks of Indian tent poles [travois] distinct,"[50] and that primitive trace led around the base of Cinnabar Mountain, past the brick-red, upended stratum of rock they appropriately named the Devil's Slide, to an overnight camp at the mouth of the Gardner River.[51] There they were joined by two white "hunters," to whom the opportunity for a convivial visit by the campfire was a real treat.

The horses fared poorly on the wisps of grass they picked from the sage-covered flat above the river, but the tired explorers made out well enough on a narrow, sandy beach where Hedges retired early to listen awhile to the music of "dashing waters & winds in cedar tops."

The party did not start until eleven o'clock the following morning, and then there was so much trouble with the packs that the advance—Lieutenant Doane, Everts and Private Williamson—soon left the main party behind. After some difficulty, the lieutenant and his companions finally found the trail of the two hunters who had camped with them the night before, and thus were set upon the same branch of the Indian trailway up the Yellowstone used by the Folsom party of the previous year. However, beyond Rescue Creek they did better than their predecessors by jogging southward onto the Bannock Trail, which led them easily to Tower Fall.

The main party was less fortunate, having been slowed by pack animals made nervous by smoke lingering from the forest fire on the slopes of Mount Everts the evening before.[52] They found the dressed carcass of an antelope Private Williamson left for them in the pass between Mount Everts and Turkey Pen Peak, then they lost the advance party's trail. They halted in indecision at a "pretty meadow by a cool stream," while a search was made for the trail. A scouting party, which pushed eight or ten miles eastward, made several unsuccessful attempts to get down to the Yellowstone River; another effort by Langford and Hauser after supper showed the way the advance had gone. As it was by then too late to move farther that evening, they camped at the meadow on the little stream called Antelope Creek by Langford and called Lost Trail Creek[53] by Hauser. A ridiculous latter-day error has turned it into Rescue Creek in the mistaken belief that Everts was rescued there which he was not, as will be shown later.

At the encampment on Rescue Creek, Gillette's horse, suddenly frightened, broke loose from its picket-pin and dashed through the sleeping camp. It was a close call for Langford, who was somehow entangled in the trailing rope and dragged into a log "which proved to be very rotten, and offered little resistance to a hard head."

Meanwhile, the advance party had reached Tower Creek, where they camped with the two hunters whose trail they had followed. Their inconvenience because of a lack of camp impedimenta was balanced by the exhilarating knowledge of having found their first hot spring. Though only a sulphurous, tepid dribble at the edge of a grassy swale near where Camp Roosevelt now stands, it was an earnest of the novel features they expected to see the next day.[54]

On the twenty-seventh, Lieutenant Doane scouted the vicinity while waiting for the main party to come up. He rode down to the mouth of the East Fork (now the Lamar River), poked about the hot springs scattered along the Yellowstone for more than a mile below the mouth of Tower Creek, and admired the waterfall a short distance from camp. As he saw it, "Nothing can be more chastely beautiful than this lovely cascade, hidden away in the dim light of overshadowing rocks and woods, its very voice hushed to a low murmur."[55]

The remainder of the party arrived during the afternoon and it was decided the expedition should lay over a day in that interesting locality. While most of the expeditioners were sightseeing, General Washburn, acting upon David Folsom's suggestion that he should seek a route on the west side of the Yellowstone River (in order to avoid that tedious detour up the Lamar River and across the Mirror Plateau made by the 1869 party), rode southward up a succession of ridges which eventually led him onto a lofty summit from which he could see their objective—Lake Yellowstone—and form some idea of the intervening terrain. The information Washburn brought back to camp that afternoon was so encouraging it was unanimously decided to apply his name to the peak he had ascended.[56]

Samuel Hauser, whose engineering instincts were dominant throughout the Yellowstone trip, proceeded to measure the waterfall Lieutenant Doane had admired. His determination, made by angulation with the help of Langford, was 115 feet, and he noted, "I named them 'Tower Falls'—from the towers & pinacles that overhang them."[57] Popular usage eventually extended the name Tower to the stream that nourishes the falls, supplanting several less appropriate designations such as Warm Spring Creek, Little Fall Creek, and Fall Creek.

In the afternoon the philosophically inclined Hedges retired to an aerie which he called Prospect Point, directly above the fall; and there he sat himself down to record something of that vista he calls "altogether the finest view I have ever had." Whoever wishes to duplicate his experience can reach his point by a stiff scramble up the slope rising directly above the north end of the highway bridge over Tower Creek, and on the top is a sturdy bench which Jack Haynes placed there many years ago for the convenience of the weary.

The party's campsite, now covered by the asphalt parking area which serves the Tower Fall area, was such a pleasant place that Everts called it Camp Comfort, and there, after an evening meal of fresh venison, there was time for writing up the day's observations, reading, smoking, and, of course, a game of cards;[58] there was even time for some pleasant josh over the naming of Tower Fall. By way of explaining what he chose to consider a violation of the party's agreement not to name natural features after themselves, Walter Trumbull wrote:

> One of the party took an unaccountable interest in bestowing upon them the name of Tower Falls, which was finally adopted. His peculiar interest was afterward satisfactorily explained, as we learned he had a sweetheart by that name, somewhere in the States. Another of the party was in favor of the name of Minaret (Minne Rhett); but that was too apparent, and he was outvoted.[59]

Tower Fall, as sketched by Pvt. Charles Moore, 1870 (the first pictorial representation of a Yellowstone feature). From Yellowstone Park Museum collection.

But there was one member of the party who was in no condition to partake of the boisterous proceedings of the camp. From the time of departure from Fort Ellis, Lieutenant Doane had been suffering from a deep-seated inflammation in his right thumb of the type called a felon. Despite several attempts to probe it "with a very dull pocket-knife," the pain had increased to a degree that allowed him no rest. While the others snored in their blankets, the lieutenant paced back and forth by the campfire with his hand wrapped in a wet bandage to subdue the "infernal agonies."

There was another sufferer in the camp, though his case was not as difficult to alleviate. The dog, Booby, had become so sore-footed he could hardly travel and it was necessary to fit him with little moccasins. It was a kindness which was amply repaid at a later date.

Breaking camp at 8 o'clock on the morning of the twenty-ninth, the expedition moved southward along the route picked by General Washburn the day before. They were following an ancient Indian trailway which ascended the long ridge flanked by Tower and Carnelian creeks on one side and Antelope Creek on the other, until the final rise of Mount Washburn was reached, whereupon that aboriginal track sidled westward around the peak toward a prominent gap (later named Dunraven Pass) and descended the Sulphur Creek drainage to reach the vicinity of the Yellowstone Falls.

Where the trail started its detour of the central peak, a party peeled off for a climb to the summit, leaving Hedges, who was poorly mounted, to confide to his diary, "Wish I had a better horse to see more country." And he had reason to lament, for the view opening from that windswept mountain top is a magnificent panorama which was accurately typified by Doane when he prefaced several pages of scenic details with the comment that it was "beyond all adequate description."[60] Indeed, where does one begin? With the drab, piled-up lavas on which he stands? With the raw cleft of the Grand Canyon at the mountain's very feet? With the silvery expanse of Yellowstone Lake southward in the middle distance? Or somewhere in the mountains that circumscribe the gaze in all directions but the southwest? Perhaps that is why Gillette wrote so little and Langford recorded nothing of what he saw.

But there was more purpose to that ascent than mere admiration of the expansive landscape. An aneroid barometer was carried up to determine the elevation of Henry Washburn's peak; and, strange to say, that single instrument was made to render four different values. Hauser entered the reading as 10,700 feet, Gillette made it 10,579, Langford said 9,800, and Doane, who may have attempted a correction for the 50 degree air temperature, used 9,966.[61]

Leaving their names on a slip of paper, the climbers descended and followed the pack train into camp, which they found in a meadow on Sulphur Creek close to the base of Mount Washburn. That evening, Washburn, Doane, and Hedges followed the drainage down a mile to a hot spring basin they called Hell-Broth Springs; and those seething, malodorous, sludge-pits provided Hedges with the inspiration for an article by the same title which he later contributed to the *Helena Daily Herald*.[62] From that basin, which is now known as the Washburn Hot Springs, reconnaissance continued down the little stream to the point where it plunged over the canyon wall to the river hidden in the depths below.

That night the guards lit huge fires to warm themselves by; in fact Jake Smith nearly burned the camp out by setting a dead pine alight. Yet Hedges noted that he "enjoyed it hugely. Easiest night I have had on guard."[63]

A short march the following day brought the party into the meadows of Cascade Creek, where they found a suitable campsite just above the canyon through which that stream reaches the Yellowstone River. Anxious to see those great waterfalls that were rumored to be as much as one thousand feet high, Hedges pushed on down Cascade Creek through that tangle he called the Devil's Den, only to find others of the party had reached the lip of the great fall before him, by an easier route. Of course he was disappointed with that first view, but a day's layover at that place brought him to a proper appreciation of the scenic grandeur.[64]

Hedges' solitary foray down Cascade Creek (named by him) was productive of another place name that has stood the test of time. Just before he reached the river he came to a beautiful triple cascade known as Crystal Falls. Even in its present condition this waterfall, with its intermediate grotto, is a delightful place.

The last day of August was given over entirely to an examination of waterfalls and their work, the party scattering widely in pursuit of particular interests. Langford measured both falls of the Yellowstone using the same method as the Folsom party in 1869—a weighted cord—obtaining an identical 115 feet for the upper, and a more nearly correct 320 feet for the lower.[65] The latter measurement had to be made in a difficult place, and the cord parted three times before the task was completed. For some unexplained reason, Langford's figure for the Lower Falls was ignored by the party's other diarists, Doane, Gillette, Trumbull, and Washburn preferring 350 feet, though there is no mention of any other measurement.

While Langford was busy with his cord and weight, Hauser and Stickney found a place two and one-half miles below the Lower Falls where they were able to descend into the canyon. That scramble not only allowed them to measure its width and depth by triangulation (the chasm was 1,300 feet across and the river was 1,050 feet below the rim),[66] but also led them to a slender ribbon of water cascading 1,500 feet from the east rim. Hauser called it Silver Thread Fall, the Silver Cord Cascade of current maps.

Lieutenant Doane and his orderly, Private McConnell, rode a mile farther down the canyon rim, then left their horses, and descended a convenient watercourse to some hot springs along the river. On the way down they came upon a flock of very tame mountain sheep, one of which McConnell killed. The descent to the river required four hours, and the return another five. It was fatiguing for the lieutenant, who was weakening from the suffering and loss of sleep caused by the inflammation in his hand. Evidently his condition was worsening, for Hedges noted: "Lieut. in pain all night. Langford & Washburn up all night with him."[67]

Hedges, who was really not a rugged, outdoor type, had a less active but more inspiring day. Going out afoot and alone, he spent several hours viewing the Lower Falls, then wandered from point to point along the canyon rim until he was filled with "too much & too great satisfaction & delight to relate."

The expedition moved southward from the camp on Cascade Creek on September 1 and passed over Alum Creek, which they named,[68] into the open, rolling grasslands of Hayden Valley. Midway across that bottom land, which is a relic of a larger, primordial Lake Yellowstone, they came to a group of low hills exhibiting thermal activity upon their western flank. Doane was inclined to call these the Seven Hills, but an examination of the area led them to suppose the hot springs and vents were manifestations of "a smothered crater covered over by an incrustation," so the name of Crater Hill was used instead.[69] Langford made this interesting comment about the formation there:

> The tramp of our horses' feet as we rode over the incrustation at the base of the mountain returned a hollow sound; yet while some of our party were not disposed to venture upon it with their horses, still I think with care in selecting a route there is little danger in riding over it.

In the meantime, the pack train had gone on four miles to a camping place near a group of such remarkable thermal features that the party again laid over for a day. There, in a slate-colored pool nearly two hundred feet across, they found their first true geyser, and it was the murky violence of its eruptions, which once flung water thirty-five to forty feet high at six-hour intervals, that led to its name,

Lt. Gustavus C. Doane in dress uniform. The photograph appeared as a tip-in illustration in William Strong's book (1876) covering the Belknap visit to the Park in the previous year. Source of photo is unknown.

Mud Geyser. Despite the novelty of the geyser, a nearby cavern in the hillside belching viscous mud with deep reverberations "resembling the reports of distant artillery" proved more interesting. Hedges' interest in this Mud Volcano, as they called it, led him to endanger his life by climbing onto the outer rim, from which he was tumbled by an unexpected, steamy exhalation. The fresh mud clinging to grass and tree limbs nearly 100 feet distant hinted that he could easily have fared worse. In a ravine 100 yards beyond that dangerous place they found clear, hot water pulsing from a green-walled, gable-like cavern which also emitted a hollow, thundering sound. Hauser called it Cave Spring, but his name stuck no better than several others that have been applied to what is now Dragons Mouth Spring.[70]

Well pleased with the novelties found in the Mud Geyser area, the party moved on toward Lake Yellowstone on September 3 with most of the expeditioners suffering from a malaise variously attributed to canned peaches, to the hot-spring impregnated water they had been drinking, and, by Hedges, to breathing what he thought were noxious gases bubbling up in the river water near where he had fished the evening before.

While the pack train was crossing the Yellowstone at what would later be known as the Nez Perce ford—an operation that consumed most of the forenoon—Washburn and Langford rode back to the Crater Hills for another look at the features in that area. This excursion nearly resulted in Langford being boiled in an alum spring where the margin had been undermined by the violent agitation of the water. He says,

> This, however, I did not at first perceive; and, as I was unconcernedly passing by the spring, my weight made the border suddenly slough off beneath my feet. General Washburn noticed the sudden cracking of the incrustation before I did, and I was aroused to a sense of my peril by his shout of alarm, and had sufficient presence of mind to fall suddenly backwards at full length upon the sound crust, whence, with my feet and legs extended over the spring, I rolled to a place of safety.[71]

Meanwhile, the main party moved up the east bank of the Yellowstone River, having a "plain trail" as far as Pelican Creek. There they became lost in fallen timber and floundered through two muddy crossings of the creek before they reached the shore of Yellowstone Lake near where the Folsom party had camped the year before.

The condition of Lieutenant Doane's thumb had been worsening each day, taking a terrible toll of his strength; it was determined before the lake was reached that an operation would again have to be attempted. As Langford was to be the acting surgeon, he prepared for the ordeal by whetting his penknife on the pommel of his saddle as he rode toward the lake. After supper that evening an operating table was improvised from a box of army cartridges, and other simple preparations were completed.

> When Doane was told that we were ready, he asked, "Where is the chloroform? I replied that I had never administered it, and that after thinking the matter over I was afraid to assume the responsibility of giving it. He swallowed his disappointment, and turned his thumb over on the cartridge box, with the nail down. Hedges and Bean were on hand to steady the arm, and before one could say "Jack Robinson" I had inserted the point of my penknife, thrusting down to the bone, and had ripped it out to the end of the thumb. Doane gave one shriek as the released corruption flew out in all directions upon surgeon and assistants, and then with a broad smile on his face he exclaimed, "That was elegant!"[72]

Doane's relief was immediate and he was able to sleep that night, and the following day and night also, a nap of thirty-six hours, from which he arose much recovered. A less beneficial effect of the surgery was permanent impairment of the use of his right hand.[73]

Since the camp could not be moved while Doane was resting, September 4 (Sunday) was spent as individual preference dictated. According to Langford, Jake Smith exclaimed, "If we're going to remain in camp, let's have a game of draw," and he probably found enough kindred spirits to organize one. Langford preferred a nap, but later he and Hedges went down the beach to a place where they found many pieces of sandstone worked into odd resemblances by the action of the waves. The Curiosity Shop, as Hedges called it, was the place referred to by those prospectors who told members of the Washburn party, prior to their departure from Bozeman, that the shore of Yellowstone Lake would yield "the dishes and cooking utensils of an ancient and more civilized race of Indians than now roam about it."[74]

The island that now bears the name of Dr. Hayden's able assistant, James Stevenson, lay so invitingly near that Gillette built a raft for voyaging to it; but the wind blew hard all day, rolling up waves that tore the frail craft apart within an hour of its launching, leaving him without a means of satisfying his curiosity as to whether human feet had ever trod the island.

General Washburn undertook a reconnaissance southward along the lake shore in the hope of finding a trail around the east side of the lake. His report of an *appearance* of a good route probably unduly influenced the vote taken that evening to decide their future course. With only Jake Smith and Sam Hauser dissenting, it was decided to go around the lake. That departure from the route followed by the Folsom party proved less fortunate than the one they had taken around the Grand Canyon.

The trek around the lake began at 9 A.M. on September 5, with the main party working their way along the east shore, sometimes following the beach and sometimes passing through the forest on convenient game trails, to a campsite in the vicinity of present Park Point. Langford and Hedges remained behind in order to measure the distance of the Teton peaks by triangulation, but they were unable to lay out a baseline of sufficient length and "abandoned the scheme after some two hours of useless labor," to hurry after their comrades.

On the following day, the route lay mostly through the forest, and progress was greatly impeded by fallen timber (a condition that would become much worse south of the lake). A difficult day, lightened only by a cursory examination of the fumarole area Doane named Brimstone Basin, ended in disappointment among the swamps where the upper Yellowstone River enters the lake. Hedges, who was then leading the pack train, attempted to cross the swamp by following a sandbar fronting on Southeast Arm, but "after struggling through the tangled willows for two hours, found the creek channel [Yellowstone River] to be a wide and deep slough, impassable for man or beast."[75] This knowledge was gained by miring some horses to their bellies before the train was backed out of that cul-de-sac. A camping place of sorts was found in a grove of pines on Beaverdam Creek.

Hedges indicates they had only salt meat to eat at their uncomfortable camp; and yet, several diarists attest that game was plentiful, if fresh tracks have any meaning. The lack of success in keeping the camp kettles supplied is explained by Doane's disgusted comment, "Our party kept up such a rackett of yelling and firing as to drive off all game for miles ahead of us."[76]

On the seventh, the pack train waited at Beaverdam Creek until General Washburn found a route around the swamp that had baffled Hedges. While his party was so employed, Langford and Doane ascended a nearby peak to get a better view of the region south of the lake. The two climbers skirted the edge of the swamp, traveling southeasterly for two and one-half miles before ascending the timbered ravine from which Cabin Creek flows. They were able to ride most of the distance to the saddle at the head of that stream, and there they tied the horses to stunted trees at timberline, then scrambled over what Langford called "loose granite" to the summit that now bears John Colter's name.[77]

The view from that lofty and exposed place was another of those unforgettable panoramas of scenic grandeur. Westward, and more than one-half mile below them, lay the estuarial swamps from which they had ascended: a crazy-quilt of bright green grass and dull red willowbrush irregularly broken by watercourses and dappled with sloughs and ponds. From that marshy labyrinth their eyes swept southward along a nearly level valley of grand dimensions through which the upper Yellowstone River descended, its serpentine course appearing to originate twenty-five miles away in a pretty lake they knew as Bridger's.[78]

From that landmark of the fur-trade era, their gaze returned along the succession of rugged summits that blocked the whole eastern horizon from south to north. But it was the northwest quarter that was of greatest interest to them, for there lay the great, blue lake they hoped to pass around. From the exposed summit where they stood, the plan of the lake was at last revealed, and Langford proceeded to sketch its details as well as he could by eye alone. That done, they noted the salient features of the topography south and west of the lake, and then began the descent to the valley and the trail of the main party.

Meanwhile, General Washburn had found a suitable ford over the upper Yellowstone River above its estuary,[79] had crossed the pack train over, and pushed on to a campsite in a meadow on the lake shore southwest of the Molly Islands. The open aspect of that encampment probably saved the two mountain climbers from spending a miserable night in the woods.

Langford and Doane easily found the trail of the main party at the foot of the mountain, and were able to follow it to the ford, where the crossing was indicated by a marker of sticks put up Indian fashion; but soon after crossing, daylight began to fail them. When the dim trace they were following at last turned abruptly up a mountain, they began to suspect they were misled, so dismounted and built a fire—to find themselves on a game trail unmarked by horse shoes. All they could do then was to blunder through the forest to the lake shore. It was their good fortune to come out at a place where the campfire of their comrades could be seen and they were soon back to their beans and blankets.

The outline sketch of Lake Yellowstone proved so helpful that General Washburn later gave Langford's name to the peak he climbed with Lieutenant Doane, while that able officer was honored by the attachment of his name to the peak north of the saddle where the horses were left. However, the map prepared by Surveyor General Washburn on his return to Helena was necessarily very crude, being

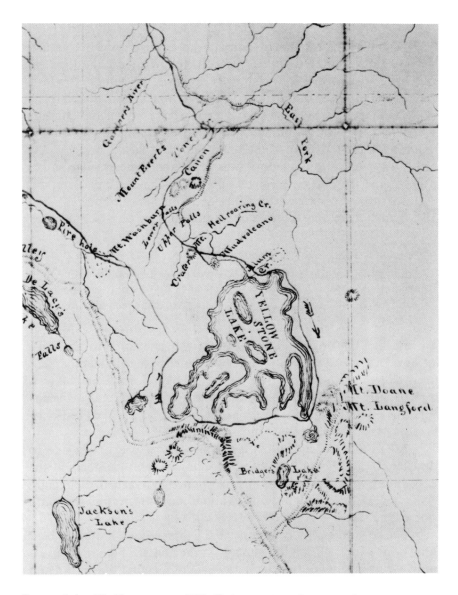

Route of the Washburn party, 1870, "being tracing of map made to accompany Washburn's report to Dept. of Interior" (notation on original map). This map was based on a penciled sketch of Yellowstone Lake and its environs that appears on p. 66 of General Washburn's "diary." The map was originally drawn in pencil on a numbered grid but was later traced over with ink, perhaps by N. P. Langford, when he borrowed the diary from Serena Washburn about 1905. The inked note on p. 67 (a vacant page opposite the map) that reads: "Photograph of map of Yellowstone Lake from Diary of Gen. H. D. Washburn Aug. 20, 1870. Probably the first map made of the lake" could be a Langford addition.

based on no better instrument than a pocket compass, and both peaks were so poorly located with respect to Yellowstone Lake that the Hayden Survey of the following year attached the names Langford and Doane to peaks far north of those they were first intended for.[80]

September 8 developed into a "terrible day for men and horses." The trees were thick and the ground strewn with fallen trunks, requiring the men to dismount often to assist the packhorses or pick a better way. As a result, fatigue was great and tempers were short. Night found the party encamped on Grouse Creek a mile from the South Arm, the distance traveled a mere four miles airline.

Again, there was some mountain climbing, of which Hedges says:

> Everts & I went up a high mountain at S. end of Lake & on left of trail, called in honor of Everts. Very steep, course rubble. came near sliding to bottom. had a splendid view of Lake found it very much cut up. We got back to camp before the train started moved out in rear with Langford.[81]

This ascent of the original Mount Everts (really the northern extremity of Two Ocean Plateau) may have contributed to the disaster that was to envelop the whole party. The ease with which Everts found his way back to the pack train created a false confidence in his woodsmanship. When he was subsequently lost, a proper search was delayed too long, as it was thought he would come in by himself.

All in all, the eighth of September was a proper prelude to disaster. In addition to the hard traveling, several members of the expedition were temporarily lost, so that they reached their night encampment filled with misgivings about the route around the south side of the lake.

The general gloom was somewhat lightened by a ludicrous bear hunt which took place after supper. In the course of a climb onto a nearby ridge to spy out the next day's route, General Washburn and Hauser stirred up an old she-grizzly and her two cubs. At the news, six hunters turned out, armed to the teeth and confident of their ability to bag those monsters; but the pursuit ended abruptly when the quarry retreated into a dense thicket. As Jake Smith put it, with scriptural inaccuracy, "I always considered Daniel a great fool to go into a den of bears."

Guard duty that night fell to Langford and Hedges, who proceeded to improve the "wee sma' hours" by broiling and eating two partridges intended for breakfast. When Newt, the head cook, discovered the birds were gone, he was quick to blame his dog Booby for the theft. The poor dog was driven out of camp in disgrace until the culprits finally confessed their sin. Thereafter, Booby had more friends than before.

The route followed from the camp on Grouse Creek was as difficult as the preceding day's. A westerly course across the Continental Divide for several miles was gradually altered to the north, bringing them to an evening encampment at the head of Surprise Creek. In the general confusion of getting all the pack animals into camp it was some time before anyone noticed that Everts was missing. Signal guns were fired and several men went back along the trail, but no real search was initiated because all felt that Everts would get back to camp or to the previously agreed-upon rendezvous at the geyser basin on the Thumb of Lake Yellowstone. Thus, Hedges could write, "All in but Everts & we felt well around the fire."[82]

Nothing was going well for Everts, who was already embarked upon the ordeal of which he later wrote so romantically.[83] He had become separated from his comrades in the afternoon, but later found a stray packhorse which he attempted to drive along. Failing in that, he rode briskly on to find camp and get help. However, he missed the way (his vision was defective) and night caught him somewhere in that tangled forest, lost but not particularly concerned. So, he picketed his horse, built a fire, and settled down to pass the dark hours as comfortably as possible.

The next day Everts started out early. He had dismounted to examine his surroundings when his horse took fright and bolted with his gun, blankets, matches—everything except the clothing he wore, a small knife, and an opera glass. By the time he had given up a frantic attempt to recapture his horse, he was thoroughly lost. He spent a second night alone in the forest, sleepless, in a thicket, and, at midday on the eleventh, he came out on the shore of Heart Lake, where he could see the geyser basin that was to be his home for some days to come.

Meanwhile, the camp moved on to the head of Flat Mountain Arm, a beacon fire was set on the ridge above, and signal guns were fired during the night; yet, the morning of the eleventh day dawned without Everts showing. All were convinced that the lost man had pushed on to the rendezvous on Thumb Bay; so the party again moved forward. Thus, Everts' arrival at Heart Lake was paralleled by the arrival of his comrades on the south shore of the Thumb of Yellowstone Lake.

Finding no indication that Everts had been there, or at the hot spring area opposite their camp, the expedition decided to lay over and begin a systematic search for him on the twelfth. But a storm set in that night, and snow hid whatever trail Everts left in his wandering course to Heart Lake. The chance of a successful search was greatly diminished by that storm, which also made the situation more precarious for the lost man; yet, the plan followed did bring rescuers very close to him.

All the men except Hedges and the cooks went out by pairs, each following a specified route. General Washburn and Langford rode south toward the Brown Mountain (Mount Sheridan),[84] and were within one-half mile of the shore of Heart Lake when Langford's horse broke through a thin turf into the underlying hot mud. The horse's legs were so badly scalded the two had to turn back when actually within sight of the geyser basin where Everts was lying in his wet clothing, absorbing the warmth radiated by a patch of stony "formation." Everts later built a rude shelter of branches on the site and remained there seven days (until the nineteenth) living mainly on the roots of thistles. He says of his shelter, "At first this was barely preferable to the storm, but I soon became accustomed to it, and before I left, though thoroughly parboiled, actually enjoyed it."[85]

The search continued until September 16, when it was decided to move the camp to the vicinity of the hot springs at present West Thumb junction. Four days of arduous searching had accomplished next to nothing: a footprint had been found on the beach of Lake Yellowstone and Jake Smith thought he saw a group of Indians; otherwise, they could only blaze trees leading to several small caches of food, in the hope that Everts would be led to one of them, if—and the question loomed large in their minds—he was still in the area, and if he remained alive through the series of storms that had put down two feet of snow.

It was on one of the worst days of the search that the dog Booby proved his worth. He had accompanied Gillette and Hauser on a check of the caches, and, when they lost their way in the snow and gloom of evening, Booby led them unerringly back to camp.

By September 17 the food supply was dangerously low; it was decided that they should begin the trek to the settlements of Montana. However, they were unwilling to entirely abandon Everts, so Gillette, the most competent woodsman among them, and the soldiers Moore and Williamson were left behind with ten days' rations to continue the search a little longer. They were authorized to go back to Bozeman by way of the expedition's outward-bound track, or to make a search and then follow the trail of the main party down the Madison River.

It was the latter course that Gillette and the soldiers followed. Working their way carefully back along the trail, they reached the general area where Everts had been lost just as he was abandoning his drafty sauna in the geyser basin at Heart Lake. On the twentieth they reached the lake at its outlet, scanned the beach line and the geyser basin on the far side for smoke, then continued down Heart River to its junction with the Snake. Had they gone over to the geyser basin, they would have seen the pitiful shelter occupied until the previous day by the man they sought, and had they been a few hours later, they would have seen smoke across the lake, for Everts returned that afternoon, defeated in his first attempt to reach Lake Yellowstone, and made a fire with a lens from his opera glass.

Gillette and the soldiers missed Everts as narrowly as Washburn and Langford had; their failure left the lost man to play out a drama of privation and suffering that has few parallels. Fortunately, he did not know what was ahead, but was content to stay by his fire two days, nourishing his body on thistle roots and treating his frostbitten feet and scalded thigh as best he could, before starting again for the rendezvous on Yellowstone Lake. By the time he reached the campsite at the West Thumb Geyser Basin, at noon on September 25, Gillette and the soldiers had been gone three days. All he could do there was to scavenge the camp refuse, adding an old table fork and a pint baking-powder tin to his equipment before moving on "in deep dejection."

The main party had left that camp on the morning of September 17, moving westward across the timbered ridges lying between Thumb Bay and the Firehole River, about as the road goes now. Much of the way was obstructed by fallen timber, but not so badly as on their route south of Lake Yellowstone. It was a dreary march in unsettled weather, with nothing scenic to break the monotony of that snowy forest but a brief glimpse of a large lake to the left of their line of travel. Doane thought the water belonged to the Madison River drainage, while Langford correctly relegated it to the Snake River side of the Continental Divide.[86] Camp was made that night on Spring Creek, within four miles of the great geysers; but they had no crystal ball, and Hedges sounded the prevailing mood when he wrote by the firelight, "much doubt as to where we are & where we should go."

But they were nearer to glory than they knew. Two hours after breaking camp the next day they rode into a scene that caused Hedges to forget all his "bad feelings of the morning." They were on the right bank of the Firehole River when the Upper Geyser Basin opened to view, and just then Old Faithful saluted them with a one-hundred-foot pillar of boiling water. In their haste to get over to the geyser they crossed the river at a bad place—a horse went down, packs were wetted and Hedges lost a glove—but they arrived in time to watch that rumbling column sink majestically onto its sinter mound. Yesterday's despondence was gone; they had reached the fabled Firehole.[87]

They established camp in a little grove of pines on the margin of a small, marshy pond opposite Beehive Geyser;[88] then the expeditioners scattered throughout the basin on a hunt for geysers. The Washburn party was fortunate in the number of first-class geysers that performed for them: six, including three that play only rarely now. Langford said, "We gave such names to those geysers which we saw in action as we think will best illustrate their peculiarities," and that fortunate procedure unquestionably resulted in a nomenclature of the highest priority. Every name is as fitting today as when first given.

General Washburn is credited with the inspiration to designate the geyser that heralded their entry into the Upper Geyser Basin as Old Faithful, and, while it does not operate with the clock-like regularity that is popularly ascribed to it, this geyser is faithful in the sense that it is the one large spouter that never disappoints the visitor by refusing to perform.

On the opposite bank of the Firehole River was a small cone, resembling an old-fashioned beehive, which later proved to be a geyser. It was so well situated with respect to the party's campsite that Sam Hauser was able to utilize his engineering skill in measuring the height of its erupted water. His figure of 219 feet remains acceptable for that rare performer they called the Beehive.

Four hundred yards northwesterly from the camp, and in full view across the little pond, was a massive cone that Trumbull did not think was doing its best on the day of their arrival. It only splashed and slopped over in a patronizing way, but its form was so like the keep of some moldered, medieval fortress that there seemed no better name for it than the Castle.

One-half mile directly north of the Castle and close to the west bank of Firehole River another geyser cone attracted their attention. It had the form of a great hollow tree stump with a part of one side broken away to expose the six-foot aperture through which its waters discharged. Upon observing an hour-long eruption in which that enormous nozzle played a constant stream to more than one hundred feet, Walter Trumbull noted: "We thought it deserved to be called 'The Giant,' as it discharged more water than any other geyser which we saw in operation."[89]

About eight hundred feet beyond the Giant was another peculiar formation with "winding apertures penetrating the sinter," immediately suggesting the Grotto as the appropriate name. As it was quiescent when discovered, several members of the party crawled into the interior to examine the vents, but, on viewing a subsequent eruption of considerable violence, one of the curious said he "felt like one who had narrowly escaped being summarily cooked."

Just at sunset there was a spectacular eruption opposite camp, on the sinter mound now known as Geyser Hill. What had first appeared to be only a large, bowl-shaped hot pool began rocketing jets of boiling water as high as two hundred feet against a backdrop of iridescent vapor. This earth-shaking geyser was obviously less powerful than the Giant, but also more beautiful, so there was only one really appropriate name for it—the Giantess.

Since half of one day and a few morning hours of another was all the time that could be spared for examining, measuring, and describing these features, beside which "the geysers of Iceland sink to insignificance,"[90] the pack train was under way at 9 A.M. on September 19. A few of the well mounted individuals lingered behind in the hope of seeing something else spectacular, but soon they, too, were moving down the Firehole River.

At Midway they admired "an enormous bluestone spring" (present Grand Prismatic Spring) and took note of a great, steaming caldron that was discharging a large volume of boiling water into Firehole River. There, they were looking at what was—or would be—the greatest of all the geysers (Excelsior Geyser, now inactive); but they were unaware of it and hurried downstream, passing with as little cognizance through the thermal riches of the Lower Geyser Basin.

That night the Washburn party camped where the Firehole and Gibbon rivers join to form the Madison, and there, by a pleasant campfire beneath the pines, the conversation is said to have turned to a discussion of the wonder-filled region they were leaving. According to Langford,

> The proposition was made by some member that we utilize the result of our exploration by taking up quarter sections of land at the most prominent points of interest, and a general discussion followed. One member of our party suggested that if there could be secured by pre-emption a good title to two or three quarter sections of land opposite the lower fall of the Yellowstone and extending down the river along the cañon, they would eventually become a source of/great profit to the owners. Another member of the party thought that it would be more desirable to take up a quarter section of land at the Upper Geyser Basin, for the reason that that locality could be more easily reached by tourists and pleasure seekers. A third suggestion was that each member of the party pre-empt a claim, and in order that no one should have an advantage over the others, the whole would be thrown into a common pool for the benefit of the entire party.

Mr. Hedges then said that he did not approve of any of these plans—that there ought to be no private ownership of any portion of that region, but the whole ought to be set apart as a great National Park, and that each one of us ought to make an effort to have this accomplished.[91]

The result of that campfire discussion on the evening of September 19, 1870, will be considered in the following chapter; for now, it is sufficient to note the absence of any mention of it in the available diaries of the party. Even Cornelius Hedges, the alleged proponent of a great, new concept, had only trivia to record: "Mon. 19 . . . No fish in river. grub getting very thin. opposite a stream comes in on right side. mud bottom . . . Tues. 20. Didn't sleep well last night. got to thinking of home & business. seems as if we are almost there."[92]

The Washburn party continued down the Madison River until the afternoon of September 22, when they reached a ranch fourteen miles from Virginia City. The next morning Langford rode ahead to the town with the news of the loss of Everts,[93] and later that day the military escort parted from the expedition to return to Fort Ellis, where Lieutenant Doane reported on the afternoon of the twenty-fourth. The return of the Helena contingent was accomplished with the arrival of the pack train on the evening of the twenty-seventh. (Langford came in from Virginia City on the coach that arrived the evening of the twenty-fifth, Washburn and Hauser coming in the next day, and Hedges and Jake Smith were just ahead of the pack train.)

They were a used-up bunch. Only Jake's clothing was fit to be seen on the street; Langford's large frame had been pared from 190 pounds to 155, and Washburn had a cold which furthered the consumption he had long suffered from. Hedges jokingly remarked that "baby seemed to know me, but Edna [probably his daughter, Edna Cornelia] said her pa was over on the Yellowstone."

Gillette and the two soldiers were back on October 2, with the discouraging news that they could find no trace of the missing man. The *Helena Herald* undoubtedly expressed the sentiment of the community in its statement, "we feel fully satisfied that everything has been done for the recovery of Mr. Everts that humanity can suggest, and to Mr. Gillette is due the highest credit and gratitude of all our citizens."[94] Yet, some of missing man's friends were not satisfied to leave his fate undetermined. The spokesman for this group was Hedge's law partner, Judge R. Lawrence, who offered a reward of $600 for Everts' recovery.

The notice of the reward offer also provided the information that "A party consisting of two men, George A. Pritchett and John Baronett, was organized and outfitted in this city, yesterday, and left this morning for the Yellowstone country, to search for the Hon. T.

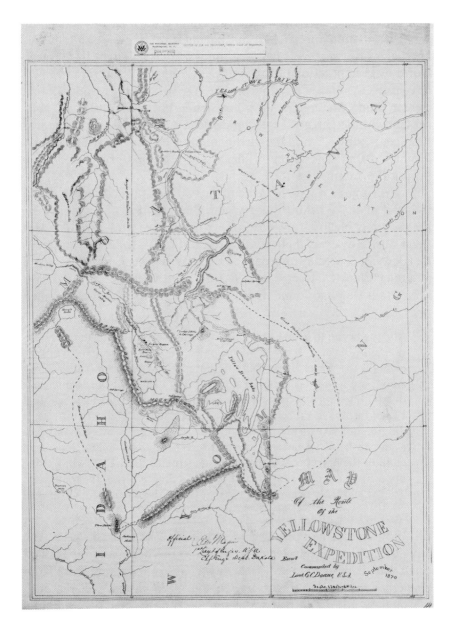

Map drawn by Lt. Gustavus C. Doane in September 1870. Record Group 77, Office of the Chief of Engineers, Q 329 - No. 30. National Archives, Washington, D.C.

C. Everts."[95] Little is known about Pritchett beyond the fact that he was a handyman and packer, but Baronett we know was a fabulous character. He was one of those younger sons set adrift in the wide world by the operation of England's ancient laws of entail, and in his adventurous life was a sailor, prospector, soldier-of-fortune, Indian fighter, guide, and much more. Yet, he was always a gentleman: soft-spoken, competent, and utterly reliable. Yellowstone Jack, as he was familiarly known,[96] had the further qualification of knowing his way around in the Yellowstone wilderness, for he had prospected there during the summer of 1869.

With a good dog to help them, the two men pushed rapidly along the trail of the Washburn party with the intention of searching the area south of Yellowstone Lake until the snows of winter should force them out. However, their mission did not prove to be that difficult. On October 6, as they approached that narrow gash, the Cut, which separates Blacktail Deer Creek Plateau from Crescent Hill, Baronett noticed his dog had found a trail he thought to be that of a wounded bear.

> My dog began to growl, and looking across a small cañon to the mountain side beyond, I saw a black object upon the ground. Yes, sure enough, there was Bruin. My first impulse was to shoot from where I stood, but as he was going so slowly, I saw I should have no difficulty overtaking him, and crossed over to where he was. When I got near to it I found it was not a bear, and for my life could not tell what it was. It did not look like an animal that I had ever seen, and it was certainly not a human being. It never occurred to me that it was Everts. I went up close to the object; it was making a low groaning noise, crawling along upon its knees and elbows, and trying to drag itself up the mountain. Then it suddenly occurred to me that it was the object of my search.[97]

At the time of his rescue, Everts was described as weighing about fifty pounds, his clothing was in shreds, and he had no shoes. The balls of his frost-bitten feet were worn to the bone, and his scalded thigh was likewise exposed. Other areas of his body were seared and blackened, while his fingers resembled bird's claws. He was both inarticulate and irrational when found, and doubtless would soon have died of exposure to the cold sleet that was then coating the ground.

Baronett was able to pick Everts up in his arms and carry him to a place where a fire could be made. There he fed him some tea with a spoon before moving him three or four miles down Blacktail Deer Creek to a camping place. The following day Baronett took the emaciated man on his horse the eleven miles to the cabin of some miners on Turkey Pen Creek opposite the mouth of Bear Gulch.[98]

While Baronett cared for Everts there, Pritchett rode to Fort Ellis to get an ambulance and a surgeon. Though willing to help, the commandant was unable to get the necessary clearance, and Pritchett had to go on to Bozeman for assistance. There, the news of Everts' survival and need brought an immediate, generous response. Charles Wright, who ran the livery stable, hitched up a light spring-wagon and started at once with Doctor O'Neil. At Fort Ellis they picked up three helpers—Harry Horr, a civilian employee of the post trader's store, and two soldiers, Sergeant Leipler and Private Mallory.

They managed to get the wagon as far as Yankee Jim Canyon, but not without upsetting it once into the river. Harry, who was quite a wag, may have dressed the story up a bit, but in his version they mistook a moonbeam for the trail, and Mallory, who went into the water with some of the freight, nearly drowned because Horr, in grabbing for him, got hold of a bag of potatoes and waded ashore with the "murphies" instead of the Irishman.[99]

Meanwhile, Jack Baronett ministered to Everts with "all the care, sympathy, and solicitude of a brother"; yet for several days it was doubted he could recover because his digestion had been so deranged by his enforced diet of fibrous thistle roots. But an old hunter who stopped at the cabin had just the remedy for that; he rendered out a pint of oil from the fat of a freshly killed bear and gave it to the sick man, thereby providing him, in one draught, with a remedy for his intestinal congestion and nourishment for his weakened constitution. Thereafter, Everts made a steady recovery, both in body and mind.[100]

When strong enough to talk, Everts gave his rescuers some idea of his wanderings. He had attempted to follow the trail of the Washburn party westward from the abandoned campsite at the hot springs on Thumb Bay, but soon decided their route was impossible for him and returned to the lake. He then began a slow trek along the shore of the lake toward the outlet, and from there followed the west bank of the Yellowstone River down to the Mud Volcano, where he came upon the outward-bound track of the Washburn party. Thereafter, he had that trail for guidance, but his physical condition was worsening rapidly. He was able to produce fire with the lens of his opera glass until he lost that valuable piece of equipment (eventually, he lost even his homemade sandals). Toward the end, he was reduced to carrying a burning brand from one overnight stop to another, but a snowstorm a day or two before he was rescued deprived him of even that slender comfort.

Ten days after his rescue, Everts was sufficiently recuperated to ride to the wagon below Yankee Jim Canyon with George Huston holding him in the saddle. He was delivered safely to Bozeman in the spring-wagon and his care was taken over by friends who came down from Helena. By the end of October he was reported as "sound in mind, hearty in appetite, with good digestion, and as jolly as can be." He was able to walk some, and to converse much with his many visitors about those experiences in the Yellowstone wilderness. As Samuel Langhorne remarked about the Yellowstone expedition, "No shadow now rests over their explorations. The lost is found and the fatted calf should be killed."[101]

The return of Everts to Helena on November 4 made it possible to plan a feast which would properly conclude the expedition. And so, on the eleventh, Everts received the following invitation:

> Dear Sir: —I am directed by members of the late Yellowstone party, as a token of appreciation of your merits, and as a mark of their heartfelt joy at your miraculous and wonderful escape, to invite you to join them in a banquet at the Kan-Kan, tomorrow at three o'clock.
>
> They make this request, believing that they are only giving expression to the universal feeling entertained by the community in which you have so long resided, and over which your supposed loss had thrown a cloud of sorrow.
>
> I am, respectfully, your ob't serv't.
>
>   H. D. Washburn.[102]

Everts accepted, "although not really sufficiently recovered" (he was troubled by a numbness of his right arm and his foot was tender and slow to heal). The banquet was a repast called "one of the most elaborate and elegant ever served in Montana,"[103] followed by toasts, and speeches, humorous recitations, and anecdotes of the Yellowstone expedition. All the gentlemen were present except Lieutenant Doane, and "each were called out, and acquitted themselves in an oratorical way much to their credit, individually and collectively."

So much for the fun; what did the expedition accomplish otherwise? Soon after his return to Helena, Cornelius Hedges began a series of articles that appeared in the *Helena Herald* from October 6 to November 9,[104] and the last—"The Yellowstone Lake" article—is of particular interest because it contains the only published suggestion for reserving Yellowstone to come from any member of the Washburn party prior to initiation of Park legislation. Hedges began with these words:

This beautiful body of water is situated in the extreme northwest corner of Wyoming, and, with its tributaries and sister lakes of smaller dimensions, is entirely cut off from all access from any portion of that Territory by the impassable and eternally snow-clad range of the Wind River Range of mountains [Absaroka Range]. Hence the propriety that the Territorial lines be so readjusted that Montana should embrace all that lake region west of the Wind River Range, a matter in which we hope our citizens will soon move to accomplish, as well as to secure, its future appropriation to the public use.[105]

The foregoing statement is certainly clear in regard to the Washburn party's desire to have the Yellowstone annexed to Montana Territory; in its other objective of "appropriation to the public use," the wording is as certainly ambiguous. Whether Hedges was asking for a reservation on a territorial basis, similar to the federal grant of the Yosemite Valley to the state of California, or whether he envisaged a truly national reservation, cannot be determined from his wording. But, regardless of his intent, he was not supported by the other members of the expedition.

Gillette, Langford, and Washburn also supplied the *Helena Herald* with information, and the latter's account was widely reprinted. The *Rocky Mountain News* of Denver headed it a "Montana Romance" and thought the general's account would "draw somewhat upon the powers of credulity," but the *New York Times* was most enthusiastic, crediting Washburn with "graphic directness and unpretending eloquence." In commenting that the account read like the realization of a child's fairy tale, the *Times* editor hastened to add, "We mean no disparagement, but the reverse,"[106] all of which was well and good, but the fact remains that his newspaper coverage was only an armchair travelogue.

Walter Trumbull wrote for the Helena *Rocky Mountain Gazette*,[107] but again it was only descriptive of the Yellowstone country, with no mention of park possibilities. In the article he later prepared for the *Overland Monthly* he recommended the area for sheep raising, though he did soften his utilitarian viewpoint slightly by adding, "When, however, by means of the Northern Pacific Railroad, the falls of the Yellowstone and the geyser basin are rendered easy of access, probably no portion of America will be more popular as a watering place or summer resort."[108]

Another article that appeared at that time was Langford's "Wonders of the Yellowstone" in *Scribner's Monthly*. This, too, was purely descriptive, but illustrated. The absurdly crude and unrealistic woodcuts used are marked with the "T.M." used by Thomas Moran. At that time, Moran supplemented a meager income from his art by

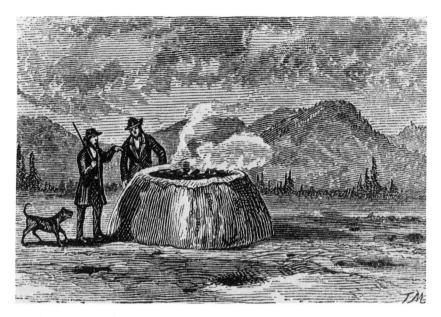

The Beehive Geyser.

Crater of the Giant Geyser. Woodcuts made by Thomas Moran from Langford's description as he saw the geysers in 1870. From *Scribner's Monthly* (June 1871).

preparing woodcuts for the use of printers, rather unglamorous hackwork that at least put meat in the kettle. Moran had made the cuts as best he could from Langford's description, and from that work came a desire to see for himself what the Yellowstone wonders were really like.

But it was through the use of the spoken rather than the printed word, that the Washburn party accomplished most. Langford, who was a nominal employee of Jay Cooke & Company, agents for the Northern Pacific Railway, while expeditioning in the Yellowstone country, probably promoted that exploration as a means of fulfilling his commitment to provide publicity. He made detailed notes while in the Yellowstone region—he says they aggregated 35,000 words[109]— and spent six weeks following his return to Helena reducing his notes to manuscript form. Both the content and the form indicate that the manuscript was intended for lecture presentation.[110]

A public announcement of Langford's purpose was made by the *Helena Herald* of November 11. Under the heading of "Lectures," the editor stated,

> Hon. N. P. Langford, we understand, is to lecture in the states this winter, on the wonders of the Yellowstone country. Mr. Langford is a good writer, and the wonderful scenes which he has to describe must insure the delight and attention of any audience—even in the plainest narration. They are eloquent of themselves. We understand that Mr. Langford will deliver his lecture here before his departure, at the request of a number of citizens. . . . The theme chosen by the lecturer, and the diffusion of knowledge in relation to our Territory among his hearers will be very beneficial to our interests—while an orator desireous of making a creditable literary effort could not be inspired by a nobler subject.

On November 18 Langford presented his lecture under the auspices of the Helena Library Association at the Methodist Episcopal Church on Broadway. At that time he used the title, "Recent Explorations on the Yellowstone," but the advance publicity informed the public that it was "the same, substantially" as the lecture to be given by Langford in the East "in filling his engagements with the Literary and Scientific Associations."[111] The newspaper was referring to Langford's agreement with Jay Cooke to give a series of twenty lectures as part of a publicity program in the interest of the Northern Pacific Railway.[112] After one more warm-up appearance on November 22 at Virginia City. Langford left for the States and his brief career as a lecturer.

The first appearance of the series was made the evening of January 19, 1871, to a small audience in Lincoln Hall, Washington, D.C.

James G. Blaine, then speaker of the House of Representatives, introduced Langford, who proceeded to "read a statement of his adventures in exploration of the Yellowstone Valley."[113] Among those who attended was Ferdinand V. Hayden, head of the U.S. Geological Survey of the Territories. Dr. Hayden (for he actually was a medical doctor, although more strongly attracted to the new science of geology) was undoubtedly quite interested in Langford's description of the region he himself had so nearly seen in 1860; and yet, those word-pictures of geyserland were less important than an idea that came to him that evening.

Hayden has been accused of "lifting" the idea for creation of Yellowstone National Park from Langford's remarks,[114] but he did not. There is no suggestion for a national park in the prepared lecture Langford read at Lincoln Hall. What Hayden got from that lecture was merely the idea to capitalize upon the current interest in the Yellowstone region by asking Congress for funds to explore it officially. Hayden's attempt to take credit for originating the park idea has an entirely different basis; he did not steal it from Langford, nor even embrace the idea until much later.

Langford presented his second lecture in the East in New York City's Cooper Union Hall on January 21. It was in concluding this particular lecture that Langford claimed to have suggested the creation of Yellowstone National Park. While Hiram Chittenden was in the process of preparing his chapter, "The National Park Idea—Its Origin and Realization," for the Yellowstone book published in 1895, Langford supplied him with a purported extract from the *New York Tribune,* January 23, 1871, which Chittenden quoted as proof that Langford had, indeed, promoted this controversial idea. As used by Chittenden, the quotation reads:

> This is probably the most remarkable region of natural wonders in the world; and, while we already have our Niagara and Yosemite, this new field of wonders should be at once withdrawn from occupancy, and set apart as a public National Park for the enjoyment of the American people for all time.[115]

A careful reading of the article from which the above was supposedly taken discloses that no such statement appeared there, nor is it in any of the reportage by New York newspapers.[116] The scholar who first discovered that Chittenden's quotation did not exist where cited corresponded with him and Langford without resolving the question of the true source.[117] Their contradictory statements only led back to Langford's stubborn avowal that "Whatever reports of my lecture have been made—whether complete or incomplete—the fact remains that I advocated the park scheme, in these few words."[118]

Nathaniel P. Langford as he appeared in the 1870s.
Used with permission of Montana Historical Society,
Helena.

Although newspaper research has not disclosed the origin of Langford's quotation, the paragraph invites analysis. Most of the opening line, to the semicolon, appears to have been taken directly from the last line of the penultimate paragraph of Langford's lecture notes, while the origin of the remainder is obscure. If Langford intended to relate Niagara to Yosemite as a public reservation, in 1871 we did *not* "have our Niagara"; the approaches to the falls were then privately owned and visitors were charged a fee to view them, after passing through an unsightly hodgepodge of tea rooms, curio shops, and advertising signs. In fact, agitation for free access to Niagara Falls bore no fruit until 1885, when the state of New York established the Niagara Falls reservation.[119] On the other hand, the passage may simply represent an intention to relate Niagara and Yosemite to Yellowstone as spectacular natural wonders.

However that may be, the quotation must be considered spurious until the question is satisfactorily answered. It is unfortunate that this quotation was used uncritically by Chittenden as evidence that Langford's lectures provided a powerful call for the creation of a park in the Yellowstone region.

There is no evidence that Langford completed his series of lectures. It appears that the Northern Pacific Railroad was not in full agreement with Jay Cooke's publicity campaign,[120] and may have limited the appearances; however, illness was the reason which Langford gave his family. His sister, Chloe Taylor, writing to her daughter on May 3, 1871, mentioned that "Louise says Eliza wrote to her that *Tan* had been there, and that he had given up his lectures—that he had seen a physician, who says, if he does not get relief from his throat trouble, he is a *doomed man* in less than three years."[121] This is in agreement with the statement of R. E. Fisk, an editor of the *Helena Herald*, who wrote from New York on May 26,

> Mr. Langford, whom I have had the pleasure of meeting several times in the city, lectured last week at the house of Jay Cooke, near Philadelphia, in the interest of the Northern Pacific Railroad Co. Mr. Langford has an engagement for a series of lectures which he will deliver in Pennsylvania the present month should his threatened bronchial trouble permit.[122]

Apparently, Langford's popularizing of the Yellowstone region in the interest of the Northern Pacific Railroad ended with that lecture at Jay Cooke's "Ogontz" estate.

Dr. Hayden's idea of asking Congress for funds to explore the Yellowstone region, inspired by Langford's Lincoln Hall lecture, had most fortunate consequences. Hayden's considerable following in

Congress included James G. Blaine, an advocate of the Northern Pacific Railroad and soon to be speaker of the House, and Henry M. Dawes. The latter, then chairman of the House Committee on Appropriations, was considered the most influential representative of the post-Civil War period—actually, "the power behind the scenes that made things move."[123] More important, it is evident from his earlier support of the Yosemite Grant legislation that Dawes already held strong conservation convictions. With such support Hayden's proposal was bound to prosper.

Thus, the Sundry Civil Act of March 3, 1871, included an item for $40,000 for the continuation of Hayden's Geological Survey of the Territories, with the working season of 1871 to be devoted to an investigation of "The sources of the Missouri and Yellowstone Rivers." The legislation also raised Hayden's salary as United States geologist by $1,000 (to $4,000 per year) and gave him a free hand in the selection of his assistants. As will be seen, Representative Dawes' part in obtaining that munificence was later acknowledged in several ways.

Although the appropriation was not available until July 1, 1871, Hayden was able to establish a rendezvous camp near Ogden, Utah, in mid-May by outfitting at Fort D. A. Russell in Wyoming Territory;[124] and he gathered the members of his expedition in the following weeks. The Union Pacific and Central Pacific railroads transported his men on free passes and moved the expedition's equipment at no cost.

The men who came singly and in small groups to that pleasant camp on an old lake terrace a mile east of Ogden were organized and outfitted by Hayden's veteran assistant, James Stevenson, of whom historian Chittenden has said: "It rarely happens that a master is so far indebted to a servant for his success, as was true of the relation of Dr. Hayden and James Stevenson." It was Stevenson's administrative ability, coupled with Hayden's capacity "to rouse in his subordinates the utmost loyalty and most enthusiastic effort,"[125] that made the Hayden Survey the success it was. Though only a little over thirty years old then, Stevenson had had seventeen years' experience in the West, and had been more or less associated with Hayden from the age of thirteen.

In addition to Managing Director Stevenson, the party included Henry W. Elliott, an artist; Professor Cyrus Thomas, agricultural statistician and entomologist; Anton Schoenborn, chief topographer (whose experience went back to the prewar days of the old Corps of Topographical Engineers); A. J. Smith, assistant topographer;

William H. Jackson, an Omaha photographer attracted to the Hayden Survey the previous year; George B. Dixon, assistant photographer; J. W. Beaman, meteorologist; Professor G. N. Allen, botanist; Robert Adams, Jr., assistant botanist (later United States minister to Brazil and a member of Congress from 1893 to 1906); Dr. Albert C. Peale, mineralogist (also a medical doctor and scion of the talented Peale family); Dr. Charles S. Turnbull, physician and general assistant; Edward C. Carrington, zoologist; William B. Logan, secretary (son of Representative John A. Logan of Illinois); F. J. Huse, Chester M. Dawes (son of Representative Henry L. Dawes of Massachusetts), Clifford DeV. Negley, and J. W. Duncan, all general assistants.

In addition to technical personnel, a guest, the artist Thomas Moran, accompanied the expedition "directly in the interest of the N.P.R.R. Company."[126] Twenty men were to serve as packers, cooks, laborers, hunters, and guides.

On June 11, the white tents were pulled down and loaded with the other impedimenta in army mule wagons, the men mounted horses that were fractious from a season of disuse, and the expedition began moving north. The immediate destination was Fort Hall, on Lincoln Creek, east of the great Snake River Plain. There, two days were taken to rest and refit before continuing northward into Montana Territory along the stage road to Virginia City.

After a brief look at the declining placers of Alder Gulch, the party continued northeast toward Fort Ellis in the Gallatin Valley, where the expedition was to receive its escort and supplies for the trip through the Yellowstone region. Upon arrival at the fort, Hayden learned that his party was to share the Yellowstone wilderness with other explorers.

General Philip H. Sheridan had been so greatly impressed by Lieutenant Doane's report on the exploration of 1870 that he had ordered two officers of the Corps of Engineers to make a reconnaissance.[127] They were: Captain John W. Barlow, chief engineer of the Division of Missouri, and Captain David P. Heap, engineer officer of the Department of Dakota. These officers left Chicago on July 2 with three assistants: W. H. Wood, a draughtsman; H. G. Prout, an assistant topographer, and a photographer by the name of Thomas J. Hine. They traveled to Fort Ellis by way of the Union Pacific Railroad and the Montana stage lines, arriving bone-weary and dusty on the twelfth. The following preparations for a six-week tour of the Yellowstone region were crowded into two days: three packers, two laborers, and a cook (all civilians) were hired; twelve mounts and ten pack mules were selected, and all the equipment,

A camp of the Hayden Survey party on Yellowstone Lake, 1871. From W.H. Jackson's photograph no. 272.

The 1871 Hayden Survey party along the shore of Mirror Lake. W. H. Jackson photograph.

supplies, and arms they required were drawn from the post quartermaster. By unceasing labor, the two engineers were able to move out a day behind Hayden's party on July 15.

Captain Taylor's F Troop, Second Cavalry, was detailed to act as escort for both parties; however, Captain Barlow had a detail, consisting of Sergeant Blade and five privates—Canter, McConnell, Lemans, Barouch, and Amer—under his personal command.

Wagon transportation was used as far as Bottlers' ranch on the Yellowstone River, but getting wagons through the narrow, rocky canyon east of Fort Ellis was still a difficult undertaking requiring three days to reach the ranch. In places the grade was so sidling it was necessary that men walk above each wagon, supporting it with ropes; even so, there was one upset and many annoying minor damages.

From the Bottler ranch, the two expeditions moved up the Yellowstone River to the hot springs they preferred to call Soda Mountain on the Gardner River (miners had renamed the river at this point Warm Spring Creek).[128] Near that great out-flow of steaming water they found a haphazard encampment of invalids who called their rude spa Chestnutville.[129] It was an intrusion into the wilderness, revealing the shape of things to come. The discovery of gold at the head of Clarks Fork the previous summer brought many men into the Yellowstone region in 1871, and, while most were interested in the riches obtainable from a placer or lode, there were those who would take up any promising opportunity. Even as the two expeditions rested at Mammoth Hot Springs, Henry Horr (one of those who brought the spring-wagon up to Yankee Jim Canyon the previous October to return the rescued Everts to Bozeman) was busy with his partner James C. McCartney staking out a claim to those springs (which he named),[130] and Matthew McGuirk would do the same at Hot River in August. The claimants saw a future profit in the supposed curative powers of those waters.

Near the mouth of the Lamar River there was another intrusion. Though Jack Baronett had failed to collect the reward offered for finding Everts, he did profit indirectly. As a by-product of that errand of mercy he received information of the discovery of gold on Clarks Fork; having chased enough golden mirages, he decided to make *his* by getting control of the only practicable bridge site on the trail to the new "mines." So, as soon as he could gather up an outfit he returned to build that structure known as the Baronett Bridge.[131] By working during the winter while the water was low, Jack was able to complete a ninety-foot stringer bridge of two spans—thirty and sixty feet—supported by a rock-filled, log-crib pier erected upon a shelf of

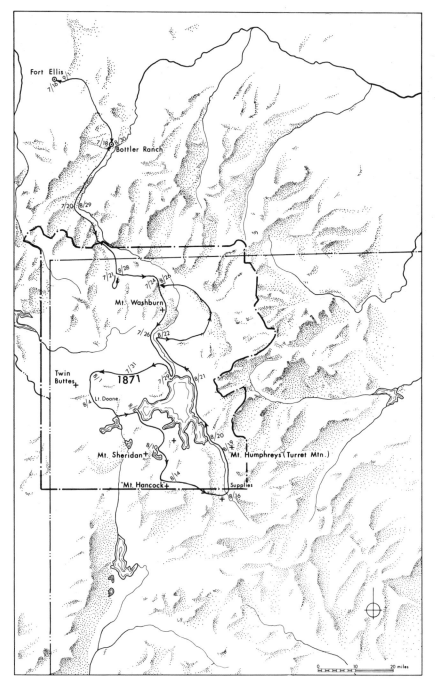

Route of the Barlow-Heap expedition, 1871. Hayden party routes are shown on page 190.

bedrock jutting out from the west bank. As originally built, the bridge was suitable only for packtrain traffic, but it was a great convenience for the miners on Clarks Fork, most, but not all, of whom paid the toll of "two-bits" per animal willingly enough. They were glad to be able to avoid the dangerous and frequently impassable Bannock ford two and one-half miles upstream—the only other place where the Yellowstone River could be crossed in that vicinity.

From a comfortable camp on Lost Creek (which Barlow called Meadow Brook), the members of both expeditions crossed the bridge to examine features near the mouth of the East Fork, (now the Lamar River).[132] Captain Barlow was particularly interested in the prominent butte immediately east of the bridge, naming it in accordance with its form, Square Butte. The name never really caught on and the U.S. Geological Survey later substituted Junction Butte. A name Dr. Hayden gave to the dark and tangled draw through which Tower Creek flows above its falls has fared better. His Devils Den remains on the map, a somber reminder that he had not forgotten that awful corner of the battlefield at Gettysburg.

From Lost Creek, the two expeditions continued their tandem progress by the Indian trail over the Washburn Range to the Falls of the Yellowstone. The topographers and scientists climbed to the commanding summit of Mount Washburn to get the lay of the land, noting in particular a mountain to the east which Captain Barlow likened to a Giant's Face staring fixedly at the zenith—the Saddle Mountain of present maps.[133]

Captain Barlow characterized the great falls of the Yellowstone River as well as anyone ever has in just a few words: he saw the upper fall "as the embodiment of beauty, the lower one that of grandeur."[134] That colorful canyon below the falls caused Thomas Moran to admit, with some regret, that its beautiful tints "were beyond the reach of human art"; nevertheless, he proceeded to do very well in capturing them in a watercolor sketch (his famous oil painting was made later from it).

Then on again, through those meadows that were recognized by Dr. Hayden as "once the bed of a great lake," of which the present Lake Yellowstone "is only a remnant"; those pleasantly swelling grasslands were to be his real memorial in a later time.[135] After a brief stop at the Mud Volcano area, where a difficult crossing of the Yellowstone River by raft proved hardly worth the effort, the journey was continued to the outlet of Yellowstone Lake, where they arrived July 28 and went into camp "in a beautiful grassy meadow or opening among the dense pines."

The *Anna*, first boat on Yellowstone Lake, 1871. The name was misspelled by the photographer in adding it to the negative. From W.H. Jackson's photograph no. 273.

The Hayden Survey camp on Mary Bay, August 19, 1871. The frame of the *Anna* has been stripped of its canvas "skin," which is drying, lower left. From W.H. Jackson's photograph no. 288.

That evening Hayden's party assembled the framework of a twelve-foot boat and covered it with a "skin" of well-tarred canvas, and the next morning were able to launch the *Anna*,[136] named for Anna L. Dawes, daughter of the senator from Massachusetts to whom Hayden was beholden for the financing of his expedition. In it, Henry Elliott and James Stevenson sailed over to the island which Hayden proceeded to name for his assistant, whom he considered "undoubtedly the first white man that ever placed foot upon it." Having proved its seaworthiness by that voyage, the *Anna* was put to work sounding the lake.

Captain Barlow was interested in exploring the north shore of the lake eastward from its outlet, but his attempt, on July 30, to swim horses across where the Fishing Bridge now stands was a failure, so he rafted over for a disappointing excursion afoot to Pelican Creek.

The leaders of the two expeditions had agreed to make a side trip to the geyser basins of Firehole River with some of the men, while the others moved around the lake shore to the geyser basin on Thumb Bay in the course of their work. But, as this reconnaissance was about to move out on the last morning in July, Dr. Hayden decided not to go by the known trail (through Hayden Valley, over Mary Mountain, and down Nez Perce Creek); instead, he accepted the guidance of two hunters who knew a shortcut. Their route by Bridge Creek and Beach Lake to Spruce Creek proved unsatisfactory for pack animals, so that Hayden came into Barlow's camp on the head of Nez Perce Creek with his stock much the worse for their toilsome crossing of the Central Plateau.

Several interesting discoveries were made in the Firehole basins. Captain Barlow found a waterfall in the southwest corner of the lower basin. Its 250-foot drop ended in a closely shaded pool of such an elfin character that Fairy Fall seemed the only fit name. In the upper basin the two parties camped separately, with the engineers stopping west of the Giant Geyser, while the geologists went across the Firehole, opposite Castle Geyser. Each was fortunate, for a group of hot springs close to the engineers contained a medium-sized geyser with an arching eruption, called Comet[137] by Captain Barlow, while a shallow pool near the other camp turned out to be a geyser of the first order. Of the latter, Hayden says:

> Soon after reaching camp a tremendous rumbling was heard, shaking the ground in every direction, and soon a column of steam burst forth from a crater near the edge of the east side of the river. Following the steam, arose, by a succession of impulses, a column of water, apparently 6 feet in diameter, to a height of 200 feet, while the steam ascended a

thousand feet or more. . . . We called this the Grand Geyser, for its power seemed greater than any other of which we obtained any knowledge in the valley.[138]

While Hayden and Barlow were in the Upper Geyser Basin, Lieutenant Doane arrived from Fort Ellis with orders for the return of all the escort except six men for each party. So, on September 9, they left the great geysers and crossed over to Thumb Bay under Doane's guidance. There they found their comrades encamped at the hot springs on the west shore.

The cavalry escort returned to Fort Ellis and the two expeditions began a circuit of Lake Yellowstone. Captain Barlow followed Hayden's trail as far as Flat Mountain Arm, then descended Beaver Creek to Heart Lake.[139] While in that vicinity, the captain climbed and named the peak the Washburn party had designated, in chameleon fashion, as Red Mountain, Brown Mountain, and Yellow Mountain. He called it Mount Sheridan, for Lieutenant General Philip H. Sheridan, hero of the Civil War battle of Cedar Run, and the officer responsible for sending the Barlow-Heap Expedition into the Yellowstone region.

From Heart Lake, Barlow's party descended Heart River to the Snake, and then traced that stream to its source before crossing the Continental Divide into the broad valley of the upper Yellowstone River. Their exploration of the headwaters of Snake River added two place names to the map: Mount Hancock, for Major General Winfield S. Hancock, then commanding in the Department of Dakota; and Barlow Peak, named in 1895 in recognition of Captain John Barlow's excellent work.

Meanwhile, Hayden's party stayed closer to Yellowstone Lake as they retraced the route of the Washburn party in the reverse direction. Dr. Hayden followed the upper Yellowstone River to Bridger Lake, which he described as "not more than one or two hundred yards in width," adding, "The lake which has been placed on the maps as Bridger's Lake has no real existence." This is such a patent misstatement when applied to a body of water over a mile in length that one suspects the geologist of not wanting the lake to exist.[140]

The Barlow party had reached the Yellowstone River near Bridger Lake—a locality the captain called Five Forks, but known through common usage as the Thorofare—and they were a day's travel south of Hayden's party, which had reached the river at its inlet into Yellowstone Lake. That spacing was maintained as both expeditions began their northward trek, leaving permanent reminders of their

William H. Jackson, photographer for Hayden's Geological Survey of the Territories, 1870-78. From a self portrait.

passage in the place names they bestowed along the way. Captain Barlow attempted to reach the summit of a "castle-topped" height midway along the east side of the valley he was moving down, but, after spending an hour in a vain attempt to find a fissure by which he could mount the last 400 feet, he had to content himself with naming the whole height Mount Humphreys (for General A.A. Humphreys, then chief of engineers),[141] while the inaccessible summit was called the Watch Tower. Meanwhile, Dr. Hayden named a peak for his assistant and moved the names of Langford and Doane to eminences far north of those they were originally given to.[142]

On the night of August 19 a severe earthquake was felt by both parties. At Beaverdam Creek, Captain Barlow noted an accompanying "rumbling and rushing sound," while Hayden was sufficiently impressed to call his encampment near Steamboat Point the Earthquake Camp. Barlow's party moved up to that place the following day and both expeditions remained there until the twenty-second, when the northward journey was continued. Hayden crossed the Mirror Plateau by way of Pelican Creek, Mirror Lake, and Flint Creek, while Captain Barlow turned up Sour Creek, which he named, working his way north to the Lamar River opposite the mouth of Soda Butte Creek (known to him as Buffalo Creek).

Both expeditions moved down Lamar Valley to cross the Yellowstone River on Baronett's bridge, which Hayden called "the first and only bridge ever built on the Yellowstone," adding, "It may become a matter of some historical importance to note this fact here."[143] West of the bridge, the explorers were on their outward bound track, which they followed rapidly toward Fort Ellis. Hayden's party left what is now the Park on August 26 and Barlow's came out two days later. Stopping only long enough at Bottlers' ranch to break up the base camp maintained there, the geologists were back at Fort Ellis on August 30, with the engineers arriving there on September 1. With the conclusion of the field work, the official exploration of the fabled Yellowstone country was finished and the period of "definitive" exploration of that wilderness was closed. There remained only to disband and return home: Dr. Hayden and a few of his key personnel going to Washington, D.C., Captain Barlow and photographer Hine to Chicago, and Captain Heap to St. Paul with his topographer.

And what were the consequences of this dual exploration? Both parties brought back incontrovertible evidence of the existence and nature of those thermal features that had been so long rumored to exist upon the Yellowstone Plateau. In the mass of field notes, sketches, photographs, and specimens they brought back was material

Bottlers' ranch on the Yellowstone River, 1871. The Hayden and Barlow parties kept a base camp here. (The sheds contain hides of wild animals killed by the Bottlers.) From W.H. Jackson's photograph no. 203.

The nearest settlement west of the Yellowstone Plateau—Gilman Sawtell's ranch at Henrys Lake, Idaho. From a W.H. Jackson photograph, 1872.

for two official reports and the beginning of an accurate map—though not all the data survived to be thus assimilated.

Captain Barlow returned to Chicago with the photographic negatives, meteorological records, and specimens gathered by the engineers. He had been back in his office but a few days when nearly all were destroyed by the great Chicago fire of October 8 to 11, 1871. All the negatives—about 200—were lost, Mr. Hine saving only 16 prints he had made the previous day.[144] Fortunately, Captain Heap took their astronomic observations and topographic notes to his headquarters at St. Paul, and from them he was able to construct the first Yellowstone map based on adequate "control"; that is, the first map on which details were shown in their proper relationship to latitude and longitude. This was a tremendous cartographic advance and Dr. Hayden took immediate advantage of it for the better presentation of his party's information.

Hayden's work suffered a calamity in the death by suicide of chief topographer Anton Schoenborn at Omaha during the return to Washington, D.C. In the face of this seemingly irreparable loss, United States Coast Survey personnel undertook to compile the dead man's field notes, and presented them in the form of maps. Otherwise, the Hayden party had done very well. They brought back geological, botanical, and zoological specimens, sketches and photographs, and voluminous notes—all of which contributed to the official report that was the culmination of the scientific work.

The information thus assembled was of primary importance to the Northern Pacific Railroad Company. In fact, the railroad had shown as deep an interest in this exploration of the Yellowstone region as it had in the Washburn party's in 1870. The Hayden party, while encamped at Virginia City enroute to the Yellowstone, was visited by a newspaper reporter who noted the party was "to cross from the head of the Yellowstone to that of Snake River and down to Fort Hall, surveying the entire route accurately, at the instigation of J. Cooke & Co., who contemplate running a branch road through this Pass to connect with the Central Pacific, if practicable."[145] Evidently, Hayden embarked upon his exploration of the Yellowstone region committed to the interest that the Northern Pacific Railroad Company had already evidenced through the Langford lectures. (General Sheridan undoubtedly had put a crimp in the plan by ordering Barlow and Heap to travel jointly with the Hayden party; being dependent upon their common escort out of Fort Ellis, Hayden was not at liberty to return to Ogden by the Snake River route, as previously planned.) The railroad promoters' deep interest in this exploration was to have a lasting effect on the future of the Yellowstone country.

Judge William D. Kelley, whose 1871 suggestion for "reserving the Great Geyser Basin as a public park forever" led to Yellowstone National Park. From a photograph by Mathew Brady, Yellowstone Park Museum collection.

When Dr. Hayden arrived at his office in Washington with the raw material for a scientific report on the Yellowstone country, he found on his desk a letter that suddenly made his data far more important than he had realized. That letter, dated October 27, 1871, on the stationery of "Jay Cooke & Co., Bankers, Financial Agents, Northern Pacific Railroad Company" and signed by A.B. Nettleton, was as follows:

> Dear Doctor:
>
> Judge Kelley has made a suggestion which strikes me as being an excellent one, viz.: Let Congress pass a bill reserving the Great Geyser Basin as a public park forever—just as it has reserved that far inferior wonder the Yosemite valley and big trees. If you approve this would such a recommendation be appropriate in your official report?[146]

Dr. Hayden did approve, and immediately set about laying the foundation for a New Creation.

CHAPTER 6

THE NEW CREATION

It is the general principle which is chiefly commendable in the Act of Congress setting aside the Yellowstone region as a national park.
—The Nation[1]

The creation of Yellowstone National Park put the federal government of the United States into the business of managing wild lands for recreational use, thereby bringing into focus a new concept of land use which had been maturing on the American scene. The "national park idea," as it has come to be known,[2] has burgeoned wonderfully, here and abroad, into park systems that are among the better expressions of man's relationship to his environment. As a result, there has been great interest in both the idea and its first working example; and also, an unfortunate tendency to confuse the two, so that the Park is often made to appear as the birthplace of the idea.

Hans Huth has said, concerning this campfire birth of the national park idea (see page 130), "If things really had happened that way, it would indeed have been something of a miracle. It would have meant that public opinion had been prepared for this supposedly new and unique idea in little more than a year."[3] But the idea was not new; in fact, it had been evolving for a very long time, and it is germane to our subject—the creation of a Yellowstone National Park—to trace the development of parks, and the park concept, from their beginnings. Only in that way can the events of Yellowstone's creation be properly related to the national park idea.

Emerson perceived the importance of parks to man when he wrote: "Only so far as the masters of the world have called nature to their aid, can they reach the height of magnificence. This is the meaning of their hanging gardens, villas, garden-houses, islands, parks and preserves, to back their faulty personality with these strong accessories."[4] Yes, the idea *is* as old as the hanging gardens built by Nebuchadnezzar for his Median wife, Amyitis, in ancient Babylon. That tiered structure supported on brick arches covered about four acres and was seventy-five feet high, resembling an artificial mountain planted with trees, vines, and flowers, and ingeniously watered from the nearby Euphrates River. There the queen could idle away the time in cool apartments, surrounded by verdure and interesting birds and animals. This private park was "the chief glory of the Great Palace,"[5] but it was not for the common people.

Nor was there any place for them in those royal gardens of the Persians, called *paradeisos* by the Greek soldier-adventurer Xenophon. These were "vast enclosures that included fruit and ornamental trees, flowers, birds, and mammals," [6] and the awe inspired by those magnificent preserves has come down to us through the Latin *paradisus* of the Vulgate Bible to that unsullied English word, paradise, a place of perfect happiness.

Alexander the Great took over the Persian royal gardens and the idea later passed from the Greek world to the Roman, where there was even a poorman's version. Exacavations at Pompeii have uncovered small courtyards where the walls were painted to resemble the lush gardens of Roman villas; but it was too early for a successful democratization. Rather it is the influence of the royal tradition, which reappeared in the Norman *parcs* of France, those "unruffled hunting estates" of the feudal nobility,[7] that is the source, with its connotation of wild property, of our word "park."

Life in Saxon England before the Norman Conquest was based upon a village community system in which the commonality of lands, that is, group use, existed under folk law. In time, most of the arable lands passed out of the "commons," leaving only the less desirable portions of a township in that category. But on those waste lands the villagers retained formalized "rights of common," such as pasturage and the taking of fuel and building materials. So things stood in England at the Conquest.

The new masters, Norman lords from France, took the ancient Saxon forest for deer parks and soon found ways to add to them from the commons. By the Statute of Merton, in A.D. 1235, Norman lawyers established the principle that the common was "the Lord's waste," to do with as he pleased, and the Statute of Westminster the Second, one-half century later, enabled the lord to enclose common lands.[8] In that manner, many commons were converted to deer parks, and yet, enough remained that no Englishman was ever a stranger to the idea of group holding and use of waste lands.

It would be logical to expect the British to merge their two concepts—of game preserves and common holding of lands—into a form that would provide the basis for true park development. But it did not happen so, even with the catalysts of industrialization and Romanticism; instead, they handed their ideas along to another people.

The colonists who settled New England brought the idea of the common to their new homes. Boston Common was established in 1634, and similar areas were features of most New England towns; but on these shores the commons came to serve a different purpose than in the mother country. As they were needed less for grazing and not at all for the supplying of fuel and building materials in a land so well provided with those commodities, these commons of the new world became the drill grounds of the militia on Training Day, and the fair grounds at harvest time. They were also haunts of itinerants and traveling shows, trysting places, and occasionally focal points for civil disorders. In brief, they emerged from the colonial period as informal village parks, giving the old English concept of commonality a new direction, toward public and park-type uses. The only progress made elsewhere in the American colonies was in Pennsylvania where Penn's original plan for Philadelphia allocated a number of squares to public use, with the intention of leaving them as tree-shaded islands within the city.[9]

Overall, it was a slow beginning impeded by Puritan attitudes toward work, nature, and recreation. Colonial New England equated idleness with wickedness, and that work ethic led to an avoidance of all the gay and frivolous things of life. As for nature, it continued to be viewed much as William Bradford had seen it in 1620: a "hideous and desolate wilderness, full of wild beasts and wild men;"[10] a wilderness to be struggled with and vanquished in accordance with the Biblical injunction to "be fruitful and multiply, and replenish the earth, and subdue it: and have dominion over the fish of the sea, and over the fowl of the air, and over every living thing that moveth upon the earth."[11] As a consequence, there was no place for recreation, as we know it, in those overserious Puritan communities. Even hunting and fishing were proscribed except as a means for procuring food.

In this regard, all Colonial conservation, whether concerned with wildlife, fish, or timber resources, tended to be defensive, the aim being to protect against waste and theft.[12] The game preserve idea did not gain a place here in Colonial days because there was no leisure class to champion it.

The eighteenth century saw the development of a philosophy which would ultimately greatly influence the New England outlook. From Jean Jacques Rousseau's concept of the "natural man"—that noble savage in his wilderness setting, living a happy and contented life—came a great upsurge of admiration for nature and a sentimental attachment to all things primitive. The basis of this Romantic Movement was a belief in the "oneness of Nature—the greater Nature, embracing God and man, stars out in space, rocks and crystals here on earth," and so "Nature invaded the consciousness of the world."[13]

Romanticism had many voices crying a love of nature, and not alone in the French of Rousseau or the German of Goethe, but also in the poetic English of Wordsworth, Coleridge, Scott, Byron, Shelley, Keats, and Blake. And these were heard across the sea, transforming the American view of nature; Hans Huth has traced with meticulous care the development of an appreciative outlook.[14] More was required than a Romantic viewpoint, however, to get the long-stalled park idea moving again.

The missing ingredient was a sense of purpose, and that was supplied early in the nineteenth century by men best called the New England philosophers. They were intellectuals whose transcendentalist viewpoint made them particularly perceptive of their surroundings,[15] and what they perceived was the change industrialism was then making in a familiar New England landscape. The spinning mills and foundries of that "inventive age" the poet Wordsworth had seen developing "to most strange issues" turned pastoral villages into squalid factory towns. Gone was the old, slow-moving and secure rustic life, replaced by urban poverty and its attendant misery and crime. To such thinkers as Henry Wadsworth Longfellow, John Greenleaf Whittier, James Russell Lowell, William Cullen Bryant, Henry David Thoreau, and Ralph Waldo Emerson, the degradation was a concomitant of civilization, and for it they saw but one antidote: a return to nature.

Thoreau presents the thesis of these New England philosophers most eloquently in this passage from his essay on "Walking":

> I wish to speak a word for Nature, for absolute freedom and wildness, as contrasted with freedom and culture merely civil,—to regard man as

an inhabitant, or a part and parcel of Nature, rather than a member of society . . . there are enough champions of civilization: the minister and the school committee and every one of you will take care of that.[16]

Both Thoreau and Emerson wrote of wondrous nature, this "mother of ours . . . lying all around with such beauty," likened by Emerson to "the music and pictures of the ancient religion." And yet, they were realists enough to know there was no returning to the natural state of man. They did not advocate primitivism, but only a limitation of the unwholesome influences of civilization by keeping closely in touch with nature. It was through such a compromise that Thoreau could say, "A town is saved, not more by the righteous men in it than by the woods and swamps that surround it," for "in wildness is the preservation of the world." And Emerson thought that every man is so far a poet as to be susceptible of these enchantments of nature, "which are medicinal, they sober and heal us."[17]

This new concept of nature—as beautiful, kindly, helpful, and restorative, rather than hideous, harsh, obstructive, and degrading— was accepted, very rapidly, by Americans. As a biographer has pointed out, "Imperceptibly Emerson's ideas passed into general currency. . . . Today his influence has spread so wide that, like atmospheric pressure, we are unaware of it. But it has played a vast part in shaping the American way of life."[18] The same can as justly be said of the influence of other New England philosophers; among them they softened the Puritan outlook of the New England mind, preparing it to contribute to the development of the park idea.

At the same time, other and less philosophical developments traceable to the influence of Romanticism were preparing the American people to appreciate beauty and enjoy leisure. Hans Huth has discussed the beginnings of a popular literature with out-of-doors themes, and also a school of painting (Hudson River) taking its subjects from landscapes.[19] Both brought nature to the fireside, but equally important, they stimulated a desire to visit scenic places. With improvement of public transportation, first by canal routes and later by railways, vacation travel to such resorts as Saratoga, White Sulphur Springs, the Adirondacks, Madison-on-Lakes, Appledore, Nahant, Newport, Mount Desert, and Mount Holyoke became feasible, and increasing numbers of the privileged traveled for pleasure.

Acquaintance with the out-of-doors led directly to the development of such leisure-time activities as walking tours, mountain climbing, camping, fishing and hunting, and even to adult games—croquet in the 1860s, then tennis and golf.[20] While such forms of recreation were not yet democratized, they *were* respectable.

The park idea, too, progressed in the climate created by that particularly American type of Romanticism generated in New England. The next step beyond the town common was taken in 1825, when Dr. Jacob Bigelow of Boston called a meeting to propose a public cemetery outside of the city. He was convinced of the "impolicy of burials under churches or in churchyards approximating closely to the abodes of the living," and was outraged by the "sad, neglected state" of such resting places. The proposal gained the support of influential people and suitable grounds were found at Mount Auburn, four miles from Boston, where the nation's first scenic cemetery was dedicated on September 24, 1831.[21]

Our concern with this prototype of the modern cemetery lies in the park use it soon began to serve. Being an area of great natural beauty, it drew numerous "parties of pleasure" and couples seeking a trysting place, leading to the suggestion that cemeteries ought to be planned "with reference to the living as well as the dead, and therefore should be convenient and pleasant to visitors."

Not long after the establishment of the Mount Auburn scenic cemetery came a suggestion for another type of park. George Catlin, the artist who ascended the Missouri River in 1832 as a passenger on the steamboat *Yellowstone*, came back with Indian portraits and an idea for turning the "strip of country, which extends from the province of Mexico to Lake Winnepeg on the North" into a huge reserve where the buffalo and the Indian

> might in the future be seen, (by some great protecting policy of government) preserved in their pristine beauty and wildness, in a magnificent park, where the world could see for ages to come, the native Indian in his classic attire, galloping his wild horse, with sinewy bow, and shield and lance, amid the fleeting herds of elks and buffaloes. What a beautiful and thrilling specimen for America to preserve and hold up to the view of her refined citizens and the world, in future ages! A *nation's Park*, containing man and beast, in all the wild freshness of their nature's beauty!
>
> I would ask no other monument to my memory, not an other enrolment of my name amongst the famous dead, than the reputation of having been the founder of such an institution.
>
> Such scenes might easily have been preserved, and still could be cherished on the great plains of the West, without detriment to the country or its border; for the tracts of country on which the buffaloes have assembled, are uniformly sterile, and of no available use to cultivating man.[22]

Catlin's suggestion was as sterile as it was impractical, and deserves no further comment beyond the fact that it may have stimulated Henry Thoreau to ask that surprisingly similar question:

The Kings of England formerly had their forests "to hold the King's game," for sport or food, sometimes destroying villages to create or extend them; and I think that they were impelled by a true instinct. Why should not we, who have renounced the King's authority, have our national preserves, where no villages need be destroyed, in which the bear and panther, and some even of the hunter race, may still exist, and not be "civilized off the face of the earth,"—our forest, not to hold the King's game merely, but to hold and preserve the King himself also, the lord of creation,—not for idle sport or food, but for inspiration and our own true recreation?[23]

If nothing else, the foregoing are evidence that at least two thinkers had pursued the park idea to its ultimate possibility prior to the middle of the nineteenth century. But they overshot the practical limits, for such an environment would be unstable because man was included among the exhibits.

A less flamboyant but sounder suggestion came from William Cullen Bryant, who seems to have been sufficiently impressed with the developing scenic cemeteries to advocate a city park for New York. It is said that he discussed this idea with friends as early as 1836, but the public proposal was made in the *New York Evening Post* on July 3, 1844,[24] and, in 1851, the project for a Central Park got under way with purchase of the necessary lands and the appointment of Frederick Law Olmsted to superintend construction.

Olmsted was a fortunate choice. He was a student of the early landscape architect, Andrew Jackson Downing, with the benefit of Downing's experience in the development of scenic cemeteries as well as insight into his hopes for the Central Park project, of which Downing was an ardent supporter. In addition, Olmsted had traveled in Europe and thus was familiar with European parks and formal gardens. Out of that background he and Calvert Vaux were able to design that prototype of all our great city parks, which, while not founded on the beauty of wild land, did simulate it through a judicious blending of formal and informal elements on a scale never before attempted. The park idea thereby reached the third stage of its growth on American soil, the city park.

It was by the same hand that the park idea was elevated to the state level. Olmsted did not always agree with the park commissioners, and finally gave up his superintendency in May 1863, leaving the completion of Central Park to others.[25] At that time he undertook the management of the Mariposa estate of General John Charles Fremont, in California, and his removal to that state brought him into fortunate proximity to the Yosemite Valley and the Big Trees.

These remarkable features of California's central Sierra were well known. An incident more than a decade earlier involving one of the Calaveras Big Trees—the Mother of the Forest—had caused James Russell Lowell and Oliver Wendell Holmes to condemn commercialization of unusual works of nature and gained public support for the conservation of similar wonders. Thus, what was needed in California in the 1860s was a catalytic personality, someone capable of marshalling existing feelings toward the protection of the scenic Yosemite Valley and the unique Big Trees. Olmsted, fresh from his work on the nation's first urban park, was just the person to channel the thoughts of influential Californians, and, within a year of his arrival, Congress had been induced to pass the act whereby the federal government gave a "grant to the State of California of the 'Yo-Semite Valley' and the land embracing the 'Mariposa Big Tree Grove.'" As signed into law by President Lincoln on June 30, 1864, the legislation required that the "said State shall accept this grant upon the express conditions that the premises shall be held for public use, resort, and recreation; shall be inalienable for all time."[26]

The significance of the Yosemite Grant is well summarized by H. D. Hampton, who says,

> The passage of the Act of 1864, granting to California the two tracts of land, did not establish a "national park" nor did it provide for one. No national laws were legislated by which the areas were to be administered and after the passage of the act Congress seems to have dismissed the areas from its collective mind. The novelty of the legislation lies in the fact that it provided for land to be reserved for strictly non-utilitarian purposes, thus establishing a precedent or parallel for the later reservation of the Yellowstone region.[27]

With the park idea raised to the state park level by means of the Yosemite Grant, we are now in position to consider the creation of Yellowstone National Park and its particular place in the development of the general idea.

It seems likely that the granting of the Yosemite Valley and the Big Trees to the state of California did set a precedent by suggesting an appropriate course of action to be pursued in regard to the Yellowstone region and its wonders. The earliest park suggestion, made in 1865 by Acting Governor Thomas Francis Meagher of Montana Territory, came from a man who was both journalist and astute politician and undoubtedly kept himself informed by the *Congressional Globe* with the same thoroughness he must have given to perusing local newspapers. That the Montana frontier was no intellectual vacuum, particularly where the Yosemite was concerned, is evident from the editorial comment in the *Virginia City Montana Post* of July 14, 1866 (quoted on page 75).

In the case of the second suggestion for the reservation of the Yellowstone, made by David E. Folsom to Surveyor General Washburn following the expedition of 1869 (see page 103), the reason for suspecting that it, too, may have been influenced by what happened at Yosemite lies in the background of Folsom and his companion, Charles W. Cook, both of whom were well-educated New England intellectuals—literate, sensitive men.

The third suggestion, restated by Cornelius Hedges at the Madison Junction campsite on the evening of September 19, 1870 (see page 130), came from a man whose background was remarkably similar to that of Folsom and Cook. While his only published statement on the subject is not sufficiently specific that we can be absolutely sure of his intent or his motivation, the language used in the "Yellowstone Lake" article seems to imply a grant to the Territory of Montana similar to the Yosemite Grant to the state of California.[28] If that is a correct interpretation, then Hedges was thinking in *state park* terms.

There is no doubt whatever of the inspiration for the fourth suggestion, which came from Judge William D. Kelley through Nettleton's letter of October 27, 1871, to Dr. Hayden (see page 155). In it he says, "Let Congress pass a bill reserving the Great Geyser Basin as a public park forever—just as it has reserved that far inferior wonder the Yosemite Valley and big trees." Kelley was definitely influenced by the Yosemite Grant legislation, with which a further connection will soon be apparent.

The time that elapsed between Dr. Hayden's receipt of Nettleton's letter (which could not have been earlier than October 29) to the creation of Yellowstone National Park was surprisingly short. On November 9, 1871, it was announced,

> Hon. N. P. Langford—who, by the way, has been back here only a few days,—yesterday received a dispatch from Gov. Marshall, of Minnesota, to return immediately to Minnesota, as important business concerning the Northern Pacific Railroad awaited him. Mr. Langford took the Overland coach this morning for Corinne.[29]

The "important business concerning the Northern Pacific Railroad" was the promotion of the park project, toward which Langford had, to that time, done nothing. (The only propaganda note struck in his lectures on behalf of the Northern Pacific, and in his article in *Scribner's Magazine*, was a low-keyed "pitch" for the railroad.)[30] Yet Langford's proven ability to talk and write about the Yellowstone region was just what was needed at that moment.

Records of the Northern Pacific Land Office show that before Langford could possibly have reached St. Paul an effort was being made to gather information useful to the project. On November 11, that office received a telegraphed reply from "Jno S. Sexton," a member of the directorate of Jay Cooke & Co., informing that *Scribner's Monthly* had "published nothing of Langford's except article in June Scribner."[31] The statement made by William Goetzmann that "Hayden joined forces with the Northern Pacific interests and Langford's Montana group and at their suggestion lobbied vigorously and with success for the establishment of the Yellowstone region as a national park"[32] would be entirely correct if changed slightly to indicate that the Montana group was called in by Northern Pacific interests to which they were subservient. Without a doubt, the Northern Pacific Railroad (speaking now of the corporate entity and not of individuals) took up Judge Kelley's suggestion and proceeded to implement it as a matter of company policy. To that end, Dr. Hayden and the Montana group were alike useful tools.

The opening of the campaign for reservation of the Yellowstone has been described somewhat differently by H. D. Hampton. According to his version, which casts the Montana group in the role of initiators, "Upon his return to Washington, Hayden was met by Nathaniel Langford, Cornelius Hedges and Samuel Hauser."[33] This does not take into account Hayden's receipt of the Nettleton letter *before* Langford left Montana, or the fact that Hedges did not leave Montana at that time.

Langford later admitted to Albert Matthews, "My real interest in the scheme was not roused to the working point till my return to Helena in the summer of 1871, when Hedges communicated his enthusiasm to me, and we joined with Clagett, our newly elected delegate to Congress."[34] However, as already noted, Langford had been back at Helena "only a few days" on November 9, and that is more in line with the facts of Clagett's availability. As Cramton has pointed out, Clagett "did not become a delegate in Congress until his election on August 7, 1871, and could not have arrived in Washington much before Congress met on December 4, 1871."[35] This brings us back to the original premise: that agents of the Northern Pacific Railroad initiated the project to reserve the Yellowstone region as a park.

Beginning in December, the sequence of events is clearer. On the seventh, the Bozeman newspaper called for a grant of the Yellowstone region to the Territory of Montana. The editor remarked that since exploration had taken place from Montana and the Yellowstone Valley had been opened by Montanans, the headwaters of that stream "should be included within the boundaries of Montana Territory," pointing out that in any event geography had made the fabled region a "barren heritage to our sister Territory."[36] This idea undoubtedly was the legitimate issue of Cornelius Hedges' "Yellowstone Lake" article (see pages 134-35).

It has been suggested that such was probably the *original* intent of the men who, early in December, undertook to frame legislation to effect reservation; but the precedent set in the Yosemite Grant could not be used exactly, because what Montana wanted as a grant from the central government lay partly or wholly in Wyoming. Obviously, to take from the one for the benefit of the other would create trouble between neighbors, but worse, it would set a precedent no thinking politician would care to have lurking about lest his own environs somehow fall victim to it. As Hampton has pointed out, "The only way to preserve the area and withhold it from settlement was to place it directly under federal control."[37]

Even so, the bill that was drawn for the consideration of the Forty-second Congress at its second session was similar in so many respects to the earlier Yosemite Grant legislation that there can be no doubt it was drawn from that model; the parallelism of the two acts is readily apparent (see opposite page for the text of the Organic Act compared to Yosemite Grant).

Thus, it is not only apparent that the existing Yosemite Grant legislation influenced the drawing of the bill for the creation of a park in the Yellowstone region, but also that Delegate William H. Clagett's claim to the authorship of that bill is ridiculous.[38] His work consisted in altering the earlier legislation to fit the new circumstances, which explains Louis Cramton's puzzlement as to how such a "remarkably well-drawn piece of legislation, it being remembered that it was pioneering in a new field," could be the "draft of an amateur who had only been a few weeks in Washington and had only served two weeks in Congress."[39]

The draft bill prepared by Delegate Clagett from the Yosemite model, with whatever other assistance he may have had, was introduced in both houses of Congress on the morning of December 18, 1871. Senator Samuel Clarke Pomeroy, Republican, from Kansas, who was chairman of the Committee on Public Lands, had asked the privilege of initiating the legislation, hence his bill (S. 392) appeared first, followed immediately by Clagett's introduction of an identical bill in the House of Representatives as H.R. 764.[40]

With that accomplished, the friends of the bill began a campaign in its support. Hayden arranged for a display, in the rotunda of the

PARALLELISM OF ACTS
to create the Yosemite Grant and Yellowstone National Park

YOSEMITE (1864)	YELLOWSTONE (1872)
". . . the said State shall accept this grant upon the express conditions that the premises shall be held for public use, resort, and recreation; shall be inalienable for all time . . ."	". . . is hereby reserved and withdrawn from settlement, occupancy, or sale . . . and dedicated and set apart as a public park or pleasureing-ground for the benefit and enjoyment of the people . . ."
". . . but leases not exceeding ten years may be granted for portions of said premises . . ."	"The Secretary may in his discretion grant leases for building purposes for terms not exceeding ten years, of small parcels of ground . . ."
"All incomes derived from leases of privileges to be expended in the preservation and improvement of the property, or the roads leading thereto . . ."	"All of the proceeds of said leases and all other revenues that may be derived from any source connected with said park, to be expended under his direction in the management of the same, and the construction of roads and bridle paths therein."

Delegate William H. Clagett, who collaborated with Senator Pomeroy on legislation to create Yellowstone National Park. From Langford, *The Discovery . . .* (1905).

Capitol, of geological specimens brought back from the Yellowstone region by his 1871 expedition, and with them some typical Jackson photographs and Moran sketches. (The large oil painting of the Grand Canyon of the Yellowstone had not yet been executed.) Copies of the issue of *Scribner's Monthly* containing Langford's article, "The Wonders of the Yellowstone," were distributed to all the senators and representatives, as were published copies of Lieutenant Doane's official report on the 1870 exploration. Clagett says that between Hayden, Langford, and himself, "there was not a single member of Congress in either House who was not fully posted by one or the other of us in personal interviews."[41]

The available newspaper coverage indicates the West favored the park project from the outset. James Hamilton Mills, the dean of Montana journalists, when referring to the action of Congress in granting the Yosemite Valley to the state of California in 1864, ended a description of the Yellowstone region by asking that "this, too, be set apart by Congress as a domain retained unto all mankind . . . and let it be *esta perpetua.*"[42] Nevada's *Territorial Enterprise* endorsed the proposal as the "grandest park in all the world,"[43] and even California, which had a few geysers of its own in Sonoma County, showed unexpected enthusiasm.[44]

On January 22, 1872, Senator Pomeroy reported his bill (S. 392) back from the Committee on Public Lands. He had been instructed to recommend passage of the measure, which he noted had been drawn at Hayden's request "to consecrate for public use this country for a public park." But, since there was an objection that consideration of the bill at that time would interfere with other business, Senator Pomeroy withdrew his report with the intention of presenting it again on the following day. On the twenty-third the necessity for such legislation was questioned and it was decided to postpone consideration for one week.[45]

When S. 392 came up for consideration in its regular order on January 30 it was defended by Senators Henry B. Anthony (Rhode Island), Thomas W. Tipton (Nebraska), George F. Edmunds (Vermont), and Lyman Trumbull (Illinois). The only hostility to it was voiced by Senator Cornelius Cole of California, chairman of the Senate Committee on Appropriations. The *Congressional Globe* reported him as saying:

> I have grave doubts about the propriety of passing this bill. The natural curiosities there cannot be interfered with by anything that man can do. The geysers will remain, no matter where the ownership of the land may be, and I do not know why settlers should be excluded from a tract of

land forty miles square . . . in the Rocky Mountains or any other place. I cannot see how the natural curiosities can be interfered with if settlers are allowed to appropriate them. I suppose there is very little timber on this tract of land, certainly no more than is necessary for the use and convenience of persons going upon it. I do not see the reason or propriety of setting apart a large tract of land . . . in the Territories of the United States for a public park. There is an abundance of public park ground in the Rocky Mountains that will never be occupied. It is all one great park, and never can be anything else; large portions of it at all events. There are some places, perhaps this is one, where persons can and would go and settle and improve and cultivate the grounds, if there be ground fit for cultivation.[46]

Senator Cole's objection was minimized by Trumbull's assurance that the law could be repealed later, "if it is in anybody's way." The Senate then passed the measure without a roll-call vote and it was sent to the House, to remain on the Speaker's table until February 27.

Delegate Clagett's bill (H.R. 764) moved less rapidly in the legislative toils. This may be, as Cramton hints, because Clagett took no further interest in his bill after introducing it.[47] For whatever reason, the House Committee on Public Lands did not ask the Interior Department for a report until January 27, three days before the Senate passed its version of the bill. In his request, the subcommittee chairman, Mark Dunnell, stated he "would be pleased to receive the report made by Professor Hayden or such as he may be able to give us on the subject," and a statement prepared by Hayden was sent him by Secretary Columbus Delano on January 29. The House Committee then authorized a favorable report on H.R. 764, using Hayden's draft as its report (which, however, was not filed until February 28).[48]

During the interval between the passage of S. 392 by the Senate and its consideration in the House, there was another flurry of publicity favoring the bill. The day following its passage by the Senate, the *Helena Herald* commented,

It will be a park worthy of the great republic, if it contains the proportions set forth in Clagett's bill; it will embrace about 2,500 square miles and include the great canyon, falls and lake of the Yellowstone, with a score of other magnificent lakes, the great geyser basin of the Madison, and thousands of mineral and boiling springs. Should the whole surface of the earth be gleaned, not another spot of equal dimensions could be found that contains on such a magnificent scale one-half the attractions here grouped together.

And the editor, being well aware who was behind this particular legislation, added: "Without a doubt the Northern Pacific Railroad will have a branch track penetrating this plutonian region and few seasons will pass before excursion trains will daily be sweeping into this great park."[49]

In an article titled "Wonders of the West—II; More about the Yellowstone," which appeared in *Scribner's Monthly,* February 1872, Dr. Hayden rephrased the thought expressed in Nettleton's letter of October 27, 1871, to ask, "Why will not Congress at once pass a law setting it [the Yellowstone] apart as a great public park for all time to come as has been done with that far inferior wonder, the Yosemite Valley?"[50] It was also during the period while S. 392 lay upon the Speaker's table in the House of Representatives that a Montana legislative councilman, Seth Bullock, asked that the Yellowstone region be added to Montana, and "be dedicated and devoted to public use, resort and recreation, for all time to come, as a great national park, under such care and restrictions as to your honorable bodies may seem best calculated to secure the ends proposed."[51]

The House took up S. 392 on February 27 in the course of considering the business on the Speaker's table. There was an attempt by Representative Glenn W. Schofield of Pennsylvania to send the bill to the Committee on Public Lands (of which he was a member), and Representative John Taffe of Nebraska made a similar attempt to send it to the Committee on Territories (on which he served). But Henry L. Dawes rose in defense of the measure, urging its immediate passage because of its meritorious nature, and his support was crucial. As the most influential man in the House at that time (one who preferred to work "more often in the committee rooms than on the floor of the House" but whose presentations were "dignified and lucid") he was deferred to. Representative Schofield withdrew his motion and no action was taken on Taffe's.[52]

The favorable report of the Committee on Public Lands was then presented by Representative John B. Hawley (Illinois) and Mark Dunnell (Minnesota), after which Dawes spoke on the purpose of the legislation, remarking that

> This bill follows the analogy of the bill passed by Congress six or eight years ago, setting apart the Yosemite Valley . . . with this difference: that bill granted to the State of California the jurisdiction over the land beyond the control of the United States. This bill reserves the control over the land . . . to the United States . . . it will infringe upon no vested rights . . . treads upon no rights of the settler . . . and it receives the urgent and ardent support of the legislature of that Territory [Montana].[53]

We know from Hayden's statement that he had been required to give "a distinct pledge" to the effect that he "would not apply for an appropriation for several years at least,"[54] that those who held the pursestrings in the economy-minded Forty-second Congress were assured that the creation of a federal park would put no additional strain upon the treasury; there being no voices raised in opposition to the bill, it was put to the vote. Upon a roll call, there were "115 ayes, 65 nays and 60 not voting." The successful passage of S. 392 was recorded in the *Helena Herald* in these words:

> Our dispatches announce the passage in the House of the Senate bill setting apart the upper Yellowstone Valley for the purposes of a National Park. The importance of this congressional enactment can not be too highly estimated. It will redound to the untold good of the Territory inasmuch as a measure of this character is well calculated to direct the world's attention to a very important section of the country that to the present time has passed largely unnoticed. It will be the means of centering upon Montana the attention of thousands heretofore comparatively uninformed of a Territory abounding in such resources of mines and agriculture and of wonderland as we can boast, spread everywhere about us.[55]

Having passed both houses of Congress, S. 392 was sent to President Ulysses S. Grant and signed by him into law on March 1, 1872, thus creating the first *national* park. That legislation completed the evolution of the park idea: from roots in the Saxon concept of holding village lands "in common," through economic and philosophical developments of the early nineteenth century leading to the scenic cemetery, the landscaped city park, the state park, to arrive at last at the idea of reserving wild lands "for the benefit and enjoyment of the people" *under federal management.*

This highest development of the park idea, which made its appearance with the creation of Yellowstone National Park, harbored possibilities not immediately apparent. In 1872 the growth of a system of national parks lay unforeseen in the future, and the extension of the matured park concept worldwide was entirely unsuspected. But with eventual realization of the worth of this "new creation" came attempts to identify a "national park idea," separate it from the sequential development of the park idea as a whole, and certify its origin in terms of author, time, and place.

But these attempts have only led to unending and unprofitable argumentation. We mire in such polemics as the *oldest*, or the *first*. There are some who champion Hot Springs National Park in Arkansas, because it has been longest in a reserved status, while overlooking its lack of essential park character, its commercialization, and the recentness of its formal designation as a national park; others prefer Yosemite National Park because the legislation by which the federal government granted that area to the state of California accomplished the first dedication of wild lands to the nonutilitarian purpose of recreation, but they ignore the forty-two years during which the area was a state rather than a *national* park; finally, there are those who favor Yellowstone National Park because its establishment resulted in the earliest federal management of wild lands dedicated to recreational use, forgetting, in their turn, the long chain of events leading back to the Yosemite Grant legislation, and beyond, on which the creation of a Yellowstone National Park was dependent.

The story is much the same when we grope for a personage to whom we may attribute this national park idea; we become enmeshed in the conflicting claims made by adherents of George Catlin, the framers of the Yosemite Grant legislation, Cornelius Hedges, and a number of others who had more or less important parts in the development of the park movement. Many years ago Louis C. Cramton decided in the course of his study of the question, Who secured the creation of Yellowstone National Park? that "It is to be regretted that in a field where there would seem to be glory enough for all, the claims to credit should be so conflicting."[56] His observation is as true when applied to the whole park idea, and it is better to simply conclude, as he did, that "many contributed," both to this "new creation"—a *national* park— and all that has subsequently developed from it.

II

PARADISE ALMOST LOST

Accuse not nature! she hath done her part;
Do thou but thine! and be not diffident
Of Wisdom; she deserts thee not, if thou
Dismiss not her, when most thou need'st her nigh,
By attrib'ting overmuch to things
Less excellent, as thou perceiv'st.

—John Milton,
Paradise Lost, *Book VIII*

Tower Fall, from a watercolor sketch by Thomas Moran, 1871 (compare with Moore's sketch, page 114). Original in Yellowstone Park Museum collection.

CHAPTER 7

MARKING TIME

*What has the Government done to render this
national elephant approachable and attractive since
its adoption as one of the nation's pets? Nothing.*
—Bozeman Avant Courier,
July 31, 1874

The "national elephant" (was the editor tempted to add the word "white"?) was born nameless and was left to shift for himself for so long he must have wondered if anybody loved him!

The immediate reaction to the setting apart of that "certain Tract of Land lying near the Head-waters of the Yellowstone River as a public Park" varied from excessive laudation (local Republicans) to angry yelpings (local Democrats), with a considerable amount of indifference between those extremes. The *Helena Herald*, which had been a promoter of the park project, turned its editorial, "Our National Park," into a panegyric for Delegate Clagett and a denunciation of the rival *Gazette*, while that newspaper commented editorially,

> In our opinion, the effect of this measure will be to keep the country a wilderness, and shut out for many years, the travel that would seek that curious region if good roads were opened through it and hotels built therein. We regard the passage of the act as a great blow struck at the prosperity of the towns of Bozeman and Virginia City which might nat-

urally look to considerable travel to this section, if it were thrown open to the curious but comfort-loving public.[1]

The editor of the *Deer Lodge New North-West* was more objective. His comment, "The same reasons that influenced Congress to set apart the wonderful Valley of the Yosemite have influenced it in this matter," was coupled to a prophecy that in time "it will become a great resort for tourists," to which he added, "This law leaves it free to be visited by all and open to scientific exploration." The editor also did what he could to allay the fears of the *Gazette* and its following, offering his opinion that legitimate rights would not suffer from the park measure (though, of course, they should not forget that settlers on unsurveyed lands, except for miners, were only trespassers).[2]

Strangely, the newspapers of the towns that should have been most concerned, Bozeman and Virginia City, remained silent. Perhaps they could not divine where their best interests lay just then, but there were those outside the territory who could tell them. The *New York Herald* said in an editorial:

> Why should we go to Switzerland to see mountains, or to Iceland for geysers? Thirty years ago the attraction of America to the foreign mind was Niagara Falls. Now we have attractions which diminish Niagara into an ordinary exhibition. The Yo Semite, which the nation has made a park, the Rocky Mountains and their singular parks, the canyons of the Colorado, the Dalles of the Columbia, the giant trees, the lake country of Upper Minnesota, the country of the Yellowstone, with their beauty, their splendor, their extraordinary and sometimes terrible manifestations of nature, form a series of attractions possessed by no other nation.[3]

The editor of *Scribner's Monthly* also realized what an asset the new park could be to the territories of Wyoming and Montana, but his jocular comment of "Verily a colossal sort of junketing-place!"[4] would undoubtedly have been less enthusiastic if he could have foreseen the problems to be mastered before we learned how to manage such a novel enterprise. But then, no one foresaw them.

Congress had placed its public park "under the exclusive control of the Secretary of the Interior," thus involving him in a land management situation for which there was no precedent. Further, there was very little help to be had from the organic act. That legislation was altruistic and quite beyond reproach where its objectives were concerned, but it was also entirely unsuited to the accomplishment of those same ends. Out of false premises on the one hand and clumsy adaptations on the other came those omissions and ambiguities that were to so trouble the early years of the new park.

As mentioned earlier, the act of March 1, 1872, was modeled upon the legislation by which the Yosemite Valley was granted to the state of California in 1864. However, the two situations were very different. In the case of the Yosemite grant, both the financing and the protection of the area could be left to the state of California; but the establishment of Yellowstone as a federal park placed those burdens directly upon the national government.

The men who drew up the bill that became Yellowstone's organic act were not unaware of their responsibility to provide financial and legal means upon which management of the area could be based— they were cognizant of both. There was a very good reason why they did not provide what was obviously needed: they knew that the economy-minded Forty-second Congress would refuse any proposal that increased the federal expenditure. (Dr. Hayden later stated that he had to give his word that "he would not apply for an appropriation for several years at least.")[5] So, the Park was presented as an area that could be managed free of cost to the national government.

The reasoning behind this conclusion evidently paralleled that of the maid who took her eggs to market in a basket on her head, "counting her chickens before they were hatched" without considering what a fall would do to her plans. From the commonly held supposition that the Northern Pacific Railroad would be extended into Montana in a year or two, opening an easy route for large numbers of tourists whose coming would create many business opportunities attractive to concessioners, it was presumed franchise fees would accumulate which would be more than adequate for the support of the Park. Such thinking was typical of the frontier, and the Earl of Dunraven later noted, " 'When the railway is made' is, in Montana, a sort of equivalent for our phrase, 'When my ship comes home.' "[6]

But it soon became a case of "If *hads* were *shads* there would have been fish for supper," for the plans of the Northern Pacific Railroad collapsed when the insolvency of Jay Cooke & Company precipitated the panic of 1873. As a result, the terminus of the railroad was stranded for six years at the town of Bismarck, Dakota Territory. No horde of tourists clamored at the gates of Wonderland, no worthy concessioners bid for privileges, no funds came forth from franchise fees, and—because of the state of penury imposed upon the Park by its promoters and the Congress—there was no progress. What did happen, then, during this period of marking time?

The act of March 1, 1872, which established a public park on the headwaters of the Yellowstone River did not specify the form of its management other than to state that the area should be under the exclusive control of the secretary of the interior. However, it seems to have been understood almost from the beginning that someone would be placed in direct charge; thus, local interests were quick to advance a candidate. In a letter dated March 28, 1872, Harry R. Horr, James C. McCartney, and J. Shaffer reminded the secretary of the interior that "Since guides are to be appointed by the government we would cheerfully recommend that you appoint George Houstin as chief guide for the National Park."[7]

It appears that the secretary had no intention of placing the new park in the care of such a local resident, however well qualified he might be; instead, he looked for a superintendent among members of the Washburn party. L.C. Cramton says that Everts was in Washington, D.C., at the time the national park bill became law and that many congressmen and others endorsed him for the superintendency. Everts would not have accepted the position without a salary, so he may have had some hopes that the Congress would provide an appropriation despite its earlier reluctance to assume such a financial burden. However, when Everts became a delegate to the Liberal Republican convention at Cincinnati, the *Helena Herald* of May 3 commented that it was "a round about way, to our thinking, for friend Everts to reach the superintendency of Yellowstone National Park."[8] Actually, his joining forces with Horace Greeley to split the Republican party was an act of political suicide, and the secretary of the interior delayed no longer in filling the superintendency.

On May 10, 1872, Nathaniel P. Langford received a letter from the secretary advising him of his appointment without salary.[9] Langford's reply from Cheyenne, Wyoming, ten days later indicates his willingness to accept the responsibility and shows that he was in touch with developments at the Park. He says:

> I have been advised here, of my appointment as Superintendent of the Yellowstone Park, and shall make immediate preparations for a thorough exploration of it. A number of parties have expressed the desire to put up small hotels for the accommodation of visitors, and it will be desirable to grant leases for this purpose to two or three persons, or at least, to one. Until a survey of the park is made by me, and my report submitted, I do not think it best to grant many leases for hotels, etc., nor these for a long time; but at least one stopping place for tourists should be put up this year.
>
> I am informed that a toll road company has graded a few steep hills on the line of travel, and are charging exorbitant rates of toll, without authority of law. I should have authority to regulate this matter, and prevent imposition upon visitors.

Will you therefore, communicate with me at Helena, Mont., advising me what power my appointment gives me, and authorizing me to make all necessary regulations for building one public house, or more if needed, and generally, for the protection of the rights of visitors, and establishment of such rules as will conduce to their comfort and pleasure.

Whatever authority is given me in this matter will be cautiously exercised, for little need be done in this behalf the present season.[10]

Superintendent Langford found he could make his inspection of the national park as a guest of the Hayden Survey, which was returning to the Yellowstone for another season's work. Congress had been particularly generous, allowing $75,000 for that project— enough to field two parties and thus accomplish a more thorough exploration of the Yellowstone region.

Preparations for the summer's work were started in May. James Stevenson, Hayden's managing director, went to Ogden to establish a base camp on an open terrace above the town in full view of the Great Salt Lake. Dr. Hayden started west himself after his final lecture at the University of Pennsylvania on May 27; Joseph Savage departed Lawrence, Kansas, with an insurance policy in his pocket, which comforted him "not a little" during his long journey over "desert wastes and mountains wild," and William H. Holmes laid aside his work at the Smithsonian Institution, packed a slim outfit of clothes, paper, pencils, paints, and other necessaries of an artist, and began his long train ride of five continuous days which eventually landed him at Ogden in the first week of June. And so they came: Rudolf Hering from Fairmont Park, Philadelphia; Professor Frank H. Bradley from Knoxville, Tennessee; T.B. Brown from California, and Dr. Josiah Curtis from Boston. Some of them were veterans of other seasons with the survey and some were greenhorns, unfamiliar with the work and the West. There were enough old hands among the teamsters, packers, guides, and hunters (men such as Shep Medara, Al Sibley, and "Potato John" Raymond) to initiate the novices in a new way of life.

At that camp, the men received instruction in their employment and were outfitted and provided with the mounts that would carry them several hundred difficult miles. In one case a less-experienced member decided on a particular horse because it was described as a "Methodist" horse. After being bucked off he inquired further and found that the reference was not to the animal's character but to the fact that it had once been owned by a Methodist minister. Mineral-ogist A.C. Peale has provided an interesting list of the names of some of the horses: Old Mortality, Cyclops, Rustler, Sowbelly, Canalboat,

Guts, Pot Gut (Tub O Guts), Baldy, Jimmy, Savage, Alice, Foxy, Nig, Stonehead, Lazarus, Jocko, Jane, Younker, Pomp, Baby, Pet, Brownie, Shoemaker, Mormon Ann, Gallatin, Whitey, Lizzie, Mrs. Jackson, Buck, Mr. Gray, Blue Skin, Bell, Mollie, Dick, Billie, and Web Foot.[11]

Dr. Peale (he, like Professor Hayden, was a medical doctor as well as a geologist) was apparently a very discerning person. His diary contains a small vocabulary which identifies a "pot rustler" as a cook; a "boar's nest" as a bed; a "dolly varden" as a black eye; a "rustler" as a particularly active person; a "Cayuse" as an Indian pony; "extract of cow" as condensed milk; a "rooster" as a pet name for a friend; and "wagon dope" as gravy. He was also sensitive to the western idiom, as this sample, titled "an ascending scale," illustrates: "you bet; you bet your life; you bet your sweet life; you bet your d____d life."[12]

With the outfitting and preparation at last completed, the survey party took to the field on June 24. Those who were to make up the northern division left by train for Corinne, where they transferred to the Montana stage line for the exhausting journey to their base at Fort Ellis, in Montana Territory. Those who were to serve with James Stevenson's southern division loaded their camp equipage into army wagons, mounted their more or less fractious horses and started for Fort Hall, Idaho, which was to be their base of operations.

Superintendent Langford, as federal bank examiner for the territories and Pacific Coast states, had been attending to those duties in Montana Territory while the members of the Hayden Survey were gathering at Ogden; he joined the southern division soon after their arrival at Fort Hall early in July. The Deer Lodge newspaper, in commenting on Langford's departure to join the expedition, mentioned that "He will explore for roads for some weeks."[13]

The southern division left Fort Hall on July 12, heading north over the arid wasteland that separated the fort from the south fork of the Snake River. The commandant of that post, Captain Putnam, had given Stevenson two fine greyhounds, one of which died of the heat on that hard march, while the other survived only by lying in a hole in moist earth until water could be brought back from the river.

The south fork of the Snake River was found to be too high for safe fording so the expedition veered westward to cross Taylor's Bridge at Eagle Rock (now Idaho Falls). Obtaining a guide at that point ("Beaver Dick" Leigh, an old trapper of cockney origin who had settled in those parts as a squaw man), the division continued up the Montana stage road to a point beyond Market Lake, where they crossed Henrys Fork and entered the Teton Valley. Since one of the

Ferdinand V. Hayden (seated) talks with an assistant, 1871. From a W.H. Jackson photograph.

Hunters Joe Clark and José bringing in meat to feed the 1871 Hayden Survey party. From W. H. Jackson's photograph no. 302.

objectives of the southern division was to explore the Teton Range, the group found a suitable campsite at the western base of the mountains and spent some time exploring the vicinity. Despite Beaver Dick's pessimism, preparations were made for an assault on the Grand Teton. In a letter written to the secretary of the interior on July 27, Langford says,

> I have the honor to report that I am now in camp at the western base of the Teton Range of mountains with that portion of Mr. Hayden's geological survey under command of his principal assistant Captain James Stevenson, for the purpose of locating a supply camp and determining the best route to be found in ascending the Grand Teton. On the 24th instant Captain Stevenson and myself ascended a spur of this route, reaching an elevation of eleven thousand (11,000) feet, opposite a saddle of the mountains, out of which the three Teton peaks rise. On the 29th instant the final attempt to ascend these giant peaks, the great landmarks of the Snake River Valley, will be made.[14]

The ascent of the Grand Teton was begun on July 29 by a party of fourteen, but for one reason and another climbers dropped out until only James Stevenson and Nathaniel Langford were left to ascend the last 300 feet of the great peak. Whether or not Stevenson and Langford actually reached the summit of the Grand Teton has been a hotly debated point ever since the Owen-Spaulding party of 1898 discovered the summit to differ materially from Langford's earlier description. Langford's poor description of the summit is insufficient reason to damn him, however, since he was habitually more romantic than accurate in his descriptions. On the other hand, James Stevenson was a man whose veracity seems never to have been questioned.[15]

This exploration of the Teton Range resulted in much new geological and geographic information. It was found that these outstanding peaks had previously been mapped thirty-two miles from their correct location. Also, the higher summits were at last given elevations that were reasonably correct.[16]

The southern division explored the Teton Range until August 8, when they continued toward the Yellowstone. Beaver Dick had convinced them that they would find the Snake River unfordable, should they descend into Jackson Hole and attempt to enter the Yellowstone region from that direction. He and Shep Medara had, therefore, been sent out to find a packtrain route (the wagons had been left at Fort Hall) which would get them to Henrys Lake, from which they could easily enter the Yellowstone region from the west. By that route they proceeded to the Lower Geyser Basin where an advanced party of the southern division met a similar party of the northern division on August 13, the date decided on seven weeks earlier.

The manner of their meeting was unusual. The party from the southern division—Jackson and Campbell, photographers, Coulter and Beveridge, botanists, and Dr. Reagles, Spencer, Sibley, and Langford—were examining a thermal area in the Lower Geyser Basin when they came upon yard-high letters scratched into the geyser basin formation which spelled out "Bill Hamilton." Langford recognized the name of an old trapper and guide whom he had first met at Bannack in 1862 and correctly presumed the man was with the Hayden party, as nearby they found the date of that very day, August 13, 1872. While scouting the vicinity for a camp they flushed one of those grouse called a "fool hen"; instead of flying, the bird stalked about on the ground until a well-aimed rock flung by Al Sibley crippled it so that they could catch it. This important success, for they were short of grub, was announced with a loud shout heard by W.H. Holmes, the artist of the northern division, who was pursuing a bear through a thicket nearly a mile away. Recognizing the sound, Holmes investigated and found eight hungry men surrounding a hot spring in which they were boiling their "chicken" in a coffee pot.[17]

The two divisions camped together in the Lower Geyser Basin, at what they called Camp Reunion, the following day. That gathering of sixty men made the geyser basin ring: " 'How are you, Jackson?' and 'How are you, Peale?' accompanied by shouts and the swinging of hats."[18]

The northern division had been traveling under a shadow. While it was being outfitted at Fort Ellis, William Blackmore,[19] a noted anthropologist who was accompanying the division as a guest, learned of the death of his wife at Bozeman, apparently from pneumonia resulting from exposure during the stage ride from Corinne, Utah. This sad occurrence, incidentally, led to the establishment of a cemetery for the town of Bozeman. In order that his wife might have a suitable resting place, Blackmore purchased five acres of land which he deeded to the town for the cemetery.

The northern division had moved out on July 20, following the Trail Creek route into the Yellowstone Valley and proceeding up the river over the almost completed toll road to Mammoth Hot Springs. They found the Springs were becoming popular as a resort for persons suffering from rheumatism and other chronic diseases. There were about fifty men, women, and children camped around James McCartney's log hotel enjoying the hot mineral baths.

A small party ascended the high peak seven miles to the north-west to make observations. Dr. Peale described the naming of that landmark:

> Mr. Gannett succeeded in attaining the highest point and depositing his instruments, when he discovered that he was in the midst of an electrical cloud, and his feelings not being of the most agreeable sort he retreated. As he neared us we observed that his hair was standing on end, as though he were on an electrical stool, and we could hear a series of snapping sounds, as though he were receiving the charges of a number of electrical frictional machines. Mr. Brown next tried to go up but received a shock which detered him. The cloud now began to settle about us, and we descended some 500 feet, and waited until the storm passed over. About four o'clock in the afternoon we succeeded in reaching the top, and Mr. Gannett found the altitude of the peak to be 10, 992 feet above the sea. We named it Electric Peak.[20]

William Blackmore's diary indicates that the Hayden Survey came into the field with a list of names to be bestowed upon mountain peaks in order to honor individuals who had been particulary helpful to the survey or the national park. The names to be used were Clagett, for William Horace Clagett, the delegate to Congress from Montana Territory; Pomeroy, for Samuel Clarke Pomeroy, United States senator from Kansas; Anthony, for Henry B. Anthony, United States senator from Rhode Island; Edmunds, for George F. Edmunds, United States senator from Vermont; Dawes, for Henry L. Dawes, U.S. representative and senator from Massachusetts; Trumbull, for Lyman Trumbull, U.S. senator from Illinois; Delano, for Columbus Delano, secretary of the interior under President Grant; Grant, for President Ulysses S. Grant; Sheridan, for Lieutenant General Philip H. Sheridan, and Sherman, for William T. Sherman, general of the army.[21] Those names were not used in 1872, although some of them appeared later on peaks within the Park.

Hayden, Holmes, and Blackmore made a side trip to the mining camp on Clarks Fork in company with Baronett, Huston, and Jack Bean, and this excursion provided the solution to an exasperating riddle: Why had the prospector A. Bart Henderson referred to Index and Pilot mountain as "Dog. t." peak? Blackmore recorded the name in shorthand in his diary and it turned out to be just the sort of obscenity a hard-bitten old prospector would be likely to use.[22]

After this visit to Clarks Fork mines, the northern division had crossed over the Washburn Range, visited the falls and canyon of the Yellowstone River and Lake Yellowstone, then went by way of Hayden Valley to the Lower Geyser Basin, where they met the southern division in the manner described. Dr. Hayden was never

Members of the Hayden Survey, 1872 (from left, W.H. Holmes, artist; unidentified; F.H. Bradley, geologist; W.H. Jackson, photographer, and his assistant C.R. Campbell, and Dr. A.C. Peale, mineralogist). From a W.H. Jackson photograph.

lacking in the ability to promote esprit de corps, and he took this occasion to speak to his assembled men, reminding them that they had had the privilege of surveying an area that had, to that time, been seen by fewer than one hundred white people, themselves included. (This, of course, was an exaggeration, for even a casual estimate would have to admit of several hundred by that time, but his statement undoubtedly did promote a feeling of accomplishment.) He also suggested that three of their guests be made honorary members of the U.S. Geological Survey of the Territories. He was reported as saying,

> This has been conferred on one gentleman heretofore, Mr. Gifford, of New York, and I now propose the names of Mr. Thomas Moran, of Philadelphia, Mr. Blackmore, of England, and Mr. Langford, of Helena, Montana Territory. Mr. Moran, by his good qualities, endeared himself to the party last summer, and by his great painting of the Yellowstone canyon and falls—now the property of the nation—has immortalized the exploration of that region. Mr. Blackmore, our guest of this season, and vice president of the anthropological society, of England, has shown himself worthy of the honor by his scientific attainments and interest in our great park. Mr. Langford is known to you all as the superintendent of the park, and the one who first made known to the world the wonders contained in its vast limits. Therefore, I now propose the names of these three gentlemen as honorary members of the United States Geological Survey.[23]

Both Blackmore and Langford took leave of the Hayden Survey at that point. The Englishman, overwhelmed by a desire to get back to his native land, was guided to Virginia City and the Montana stage line by Bill Hamilton. Langford and his nephew-assistant, with their packhorse loaded with "specimens," began a leisurely journey through the northern part of the Park, which they reached by way of the Falls of the Yellowstone and the trail over the Washburn Range.

As superintendent, Langford undoubtedly had in mind doing something about the Bozeman toll road, which was being extended into the Park from the north. The road was a scheme originated by A. Bart Henderson, whose diary contains this entry:

> Monday July 24, 1871 arrived at Bottler's ranch. Here I remained a few days, resting and viewing out a road which I located on the twelve day of Aug. 1871. It is to run from Bozeman to the Yellowstone Lake, by the Mammoth Hot Springs, built for the benefit of the travel to & from Wonderland, & to be a toll road.[24]

An item in the Bozeman newspaper indicates that work commenced on the toll road between Bottlers' ranch and Mammoth Hot Springs in September 1871.[25] Only a little over a month later the same news-

paper reported the road "about completed."²⁶ A more detailed report
a few days later told that the crew had conquered the Point of Rocks
and the road was completed up to the mouth of the present Yankee
Jim Canyon, where Henderson's camp was then located. Despite his
limited progress, that optimistic road builder continued to maintain
that his toll road would be an accomplished fact by springtime.²⁷
Actually it was nearly a year before the first wagon passed through
Yankee Jim Canyon.²⁸ After Bart's brother, James, broke his leg in
mid-October, the work on the road became sporadic, and in July of
the following year it was reported still two miles short of Mammoth
Hot Springs.²⁹

Very probably Bart's resources were inadequate, for he seems to
have formed a partnership with J.V. Bogart, Leander M. Black, and
L.S. Willson—all of Bozeman—and C.J. Lyston of Helena, as the
"Bozeman City & Yellowstone National Park Wagon Road and
Hotel Company." The group proposed "to make all principal points
and objects of interest in the park accessible, as far as possible, by
wheeled vehicles" and sought authority from the government to build
station houses along the route and "a commodious hotel for the
accommodation of visitors." A bill to incorporate, with a capitaliza-
tion of $500,000, was introduced in the first session of the Forty-third
Congress by Representative Isaac C. Parker of Missouri, April 27,
1874. The bill was referred to the Committee on the Territories but
was never reported back. That failure to obtain a federal charter
seems to have deflated the scheme; the portion of the road constructed
through Yankee Jim Canyon passed into the hands of James George,
better known perhaps as Yankee Jim, who operated it as a toll road
until about 1910.

At the time of Langford's tour of inspection the Bozeman toll
road had not yet entered the Park, so there was no action he could
take. However, one could logically suspect that he was responsible for
the defeat of the toll road proposal in Congress two years later.

Hayden's northern division was the first to leave the Lower
Geyser Basin. As they passed down the Firehole River on August 20
they "encountered a party of officers and soldiers from Fort Ellis and
other northern posts, under the leadership of Colonel Gibbon, who
had been visiting the wonders of the Yellowstone."³⁰ According to
Colonel Gibbon, his detachment had run entirely out of provisions
and had been subsisting on roots, squirrels, and blue jays when they
met Hayden's party. They were given flour and sugar, and the stream
they had descended with such difficulty was named Gibbon's Fork.³¹

The party continued down the Madison River, traced the river
nearly to the three forks of the Missouri, followed the Gallatin River

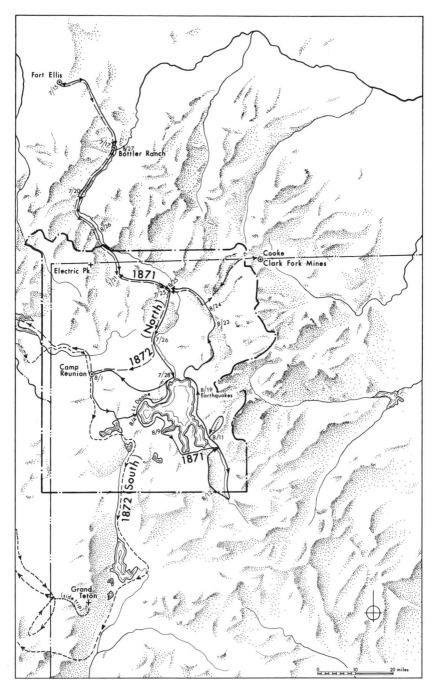

Fort Ellis

7/15

7/17

8/27
Bottler Ranch

7/20

8/26

Cooke
Clark Fork Mines

Electric Pk.

1871

7/21

7/25

(North)

7/25

8/24

8/23

7/26

1872

Camp
Reunion

8/1

7/28

8/19
Earthquakes

8/11 Doane

8/4

8/9

8/11

1871

1872 (South)

8/12

Grand
Teton
(side trip)

0   10   20 miles

Routes of the Hayden Survey parties, 1871 and 1872. Barlow routes are
shown on page 145.

back into the mountains, and made the crossing over the range lying between the Gallatin and the Yellowstone; then they followed the Yellowstone down through the first canyon. Thereafter, the northern division moved up Shields River and crossed over Flathead Pass back into the Gallatin Valley, where the season's work was terminated September 11.

Stevenson's southern division remained in the geyser basins until September 3. During that time W.H. Holmes named the Great Fountain Geyser, of which he says: "Among the several geysers, the names of which I had the honor of giving, the most remarkable and beautiful is the Great Fountain."[32] The southern division met an interesting party of tourists in the geyser basins. Camped near them part of the time was a party from Bozeman which included Mrs. Hiram H. Stone, the first lady on record to visit the geyser basins. This party also included the Reverend W.S. Frackleton, who is credited with holding the first divine services in Yellowstone Park. The visitors were conducted to the geyser basins, from Mammoth Hot Springs, by E.S. Topping, who had discovered a new route to the geysers via the Norris Basin and Gibbon River while trapping in that area with Dwight Woodruff.[33]

From the geyser basins the southern division moved up the Firehole River, discovering Bechler River on August 5, and then examined Shoshone and Lewis lakes, which they named as they descended the Lewis fork of the Snake River toward Jackson Hole.[34]

The southern division continued through Jackson Hole and down the Snake River exploring the great canyon by which it passes around the southern flank of the Teton Range, arriving at Fort Hall on October 11. The season's field work officially ended with a large banquet given by the board of trade at Corinne, Utah, as a "tribute to science."[35]

The accomplishments of Hayden's Geological Survey of the Territories during the summer of 1872 were remarkable. Reconnaissance mapping of 9,000 square miles of previously poorly known territory was accomplished, although the subsequent death of Chief Topographer Burck led to a problem reminiscent of that which followed the death of Antoine Schoenborn in 1871; in this case too the field notes were plotted at Washington, D.C. Many more features had received names in the course of the summer's work, and both Langford and Rudolph Hering reported on the wagon road and railroad possibilities in the area inspected by the survey. In this matter of railroad access to the Yellowstone region, Hering's statement that "a project for such a road has already been conceived, but encountered pecuniary difficulties sufficient to impede its immediate construction"[36] is probably a reflection of the problems which were even then engulfing Jay Cooke & Company, and with it, the Northern Pacific Railroad. Anyhow, his proposal was oriented toward the south, not the north. He thought a line could be constructed from the Central Pacific Railway at Corrine, Utah, to cross the divide to the Snake River plains, from whence the road could ascend Henrys Fork to Raynolds Pass and from there into Montana; and he proposed a branch from this line up Falls River to Yellowstone National Park, branching again in the vicinity of Lewis Lake, with one spur running to the geyser basins and the other to Lake Yellowstone and the Grand Canyon at the falls. Regardless of the interest behind Hering's work it was an idle exercise, for the onset of the panic of 1873 stopped all railroad construction in the United States for the next six years.

At the conclusion of his tour of Yellowstone Park, Superintendent Langford wrote his one and only report on the area. In it he recommended that the Wyoming portion be placed in Montana, with Gallatin County having jurisdiction over it. He thought the government should retain title to all the land within the Park, and he mentioned that he had refused all applications for privileges until the Congress would establish policies to govern the operation of concessions. In his recommendation for the protection of the wildlife and forests, he particularly asked for stringent penalties to cover the careless use of fire. Langford devoted considerable space to the problem of roads to and within the park area. He saw a need for access roads from the north between Bottlers' ranch and Mammoth Hot Springs; from the west, between Henrys Lake and the Lower Geyser Basin, and from the southwest by way of Falls River to the same place. His proposals within the Park roughly approximated the figure-eight road system of today; that is, he favored a direct connection between Mammoth Hot Springs and the geyser basins, with a road extending eastward from Old Faithful to Yellowstone Lake and its outlet, then northward along the Yellowstone River to the falls and canyon, over the Washburn Range to Tower Fall, and down the Yellowstone to Mammoth Hot Springs. In addition, he foresaw a road from the Lower Geyser Basin to a junction below the outlet of Yellowstone Lake. Langford was satisfied that "if the park was rendered accessible by good wagon roads it would immediately prove a source of considerable revenue to the government, and in a few years would largely repay any expenditures needful for its present improvement."[37]

Superintendent Langford undoubtedly believed that the government should make the initial improvements in the area, for he concludes his report with the statement, "Our Government, having adopted it should foster it and render it accessible to the people of all lands, who in future time will come in crowds to visit it."

Yellowstone National Park was, in fact, practically inaccessible; it could be reached only with great difficulty. For the visitor there were two possible routes: by Union Pacific Railway to Corinne, Utah, near the mouth of Bear River, and then by dusty, bone-jolting stagecoach northward across Idaho into Montana Territory; or, by Missouri River packet from Bismarck, Dakota Territory, to Fort Benton or such other Montana landing as the seasonal fluctuation of the river allowed; then it was again a matter of tedious staging to reach one of the outfitting towns, Virginia City or Bozeman. Regardless of which route the visitor came by, there were only those two jumping-off places for a park tour, and beyond them he was largely on his own.

Of these two routes to Montana and the vicinity of the Park, the first, the Montana Stage Line from Corinne, was the more rapid but also more difficult. A stagecoach journey of any length, anywhere in the West, was a fearful undertaking, and that was particularly true of this trip to Montana. As Lord Dunraven noted, the traveler on arrival at Corinne was like the young bear, with all his sorrows to come.

In 1872 Wells Fargo and Company ran daily stages from Corinne over a well-worn but unimproved prairie trail 438 miles to Virginia City. By changing horses at relay stations spaced ten to fifteen miles apart it was possible for drivers to make from six to fifteen miles an hour; even so, a trip required three and one-half days of nearly continuous "dash and jolt" (a service that cost the passenger thirteen cents per mile, with an additional charge of ten and one-half cents per mile for baggage in excess of twenty-five pounds).

For passengers who lacked the physical and mental stamina—and few could endure the strain for more than forty-eight hours—there were primitive stopover arrangements at some of the relay stations. One such, the Sand Holes, was remembered by a traveler of that day as a place "of dust, primarily; and wakeful misery, only aggravated by little catnaps."[38] Other travelers, less demanding in regard to creature comforts, could roll up in warm, dry blankets on the floor of a one-room frontier "hotel" in utter content, but they, like the sagebrush, were usually a product of the land, or very well seasoned.

But the dust!—that nuisance of stagecoach travel which was so inescapable, except when rain or snow created equally disagreeable conditions. It was often "thick, blinding, making a dense cloud all about us, so that the driver cannot see to drive, the horses follow the road, or one man to recognize his neighbor."[39] Yet the same writer admitted "the day's ride was not without its enjoyments; when the dust got tired, for a moment, of circulating." Senator James A.

Garfield found the dust so irritating on his 1872 journey in Montana Territory that he had to forego washing his face on the return trip to "avoid the bad effects of the alkali dust on the skin."[40]

Add to those unavoidable difficulties the vagaries of drivers who "often exhibited wonderful skill running on two or three wheels, and by taking the average between a tip this way and that managed to keep their coaches right side up," to which our informant adds that the stagecoach driver "never refuses to 'take a smile' and always drives with the 'spirit' as well as the 'understanding.' "[41] As if riding with reckless, and sometimes drunken, drivers was not enough, there was also the constant hazard of road agents. A. C. Peale's diary notes that at Virginia City "we saw in the paper that the overland coach was robbed near Pleasant Valley. Logan, Burck & Hamp were aboard. Logan had about $400 in cash with him and must have lost it all. The robbers got $700 from the passengers." He was later able to add, "We passed the place where Logan was robbed in safety. We have six revolvers & three derringers and if we had been attacked there might have been some fighting."[42]

It was a rough mode of travel and the only improvement ever made was the eventual shortening of the stage lines. By 1875 the northward extension of the narrow-gauge Utah & Northern Railway to Franklin, in the Idaho end of Cache Valley, reduced the stagecoach journey to Virginia City by eighty-four miles; further improvement in the painful journey to Montana Territory was accomplished after the Utah & Northern became a part of the Union Pacific system in 1877. Eagle Rock, Idaho, was reached in April 1879, which shortened the stage line (by then in the hands of Gilmer & Salisbury Company) to 228 miles to Virginia City, or 300 miles to Bozeman.

The Missouri River route was for the traveler who valued his comfort more than his time. After 1872, when the Northern Pacific Railroad reached Bismarck, Dakota Territory, a river voyage of 834 miles, requiring two weeks under fortunate circumstances, put the traveler on the Fort Benton levee; from there he could go, via Helena, to Bozeman (250 miles), or to Virginia City (390 miles) by regular stagecoach or by mail-jerky. That part of the journey was just as exhausting and uncomfortable, mile for mile, as the southern route. Also, there were all the other hazards, both physical and mental, which were common on all stagecoach routes: the chance of a runaway or upset, the danger of attack by Indians or hold-up men, and the possibility of abuse by drunken fellow passengers or stage company employees.

Having arrived at the outfitting point, what did the visitor find? Here are some contemporary opinions. Lord Dunraven says,

Virginia City. Good Lord! What a name for the place! We had looked
forward to a haven of rest . . . to forget our woes and weariness; an
Elysium where we might be washed, clean-shirted, rubbed, shampooed,
barbered, curled, cooled, and cocktailed. Not a bit of it! . . . there was no
luxury. A street of straggling shanties, a bank, a blacksmith's shop,
a few drygoods stores, and barrooms, constitute the main attractions of
the "city."[43]

He thought the whole place a delusion and snare, but softened his
opinion a little by admitting that the inn was clean and comfortable,
that he enjoyed the deer, antelope, and bear meat served there, and
that the people were exceedingly civil and obliging. Americans tended
to take Virginia City pretty much for granted. Captain Barlow, in 1871,
only commented on its "small houses and narrow, crooked streets—
the people being American miners and Chinese in about equal portions"; A. C. Peale considered the town "very dull. Although a
considerably larger place than Bozeman it is not nearly so lively.
There are not so many people in the streets," while General Strong in
1875 stated, "From all I can learn however, Virginia City has seen its
best and most prosperous days as it has been steadily loosing ground
for two or three years passed." In contrast, the town of Bozeman drew
no comment except from Lord Dunraven who thought it a "clean, all
alive, and wide awake town."

Actually, there was considerable rivalry between these two Montana towns in regard to the park tourist business. Bozeman was only
seventy-three miles from Mammoth Hot Springs, while Virginia City
was ninety-three miles from the Lower Geyser Basin; also, the building of the Bozeman toll road made the Yellowstone Valley route
much the better of the two. However, the people of Virginia City set
abut shifting the odds in their favor by constructing what was called
"the Virginia City and National Park Free Wagon Road." During the
summer of 1873 more than $2,000 was contributed to a construction
committee which forwarded provisions, tools, and laborers to Gilman Sawtell at Henrys Lake, and with that help he extended the
wagon road that he had already built to his ranch, by way of the
Madison River and Raynolds Pass, on over the Targhee Pass into the
Madison Valley and up the Madison and Firehole rivers to the Lower
Geyser Basin. This ambitious undertaking was roughed out that fall
and was considered a "credit to the energy of our people."[44] Those
traveling by the Virginia City route had to go in their own convey-
ances, of course, for there was no public transportation, nor were
there any accommodations to be had in the geyser basins. On the
other hand, beginning in July 1874 visitors could reach Mammoth
Hot Springs from Bozeman by means of "Zack Root's express," which

left every Monday morning for the Springs with freight and passengers.[45]

At the Springs there was a hotel that could provide accommodations of a rude sort, though opinions concerning this hostel, and the services available there, varied greatly. Variously known as "Horr and McCartney's Hotel," "Mammoth Hot Springs Hotel," and "National Park Hotel," this one-story log building of twenty-five by thirty-five feet, with an earth-covered slab roof, was built in the summer of 1871 by Harry Horr and James McCartney of Bozeman. The Park's first guidebook considered the accommodations "fair";[46] but the Reverend Stanley, in his directions for tourists, comments: "There was no hotel when we were there, though the gentlemanly proprieters will do all they can for the comfort and pleasure of visitors."[47] The reality lay somewhere between those extremes. According to Hayden, the accommodations were "very primitive, consisting, in lieu of a bedstead, of 12 square feet of floor-room," with the guest providing his own blankets, and he adds that the "fare is simple, and remarkable for quantity rather than for quality or variety."[48] Lord Dunraven called it "the last outpost of civilization—that is, the last place where whiskey is sold."[49]

As shabby and inadequate as McCartney's hotel may have seemed, it was all there was in the way of facilities for the public within the Park, unless we include that string of pack and saddle horses which John Werks brought into the area in 1873. His charge for a good horse was $1 a day, and he operated his cayuse line with the help of George Huston and Frank Grounds. Later, he made connections with Zack Root's express, enabling visitors to go on to the geyser basins. These men also served as guides, along with Julius Beltizer and Ed Hibbard. As business was not rushing, they spent their spare time at the Springs, coating objects for sale to the visitors; horseshoe nails and wire or horsehair baskets, motifs, and initials, when immersed one or two days in the mineral springs, took on an alabaster-like appearance and became the basis of a primitive souvenir industry.

Visitors were not numerous in those early years: 300 in 1872 and no more than 500 in any of the years prior to 1877. They seem to have come for a variety of reasons. Invalids came to the Mammoth Hot Springs to soak their infirm limbs in the hot water, which was considered beneficial for anything from rheumatism engendered by exposure and hard work of the frontier to that equally prevalent and less honorable infirmity by tradition incurred in bawdy houses.

General Gibbon described McCartney's bathhouse as it was in 1872:

Bathhouses of J.C. McCartney on the Hymen Terrace, Mammoth Hot Springs, 1871. From a W.H. Jackson photograph.

A small tent is pitched a short distance from the main basin, and looking in you find an oblong hole, dug in pure white soil large enough to contain the human form. It is full of water, led from the spring through a trough hollowed out in the ground. This is the primitive bathing establishment of the place. They have become more luxurious out there since, and have put up several plank bathhouses, with real bathtubs in them. The tubs are not made of white marble, nor are the floors covered with Brussels carpets. These things will come in time. Already, these different bathhouses have established a local reputation with reference to their curative qualities. Should you require parboiling for the rheumatism, take No. 1; if a less degree of heat will suit your disease, and you do not care to lose all your cuticle, take No. 2. Not being possessed of any chronic disease I chose No. 3, and took one bath—no more.[50]

Sometimes the waters seem not to have lived up to their reputation, as in the case of a Mr. Richards, who went to "McGuirk's Medicinal Hot Spring" on the Gardner River below the Mammoth Hot Spring Terraces. He came there suffering from a pulmonary complaint and in a short time seemed to be entirely relieved, and so left for Bozeman. However, he got no farther than Bottlers' ranch when he died suddenly from internal hemorrhage.[51]

Early visitors included a few world travelers such as Lord Dunraven and Al Jessup. The latter was a much-traveled gentleman who had made a tour of the world, seeing all the sights of Europe and Africa. He had hunted the polar bear in the Arctic seas and chased the tiger in the Indian jungle, in fact, had "braved every danger of land and deep," and he was eager to see the new national park in wintertime. He arrived at Bozeman in mid-December of 1872 and outfitted for a winter junket. His "party" with their retinue of guides, hunters, and servants, made an imposing appearance as it filed out of town for the purpose of "visiting the geysers, hot springs and other curiosities of the region." Apparently, he spent most of the three months in the Park, but the record is incomplete due to his subsequent death in Colorado, which, it was reported, resulted from his rashness in taking part in a very one-sided duel—with a rifle against a man with a shotgun.[52]

There were also parties of socially prominent local people who were out to "make the grand round." A single issue of the Bozeman newspaper carried items on three such parties. One from Deer Lodge included Granville Stuart, two judges, and four other men of the town, who returned speaking of the geysers "in rapturous terms." Another party of seven included four ladies. The editor comments that this group "amused themselves fishing, dancing, riding and viewing the wonders . . . 'fun' was their only thought from morn 'till night."[53]

Artist's conception of descent into a solution cave at Mammoth Hot Springs. From a sketch by T.H. Thomas in *The Daily Graphic* (Aug. 11, 1888).

In addition to those rather aristocratic forays there were the visits of the "great unwashed," those wagon tourists who came and went largely unheralded. Captain Ludlow typified them as prowling about "with shovel and axe, chopping and hacking and prying up great pieces of the most ornamental work they could find. Men and women alike joining in the barbarous pastime."[54] Perhaps this is unfair, for how were those plain country people, who had come in by the new Virginia City road, to know how they should act? No one had told them. Indeed, it was only in the rudeness of their action that they differed from the scientific visitor who used his hammer to break off a piece of exquisite hot-spring filigree for his specimen sack. These people were vandals all, whether their trophies served a parlor knick-knack cabinet or a museum exhibit case; the waste was as great whether those severed fragments ended up in the storeroom of a scientific institution or were jettisoned from the family wagon to ease a sweating team on a long, hard hill.

Nor was the breaking of delicate formations the only vandalism practiced. Some was accomplished with rifle and shotgun. Everyone came armed and as often as not shot animals and birds indiscriminately as sport. For instance, Mr. Thomas Bliven was reported to have come upon six bears near the Yellowstone Falls and killed five of them,[55] and Mr. Thomas E. Sherman describes the fate of a trumpeter swan thus:

> Against a great tree near our camp a huntsman had left a proof of his marksmanship, a huge swan, delicate in plumage, hung with outstretched wings, nailed to the rough bark. What a mass of down on its swelling breast, what power in those long, tapering wings, what a silky gloss on the neck, once proudly arched, now drooping like a bruised reed. It must have been a beautiful creature as it glided over the ripples of the river, or sailed through the clear air, and precisely because it was so goodly to the eye, it was laid low by a bullet, its whiteness sullied by its own blood, those wings stretched 'round a tree.[56]

Such senseless slaughter, combined with the activity of meat and hide hunters, within two or three years of the founding of the Park drove the four-footed animals away from traveled routes and the frequented areas.

Fortunately, the destruction of park values by vandalism, hunting, and the careless use of fire did not go entirely unnoticed. The frontier editor who termed it "mockery" to set apart such natural wonders without some provision for their protection,[57] was seconded by perceptive men among the belated explorers and early junketeers who were in the Park during its primal period.

Hayden's double-barreled exploration of 1872 was followed the next year by a lesser effort of the Corps of Engineers. This party was organized by Captain William A. Jones at Camp Brown on the Wind River Reservation, having for its purpose a "reconnaissance of northwestern Wyoming, including Yellowstone National Park."[58] Guided by Sheepeater Indians who had formerly lived in the Yellowstone region, Jones' expedition entered the Park on August 2, 1873, by way of the pass that now bears his name.

As he thought this was the first crossing of the "Yellowstone Mountains" south of Colter Pass, Captain Jones presumed to rename this barrier range the Sierra Shoshone.[59] From that crossing, the expedition proceeded to the outlet of Yellowstone Lake, where two topographers (Paul LeHardy and his partner, Gabbet) decided to abandon their horses temporarily for a float trip down the Yellowstone River. Loading their bedding, firearms, some food, and a gridiron on a raft, they poled out into the sluggish current for what they expected to be a pleasant voyage of a day or so to the falls, where they would meet the pack train.

The first three miles were delightful, but, on approaching some cascades, they found the clumsy raft unmanageable, and realized it was

> now too late for anything except to trust to luck. On the crest of the rapids there appeared an opening we could shoot through, but upon reaching this gap we perceived, half way down the chute, a conical rock and instantly our heavy raft straddled it, the rear end being at once sucked to the bottom. The water fortunately was only about two feet deep.[60]

Unable to pull the raft off the rock, they threw their outfit to shore (breaking LeHardy's precious French shotgun in the process), and tramped down the river carrying what they could. It is from that misadventure that LeHardys Rapids received their name.

While awaiting his topographers, Captain Jones measured the height of both falls of the Yellowstone River, obtaining for the Upper 150 feet, and for the Lower 329 feet. Neither value was a particular improvement on previous determinations.

From the falls the expedition toiled along the east rim of the Grand Canyon, crossed the Yellowstone River at the Baronett Bridge, and proceeded down to Mammoth Hot Springs. There they were resupplied from Fort Ellis, after which they went to the geyser basins by way of the trail over the Washburn Range and down Nez Perce Creek. The rough country between the Upper Geyser Basin and West Thumb Bay wore out the odometer cart, which they abandoned by the trail.

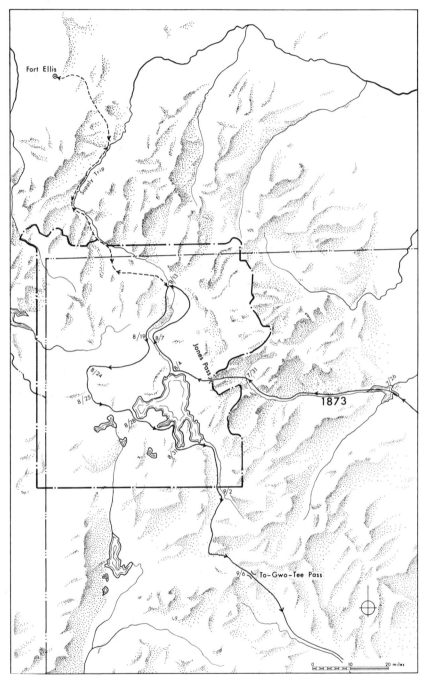

Route of the Jones expedition, 1873.

Their route from the West Thumb Geyser Basin took the expedition south of Yellowstone Lake to the upper Yellowstone River, then over Two Ocean Pass, which was at last "discovered," into Jackson Hole, and from there over Togwotee Pass (named for a Sheepeater guide) into the Wind River Valley, which led them back to Camp Brown.

The contribution of the Jones expedition was essentially geographical. The "discovery" of two passes through the supposedly impassable Absaroka Range encouraged those dreamers who were hoping for a practicable road between Wyoming and Montana by that route. As the editor of the *Avant Courier* said, "it will bring Bozeman within 300 miles of the Union Pacific Railroad and will save Montanans time and expense for over 200 miles of railroad travel and from 75 to 150 miles of staging."[61]

This interest of Montanans in shortening their line of communication with the states led to introduction in the Forty-third Congress of a bill for a Green River to Fort Ellis wagon road to pass through the Park. However, H.R. 2854 was not approved. As the railroads approached Montana from the east and south, interest in this wagon road died away there; in Wyoming, however, there was continual agitation for its construction as a connection between that territory and the Park. Senator Joseph M. Carey became interested in such a road in 1891, and it was authorized as the Washakie Military Road through the act of June 4, 1897. Work was begun by the Corps of Engineers, who built a rudimentary wagon road between the Buffalo fork of the Snake River and the Wind River Valley before the funds ran out in August 1902.[62] The road was never finished and probably was of very little value.

An expedition of more importance to the Park than the Jones effort was sent into the area under the command of Captain William Ludlow in 1875. This officer of the Corps of Engineers came up the Missouri River accompanied by his brother, an assistant named W. H. Wood, two young scientists who would later make names for themselves—George Bird Grinnell and E. S. Dana—and Lonesome Charley Reynolds, who was to be their guide. From the steamer landing at Carroll, Montana Territory, they crossed overland to Fort Ellis, where they gathered a modest outfit and departed for the Park on August 11, 1875.

The visit of this party was so hurried (only thirteen days in the Park) and the route was so routine (the tourist trail from Mammoth Hot Springs to the geyser basins by way of the Washburn Range) that it might be dismissed as a minor junket, except for the importance of its consequences.[63]

In his official report Captain Ludlow commented on the twin problems of vandalism and indiscriminate slaughter of wildlife, suggesting the solution that became the Park's salvation a decade later. As he saw it,

> In the absence of any legislative provision, recourse can most readily be had to the already existing facilities afforded by the presence of troops in the vicinity, and by the transfer of the Park to the control of the War Department. Troops should be stationed to act as guards at the Lake, the Mammoth Hot Springs and especially the geyser basins. A couple of signal sergeants might profitably be employed in keeping meteorological and geyser records, which would be of great interest and value ... before any improvements can be judiciously undertaken, an indispensible preliminary would be a thorough topographical survey, which having been completed, would serve to indicate where roads and bridal paths could best be opened, or most improved. The boundaries of the Park could, at the same time, be run and laid down on the ground. A survey might properly be under the charge of an Engineer officer. Rough bridges could be constructed, where needed. After the construction by the Engineer officer, [they] should be under the charge of an officer detailed to make constant inspection of them, and of the detachments doing guard and police duty. Visitors should be forbidden to kill any game and the hunters should have their arms and spoils confiscated besides being liable to prosecution. For the accomplishment of these purposes, it would certainly be most convenient and expedient to take advantage of the presence and organization of the military, and to entrust the care of the Park, at least temporarily, to the War Department; at least until such time as a Civilian Superintendent, living in the Park, with a body of mounted police under his orders, can suffice for its protection.[64]

Captain Ludlow's suggestions were to provide the blueprint for Senator George Graham Vest's successful defense of the Park. That was not the whole contribution of the expedition, however. Because of his introduction to the Park during that brief visit, George Bird Grinnell became its unvarying champion. As editor of *Forest and Stream*, he later earned Captain Hiram Chittenden's accolade as being "one of the most steadfast and watchful guardians the Park has ever had."[65]

Almost on the heels of Ludlow's party came a lone explorer. He was Philetus W. Norris, whose bad luck had kept him from being a forerunner of the Washburn party in 1870. His departure from Bozeman "with about one hundred boxes, ranging all the way from a match to a drygoods box, which he proposes filling with 'specimens,'" brought forth the editorial complaint: "Must this robbing the Park of is treasures be kept up continuously and especially by vandals from the East? Where's Langford? 'Sic 'em!' "[66] Norris was a collector for the Smithsonian Institution, and appears to have been quite conscientious about consigning his gleanings to the national museum.

The route followed by Norris was the same as Ludlow's except that he returned from the geyser basins to Mammoth Hot Springs by that direct route established the year before by the French Canadian guide, Julius Beltizer.[67] It was this route that Norris was to turn into "his" road three years later.

Norris enjoyed a particularly close rapport with such old mountaineers as George Huston, C. H. Wyman, and Jack Baronett; from what they told him he was convinced that all was not well in the new national park. From them he learned that hide-hunters were taking a terrible toll of the Park's ungulates. That very spring the Bottler brothers had killed an estimated 2,000 elk in the vicinity of Mammoth Hot Springs (and other hunters at least as many more), and "as the only part of most of them saved was the tongue and hide, an opinion can be formed of the wanton, unwise, unlawful slaughter of beautiful and valuable animals in the Great National Yellowstone Park."[68] This, and other observations on the ineffectualness of Langford's superintendency of the Park, became the basis later for Norris' successful bid for the position.

Two other observations made by Norris in 1875 are worth noting here, one because it is so wrong, and the other because it is so right. From some source, perhaps one of his prospector friends, Norris understood that Mary Lake, on the divide between Alum and Nez Perce creeks, had been named by T. C. Everts, of the Washburn party. Edwin J. Stanley, however, was a witness to the ceremony on August 29, 1873, when "some members of our party unfurled the Stars and Stripes, and christened it Mary's Lake, in honor of Miss Clark, a young lady belonging to our party."[69] Norris did much better in his speculations on the relation between earthquakes and geyser activity. Upon observing an increase in geyser activity following an earth tremor, he concluded that tremors were not only related to the increased activity but were essential to the longevity of a geyser. He reasoned that deposition of minerals within the geyser's plumbing tended to seal it off, inhibiting its functioning, but that earth shocks produced crustal movements which reopened old passages or created new ones.[70] Just such a view has gained general acceptance since the 1959 earthquake.

Another party that was in the Park that summer of 1875 commented on the destruction of its wildlife and so contributed to the developing picture of official neglect. This was the Belknap party,

Elk killed by Frederick Bottler near Yellowstone Falls, 1875. This photograph has been credited to both W.H. Jackson and L.A. Huffman. Yellowstone Park Museum collection.

"Fishing in the Park." From an engraving credited to "R.M.H. K.C.," which appeared in W. W. Wylie's 1882 guidebook, *Yellowstone National Park,* p. 54.

consisting of Secretary of War William W. Belknap, General R. B. Marcy, General James W. Forsyth, General W. B. Sweitzer, Colonel George L. Gillespie, and William E. Strong. They were guided through the Park by Lieutenant Gustavus C. Doane on what was to be the first of the several military junkets which were features of the early years. Usually disguised as "inspection" trips they were actually pleasure excursions of a luxurious sort (in one instance, requiring 150 men and 300 horses).

This particular excursion was not so pretentious as later ones, an escort of twenty-four men of the Second Cavalry being deemed sufficient, and its route in the Park was the usual one from Mammoth Hot Springs to the geyser basins, with a side trip to Yellowstone Lake. It was in no sense an exploration, though there was an attempt to fasten Secretary Belknap's name on the largest island of the great lake.[71] Rather, it was a carefree quest for good fishing, which they found, and good hunting, which largely eluded them. Indeed, it is only because of this sporting instinct that Belknap's expedition has an important place in the Yellowstone story.

These men represented a new type of visitor, the soldier-sportsman of the post-Civil War era, and through all the troubled years preceding passage of the Lacey Act such men were to give the Park support essential to its survival. In this instance, it was their published witness to the wanton destruction of the Park's wildlife that is important. In "The Game and Fish of the National Park," a section of his book, William Strong says, in part:

> In 1870 when Lieutenant Doane first entered the Yellowstone Basin, it was without doubt a country unsurpassed on this continent for big game. Large herds of elk, mountain sheep, the black and white-tail deer, and the grizzly, cinnamon and black bears were numerous. The Yellowstone Valley was swarming with antelope, and the mountain lion was frequently killed. During the first five years the large game has been slaughtered here by professional hunters by thousands, and for their hides alone. When the snow falls and the fierce winter storms begin in November and December, the elk, deer and sheep leave the summits of the snowy ranges and come in great bands to the foot-hills and valleys, where they are shot down shamefully by these merciless human vultures. An elk skin is worth from six to eight dollars, and it is said that when the snow is deep, and a herd gets confused, one hunter will frequently kill from twenty-five to fifty of these noble animals in a single day. Over four thousand were killed last winter by professional hunters in the Mammoth Springs Basin alone. Their carcasses and branching antlers can be seen on every hillside and in every valley. Mountain sheep and deer have been hunted and killed in the same manner for their hides. The terrible slaughter which has been going on

since the fall of 1871 has thinned out the great bands of big game, until it is a rare thing now to see an elk, deer, or mountain sheep along the regular trail from Ellis to the Yellowstone Lake. There is undoubtedly considerable game still left on the west side of the Yellowstone, which, in the summer months, seeks the highest mountain summits to escape the flies and mosquitoes; and on the eastern side of the Yellowstone, commencing at the Lake and following the gigantic mountains northward, large game is probably as plentiful to-day as it was on the western side when Doane first explored this country. But few years will elapse before every elk, mountain-sheep, and deer will have been killed, or driven from the mountains and valleys of the National Park. Already the hunters are looking to the eastern shore of the Yellowstone, and without doubt this coming fall and winter immense numbers of elk will be shot in this region for the paltry sum paid for their hides. It is an outrage and a crying shame that this indiscriminate slaughter of the large game of our country should be permitted. The act of Congress setting aside the National Park expressly instructs the Secretary of the Interior to provide against the wanton destruction of the game and fish found within the limits of the Park, and against their capture or destruction for merchandise or profit. No attempt has yet been made, however, to enforce the act in the Park, and unless some active measures are soon taken looking to the protection of the game there will be none left to protect. [72]

Strong ended with the question, "How is it that the Commissioner of the Park allows this unlawful killing?" which put Superintendent Langford in the same unenviable light as the man who was asked if he had stopped beating his wife. Regardless of the answer, there was bound to be a residue of odium.

A book by another sportsman appeared in 1876 and it, too, was influential, though in a different manner than Strong's. It was *The Great Divide*, published in London by Lord Dunraven as a reminiscence of his visit to the Rocky Mountains in 1874.[73] His comments on the Yellowstone Park area are discerning, often amusing, and replete with charming vignettes of the Yellowstone country in that day. His book introduced many Britons, and other Europeans, to Yellowstone National Park. He made Wonderland something more than an American park, and for that service Henry Gannett of the Hayden Survey put Dunraven's name on the peak just west of the pass by which the tourist trail crossed the Washburn Range.[74] Superintendent Norris later applied the name to the pass also.

The period 1872 to 1877 was thus dominated by a series of minor explorations which, though generally useful, were rather routine. Lieutenant Doane's attempt to explore the Snake River from its

Hunters with their bag of grouse, at Mammoth Hot Springs before 1883. From Yellowstone Park Museum collection.

Sportsmen camped at Yellowstone Lake in 1882 display fish and waterbirds killed there. From F.J. Haynes' stereo-photo no. 1283.

source to its junction with the Columbia during the winter of 1876-77 now seems bizarre and useless by contrast. It was the sort of project one might expect the adventurous lieutenant to originate, but he was too experienced an officer to propose it for the harshest season of the year. Undoubtedly, both the plan and the man were victims of bureaucratic bungling as to timing. The record begins on October 4, 1876, with telegraphic instructions from headquarters, Department of Dakota, to the commanding officer at Fort Ellis, ordering Lieutenant Doane to make the exploration with a detail of one noncommissioned officer and five privates. He was to be supplied with sixty days' rations, camp equipage, and a small boat.[75]

Special Orders no. 142, issued at Fort Ellis on October 7, detailed the men who were to accompany Doane: Sergeant Fred E. Server, "a splendid daring soldier . . . of perfect physique and iron constitution," and Private F. R. Applegate, a wiry Marylander "full of expedients and knows all about managing small craft"; both were drawn from Company G of the Second Cavalry. Company F provided Private Daniel Starr, a huge, reckless jokester who had operated Hayden's canvas boat on Yellowstone Lake in 1871, and Private William White, a solemn, romantic, but fearless fellow. Private C. B. Davis of Company L was a born cook, happy when he had "a dishcloth in one hand and 'something dead' in the other," and lastly there was Private John B. Warren of Company H, a stubborn Englishman who was an indefatigable fisherman. They were to be accompanied to the launching site by the post carpenter, Private Morgan Osborn, and a teamster, Private John L. Ward, of proven ability as a woodsman. It was a good crew.

The boat had been built in the post carpentry shop before the expedition was authorized (which leads to a suspicion that Doane sparked the venture). It was a 22-foot double-ender with a beam of 46 inches and depth of 26 inches, strongly up-curved fore and aft. After construction the boat was taken apart and packaged in two bundles convenient for mule transportation. It would be reassembled with wood screws upon reaching the launch site.

The outfitting of the party was the result of careful planning. For shelter, they carried an Indian lodge made of canvas from wagon covers, and their clothing included buffalo coats, rubber boots, and heavy underclothing. Sidearms were left behind as useless (but carbines were carried for hunting), and the army ration was supplemented with such non-issue items as tea. All in all, they were as well supplied as the time and place allowed.

The expedition left Fort Ellis on October 11, with their supplies in a wagon pulled by eight mules, the knocked-down boat packed by two more, and the men mounted. All went well until the third day, when an unruly wheeler wrecked the wagon on a grade in Yankee Jim Canyon. As a result, it was necessary to pack the supplies farther than had been anticipated, while the snowstorm which caught them north of Mount Washburn on the nineteenth caused additional delay. Thus, they did not reach the outlet of Lake Yellowstone until the twenty-third; with two days to assemble their craft, they were able to launch it on the twenty-sixth.

In order to save their nearly exhausted mules the strain of packing loads around the lake, all the supplies were put into the boat, which was towed along the shore by a mule. That worked well enough for fifteen miles, but at Pumice Point, where it was necessary to cast off the line and row around the rocks, a large wave swamped the loaded boat and it sank instantly. Everything was saved but time was lost drying the cargo and repairing the damaged hull.

Repacking the mules, Doane set out around Thumb Bay, intending to carry the supplies to Heart Lake, then return to the south shore of the bay to meet Starr, Applegate, and Ward, who were to take the boat directly across. But when he returned to the lake the following day, Doane found no sign of the boat. Doane and Sergeant Server tramped the beach until dark, anxiously noting the rising wind and decreasing temperature. They had just come to the conclusion that the boat had foundered in the sleet-lashed waves, when they heard the "boisterous and double-jointed profanity" of Starr above the roar of the storm. When the boat was safely beached, there was ice an inch thick on the oars, and the crews' "hair and beards were frozen to their caps and overcoats and they were sheeted with glistening ice from head to foot."

Once started upon the stormy crossing, the crew had found themselves helpless to do anything but hold their craft's bow to the wind, for it would not bear a cross-sea. They had labored hour after hour at the oars, bailing desperately each time a wave caught them unawares and came tumbling aboard. Such a voyage made their survival seem miraculous.

Doane's party exchanged clothes with the nearly frozen boatmen and thawed them out by a roaring fire. The following day, the boat's shroud of ice was chopped away and it was placed on "slipper-poles" and dragged to Heart Lake. On November 2 the carpenter and teamster started for Fort Ellis with the extra animals, and three days later, after extensive repairs, the boat was launched a second time.

The plan was to transport the expedition's supplies down the outlet stream while several men paralleled the boat's progress with the seven horses and four mules they had retained. But ice and low water prevented the boat from performing its transportation function; the weakening animals had to double-trip to move the supplies and equipment forward. As Doane noted in his diary, "The problem was to get to where the boat would carry the property and make distance before the animals gave out."

The party reached the forks of the Snake River on November 21, where the volume of the stream was at last sufficient to be called navigable. There the boat was able to relieve the suffering pack stock. It would be nice to be able to say that all went well after Yellowstone Park was put behind them, but it was not so. As they struggled through Jackson Hole, living mainly on fish caught by Warren and on horsemeat (Doane remarked that "the worn out U. S. Cavalry plug was never intended for food") they continued to be plagued by minor disasters, and dysentery, until their craft was finally wrecked in the canyon by which the Snake River passes the southern flank of the Teton Range. Thus bereft of most of their scant equipage, Doane's party had to abandon the river and make for Fort Hall, which they reached on January 4, 1877.

Lieutenant Doane found more than succor at that post: orders terminating the venture awaited him there. His commanding officer, Major James Brisbin, had succeeded in having him ordered back and, though Doane read a petty motive into it, the fact remains that Brisbin was right. A continuation of the ill-fated expedition could only have led to additional suffering and eventual loss of some or all of those determined explorers.

In retrospect, it must be admitted that Doane's winter expedition accomplished nothing. There was no gain in geographical knowledge despite a considerable expenditure in supplies, animals, and equipment, and if anything at all came out of that misguided venture, it was entirely in the realm of the spirit: one more illustration of what motivated men will endure. One and all, those adventurers returned to Fort Ellis angry about the recall order that kept them from risking further danger on Snake River.

As for Superintendent Langford and his administration of the Park after 1872, the available record indicates that he entered the Park only twice while serving as its superintendent, once as a guest of the Hayden Survey in 1872, and again briefly in late August of 1874. The second visit seems to have been made for the express purpose of evicting Matthew McGuirk from his claim at Boiling River.[76] That, and perhaps a visit by David E. Folsom to the Park following his appointment as assistant superintendent in 1873, was the extent of "on site" management.

Nathaniel P. Langford, circa 1900. From Yellowstone Park Museum collection.

Although Langford did not submit a formal report following his second visit (he submitted only one, for 1872), he did recommend that Congress appropriate $100,000 for the "survey of boundaries and for roads," adding that the "duty of preserving the Park from spoliation . . . cannot be performed without moneyed aid."[77] This is not a great retreat from the position of the Park's promoters: that the area could be managed free of cost to the government. Langford merely thought some pump-priming was necessary in the form of road construction with public funds to attract concessioners who "would immediately prove a source of considerable revenue to the Government, and in a few years would largely repay any expenditures for its present improvement."[78]

Yet, Langford's official actions did not accord with that viewpoint. The secretary of the interior received many applications from persons seeking such privileges as the construction and operation of toll roads, hotels, stores, and a sawmill, and these were duly referred to Langford, who routinely rejected all proposals, the good with the bad. He was probably stalling in the hope that the Northern Pacific Railroad would resume its westward construction and become a contender for the prize (and the preferred one, without a doubt).

Meanwhile, the secretary became increasingly annoyed at Langford's negative attitude, which did nothing to relieve him of the pressures applied by privilege-seekers. The official correspondence became increasingly strained, from that and other causes, during 1873 and 1874, when communication ceased entirely.

The "other" cause for dissatisfaction with Langford's super-intendency was probably less within his control but was real. Yellowstone Park was not yet two years old when the secretary of the interior received the first of those letters, memorials, and reports which, in one way or another, emphasized that all was not well in Wonderland. A dignified and rather impersonal communication from Governor Potts of Montana Territory[79] was soon followed by a somewhat critical petition which is best called the "Bozeman memorial." In it, seventy citizens of that town, and one from Central Park, informed the secretary of the interior that

> We, the undersigned, respectfully represent that the preservation of the great national Yellowstone Park demands the appointment of a salaried commissioner and assistants, and an appropriation by Congress for the building of roads through and for protecting said park.
> We are urged to this request by the vandalism that is rapidly denuding the park of its curiosities, driving off and killing game, and

rendering it a disappointment to all those who desire to see this grand domain left in a state of nature.

That the necessity of such action may be seen, we respectfully request the immediate appointment of a Congressional Commission, empowered to visit the Park early during the coming summer, with instructions to enquire into the need of the measures herein suggested, that the same may be duly reported to Congress, and the mentioned relief speedily obtained.[80]

Gilman Sawtell, whose letter reached the secretary of the interior through Senator George G. Boutwell of Massachusetts, was more blunt. He stated that Langford had not even visited the Park during the previous year, that a change was needed, and that he himself was better qualified to look after the area because he resided near it.[81]

On the other side of the Park, H. R. Horr, who had claimed land jointly with James McCartney at Mammoth Hot Springs, wrote the secretary of the interior complaining of the vandalism of visitors and asking that Congress take action to protect the wildlife from hide-hunters and from men catching elk and buffalo calves within the area.[82]

Such local complaints, supported by the published report of Captain William Ludlow and William Strong's comments on the depletion of the Park's game animals, were bound to create an image of official neglect. Thus, when Philetus W. Norris wrote that in his explorations in the Park (1875) he had "found no superintendent or other agent of government" to control the vandalism and slaughter of its animals, the secretary of the interior was pleased to accept his offer to assume the superintendency, and an end was put to that period of aimless marking time. Norris was a man of action.

CHAPTER 8

WARFARE IN WONDERLAND

The next moment soldiers came running through the wood, at first in twos and threes, then ten or twenty together. . . . The confusion got worse every moment, and Alice was very glad to get out of the wood into an open place.
—Alice's Adventures in Wonderland, *(1865)*

On April 19, 1877, Philetus W. Norris received word in Washington, D.C., that the new secretary of the interior, Carl Schurz, had appointed him superintendent of Yellowstone National Park. So he sat down and wrote a letter to James C. McCartney, proprietor of the hotel and bathhouse at Mammoth Hot Springs, informing him that

> Under authority this day received from the Hon. Sec'y of the Interior . . .
> you are hereby appointed assistant superintendent until my arrival there
> via the Yellowstone River route, I trust sometime in June if not too
> much annoyed by Indians.
> Please guard well and enjoin upon others to do so, against wanton
> slaughter of game spoilation of geyser cones or other curiosities, and
> especially against forest fires—Further instructions and information
> will soon be published in the "suburban," and extra copies sent you for
> the general information of mountaineers.

After inquiring about old acquaintances, Norris asked if the snow would allow him to reach the Park from the Crow Agency by ascending Stillwater River to the "Big Horn Range, where I have great hopes of finding a pass and cut-off route to Clarks' fork mines and Soda Butte . . . or must I ascend the main river through the canon?"[1]

Leaving Washington, D.C., late in April for his home at Norris, Michigan (a town founded by him in what is now a suburb of Detroit), he stopped only long enough to get out the promised edition of his newspaper—the *Norris Suburban*—notifying all of his appointment to the superintendency of Yellowstone Park and his temporary delegation of authority to McCartney; included was a reprint of the act of Congress that established the Park and the rules and regulations promulgated by the secretary of the interior for its management. With that done, and with a bundle of warning signs printed on stout linen for posting at suitable places within the area, Norris left for the Yellowstone country.

His route took him by rail across Dakota Territory to the town of Bismarck, where he transferred to a Missouri River steamboat for the voyage to Fort Buford at the mouth of the Yellowstone River. At that point, reached on June 18, Norris transferred to one of the ill-suited craft then hauling military freight on the Yellowstone and continued upstream to the mouth of the Tongue River, which was as far as the packets could take him. With two companions, he then proceeded up the north bank on captured Indian horses furnished him by General Nelson A. Miles.

The journey up the Yellowstone was without incident except for a side-trip that illustrates Norris' humanity. That none-too-safe detour of forty miles to the Custer battlefield on the Little Big Horn River, under the guidance of "Yellowstone Jack" Baronett, allowed him to obtain the mortal remains of his old friend, scout "Lonesome Charley" Reynolds, for later interment in Michigan.[2]

Norris obtained an outfit at the town of Bozeman, consulted with local people regarding the use then being made of the waters of the Mammoth Hot Springs, and hied himself off to look at the mining operations at Bear Gulch and on the head of Clarks Fork, where he obtained Adam "Horn" Miller as guide. Together they set out to examine the Slough Creek-Rosebud route that Norris hoped would provide a suitable northern approach to the Park.

But his exploration was far from complete when word came that General William T. Sherman intended to tour the Park with a small party. Norris put his favorite project aside and hastened down the Yellowstone River to meet the general at Bottlers' ranch. According to a letter Sherman wrote to the secretary of war on August 3, he saw "no seeming danger" in that vicinity, and so proposed to start for the Park on the following day with an escort of four soldiers. He was convinced that Indians would not enter the area which was "to their superstitious minds associated with hell by reason of its geysers and hot-springs."[3]

Meeting the Sherman party, which also included the general's son, Thomas Ewing, and Colonels Poe and Bacon (with a packer and three teamsters to handle the transportation), Norris moved with them to Tower Fall, intending to serve as their guide for a quick tour of the Park. On the morning of the seventh, Norris was out in advance of the others when a stirrup strap broke. He was thrown from his horse and fell among rocks, injuring his back and neck. As a result he could accompany the general's party no farther but had to begin a "most reluctant return to Mammoth Hot Springs."[4]

The official tour was continued under the guidance of the packer, who included an ascent of Mount Washburn in the itinerary. Of this, the general says: "Any man standing on Mount Washburn feels as though the whole world were below him. The view is simply sublime; worth the labor of reaching it once but not twice."[5] His son was caught up in a different and more serious meditation:

> While I am reveling in enjoyment of the panorama before me, and the emotions it awakens, the millions in the crowded cities of the East are trembling lest the railroad strikers, who, socialists, should lay waste to their fireside, while not far to the west a column of troops is hotly pursuing a band of hostile Nez Perces. . . . One of our party has found under a loose stone a small tin box containing the names of many visitors who have climbed the peak. Among others, of General Belknap and party. At the bottom of the list containing the names of those who accompanied him are scribbled the words, "We drink to the next travelers in Chaune." Time was when such a scene as this would have awakened in men's minds only reverence and awe, but now "pleasure in the mountains is never mingled with fear or tempered by a spirit of meditation, as with the Medevial, but is always free and fearless, brightly exhilarating and wholly unreflective, so that the painter feels that his mountain foreground may be more consistently animated by a sportsman than a hermit. Society in general goes to the mountains not to fast but to feast and leaves their glaciers covered with chicken bones and eggshells."[6]

The general's little party made the circuit of the Park in very good time, and at Upper Geyser Basin they confided to George Huston (who was loitering there in hope of finding a party to guide) their opinion that the hostile Nez Perce Indians would not invade the geyser regions because of superstitious fear. How wrong they were, and what the consequences would be, will soon be seen. As for Sherman's visit, he and his party left the Park the way they had entered it and were back at Fort Ellis on August 18, proud of having brought back "every horse and mule in good order."[7]

General Sherman was surprised to learn of the unexpected turn the Nez Perce War had taken during the fifteen days he was sightseeing in the Park. The facts are these: the military campaign against the Nez Perce Indians had begun two months earlier—in mid-June—when non-treaty bands became embroiled with whites who had settled upon their ancestral lands; revenge slayings by irresponsible young men led to pitched battles with regular troops and Idaho volunteers. The embattled tribesmen came off best in those early encounters, yet they recognized the futility of continued resistance; thus, a retreat across the mountains of Idaho toward a fancied security on the buffalo plains of Montana was undertaken. But the illusion that they would be allowed to escape in peace was snatched from them in a vicious dawn attack on their unsuspecting village in the Big Hole Valley of western Montana. There, caught "sleeping" in the most literal sense, they nevertheless crippled the attacking force and escaped. From that experience the Nez Perce Indians learned that the United States Army was everywhere their enemy, that the citizens of Montana were not as friendly as they had supposed, and that their only hope lay in an alliance with their old friends of buffalo-hunting days—the Crow Indians. Thus, even while General Sherman was in the Park, the Indians were pushing desperately eastward on a course intended to bring them into Crow country with the least contact with white settlements. Their route crossed the Yellowstone Plateau, directly through the nation's pleasuring ground, which they seem not to have known was off-limits to them for superstitious reasons.

Yellowstone National Park thus became the vast and rugged arena for a two-weeks' struggle resembling a military version of that childhood game known as blind man's buff. In that rough wilderness, described by an army scout as "the most outdoors country on earth," a confusing place for pursued and pursuers where horses and men wore out, communications snarled and transportation staggered, the war was resumed in a series of vicious but indecisive confrontations. Entirely by chance, several parties of pleasure-bent tourists were involved, effectively drawing the interest of the press and public from the fact that the army had again muffed a chance to catch the Nez Perces.

Several parties of tourists were in the Park on the eve of the Nez Perce invasion, one of them camped on Tangled Creek to the west of

Fountain Paintpot, in Lower Geyser Basin. This Radersburg party consisted of nine persons: George F. Cowan and his wife Emma, her brother and sister, Frank and Ida Carpenter, Charles Mann and Henry Meyers—all of Radersburg, located between Three Forks and Helena, Montana; with them were three Helena friends of Frank Carpenter—A.J. Arnold, William Dingee, and Albert Oldham—and William H. Harmon of Colorado, who had joined them from the Storey-Riche party (which had departed for Bozeman, Montana, the day before). That evening of August 23 was the eighth day in the Park for these tourists, who had entered Lower Geyser Basin on the fifteenth—just as General Sherman's party was leaving. (Their brief contact with Sherman, when reviewed in the light of subsequent events, would cause the tourists to think the illustrious officer was running from the Indians; but he wasn't.) They had had a satisfactory tour of the geyser basins under the gratuitous guidance of George Huston, the old Bear Gulch miner, and they had no particular feeling of danger, for George had duly passed along Sherman's view that superstitious dread of the hot springs would keep the hostiles out of the geyser region. That erroneous notion kept the Radersburg party in the Park and in the path of the approaching Nez Perce Indians.

Something over a mile north was the camp of a solitary prospector, John Shively, who was relaxing while considering where to look for his lost horses. He had already made arrangements with the Radersburg party to transport his outfit in their baggage wagon if he did not find his animals before the time of their intended departure for home on the following morning.

Another party of importance in the developing debacle was the group of eager young men we will call the Helena party. It was made up of Andrew Weikert, Richard Dietrich, Charles Kenck, Frederic Pfister, Jack Stewart, Leonard Duncan, Joseph Roberts, August Foller, Leslie Wilke, and Benjamin Stone, a black cook. They went into camp at the Falls of the Yellowstone River the evening of the twenty-third, unaware that anything more than the pleasures of a carefree excursion lay ahead of them. Somewhere in the same general area was a recently discharged soldier by the name of J.C. Irwin who was sightseeing afoot and alone.

Thus, the center of the stage was occupied by two tourist parties and two singles—a total of 23 persons. Waiting in the wings, in a manner of speaking, were other characters of the drama. Along the northern verge of the Park was a miscellany of miners and settlers, and a small party of English tourists who had just "done" Wonderland under the guidance of the flamboyant but improvident

"Texas Jack" (John Omohondro). He and his dudes had settled down north of Mount Washburn and were enjoying some trophy hunting before leaving Yellowstone country. To the west, there were about 600 Nez Perce Indians—men, women, and children, who had just entered the Park by way of the Madison River. Regardless of their feelings about geysers (and there is no evidence they had any), they had a compelling reason for wanting to "get lost" in the Yellowstone wilderness. Behind them, and no farther away than Henrys Lake, Idaho, was General Oliver O. Howard's force of 600 men , including volunteers and Indian scouts, all anxious to overtake the fugitives for reasons varying from wounded martial pride to a desire to possess Nez Perce horses.

The outriders of the invasion reached the Lower Geyser Basin late in the afternoon and two of them, Yellow Wolf and his cousin *Ots-kai*, captured the old prospector as he was cooking his evening meal. By the time Shively was handed over to other Indians it was nearly dark, so that Yellow Wolf's scouting party, reinforced to five Indians, found themselves in danger of miring their horses in the marshy ground of the Fountain Flats. Therefore, they stopped for the night, despite the tantalizing flicker of a campfire to the south, where members of the Radersburg party were staging a minstrel show of sorts in celebration of their last night in the Park—or so they thought![8]

Arnold and Dingee were up early on the morning of the twenty-fourth to prepare breakfast. While Arnold built the fire, Dingee took the coffee pot and went over to Tangled Creek to get water, and there he found several Indians sitting their horses and watching him. After an exchange of "How," Dingee went back to camp with the Indians trailing behind him. In the conversation that was struck up by *Hin-mah-to-sin-mikt*, or Henry, who acted as interpreter for the Nez Perces, the Indians first tried to pass themselves off as Snakes but, when that proved unconvincing, admitted to being Nez Perces.

The Radersburg party was fortunate, for Yellow Wolf had wanted to charge the camp in the predawn grayness, but Henry had talked him out of it and they had already decided to take the tourists prisoner before Dingee showed up.

The camp was soon aroused, but no one had much appetite for breakfast except the Indians. Upon a hasty consultation the men decided to pack up and start for home if they could, and while the wagon was being loaded the Indians asked for coffee, bacon, and sugar, and other articles of food which Arnold proceeded to give them. George Cowan observed what was going on and put an end to the generosity, and "not very mildly, either," according to his wife. She always thought that his tactlessness in this matter was the reason for the attack on the party later that day.[9]

The Radersburg tourists were not molested as they started down the rough wagon trail leading out of the Lower Geyser Basin, but Yellow Wolf's scouting party accompanied them. They were allowed to pass the squaw camp which was moving up Nez Perce Creek, but near the mouth of the creek they were stopped by a line of about fifty mounted warriors. Mrs. Cowan says, "We were told to backtrack, which we did, not without some protest, realizing, however, the utter futility. The Indians pretended all this while to be our very good friends." So the tourists followed in the wake of the squaw camp for about two miles until they reached a place where fallen timber prevented any further progress with the wagon and buggy.

At that point, the vehicles were "ransacked and destroyed." While several Indians busied themselves cutting spokes from the buggy wheels to use in making whip handles, another tied several yards of pink mosquito bar to his horse's tail and went dashing about, and an ugly old Indian made himself a turban out of a fine piece of swansdown Mrs. Cowan had obtained at Henrys Lake. She observed that the Nez Perces were "light hearted and seemed not to worry over the outcome of their campaign."

Six miles above the place where the vehicles had been abandoned, the tourists—or perhaps we should call them captives— came up with the squaw camp, which had halted for the noon meal in the open meadow near the crossing of Cowan Creek. At that place they were told by Poker Joe[10] that the Indians had decided to release them if they would trade their good horses and saddles for worn-out Indian ponies adequate to take them back to the settlements. Having no real choice in the matter they handed over their horses, but not before Oldham had philosophically remarked that "this was the easiest crowd to trade with he ever saw." The Indians also took all their guns except Oldham's Ballard rifle, for which they had no ammunition and which was defective. As soon as he had the squaw camp moving again, Poker Joe came to the tourists and told them they could go, but he warned them to go into the timber, stay off the trail, and go fast as "Injuns heap mad. They kill maybe."

The little party did as ordered but after one-half mile of struggling over fallen logs and around mirey places all but Arnold and Dingee returned to the trail, where they were overtaken by a party of twenty to thirty Indians. These insisted the chiefs wanted to see them again; so the tourists were turned around and marched eastward in the wake of the squaw camp. They had passed the site of the noon stop and were just at the foot of Mary Mountain when shots rang out. Ida Carpenter, who was riding beside Albert Oldham, and somewhat behind the Cowans, had a good view of what happened. She says:

> I saw two Indians on horses coming down in front of us at a full gallop. They stopped suddenly and fired, and George jumped or fell from his horse. At the same moment Albert Oldham dropped from his horse, being shot by an Indian a little way above and behind us. Emma jumped from her horse and ran to Cowan, and the Indians made a rush and surrounded her and George.

When Cowan jumped from his horse he could not stand and rolled down hill until he came up against a pine tree. His wife reached him before the Indians did and seeing he was wounded above the knee surmised he had not been mortally hit and threw her arms around his neck to shelter him from a fatal shot. By the time Ida could dismount and run forward to help her, an Indian had pulled Mrs. Cowan back sufficiently to have a shot at Cowan's head. She remembers being "roughly drawn aside. Another Indian stepped up, a pistol shot rang out, my husband's head fell back, and a red stream trickled down his face from beneath his hat. The warm sunshine, the smell of blood, the horror of it all, a faint feeling and all was blank."

The shot that felled Oldham had struck him in the left cheek and passed downward, cutting his tongue and coming out beneath the jaw on the right side. Oldham struggled to his feet in the bottom of the little draw into which he had fallen, just in time to see the Indian who had shot him descending from the trail. He had kept his hold on his Ballard rifle and pointed it at the Indian and tried to fire; not knowing the gun was useless the Indian dodged into cover, giving Oldham a chance to find a hiding place in the bushes. There he lay for thirty-six hours, suffering intensely.

When the firing started, Frank Carpenter was thirty or forty yards behind the Cowans, riding beside an Indian. His first impulse was to bolt, but on looking around he saw that he was covered by several guns. He later declared that his life was spared because he had the presence of mind to make the sign of the cross, yet it seems unlikely this could have had any effect, as the Nez Perces were not even Christians, let alone Catholics.

The remainder of the party—Meyers, Mann, and Harmon— meanwhile ran toward a marsh covered with willows and high grass, with the Indians following and firing at them. The two men who stayed in the woods, Arnold and Dingee, saw they were being followed so abandoned their horses and started afoot toward Gibbon

River, dodging a few parting shots. Arnold, who had a watch, says it was three o'clock when they reached a place of safety; by dark they were at Gibbon River, something over six miles from the place where they had been attacked. Not daring to light a fire and "as we had neither coats nor blankets, we amused ourselves that night by crawling over fallen trees to keep warm."

George Cowan lived to remember the revolver within three inches of his face: "The next instant there was a flash, a deafening report, and a faint scream from my wife rang in my ears. My head felt as if a great weight had fallen upon it and crushed it, and everything became dark." He regained consciousness several hours later and was pulling himself upright by holding onto tree branches when he noticed an Indian nearby, sitting on a pony, watching him. Cowan started to hobble away but the Indian dismounted, dropped to one knee and fired a shot after him. The ball struck him in the left side above the hip and came out over the abdomen. Cowan lay where he had fallen expecting the Indian to come up and finish him off; when he finally realized he had been left for dead he found he could make some progress dragging himself with his elbows, and in that way he got into a willow thicket. He managed to cross Nez Perce Creek and crawl one-half mile down it before stopping to rest sometime after midnight.

The attack on the Cowan party had been the irresponsible action of a ragtag group of Indians bringing up the rear. No further injury was done the members of the party because a chief, on hearing the first shots, had ridden rapidly back to restrain the would-be murderers. He shepherded Frank Carpenter and the two women up the trail toward the Squaw camp. After the shooting of her husband, Mrs. Cowan was not aware of anything until they were well up Mary Mountain, when her brother, Frank, was able to ride up beside her. She was pale and looked years older and Frank's assurance that the Indians would not harm them further seemed to her to have come too late.

The Indians camped that evening in a meadow east of Mary Lake. Mrs. Cowan and her brother were assigned to Chief Joseph's camp, while Ida and the prospector Shively were left with Poker Joe. Mrs. Cowan sat on a blanket by the campfire crying that evening, when her brother, thinking to assuage her grief, handed her an Indian baby to hold. The mother was pleased, and yet troubled by Mrs. Cowan's grief, she asked Frank, "Why cry?" He told her they believed Mrs. Cowan's husband had been killed, and the woman replied "She heartsick." Mrs. Cowan remembers Chief Joseph sitting by the fire "somber and silent, foreseeing in his gloomy meditations possibly the unhappy ending of his campaign. 'The noble Redman' we read of was more nearly impersonated in this Indian than in any I have ever met. Grave and dignified, he looked a chief."

On the morning of August 25 the Indians moved down Trout Creek toward the Yellowstone River. Near Sulphur Mountain outriders found the solitary sightseer, James Irwin, hiding in a ravine. Irwin was such an unkempt looking individual that Mrs. Cowan could not later bring herself to trust him. She preferred to consider him a deserter, which he was not, having been recently discharged from the Second Cavalry at Fort Ellis. However, Irwin did inadvertently disclose to the Indians the presence of the Helena party in that vicinity.

The Helena party discovered the Indians for themselves when they rode out from their camp near the Falls of the Yellowstone to see the thermal features at Sulphur Mountain. While climbing to the top of one of the small hills, Leonard Duncan sighted what he thought to be a large party of tourists, or many elk. Three scouts were sent out and reported that a large number of Indians were crossing the Yellowstone River. The boys then decided upon a retreat to the vicinity of the falls, but instead of going back to their old campsite they went to Otter Creek, nearer to Hayden Valley, and settled there to wait until the Indians should move out of the area. Duncan did not feel safe and took his blankets one-half mile from camp and bedded down for the night. The others accused him of being like Potiphar's wife, saying that he "had Joseph on the brain." Andrew Weikert admitted later that he spent a sleepless night. As he put it, "I felt as though someone ought to stay awake; if the truth was known, I felt pretty nervous."[11]

Two members of the unfortunate Radersburg party reached safety late in the afternoon of the twenty-fifth. S. G. Fisher, in charge of General Howard's Bannock Indian scouts, found William Harmon about six miles below Madison Junction, in a state of exhaustion. Soon after they had made camp at the forks of the Firehole and Gibbon rivers, two of the Bannock scouts came in with Charles Mann, whom they had found a short distance above the camp. His narrow escape from death was apparent from a bullet hole through his hat.[12]

After crossing the Yellowstone River at the ford a short distance above the Mud Volcano, the Indians halted on the east bank, and there a council was held to determine the fate of the prisoners. It was decided to release the two women, who were to be guided to the settlements north of the Park by ex-soldier James Irwin; Mrs. Cowan, however, insisted that her brother, Frank, should guide them out. After further deliberation the Indians agreed to that. The little party was given two worn-out horses for the women, some clothing, bedding, bread and matches. Poker Joe accompanied them across the ford and for a short distance beyond, then told them to "ride all night, all day, no sleep." He shook hands with them and repeated his warning to move rapidly. They did so, but mistrusting the Indians and knowing further that a large party of warriors had gone in that direction looking for the camp of the Helena party, they stayed off the trail in the edge of the timber, which was hard on their horses. It was noon the following day when they spied soldiers camped in the meadow near present Tower Junction, a small detachment of the Second Cavalry out of Fort Ellis under Second Lieutenant Charles Schofield, who was using Mount Washburn as an observation post. The lieutenant obtained from the three, who thought themselves the only survivors of the Radersburg party, the information he had been sent out to get.

About the time that Mrs. Cowan and her brother and sister reached safety at Lieutenant Schofield's camp, the Nez Perce warriors found the Helena party at the forks of Otter Creek. All the boys except Weikert and Wilke, who had gone out to scout for Indians, were lying about the camp. The black cook was joshing Duncan, who seemed downhearted, telling him he ought to be thinking of his girl instead of Indians. At that, Joe Roberts said, "Ben, you are gassing so much, what would you do if the Indians do come down on us?" and Ben answered, "Joe, you look out for yourself, for when the drum taps come I'll be there." That raised a laugh. Moments later several shots rang out, they all jumped and stood confused until they saw several Indians running in on them, firing as they came. Everyone left the camp on a run.

Ben later remembered starting down the hill and turning three somersaults on the way. An Indian fired at him as he fetched up at the bottom, the ball plowing the ground alongside of him, and Ben rolled over into the little stream, where he lay for three hours nearly submerged, while the Indians plundered the camp. John Stewart, the last to leave the camp, got into a patch of brush but had passed into the open again when he saw Charles Kenck ahead of him. He took a few steps and received a shot in the leg, at the same time hearing Kenck cry out, "Oh, my God." Fifty feet farther Stewart was dropped a second time, by a bullet in his hip, while two Indians ran past him pursuing Kenck. A moment later he heard two shots, and again Kenck cried out. One of the Indians came back to Stewart holding his gun on him; the wounded man begged for his life, whereupon the Indian asked him if he had any money and Stewart gave him $263 and a silver watch. The Indians were so elated that they walked off.

Stewart washed his wounds and called to Kenck but got no answer. Too weak to climb up the slope where the Indians had caught Kenck, he crawled back to camp. There he found a little food, and believing himself to be the only survivor, he took his overcoat and what food he could carry and began a painful retreat along the trail he knew would take him over the Washburn Range toward Mammoth Hot Springs.

Weikert and Wilke, the two who had gone out in the morning to scout for Indians, had got as far as Sulphur Mountain. Believing the Indians had moved on, they were returning to Otter Creek and were only a short distance into the timber that skirts the Yellowstone River south of Otter Creek when they ran into an ambush. Weikert turned his horse and made a run for it. The first volley missed him but the second took a chip out of his shoulder bone, and his horse stumbled and fell. He was able to catch his horse, remount, and get out of there without further damage. Wilke managed to get out of the timber well ahead of Weikert.

Weikert and Wilke circled around and rode rapidly for the camp on Otter Creek, hoping they could warn the boys. On entering camp they knew from the wreckage and the broken shotguns—which the Indians had smashed against tree trunks because they didn't want them—that the camp had been attacked, so they retreated to Mammoth Hot Springs.

Stewart meanwhile had not hobbled far before he came upon his mare standing quietly. With transportation thus fortunately provided, Stewart had gone but a mile beyond Cascade Creek when he saw Ben Stone ahead of him. While the two were stopped, eating the lunch Stewart had brought with him, Weikert and Wilke rode up. There remained only the long, slow journey over the Washburn Range and down the Yellowstone Valley, during which Weikert and Wilke gave up their horses to the wounded Stewart and the exhausted Stone. They arrived at Mammoth Hot Springs between 3 and 5 A.M. on August 27. At McCartney's log cabin hotel they found Mrs. Cowan and her brother and sister, and Fred Pfister of their own party. Fred had reached the soldiers' encampment about dark on the twenty-sixth and had moved back with the detachment to Mammoth Hot Springs.

After Mrs. Cowan and her sister and brother had been released by the Indians at the noon stop opposite the Mud Geyser, the squaw camp had moved on to Indian Pond, east of Pelican Creek. They had left behind an aged Nez Perce woman to die. The following day Fisher's Bannock scouts, those savage auxiliaries of General Howard's advancing army, pounced upon the old woman and killed and scalped her. Fisher had had great difficulty controlling his Indians for they were dissatisfied with their meager rations and not at all anxious to close with the Nez Perce Indians. Their principal concern was to gather up a few horses and make off with them, and Fisher had to keep a close watch on the captured stock. Charles Mann had remained with Fisher in the hope of locating other members of his party.

Early on the morning of August 27, Lieutenant Schofield and his detachment left Mammoth Hot Springs for Fort Ellis, taking Fred Pfister with them. That same morning two more survivors of the attack on the Cowan party showed up at General Howard's camp at Henrys Lake. Also that morning, Leonard Duncan came into Mammoth Hot Springs with the good news that Richard Dietrich, completely exhausted, was about two miles out on the trail. Weikert, whose shoulder wound had been dressed by an English physician visiting at the hot springs, took an extra horse and went out after Dietrich.[13] At this point three members of the Helena party remained unaccounted for: the two youngsters, Roberts and Foller, who had come on the Yellowstone vacation in Weikert's care, and Charles Kenck, whom they had good reason to believe lay dead at the Otter Creek campground. Weikert felt his responsibility for the two lads and wanted to go searching for them, but could find no one to go with him at that time.

As Weikert was bringing Dietrich in, Mrs. Cowan was leaving the Springs in a wagon belonging to Henry Bird Calfee, the Bozeman photographer, accompanied by Texas Jack's English tourists. Mrs. Cowan has this to say about their departure:

> We had traveled only a few miles when the guide for the Englishmen declared he had sighted Indians through his field glasses in the direction of the trail over which we had come the night previous. He was quite positive, although no one else could see them. Finally he made a detour in that direction. He was soon out of sight, but in a very few minutes we heard several shots fired in rapid succession. Presently the guide came dashing up to the wagon, declaring he had been fired upon by the Indians, and as evidence exhibiting a stirrup with a bullet hole straight through the bottom of it. The Englishmen, however, seemed sceptical.[14]

That ride in the heavy wagon behind Calfee's wild mules was a rough one, but they arrived safely at the Bottler ranch before dark.

The evening of the twenty-seventh the Nez Perce Indians camped about four miles up Pelican Creek from Mary Bay. They probably were in no hurry as they were far ahead of General Howard's column, which had only left Henrys Lake that morning. Two more survivors of the attack on the Cowan party were rescued on the twenty-eighth by General Howard's scouts as they pushed up the Madison River into the Park. Of this General Howard writes,

The first man [Meyers] we encountered, breathless, hatless, almost starved, with his feet wrapped in rags, was so wild he could give no intelligible account of himself. It was: "Three Indians fired on me, and I got away. They are all killed. The rest all killed!" The next one was Mr. Oldham, a tall, stout young man, with very straight, black hair. He was shot through both cheeks and of course could hardly speak.[15]

When the main column came up later, Oldham was put in an ambulance and hauled along by the soldiers.

By the evening of August 28 Captain Fisher had pressed close enough to the Nez Perces to be able to see the smoke of their campfires on the headwaters of Timothy Creek but was unable to get his Bannock scouts to move forward for an attack. Realizing that it was both dangerous and useless to pursue the Nez Perces so closely with his unreliable allies, Fisher decided to return to the Yellowstone River and await General Howard's arrival there.

Word of the Nez Perce invasion of the Yellowstone region percolated to the outside world with those refugees who had left the Park so hurriedly. Some idea of their wild, rumor-freighted stories can be gathered from the item that appeared in the *Avant Courier's* issue of August 30.

Monday, Aug. 27th. Nez Perce in the geyser basins struck the Helena and Radersburg parties. They killed 7 men and took Mrs. Cowan and sister and brother prisoners. They attacked another party of 10 and killed 9.

That sanguinary and exaggerated information, flashed eastward by telegraph, was the first knowledge Superintendent Norris had that his park had become a battleground. He had just arrived at St. Paul (via horseback to Bottlers' ranch and flatboat and steamer down the Yellowstone and Missouri rivers to Bismarck, where he had boarded a Northern Pacific train) when the news of the depredations in the Park reached him. His reaction was to castigate himself for deserting his duty, yet he could not have influenced events in the Park had he been there.

At Bottlers' ranch, Mrs. Cowan, Frank, and Ida had met an old friend, Dave Boreum of Bozeman, who offered to take them to town in his carriage. They made fifteen miles before stopping for the night at a ranch house on Trail Creek. That evening Crow Indians apparently tried to help themselves to a few horses; shots were fired, and soon that part of the country was in considerable uproar. As Frank Carpenter says,

The following morning the scene about the ranch was rather rumpled. It seemed as if everybody in the country, with all their moveable property had assembled here during the night. There were horses, packs, saddles, household goods, from a stove poker up, women, children, wagons, etc., etc., piled around promiscuously.

Undoubtedly, everybody's nerves were just a little more than edgy.

That morning James McCartney, proprietor of the hotel and bathhouse at Mammoth Hot Springs, agreed to accompany Andy Weikert to the campsite of the Helena party at Otter Creek to bury Kenck and, if possible, find out what had happened to Roberts and Foller. An ambulance was coming up to the Springs to get Stewart, and Weikert wanted Dietrich and Stone to accompany it to Bozeman, but Dietrich didn't care to leave until he knew what had happened to the remainder of their party. As McCartney and Weikert were leaving, Dietrich asked quizzically, "Andy, you will give me a decent burial, won't you?" Weikert agreed readily, never realizing that he would have to do just that.

The mission Weikert and McCartney were embarking upon was more dangerous than they suspected. On the way out they must have passed, unseen, a band of twenty or thirty Nez Perces moving toward Mammoth Hot Springs, but the two men pushed on to within two miles of the old camp on Otter Creek, then stopped for the night. The following day, the thirtieth, they found Kenck's body and buried it, then hunted most of the remaining hours of daylight for Roberts and Foller without finding a trace of them. Staying a second night in the canyon area, they began their return to Mammoth Hot Springs on the last day of August, loaded with such camp gear as they had been able to salvage.

Weikert and McCartney were not the only ones abroad on an errand of mercy. The old miner, George Huston, joined forces with Jimmy Dewing, and the two of them went up the Yellowstone River with the idea of finding Cowan's body and burying it. What they found was a Nez Perce war party in Hayden Valley and only got away after a strenuous chase. Meanwhile, the man they were searching for was found alive on Nez Perce Creek by General Howard's scout, Colonel J. W. Redington, who could do no more for him than make him comfortable with a pair of blankets until the soldiers should come up. That same afternoon the two boys, Roberts and Foller, who had lit out of the camp on Otter Creek with bullets thudding around them at every jump, met some of Howard's soldiers and obtained food. It was their first real nourishment during the three days they had been traveling westward through trackless wilderness. Despite their harrowing experience, they were in reasonably good condition and continued on to Virginia City on their own legs.

Meanwhile, the outside world was beginning to take note of events in the Yellowstone country. Upon receipt of Lieutenant Schofield's information that the Nez Perces were in the Park, the commandant at Fort Ellis sent Lieutenant Gustavus Doane to the Crow Agency to recruit tribesmen for service with the few soldiers that could be spared from that already depleted garrison. Independently of the military, citizens of Bozeman volunteered to go back into the Park with Frank Carpenter to recover the body of George Cowan, and late on the afternoon of August 29, both groups—Doane with his Crow scouts, and Carpenter and the civilians—left Bozeman.

The course of the Nez Perce Indians across the Mirror Plateau, under the guidance of the old prospector, Shively, would have brought them from their encampment on the head of Timothy Creek to the Lamar River in another day, the evening of the twenty-eighth. However, it appears that they became suspicious of their guide and put the route-finding in the hands of a Shoshoni Indian who seems to have known less about the country. Under their new guide they turned northwest on the twenty-ninth and were soon on Broad Creek, so that several days were lost hacking a way through nearly impenetrable forest before they were again on waters leading to the Lamar River. Their slow progress, and their lack of accurate information, were probably to blame for more raids into surrounding territory.

Just such a scouting party was approaching Mammoth Hot Springs on the morning of August 30. The ambulance from Bozeman had departed with the wounded Stewart and Leonard Duncan, but Richard Dietrich and Ben Stone stayed behind, and with them was a Jake Stonner. Shortly after the ambulance left, Jake went out hunting and, happening to look toward Lava Creek, he saw several large parties coming toward the Springs. Suspecting they were Indians, he went out to where Dietrich was taking care of the horses and warned him to hide until the danger had passed. Dietrich did so. When the Indians arrived at McCartney's hotel, Ben Stone ran out of the back door and up the gulch, where he eluded the Nez Perces by hiding in a tree. After dark he went up on the hill and stayed through the next day. For the time the men were safe.

Apparently this or another party of raiding Indians set fire to the Baronett Bridge that day; the stringers burned through near the east abutment and fell into the water extinguishing the fire, leaving the bridge partially destroyed. Indians were also seen on Clarks Fork, near the new smelter that the miners had prepared for a siege. General

Howard's column reached George Cowan that afternoon and he was put in the ambulance with Oldham. When the evening encampment was reached, Arnold, who had accompanied the troops in the hope of finding some of his party, went looking for someone to attend to the wounded men; but he found that the surgeons had gone off with the officers to look at the geysers and it was very late before the wounds were probed and dressed.

Arnold says that "Neither Cowan, Oldham, or myself were in any way indebted to the surgeons or the officers for anything." Although Cowan wanted to be sent out of the mountains by way of Henrys Lake, General Howard decided to take him along with the troops, this subjecting him to unnecessary discomfort.

That night the surgeons roughly probed the wound in Cowan's head by candle light to remove the bullet flattened on his skull. The squaw camp was on Deep Creek on the Mirror Plateau at that moment, and Lieutenant Doane's mixed force was camped at Bottlers' ranch. Somewhere in the vicinity of Mammoth Hot Springs was the band of Nez Perce raiders and the two fugitives, Richard Dietrich and Ben Stone, who were sleeping out in the brush for a very good reason.

The last homestead in the Yellowstone Valley below Mammoth Hot Springs was Henderson's ranch, established by James Henderson in 1871. After Henderson was injured he had left the ranch in the hands of his grown son, Sterling, who provided Bear Gulch miners and others in the area with mail service and supplies; and those settlers who had remained in that part of the Yellowstone Valley had gathered there. When a party of Nez Perce raiders came into sight of the ranch on the morning of August 31, three of its defenders were down at the river, 300 yards away, fishing, as no trouble had occurred for several days and they had somewhat relaxed. Sterling Henderson and John Werks were at the house. Werks got up from a nap and walked outside just in time to see the first eight Indians begin their charge down the open slope nearly a mile to the east. He called Sterling and together they took the rifles and ammunition to the men on the river bank (Joe Brown, George Reese, and William Davis). By the time the Indians were dismounting at the buildings the five defenders had reached some large boulders about 100 yards from the house. They opened fire as the raiders were attempting to drive the horses out of the corral, thereby starting a peculiar little battle.

At the first volley the Nez Perce horses ran out in the open toward the rocks where the whites were sheltering. Left afoot, the Indians had to take cover behind the house and barn. The combatants held their positions for about two hours firing only occasional shots until an Indian tried to reach the horses and was driven back to cover by a volley. Meanwhile, ten mounted Nez Perces sat their horses on the terrace behind the ranch watching the fight, and when the whites finally gave up the contest by crawling back to the river and crossing it in a boat, the mounted group followed them to the water's edge to fire a few parting shots. The others then set fire to Henderson's house, gathered up all the horses in view, and started toward Mammoth Hot Springs.

Lieutenant Gustavus C. Doane was just then rounding Cinnabar Mountain with his Crow scouts, civilians and cavalrymen. When he saw smoke billow up from the burning ranch house, he put his command to the gallop and recovered nineteen horses from the fleeing raiders. There were no casualties in that two-hour battle over a ranch house and some horses, but, as the raiders fled back past Mammoth Hot Springs, they surprised Richard Dietrich, who had returned to the hotel building to get something to eat. He probably failed to connect the sound of horses hooves coming from that direction with the Nez Perce raiders and carelessly walked out the front door, where he was shot down. When Lieutenant Hugh L. Scott rode up with a handful of cavalrymen a short time later, Dietrich's body was lying by the stoop, still warm. Finding no trace of Ben Stone, the cavalrymen presumed he, too, had been killed; so they carried Dietrich's body into the cabin and continued their pursuit of the Nez Perces to Lava Creek.

McCartney and Weikert, on returning from the sad chore of burying Charles Kenck, had the misfortune to meet those same Indians near the Blacktail Ponds. Since the Indians numbered eighteen the two saw nothing to do but to cut out and run. After a hot race of a mile, with the bullets singing around them, they reached a brush patch on the slope of Mount Everts, where the Indians left them alone. Weikert's horse had been killed and a chunk had been shot out of his boot, while McCartney's horse went bucking off with his saddle turned under his belly. After the Indians left, the two continued afoot to Mammoth Hot Springs and, seeing no sign of life there and the door of the hotel open, they entered, struck a match to a candle and were shocked to find Richard Dietrich lying dead on the floor. Fearful that some of the others might have been killed there also, they searched the place thoroughly, then started down the road toward Henderson's ranch. Doane's little command was camped at the ranch and Weikert and McCartney nearly fired upon a sentry who showed himself before challenging them. They were glad to be back among friends, and particularly glad that Ben Stone had come in just ahead of them.

Ben had had his share of difficulties, including an encounter with a bear in a brush patch. Ben said, "As I was there first I determined to stay. When it came to bears or Indians, I had had enough of the latter and was willing to try bears for awhile." After dark the second night he started moving cautiously down the road toward Henderson's ranch and must have been just ahead of McCartney and Weikert—and may have made some of the noises that sent those two into frequent hiding.

The Nez Perce encampment was still on the Mirror Plateau at that time. The next morning (September 1) Irwin asked Shively where the stream they were on flowed to. When Shively told him, he got permission from the Indians to go down to the creek for a drink, and vanished. The Indians didn't seem too concerned about Irwin's escape, but they warned Shively that if he tried it, that would be another matter. That evening, as Irwin was hiking down Pelican Creek, he was surprised by an armed man who ordered him to halt. It was Captain Fisher, who was again moving toward the Nez Perces with a few of his Bannock scouts. He sent the ex-soldier back to General Howard, who was then camped at the Mud Volcano, and Irwin later proved quite helpful by guiding the wagon train over the Washburn Range to the Baronett Bridge.

Howard had had to lay over several days because his wagon train could not move forward from the encampment on Nez Perce Creek at the foot of Mary Mountain. While they were waiting there for Captain Spurgin's "skillets" to cut a road up the mountain, some of Captain Fisher's Bannocks, who had been discharged and were returning home, ran off the team mules and a detachment of cavalry had to go after them. Lieutenant Doane's command at Henderson's ranch was also stalled, for he had received orders from Fort Ellis to await the arrival of Lieutenant Colonel Charles C. Gilbert of the Seventh Infantry and, though the energetic Doane chafed at this restraint when he was so close to the Indians, he nevertheless obeyed. He did send a detail to Mammoth Hot Springs to bury Richard Dietrich, which was accomplished by using one of the wooden bathtubs from McCartney's bathhouse for a coffin. He also sent John Werks and Jack Baronett on a scout toward the Baronett Bridge, and he gathered in all the miners and settlers in that part of the Yellowstone Valley at Henderson's ranch so they could be evacuated.

The next day Baronett and Werks returned bringing two scouts, J. S. Leonard and John Goff, who had come through Clarks Fork country from the command of General S. D. Sturgis, then trying to block up the eastern exits from the Yellowstone region in case the Nez

Perces should attempt to leave that way. Everything had gone well for the scouts until after they passed the Baronett Bridge; then, somewhere on the Blacktail Deer Creek Plateau they were ambushed. The first shots dropped an Indian boy who had been raised by Goff and was accompanying them, and Goff was wounded in the neck. The two scouts managed to hold off the Indians, but when found by Baronett and Werks they were in bad shape. The fate of the Indian boy was never determined. That evening the old prospector, Shively, who had escaped from the Indians on the Mirror Plateau the night before, crossed the Baronett Bridge on the partially burnt stringers and made his cautious way toward Mammoth Hot Springs.

On September 3 Lieutenant Colonel Gilbert arrived at Doane's command with some additional cavalry and it was soon apparent how the war had been going. It appears that dispatches sent by General Howard from Virginia City to explain his long delay at Henrys Lake had been interpreted by his superiors as a lack of military initiative, rather than a necessary halt for resupply. Since General Howard was operating outside his departmental limits, it was decided to replace him with Lieutenant Colonel Gilbert of the Seventh Infantry. Thus, Gilbert's concern was not with the Nez Perces who were then so close to him, but with this opportunity to take over General Howard's command. He ordered Lieutenant Doane to accompany him to Henrys Lake, which he proposed to reach by crossing to the West Gallatin River and following it up to the Madison Valley and over Targhee Pass. So, all the citizens and the Crow auxiliaries were sent down the Yellowstone Valley and the march was begun. Colonel Gilbert was no cavalryman and he pushed the horses and men so hard that the entire outfit broke down. (Thirty head of horses were later brought into Fort Ellis without saddles or equipment.) He arrived on the Madison River to find that General Howard had already passed into the Park; he never did catch up with General Howard. The irony of it was that if he had followed Lieutenant Doane's advice and pushed up the Yellowstone instead, he would have met General Howard at the Baronett Bridge.

Howard's wagon train reached the Lower Falls of the Yellowstone on September 3, after having been lowered down the steep bluff south of Otter Creek with snubbing lines. The rope burns on the trees at Spurgin's beaver slide, as the place is called, can still be seen. Howard's command had already shifted to pack mules and in that manner reached the Baronett Bridge on the fifth, while the slow-moving wagon train, for which a roadway had to be chopped out of the forest over the Washburn Range by way of Dunraven Pass, did not reach that crossing until the twelfth. All that time George Cowan was being pulled along in an army ambulance with very little care except what Arnold and the teamsters could give him.

The old prospector, John Shively, was moving almost as slowly as the wagon train. He reached Mammoth Hot Springs on the evening of September 3 to find the place deserted, and on the fourth he arrived at Henderson's ranch, where he found a cache of supplies left behind by Lieutenant Doane. He had the good luck there to meet J. B. Shuler, who supplied him with a mount so that he could ride on toward Bozeman.

Captain Fisher's remaining Bannock scouts came up with the rear guard of the retreating Nez Perces three miles up Cache Creek from the Lamar River during the afternoon of September 4. The result was a peculiar engagement. The Nez Perces were not sure what Indians they were up against and kept halloing to the Bannocks in several languages, saying, "We don't want to fight you, for if you are Crows, Bannocks, or Snakes you are our friends. Let us talk and smoke together." Though more than a hundred rounds were fired, the only damage done to the Bannocks was one horse disabled by a shot through the jaw. After dark, the Bannocks abandoned their extra animals and slipped away from a situation in which they were badly outnumbered. Along Cache Creek, near its junction with Lamar River, Captain Fisher found the carcasses of cattle belonging to a rancher named James C. Beatty. The Indians had evidently spent some time drying meat for subsistence during the next stage of their retreat.

Two weeks of warfare in Wonderland ended on September 6, when the Indians passed down Crandall Creek toward Clarks Fork. That same day Shively reached Bozeman, but George Cowan did not get there until the twenty-fifth, and not without two further misadventures. On the last lap of his journey out of the Yellowstone wilderness, while he was coming through Spring Creek canyon east of Fort Ellis, the wagon overturned spilling him down the slope, and, when he was at last put to bed in a Bozeman hotel, the bedstead collapsed, rolling him out on the floor. At this final indignity, he suggested they try artillery if they couldn't kill him any other way! Cowan reached his home at Radersburg on October 5 and recovered fully from his injuries. Several times in later years he visited the Park, and on such occasions would tell tourists of his experience during the Nez Perce War, showing them the bullet that had been removed from his skull. It had been made into a fob for his watch.

Andrew Weikert later claimed that he brought the bodies of Kenck and Dietrich back from the Park by wagon in mid-October.[16]

The fact is that there had been a heavy fall of snow on the Washburn Range and he was unable to reach the grave of Charles Kenck at Otter Creek; so, he made arrangements with James McCartney to go in and get the body as soon as the snow settled.[17] Weikert did make good his promise to give his friend Dietrich a decent burial but even that was marred by one last accident. As the funeral procession was moving down Broadway, in Helena, a team driven by Marshal Wheeler got out of hand, ran away and upset a carriage. James McCartney delivered Charles Kenck's body to Bozeman on November 1.[18] Kenck was buried at Helena.

Poker Joe, whose humanity undoubtedly saved a number of the Yellowstone tourists from death, was himself a victim of the war. He was killed in the first day's fighting at the Bear Paw Mountain battle, where the valiant retreat of the Nez Perce Indians finally ended in their defeat at the hands of General Nelson A. Miles. Even in defeat the Nez Perces had made their mark, for the editor of *The Nation*, while commenting on their manly and unflinching bravery and the fact that they had proved as good soldiers as the regulars, added that their "un-Indian-like humanity towards those who fell into their hands has greatly strengthened their title to the best treatment."[19]

It would seem that the events of the summer of 1877 were war enough for a new undeveloped park, but there was more to come. By the time Superintendent P. W. Norris reached the Park during the last week of July 1878 it was already apparent that hostile Bannock Indians might, like the Nez Perces, raid through the Park from the west, and so he decided to forego the building of a headquarters at Mammoth Hot Springs and concentrate on constructing a wagon road to connect the Springs with the geyser basins and the military road built by General Howard's troops the previous summer. Leaving all official and personal valuables in storage at Bottlers' ranch, Norris assembled a party of twenty armed and mounted mountaineer laborers and proceeded to build the Norris road. From Mammoth, the route climbed steeply up over the terraces to Snow Pass, crossed Swan Lake Flat to the Gardner River, which was rudely bridged, then followed the edge of Willow Park to Obsidian Cliff. There, considerable labor was expended in constructing a corduroy road across the lower end of Beaver Lake and in pecking out a narrow grade around the foot of Obsidian Cliff. Since picks, shovels, axes, and iron bars were hardly adequate for the rock work that had to be done, Norris resorted to building fires on the rock and dashing cold water on the heated stone to fracture it.

From Beaver Lake the road climbed over the divide to Lake of the Woods and passed down Solfatara Creek to Norris Geyser Basin, then followed the Gibbon River, much as the present road does, to a point midway in Gibbon Canyon, where it climbed out on the east side in order to pass around Gibbon Falls. It then crossed Canyon Creek and ascended over dry, pine-covered benches to come out in the Lower Geyser Basin near the mouth of Nez Perce Creek and join Howard's road. Norris extended his road on to the Upper Geyser Basin and his baggage wagon was the first vehicle to get that far. W. H. Holmes, a geologist working for the Hayden Survey in the Upper Geyser Basin, records the arrival of the road builders thus: "Just below the middle geyser basin, we were accosted by a horseman with gaudy buckskins and feather who issued suddenly from the woods. It was Col. Norris, Superintendent of the park. He was on his way to the upper basin. His men were just behind him cutting a wagon road up the valley."[20]

Norris' accomplishment in putting through sixty miles of road in less than a month without adequate prior exploration of the route was no less than monumental; particularly so at a time when conditions required unusual vigilance, which used some of his limited means in guarding the camps, working crews and stock. The work was accomplished with hardly a moment to spare, for the road builders arrived on the very day that topographer A. D. Wilson and Harry Yount straggled in afoot from Henrys Lake, where their camp had been fired upon by Indians who stole their animals. The scout who came over the new road from Mammoth Hot Springs with mail on the twenty-eighth reported finding a large Indian trail crossing it, correctly presumed to have been made by the seventy or eighty Indians who shot up Wilson's survey party.

Faced with such evidence of the presence of hostiles in and around the Park, Norris gathered Hayden's topographers and surveyors and took them back to Mammoth Hot Springs with his road crew. There he found a Gatling gun battery that General Brisbin had sent up from Fort Ellis for their defense. It turned out to be unnecessary, for General Nelson A. Miles located the hostile Bannocks on Clarks Fork and attacked them with thirty-five soldiers and seventy-five Crow scouts on September 4, 1878, killing eleven of them. The remainder were captured, with all their horses and camp equipment, at a cost of two attackers killed.

With the capture of the Bannocks, the brief period of warfare in Wonderland was closed. Evidence of the conflict remained for a time along the route of the Nez Perce retreat through the Park—the bones of horses, shreds of cast-off blankets, oddments of clothing, and camp equipment abandoned along the way. A permanent reminder was the road built for General Howard's wagon train. Also, for a time, visitors entering the Park from the east via Clarks Fork passed that pitiful monument made of "bones of men on which were piled stones, and [a] man's breeches thrown over these for a shroud or as a rememberance of the shriveled thing below being human."[21]

Bannock War soldiers at Henrys Lake, 1878. This photograph, taken by Thomas H. Rutter, of Salt Lake City, is sometimes incorrectly used as portraying a military camp in the Lower Geyser Basin of Yellowstone Park.

CHAPTER 9

PIONEERING
IN A PARK

*Norris did the preliminary work with an unselfish
devotion and enthusiasm that shortened his life. In
all that relates to the Yellowstone Park he should be
gratefully remembered.*
                                    —*G. L. Henderson in*
                Yellowstone Park Manual and Guide, *1885*

Superintendent Norris was a pioneer whose life "was spent in
dealing first blows in the subjugation of a primeval wilderness."[1] His were frontier instincts: boundless curiosity and
impatient energy, coupled with a vast indifference to hardships and
hard work, and with that, a streak of Yankee ingenuity and
imagination. He was a kindly, sincere man, whose sense of stewardship had a biblical purity as evident to the mountaineer as it was to the
savant. Admitted to the fellowship of both, he was a natural leader of
the former and a respected colleague of the latter. His weakness was
his view of himself as a pioneer and his desire to be remembered that
way; and through the image he created—a figure in gaudy buckskins,
hurrying through a wilderness without finishing what he set his hand
to—he gave his enemies a way to pull him down.

The best defense of the rough and ready methods used by
Superintendent Norris in the opening of the Park is his lack of fiscal
means. If "money makes the mare to go," Norris had a very small

Superintendent Philetus W. Norris in buckskins (a studio portrait but typical of his dress). From Yellowstone Park Museum collection.

whip. The first appropriation made for Yellowstone National Park was $10,000 for the 1879 fiscal year (available July 1, 1878); and that, with a like amount in fiscal year 1880 and $15,000 each in the two subsequent fiscal years—with some additional allowances for salary and deficiencies—gave him a total of $53,425.17 of appropriated money. Of that amount, approximately $7,500 was for his salary of $1,500 per annum, leaving about $45,925 available for the four working seasons. Thus, he had a little less than $11,500 per year for purchasing equipment and supplies, and hiring men and animals. The marvel is that he accomplished so much with so little.

As soon as funds were available in 1878, Norris organized the party of twenty "well armed, mounted, equipped, resolute and reliable mountaineer laborers" who built the road now identified with his name.[2] This first project was born of military necessity. The Park was threatened with an invasion of hostile Bannock Indians who seemed about to move through the area as the Nez Perces had done the previous summer, and a road connecting Mammoth Hot Springs with the geyser basins on the Firehole River was needed to move troops within the area. It was hastily built (only thirty days of elapsed time for sixty miles of road) and crudely made. Grades were often so steep as to require double teams; stumps were cut just low enough to clear the axle of a Bane wagon; and bone-jolting corduroy was frequently used, but bridges seldom; sidehills were negotiated by laying logs parallel to the roadway on the low side and scraping down a little earth and rock against them. All in all, it was only a fair wagon trail, no more, but a remarkable achievement considering the speed with which it was constructed and its low cost of less than $100 per mile. Norris' reputation as a road builder would have fared better had he subsequently improved this rude track, but he left it essentially as first built.

Norris was almost unable to pay his crew of laborers at the conclusion of the season's work. The funds appropriated for the Park had been deposited in the First National Bank at Bozeman, Montana. Late in August it became evident that the bank was insolvent, and steps were taken to appoint a receiver. This, of course, left Norris temporarily without funds and, though they were ultimately replaced, he was dependent upon the kindness of his friends, the Bottler brothers, to meet the payroll. There is an interesting sidelight to this: the United States grand jury that returned seven indictments against George W. Fox, the president of the bank, noted that at the annual examination of the said bank by the United States Bank Inspector, N. P. Langford, in the year 1877, the books of the said bank would have disclosed, if scanned with ordinary scrutiny, such multiplied evidences of fraud and insolvency as would have required it to be placed in liquidation for the protection of its depositers, creditors and stockholders, and as a just punishment for its disobedience to many provisions of the law regulating its organization and business: and we believe that had this been done when these facts were first discovered from an inspection of the books and papers of said bank, that many losses from which innocent persons are now suffering would have been prevented.

And this Grand Jury further believes that the responsibility of the disaster to the said bank rests largely upon the shoulders of the United States Bank Examiner, as he was evidently guilty of gross neglect of those duties which the law especially directs him to perform in such cases, but which it would appear were totally neglected.[3]

That fall of 1878, Norris helped Jack Baronett rebuild his bridge, burned the previous year by the retreating Nez Perce Indians. Having a knowledge of the millwright's trade, as well as being the kind of person who could build anything, Norris converted the bridge from a simple stringer packtrain bridge to a stout structure with trusses capable of bearing wagon traffic.[4]

During the three seasons subsequent to 1878, Superintendent Norris extended the park roads and trails as shown in the accompanying sketches. In 1879 he built a road to the forks of the Gardner River, that is, to the mouth of present Lava Creek, and also built eastward up Nez Perce Creek along the route of General Howard's military road to Mary Lake. In 1880, he continued this road through Hayden Valley to the vicinity of the Crater Hills, from which a spur was built southward to the outlet of Lake Yellowstone, and a shorter section was built northward to Alum Creek. Much of the effort that summer went into an attempt to find an alternate route that would avoid the many crossings of the Madison River made by the Virginia City road in the canyon below Madison Junction. This effort was spurred by a proposal of the Gilmer & Salisbury Company to establish a mail service into the Park from the west, and of course, the river route was unsatisfactory for stagecoach travel without extensive bridging.

The route that Norris established left the Virginia City road about six miles within the western boundary of the Park at the point where the Riverside mail station would soon be built, and climbed steeply onto the Madison Plateau south of the river. This part of the road was known both as the Norris slide, from its steepness, and as

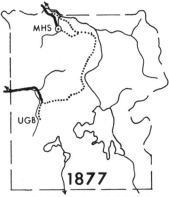

1877

Roads 32 mi.; Trails 108 mi.

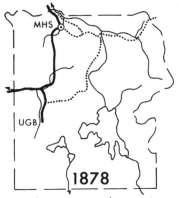

1878

Roads 70 mi.; Trails 97 mi.

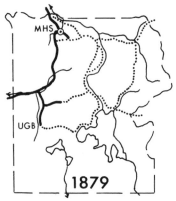

1879

Roads 89 mi.; Trails 222 mi.

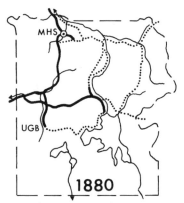

1880

Roads 124 mi.; Trails 191 mi.

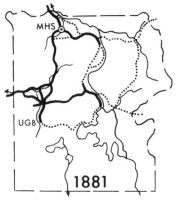

1881

Roads 153 mi.; Trails 204 mi.

DEVELOPMENT
of
ROADS and TRAILS

UGB : Upper Geyser Basin
MHS : Mammoth Hot Springs

1877-1881

the ten pin alley from its high cut stumps. After crossing the relatively flat Madison Plateau this road descended to the junction of Nez Perce Creek and the Firehole River, where it joined the Norris road. This road figured later in the star route mail frauds of 1881.

During his last working season, Superintendent Norris extended his road from the forks of the Gardner River across the Blacktail Deer Plateau, through "the cut" (sometimes called the Devil's Cut or the Devil's Gut), down Elk Creek into the meadows known as Pleasant Valley, and then across the top of Overhanging Cliff to Tower Creek. That was as far as Norris got with this road, which he had intended to build over the Washburn Range by way of Rowland Pass, east of the principal summit of Mount Washburn, and on to a junction with the spur road he had left dangling at Alum Creek beyond the Falls of the Yellowstone. At this time an improvement was made in the original Norris road by building a cut-off from the crossing of Canyon Creek below Gibbon Falls directly over the pine-covered benches to the mouth of Nez Perce Creek, thus avoiding some difficult road down Gibbon River to Madison Junction and up the Firehole River, as well as shortening the distance between Mammoth Hot Springs and the Lower Geyser Basin. A short spur road up Sentinel Creek to the Queen's Laundry Spring completed Norris' road building.

The trail building undertaken by Superintendent Norris was equally ambitious. In 1879 he located a horse trail around the south side of Bunsen Peak very much as the present scenic road goes, and found a new route for a trail over the Washburn Range by way of Rowland Pass. This trail was intended for development as a segment of the road between Tower Creek and the Falls of the Yellowstone, and, in fact, was swathed out by Norris' crews but never graded. Had the road been built along his location, we might not have had the very scenic crossing by way of Dunraven Pass as later built by Captain Chittenden of the Corps of Engineers, though the upper loop of the Park's figure-eight road system would not have differed materially from the form it ultimately took.

Another segment of the Park's future road system, which was sketched in by Superintendent Norris with a trail, made it possible for visitors to go from the Upper Geyser Basin eastward through Norris Pass to the Thumb of Lake Yellowstone, and then around the lake shore to the outlet, where they were again on one of Norris' primitive wagon trails.

The opening of a trail that gave access to much of the east side of the Park was a direct result of an attempt by Superintendent Norris to explore the Hoodoo region just east of the Park in 1878. In company with Adam "Horn" Miller, George Rowland, and others, an attempt was made to reach that region from which Miller had been driven by hostile Indians in 1870; however, signs of Indians in that area, or perhaps just a general edginess resulting from the recent Bannock incursion upon the Park, deterred them from reaching the Hoodoos in 1878.[5] They did lay out a passable trail beginning on the Lamar River near the mouth of Soda Butte Creek and crossing Amethyst Mountain and down Pelican Creek to its entrance into Lake Yellowstone. During the summer of 1879, a trail was opened along that route and connections were made from its terminus on the lake with the Stinkingwater (now Shoshone) River, via Jones Pass, and with the Mud Geyser area by way of the Nez Perce ford.

When Superintendent Norris first took over management of Yellowstone Park there were 32 miles of road and 108 miles of trail within its borders; when he was replaced five years later (less twelve days) there were 153 miles of road and 204 miles of trail. While historian Hiram Chittenden considered Norris' road work ill-conceived and poorly executed, he nevertheless thought it deserving of praise, remarking, "All the difference between poor roads and none at all may justly be placed to his credit."[6] It can also be added that the roads and trails that Norris built had something never before found in the Park—sign boards. At important intersections, and at many named features, he provided wooden sign boards stenciled in black paint, and, while his signs were often criticized as being rather inadequate, it must be remembered that every piece of board he used had to be hauled from Bozeman, Montana, over rough wagon roads, and usually had to be packed on animals for considerable distances.

Superintendent Norris was also a pioneer in the sense that he constructed the Park's first government buildings. He was getting out timber for a headquarters building at Mammoth Hot Springs in 1878 when word was received of the possibility of troubles with the Bannock Indians; so he put aside that project for the season in order to build the Norris road. In 1879, construction of the headquarters building was continued. Norris had picked a site dictated more by its defensible nature than by convenience. Apprehensive of future Indian raids, he could see only the exposed summit of that pile of glacial gravels now called Capitol Hill, and it was there that work was begun in 1879.

Of this structure, Superintendent Norris says:

> By hewing the timber and making the shingles upon the mountain terraces and hauling them to the site upon the mound, we had, during

The Norris blockhouse on Capitol Hill, Mammoth Hot Springs. From Yellowstone Park Museum collection.

"Colonel P. W. Norris and Party Entering the Upper Fire Hole Basin, Yellowstone National Park, with the first wagon ever there. August 30, 1878." W. H. Jackson photograph.

July, erected in first-class manner a block-house 40 by 18 feet, two tall
stories high, with, for use as well as safety from mountain storms, substantial block-house leantos or wings upon three of the sides, and an
8-foot balcony to both stories of the other fronting the active hot spring
terraces. Upon the main building is an octagon turret or gun-room, 9
feet in diameter and 10 feet high, well loop-holed for rifles, and all sur-
mounted by a national flag 53 feet from the ground, upon a fine flag-
staff or liberty-pole passing from a solid foundation through and
sustaining all the stories, turret, and roof thereof.[7]

Though the Norris blockhouse was razed in 1909, evidences remain.
A short walk from the Jupiter Terrace parking area will take one onto
the west end of Capitol Hill, where the foundation stones and
partially filled-in cellar, with the butt of the flag pole mentioned by
Norris still firmly set in its center, can yet be seen within a patch of tall
rye grass.

This headquarters fortress was later given such necessary
appurtenances as a barn, a smithy, and an open reservoir on the
divide to the west, where water from the terraces was impounded for
domestic use. There was also a pasture, south of Capitol Hill,
enclosed by nearly two miles of "Montana fence," and a garden on the
bank of the Gardner River where Matthew McGuirk located before
the Park was established. But the combination of a short growing
season and frequent vandalism made the garden less profitable than
Norris had hoped it might be.

The same summer that the Norris blockhouse was built at
Mammoth Hot Springs, a party of Norris' men constructed a
"loopholed, earth roofed log house" in the Upper Geyser Basin. This
building, on the bank of the Firehole River between Castle and Lion
geysers, had a good stone chimney, and Norris put in a supply of
firewood with the intention of remaining there at least part of the
winter to study the geysers; but, "finding the sulphur-charged
condensed steam and fogs of the Geyser Basin were too suffocating to
long endure, and that the unusual deep snows had seriously blocked
the passes and gorged the Madison and other streams in their
canyons, the project was reluctantly abandoned."[8]

A blacksmith shop was built in the Lower Geyser Basin in the
woods very near where the highway now crosses Nez Perce Creek, but
the most unusual building of all was erected several miles to the west
of that point, in the valley of Sentinel Creek, at a hot spring feature
that Norris named the Queen's Laundry. There, a two-room bathhouse with an earth-covered, puncheon roof was begun in the fall of
1881. The end of work that fall found the building yet unfinished and,
as Norris was replaced before the next season, work on the building

was never resumed. This peculiar little structure still stands on the sinter slope below the Queen's Laundry Spring. The roof has fallen in, but the wall logs have become so heavily impregnated with mineral from the hot spring waters, during the intervening years, that they remain quite sound. One room had evidently been fitted up for bathing, as there is evidence of a trough for leading hot water in through the rear wall, but the other room was never completed; in fact, the doorway into it was never cut out. And there the Queen's Laundry bathhouse stands today, an interesting relic of the administration of the Park's second superintendent, and the first government building constructed specifically for the use of the public in any national park.[9]

While much of the exploration accomplished by Superintendent Norris had for its objective finding suitable routes of travel within the Park, some of his wanderings served only to satisfy his scientific curiosity. Such was his successful exploration of the Hoodoo basin in the year 1880, guided by Adam "Horn" Miller and accompanied by Henry Bird Calfee, the Bozeman photographer; his assistant, William H. Parker, who, as "Professor" Parker, later lectured for Calfee at presentations of his stereopticon show built around views that he took in the Park; and two of Norris' employees, George Rowland and another man known only as Handford. The party not only found the weird erosional features that so resemble those in the Garden of the Gods near Denver, Colorado, but also found the decaying lodge poles of a large Indian encampment which Norris estimated to have included as many as forty lodges with, among their decaying remains, evidences of what was assumed to have been plunder taken on forays in previous years. Names given at this time that remain on the map, in addition to Hoodoo Creek, Hoodoo Basin, and Hoodoo Mountain, are Calfee Creek, Miller Creek, and Parker Mountain.[10] Norris discovered Sylvan Pass in 1881, and though he claimed many other discoveries, most of these features were already known before his time. However, he was responsible for giving names to many of the features in the Park. In addition to those already listed, place names of his that remain in use are: Rustic Falls, Monument Geyser Basin, Beaver Lake, Obsidian Mountain, Excelsior Geyser, and several immortalizing himself. This egoistic tendency was not lost on park visitors, one of whom offered the following instructions for getting out of the geyser basins:

> Take the Norris wagon road and follow down the Norris fork of the Firehole River to the Norris Canyon of the Norris Obsidian Mountain; then go on to Mount Norris, on the summit of which you will find

Monument Park or the Norris Blowout, and at its northerly base the
Norris Basin and Park. Further on you will come to the Norris Geyser
plateau, and must not fail to see Geyser Norris. The Norris Falls of the
Gibbon are worth a visit. The next point of interest is the Gibbon, half a
day's ride from the Norris Hot Springs.[11]

While the foregoing is certainly overdrawn, it does not stand alone.
Another visitor complained that Norris "has honored the park by
bestowing his lordly name upon numerous attractions . . . Mount
Norris, Norris Geyser Basin, Norris Fork of the Gibbon, Norris cut
off, Norris Obsidian-glass Road, Norris Plateau, Norris Geyser,
Norris Museum, Norris Paint-Pot, Norris Falls, Norris Pass, Norris
Pile Spring,"[12] and there was the newspaper man who said that he
thought that he had come to see the Yellowstone Park, but found he
was "simply paying a visit to 'Norris Park.' "[13] But Norris should be
forgiven for this foible.

The pioneer in Superintendent Norris opened the Yellowstone
Park, providing it with an indispensable minimum of roads, trails, and
buildings; but the scientist in his nature was equally important to the
area. His curiosity in this regard was limitless. He observed a total
eclipse of the sun from the summit of Sepulcher Mountain on July 29,
1878, and kept a meteorological record that is the beginning of the
Park's weather records; he began the recording of geyser eruptions,
being the first to note a relation between thermal activity and the
occurrence of earthquake tremors; and he collected assiduously for
the Smithsonian Institution in Washington, D.C., in one instance
shipping an entire geyser cone for display there. Yet, his scientific
interest in the thermal features also took a practical turn in several
instances. Coming to the conclusion that the Liberty Cap, at
Mammoth Hot Springs, was in danger of toppling, he had it braced
with timbers; and similarly concluding that the scabrous appearance
of the Devil's Thumb was evidence of its deterioration from lack of
rejuvenating hot spring waters, he built a trough to convey water to its
top from nearby springs. Norris was very much concerned about the
wildlife in the Park, particularly in the obvious decline of its
ungulates, and this led him to initiate the first wildlife management
undertaken in the area.

It is in the fields of history and prehistory that Norris accomplished most. Not only did he record many interesting facts he had
learned from prospectors with whom he was constantly associated,
thus preserving an invaluable record of their activities in the
Yellowstone region during the mining era of the sixties, but he also
related his observations to historic sources. As an archeologist,

Norris was entirely self-taught and was an amazingly competent observer in a day when the science of archeology was less than a decade old. He recognized evidences of prehistoric occupation of the Yellowstone country (clearly differentiating between those evidences and traces of modern Indians in the area). In this field, too, he was an indefatigable collector, shipping to the Smithsonian Institution artifacts that included fragments of soapstone cooking pots, *atl-atl* weights, hide scrapers, and stone knives, lance heads, and projectile points.

Something of the enthusiasm with which Superintendent Norris worked for science can be seen in the instructions he gave his road crews in 1881. Addressing his "mountain comrades," he said:

> While labor in the construction of roads and bridal paths will be our main object, still, with trifling care and effort, much valuable knowledge may be obtained of the regions visited, especially by the hunters and scouts, all of which, including the discovery of mountain passes, geysers, and other hot springs, falls and fossil forests, are to be promptly reported to the leader of each party.
>
> As all civilized nations are now actively pushing explorations and researches for evidences of prehistoric peoples, careful scrutiny is required of all material handled in excavations; and all arrow, spear, or lance heads, stone axes, and knives, or other weapons, utensils or ornaments; in short, all such objects of interest are to be regularly retained and turned over daily to the officer in charge of each party for transmittal to the National Museum in Washington.[14]

Norris' interest in prehistoric things was not restricted to the Park. By continuing his investigations northward along the Yellowstone Valley into Montana Territory, Norris gained the particular distinction of being Montana's first archeologist.[15] Fittingly, it was archeology—the investigations of the mound builders of the Mississippi Valley—which occupied the last years of his life.

The garrulous reports in which Superintendent Norris detailed the opening of the Park, his explorations, and his scientific investigations also contained many suggestions, practical and otherwise, for the management of Yellowstone Park. Knowing the difficulty of administering an area not wholly within one legal jurisdiction, Norris was an early advocate of what was later to become the troublesome segregation issue. (Segregation in this case refers to the elimination from the Park of lands considered to be unnecessarily contained within its boundaries.) Norris advocated eliminating those areas lying north and west of the boundaries of Wyoming Territory, a two and one-half-mile strip on the north and a three-mile strip on the west. He was at first inclined to this view through the fact that the mining region on

Clarks Fork was thought to be included in the "Montana strip," and also that everything north of the forty-fifth degree of latitude eastward from the Yellowstone River was already a part of the Crow Indian Reservation. Thus, he proposed to get rid of both problems at the same time, though he preferred to have all the Park treated as a part of Montana Territory for judicial purposes.[16] Later, he changed his mind concerning the matter of legal jurisdiction, advocating the inclusion of the Park in a county of Wyoming Territory and the use of Wyoming law.[17] Unfortunately, just such an expedient finally was resorted to, with disastrous results for the Park.

In his first report (for the year 1877), Superintendent Norris made a recommendation that eventually flowered into the first game management program undertaken on any federal land. He had been so appalled by reports of the wanton slaughter of elk, deer, antelope, and big horn sheep, which reached him in the Park in 1875, that he proposed saving the remaining bands of animals by turning the northeast corner of the Park, particularly the grassy valley of the Lamar River, into a great game preserve where "two or three spirited, intelligent herdsmen might (in addition to profitably rearing domestic animals) also thoroughly protect and, by capture of the young, gradually domesticate any desired number of them."[18] This proposal resulted in the employment of Harry Yount as gamekeeper on June 21, 1880. A cabin was built for Yount in the angle between Soda Butte Creek and the upper Lamar River, and there "Rocky Mountain Harry" spent a solitary winter among the herds he was somehow supposed to singlehandedly protect. In the well-written report that accompanied his resignation the following fall, he commented:

> I do not think that any one man appointed by the honorable Secretary, and specificly designated as a gamekeeper, is what is needed or can prove effective for certain necessary purposes, but a small and reliable police force of men, employed when needed, during good behavior, and dischargable for cause by the superintendent of the park, is what is really the most practicable way of seeing that the game is protected from wanton slaughter, the forests from careless use of fire, and the enforcement of all the other laws, rules, and regulations for the protection and improvement of the park.[19]

Although Norris very early recommended hotel facilities for the visiting public at the canyon, at the outlet of Yellowstone Lake, and in the Upper Geyser Basin, as well as at Mammoth Hot Springs, only one such development appeared during his superintendency, and that was in connection with a mail route and stage line opened from Virginia City into the Lower Geyser Basin in the fall of 1880. As the

Harry Yount, the Park's gamekeeper under Superintendent Norris. From
Yellowstone Park Museum collection.

park terminus of the "Virginia City and Hot Springs line," George
Marshall had built that summer a facility described as a fine shingle-
roofed mail station and hotel, with barn and outbuildings, situated on
a cold rivulet at the foot of the cliffs just west of the forks of the
Firehole River. Mrs. Carrie Adell Strahorn, who claims to have been
a passenger on the first stage to come through on that line early in
October, admits to a twinge of disappointment when she saw the
unfinished little log house.

> Next morning there was an early review of our surroundings; the log
> house was far from being finished, and the part we occupied was parti-
> tioned off with a canvas wagon cover. The second floor was only partly
> laid, and a window or two was missing in the upper part while the
> unfilled chinks between the logs allowed the rigorous October breezes
> to fan us at will. At that time the office and sitting room and dining
> room were one, and a single stove did its best toward heating the whole
> house.[20]

Rude and unfinished though it was, George Marshall and his wife,
Sarah, lived there through the cold, snowy winter that followed, and it
was there that the first white child was born in Yellowstone Park, January 30, 1881. Her father claimed that she was named Rose Park by
Governor John W. Hoyt of Wyoming Territory; " 'Rose' because
roses were scarce in the Park and 'Park' because she was born in
same."[21]

The stage line was an early casualty of the great star route mail
fraud scandal, but George Marshall hung on in the Park in the hope of
obtaining a franchise for a hotel at that point. His encouragement in
this came about during the summer of 1880, when a party including
Secretary of the Interior Carl Schurz was forced to camp out in the
Lower Geyser Basin on a rainy night. The following morning the
secretary, in conversation with Marshall, stated that he would have
given $20 to have gotten into a house that night, and he suggested that
Marshall should prepare to keep travelers, and promised him a lease
for erecting a hotel.[22] George Marshall did eventually get his lease,
but it was never profitable to him and he finally sold his interest.

McCartney's hotel at Mammoth Hot Springs seems never to
have really recovered from the impact of two Indian wars. Jim tried to
operate by subletting the hotel to others, but that expedient was
satisfactory only in the summer of 1881, when the hotel was managed
by Mrs. James Jobb, and we may presume that James McCartney
had already been evicted from his claim at the Mammoth Hot
Springs, for Superintendent Norris proceeded to tear down four of
the five buildings on it, and the hotel building was used by the
government after that year.[23]

Other suggestions made by Norris for licensing guides and developing concessions within the Park were long ignored. Indeed, events already maturing in 1881 made any such orderly development an impossibility: the Park had attracted the interest of several monopolistic groups.

The Northern Pacific Railroad, which had much to do with the creation of Yellowstone National Park, had intended to take advantage of its preferential situation as soon as the main line was extended to the vicinity of the Park. The panic of 1873, however, by halting all further railroad expansion for a time, delayed the Northern Pacific's attempt to take over Wonderland. In 1879 the railroad was able to resume construction, building 125 miles of track across Dakota Territory from the town of Bismarck, and the following year, under the presidency of Frederick Billings, the railroad took up its former interests, among them the long delayed park project.[24]

Meanwhile, J. Gould had gained control of the Union Pacific Railroad system, which, by 1878, included the Utah & Northern narrow gauge railway struggling northward from Ogden toward Montana. With rails laid to Beaver Canyon by late fall, and with excellent prospects for entering Montana the following season, the Union Pacific management saw an opportunity to beat the Northern Pacific to the Yellowstone Wonderland by building a branch line from Virginia City into the Park from the west. Consequently the Berthold party of Union Pacific Railroad surveyors was sent to find a suitable route up the Madison River to the geyser basins, which they did. On a map included with his report for the year 1879, Superintendent Norris showed this preliminary location. His obvious enthusiasm for the possible railroad connection from the west did not set well in the town of Bozeman, Montana, which knew its best interests to coincide with those of the Northern Pacific Railroad.

Superintendent Norris probably would have been forgiven that indiscretion, (particularly since the Utah Northern had turned instead from Dillon toward Butte, ruling out for the moment a branch line into the Park) had he not blundered again. A weekly mail service between Bozeman and Mammoth Hot Springs, via Hayden and Chico in the Yellowstone Valley, had been authorized in July 1874 but had not proved satisfactory to residents of the upper Yellowstone Valley. In response to their requests for better service, Montana's delegate to Congress took up the matter in 1879. As a result, Congress suspended the service in favor of a new route from Camp Brown, Wyoming Territory, through the Park to Bozeman. Superintendent Norris first learned of the change when he was approached by G. W. Nelson, a stage driver who had bid on the route as a "dummy" for the Gilmer & Salisbury stage line, and who, as the nominal contractor, wanted Norris to find a mountaineer willing to carry the mail over the 200-mile route through uninhabited country. Such a man could not be found for less than $10,000 and the route from Camp Brown was therefore represented as impracticable, the contractor suggesting an alternate route from the Utah & Northern station at Red Rock, by way of Henrys Lake and Lower Geyser Basin to Mammoth Hot Springs and Bozeman. As the service was represented as operating in connection with a line to be operated by Gilmer & Salisbury, both Superintendent Norris and the postmaster at Bozeman endorsed the idea, but only on the basis of weekly service, and that in the summertime.

Norris was understandably surprised when, on meeting Mr. O. J. Salisbury in the Park early in July, 1880, he learned the contract had been let for daily service, year round, from Red Rock to Mammoth Hot Springs, and that Mr. Salisbury was checking the route and arranging facilities for his mail carriers. Though he did not approve of the arrangement, Norris accompanied Mr. Salisbury back through the Park to select sites for mail stations. They chose three: one at the site of the present Norris soldier station, another in the Lower Geyser Basin near the mouth of Nez Perce Creek, a third on the Madison River about four miles inside the western park boundary. They decided the old Virginia City stage route, with its many fordings of the Madison River below its junction with the Gibbon, was impracticable, and Norris located an alternate route across the Madison Plateau from the Riverside mail station directly to the Lower Geyser Basin.[25]

While Norris was laboring on this stage road with his force of thirty men, two wagons, and a pack train, the Red Rock to Mammoth Hot Springs mail route was abandoned as impractical; the contractor sought a further change to service between Virginia City and Mammoth Hot Springs.[26] Once in operation, the Virginia City and Mammoth Hot Springs route worked a hardship on tourists who had expected to reach the Park by stagecoach from the Utah & Northern line. The editor of the Bozeman newspaper called it "a great wrong to the travelling public."[27] The new route was too much for the people of Bozeman; they read into it a sinister design. As the Bozeman editor put it, "J. Gould proposes to head off the Northern Pacific," and he informed his readers by way of a letter from a park tourist that Norris "is engaged in building a stage road to the Madison River for Gilmer and Salisbury, mail contractors, and the money is being thus used that was appropriated by Congress for the purpose of improving and keeping open the roads . . . does this mean subsidy or insanity?" As an afterthought, he added that the superintendent and contractor "seem to be running this particular line to please themselves."[28]

Superintendent Norris was thus labeled an ally of Virginia City interests, and the Bozeman press was hostile to him from then on, seizing every opportunity to attack his work and his character. The following letter of October 13, 1880, from Norris to Assistant Secretary Bell is revealing:

> My ever true friend
> No mails upon the Henry Lake route for several days nor do the local contractors here show much signs of a purpose to carry it this winter, so I write this hasty note & send by man going to Bozeman with the mail. I have not replied to newspaper attacks as I firstly knew little of them having been active in my duties in the mountains and second deemed them casual but from the reply made by the editor of the Bozeman paper to a prominent merchant of that place, who upon return of a tour of the park and remonstrating with him as to those false statements in regard to myself and the park received as I learned the reply that if I was allowed to publish another report I would become too popular for removal and as he is not the man *we* want there, strong influences are organizing for his removal and of this fact I am daily more aware, although never before so popular with the mass of the people here as now.
> I now only write to you this intention so that you may defer action upon any move that may be made in the interest of ex-marshall Wheeler or others until I explain who it is that desires my removal and why— which I will soon furnish even if our daily mail stops because Stevens will not falsly swear to mail reports sent prepared for that purpose—and I refuse to become a member of a syndicate for absorption of the best hotel and other sites in the park.
> I desire this *confidential* to all save the honorable Secretary if deemed necessary.[29]

In that letter, both horns of Norris' dilemma are exposed. On the one hand, he was considered a friend of Virginia City interests because he had rendered such service to the mail contractor as he thought it his duty in order that the mail should go through; for that supposed alliance he was under attack and marked for removal from the superintendency. On the other hand, he had no friends at Virginia City either because of his refusal to protect the scheming mail contractor. And further, since that contractor was but one link in a gigantic fraud that reached to the very top of the Post Office Department, his obstinacy was politically dangerous and would have inevitably cost him some support even if he had not set about exposing the swindle.

Whether or not Norris was aiming too high when he wrote to the *New York Tribune* describing his particular specimen of unnecessary and costly mail service is something that cannot be determined now; however, he helped to publicize the whole star route fraud. The swindle worked this way: When a new mail route was to be established, persons in collusion with Assistant Postmaster Brady would make a ridiculously low bid, usually through a "dummy," and the contract would be let on that basis. Then the contractor would "discover" certain conditions that made it impossible for him to fulfill his contract at the figure he had bid and would request more money. By arranging several such required changes it was possible to bloat the contract figure to magnificent proportions. In the case of the Virginia City to Mammoth Hot Springs star route, the cost of the service reached $20,000, of which one-quarter went to the expeditors. So widespread was this practice in the West that Brady and his confederates made a fortune before their dishonest practice was halted.

The newspaper campaign against Superintendent Norris was, at first, merely critical of his road building; but in that he was fairly well supported. There were those who would testify that Norris had been neither idle nor remiss and that too much had been expected from too small an appropriation;   among these, no less a person than Lieutenant General Philip H. Sheridan said: "Mr. Norris, the Superintendent of the park, is doing a good work in making wagon roads to the principal points of interest and trails to the less important ones."[30] Failing to make headway in the matter of Norris' road building, his detractors turned to magnifying eccentricities of his character and to intimations that he considered himself above the law in "Norris Park." He was accused of slaughtering more game than anyone else, of being strict against the carrying away of specimens, at the same time shipping off "tons" of curiosities for his own cabinet, and of allowing tourists to wantonly destroy geysers and hot springs "without let or hinderance." He was presented as eccentric in appearance, wearing

> A broad-brimed white hat, looped up at the side and decorated with an eagle's feather. Long white hair reached far down upon his brawny shoulders; a white waving beard ornamented his breast. He wore a buckskin hunting shirt, decked with long, flowing fringe. He wore a belt full of cartridges, and had a revolver hanging at his side. He also carried a hunting knife. He swung a tomahawk in his hand. He rode a gallant steed. I was struck with awe.[31]

Fun was poked at Norris' poetic efforts, which were not very good, but not as bad as the following would hint. According to this little fabrication, one of Norris' workmen reported finding in a hot spring the petrified remains of a soldier "with his musket at right shoulder shift, Hardie's tactics," whose demise was attributed to his desperate attempt to avoid hearing any more of Norris' poetry. The editor of the Bozeman newspaper commented that "placing the work and appropriations in the hands of an old rattle brain whose highest ambition appears to be writing doggerel verses and stocking private cabinets and museums is worse than child's play."[32] He later concluded that, since Colonel Norris was the greatest curiosity in the Park, a subscription should be taken up to buy "a sign board 'well painted and lettered,' that might be permanently affixed to some prominent part of his body," adding, "seriously, isn't it about time a suitable superintendent was appointed . . . rather than retain the present incumbent who makes himself the laughing stock of everybody he meets?"[33]

This maliciousness had a purpose: to get rid of a superintendent who was considered inimical to the plans of certain persons for Yellowstone National Park. In August 1881, as the Northern Pacific track approached Miles City, Montana, word began to circulate that an eastern company contemplated applying for hotel locations in the Park.[34] Simultaneously, three Bozeman men—Peter Koch, Walter Cooper, and G. W. Wakefield—organized the Bozeman and National Park Railway, which was a paper corporation. Through it they hoped to control a branch line to the geyser basins by way of the West Gallatin River at such time as the Northern Pacific Railroad should reach the town of Bozeman. This group later reorganized as the Yellowstone Park Railroad, but their hopes were dashed by a St. Paul dispatch that announced:

> Six prominent capitalists of St. Paul & Minneapolis, including Senator Windom, J. B. Gillfillen, of Minneapolis, E. H. Bly, of Bismarck, and Mr. Hobart, of the Northern Pacific, have agreed with the Northern Pacific to build a railroad, standard gauge, from the point on the Northern Pacific nearest the park, to the geysers and Yellowstone Park; or, to speak more definitely, forty miles of road outside of the government park reservation and forty miles within it, the cost to be $420,000 per mile, and allowing for contingencies, nearly $2,000,000. Sixty thousand dollars are to be put up by the six as an earnest of good faith, and the Northern Pacific will then furnish the money to build and equip the road, taking a mortgage as security. The six men will build a large hotel, being assured by the Government of a monopoly therein. A large influx of summer visitors is expected annually.[35]

The Bozeman group that had served the Northern Pacific so well by discrediting Superintendent Norris was written off the following week when C. T. Hobart disavowed any connection with them, stating that the "Northern Pacific will construct its own branch line." He meant that a decision had been reached to build to the Park by way of the Yellowstone River from Benson's Landing rather than up the West Gallatin from Bozeman, and arrangements were begun for Location Engineer Grant to begin a preliminary survey for a park branch line by way of the Yellowstone River.[36]

Meanwhile, Superintendent Norris continued to complain of an organized raid on the Park, in one instance stating "the land sharks who propose this have threatened to have the superintendent of the park, who has already protested against the action discharged," to which the editor of the Bozeman newspaper demurely replied, "Nobody, either east or west ever dreamed of jumping the national park except Norris. From the first he has acted as though he has had a life lease of the entire reservation."[37] But Superintendent Norris was essentially right; a scheme to take over Yellowstone Park had nearly matured and so had proceedings to get the incumbent superintendent discharged. A week later, his "life lease" on the Park was terminated by the announcement that he would be succeeded by Mr. P.H. Conger of Iowa. In commenting on the impending change, the editor of the Bozeman newspaper stated: "One of his delusions was that Senator Conger was one of his staunch supporters."[38] It was all too true. Omar D. Conger, as a representative and senator from the state of Michigan, had been a chief supporter of Superintendent Norris, but he was also a railroad man and he had a brother who needed patronage; so Norris was replaced on March 31, 1882, by Patrick Henry Conger.

Somewhat anticlimactic to the story of Norris' regime, but very revealing, is an article titled "Save the National Park from Ruin," which appeared in the *New York Sun*, under the name of Samuel Wilkeson, secretary of the Northern Pacific Railroad Company. In it he attacked the ex-superintendent in a manner so savage as to be almost unbelievable, particularly as it could serve no purpose unless, of course, the railroad felt the need to justify, after the fact, the action it had taken against an able and honorable man.[39]

CHAPTER 10

PETERFUNK'S GHOST

*We are led to infer that Peterfunk Windy Norris'
cake is dough; in other words he has gone where the
woodbine twineth; or to speak plainly, he has received the grand bounce. It is extremely sad . . .
Good-by Peter. Farewell Windy. We shall never
look upon thy like again.*
—Bozeman Avant Courier
January 26, 1882

The editor who wrote the foregoing was right about one thing:
Yellowstone Park would not see the like of Superintendent
Norris for some time—or, more precisely, not during the
four years and nearly five months covering the superintendencies of
his three civilian successors. Patrick Henry Conger, the man who took
Norris' place on April 1, 1882, was described as of strong intellect and
ripe experience in business affairs.[1] But the editor would soon find
out how far astray his first impression had taken him. The "Major"
(his was a purely honorific title earned during his superintendency of
the Sioux Indian Reservation at Yankton, Dakota Territory) had
character flaws which became all too evident in the course of his
tenure in the Park. Historian Chittenden has noted:

Of this Superintendent, it need only be said that his administration was throughout characterized by a weakness and inefficency which brought the Park to the lowest ebb of its fortunes, and drew forth the severe condemnation of visitors and public officials alike.[2]

Conger's trouble was that he was one of those persons who made promises easily and as easily disavowed them; he was petty in his relations with his subordinate employees, feuding with them often; and he lacked the courage to enforce rules and regulations, even when he was under direct orders to do so. Add to that an ossified political outlook, and he was hardly the man for the job.

Following the removal of Superintendent Norris, his able and loyal assistant, Clarence M. Stephens, remained in the Park serving as its acting superintendent. Stephens evidently did not relish the turn of events and on May 18 he wrote the secretary of the interior requesting that he be replaced as soon as possible.[3] The secretary sent Conger a blunt order to proceed at once to the Park,[4] an unnecessary order as the superintendent was already on his way.

Conger arrived in the Park on May 22, by way of the Utah & Northern Railroad and the stage line to Virginia City, from whence he proceeded by private conveyance to the geyser basins. He came accompanied by his son, Cassius M. Conger, and George Graham, a blacksmith he hired at Virginia City. Of their arrival at park headquarters late at night, Conger says: "All was dark and silent, but we soon made ourselves heard. A light gleamed through the windows, the door was thrown open, and we were invited in by Mr. Stephens, the superintendent in charge, with a generous cordiality seldom found elsewhere than in these mountains."[5]

Mr. George L. Henderson, Stephens' replacement, arrived at park headquarters early in June. He came with his grown son, Walter J., and four daughters, Helen L., Jennie H., Barbara G., and Mary R., by way of the Northern Pacific Railroad to its terminus near Miles City, Montana, and from there by wagon to the Park.[6] Henderson's first impression of Conger was good. He says: "I was much pleased to find that the superintendent had not only a good library, but was well posted on literary matters . . . he did me the honor to invite me to take what books I might choose to read."[7] However, he soon became aware of the exaggerated animus that Conger held for his predecessor, Norris, and "all who spoke of him with respect. His ill will was manifestly shown to all old employees who had been under Norris."[8]

Superintendent Conger immediately did what Norris had too long neglected; he put crews to work on the roads: bridging, removing rocks and stumps, easing the grades a little here and there, and providing drains and corduroying. The editor of the Bozeman newspaper could soon remark that returning tourists "concur in the opinion that Major Conger is 'the right man in the right place.' "[9] Though Conger hinted at considerable new construction, his contribution during more than two years in office was limited to bridging the Gardner River and in extending the road from Alum Creek, in Hayden Valley, northward along the Yellowstone River to the Upper Fall; otherwise, what roadwork he did was merely improvement.

While Superintendent Conger's report for 1882 was, as he said, "prosy" in regard to his maintenance work, he was too brief about some of the important happenings of that summer. The notable junket of General Philip H. Sheridan that year (his second such in the Park) received no more notice than a listing of names; yet, it was the Sheridan party, with its 150 men and 300 horses and mules, that cut the first trail up Snake River from Jackson Hole to the Thumb of Lake Yellowstone. The Sheridan trail, as it was called, served as a useful thoroughfare until a road was at last built in August 1895. The superintendent failed to mention that this party was charged with carelessly allowing their fires to burn over considerable areas of the Park—15,000 acres, if we can accept a newspaper estimate.[10] Jack Baronett, who was waiting in the geyser basins to conduct Sheridan's party through the Park and out by way of Clarks Fork, witnessed a number of powerful eruptions of the great geyser that Norris had named Excelsior, and took the liberty of renaming it Sheridan Geyser in the general's honor. The new name did not stick, however.

Superintendent Conger had no way of knowing, of course, just how important General Sheridan's visit was to become in the history of the Park. Upon reaching "civilization" near the mouth of Clarks Fork, Sheridan came upon construction parties of the Northern Pacific Railroad, and the construction superintendent obligingly took the general to the Billings town site, twelve miles to the east, in the caboose of a work train. It was there, at the end of the track, that General Sheridan received the news of which he says: "I regretted exceedingly to learn that the national park had been rented out to private parties."[11]

That was the first intimation of the actual plans of the men who were to become known corporately as the Yellowstone Park Improvement Company. This was the very development Norris was protesting at the time he was removed from the superintendency. Public announcement had merely stated that "a couple of Dakota men are negotiating, with fair prospects of success, with Acting Secretary Joslyn, of the Interior Department, for the necessary ground in . . . the Yellowstone National Park, upon which to construct roadways and erect hotels and other buildings for the accommodation and convenience of visitors."[12] There was nothing too bad in that—until the terms of the agreement began to appear. The arrangement called for the company to pay a rental not to exceed $2 per acre for the land occupied in the Park, which was to include tracts of 640 acres (a square mile) at each of the seven most desirable sites in the Park. The lessees were to have the privilege of cutting timber for telegraph poles and fuel and were to be granted such favorable lands within the Park as they might need for raising vegetables and forage. The contract was to be between the secretary of the interior and Messrs. H. F. Douglas of Fort Yates and C. T. Hobart of Fargo, the latter representing a joint stock company with a board of directors of twenty-five persons, including Roscoe Conkling, a New York lawyer; Rufus Hatch, a retired New York banker; and a good many others (five lawyers, four merchants, two bankers, four capitalists, one civil engineer, one ex-commissioner of the General Land Office, one president of a steamship line, one Northern Pacific Railroad division superintendent, one editor, one judge of the Supreme Court, one artist, one manufacturer, and one stock broker).[13] It was made evident by the same source that Mr. Hobart was kingpin of the operation and was to be both construction superintendent for the proposed Northern Pacific branch line into the Park and vice-president of the improvement company. The other key person was Mr. Hatch, who had been brought into the project for the particular purpose of furnishing $500,000 in capital to begin the work. But while such things were being talked of, and before this "syndicate" had a properly executed lease in hand, two steam sawmills and a shingle mill had arrived at the end of track and were awaiting transportation to the Park.[14]

This nefarious scheme can best be explained in the words of the editor of *Forest and Stream,* who later wrote:

At first its promoters, if their own story was to be believed, were working solely and simply for the interests of the people of this country. They related with tears in their eyes most heartrending stories of the slaughter of game, and told about the destruction of geysers and other natural wonders. It is true that none of these statements were very new, for all that they spoke of had been going on for years, and was perfectly well known to every man who kept himself at all informed as to what is taking place in the Park, but they talked about "vandals," and quite made it appear to people ignorant of the subject that they were acting almost entirely from philanthropic motives. It is true that they mentioned incidentally that they wished in return for the benefits that they were going to confer upon the people, to have a monopoly of the hotel, stage and telegraph privileges in the Park, but they said that this would be a small matter, and that they would really scarcely pay expenses. A little later it appeared that they were to charge for the guides and the horses which tourists would require while in the park, and were to have the sole right to all timber and arable lands; and now we are told quite as a matter of course that this company is going into the cattle business, and that the Park, which has been set apart for the people, is to be turned into a big stock range for the benefit and behoof of the Yellowstone Park Improvement Company. Truly the modesty of these monopolists is startling, but not more so than the meekness with which the people endure this monstrous invasion of their rights.[15]

Of such grave matters Superintendent Conger gave bare passing notice in his annual report, and of another development of considerable import he said nothing. Only a few days after Conger received his appointment, an old-timer by the name of John Yancey sold his one-third interest in a partially developed mine on Crevice Mountain for a rather good figure and moved into the Park to settle on the road between Mammoth Hot Springs and Cooke City in that attactive little vale known as Pleasant Valley.[16] While his squatting in the Park may not have had prior approval, "Uncle John" was nevertheless allowed to remain, and very likely he had oral permission from Superintendent Conger, as had those other squatters—Cutler and Jackson in the Lamar Valley, and Tate and Scott near Soda Butte. These entries were to become thorny issues.

Things were happening outside the Park as well. As the main line of the Northern Pacific Railroad advanced rapidly up the Yellowstone Valley, the little town of Clark City, which stood three miles west of Benson's Landing, was rechristened Livingston in honor of Johnston Livingston, a director of the Northern Pacific Railroad Company.[17] By the end of November the new town boasted 130 houses and tents, of which ten or twelve were considered to be quite respectable. Among the total there were six hotels and restaurants, four stores, five feed stables, two butcher shops, two wholesale liquor houses, thirty saloons, and a lumber yard; the population of the place was estimated to be 600. Being a railroad town, that is, on railroad property, the Northern Pacific surveyors had laid it out parallel to the main line so that the streets, as surveyed, crossed the existing streets of old Clark City on a diagonal, causing confusion in regard to property lines and rights.

The railroad's surveyors had been active through most of 1882, running a preliminary line up the Yellowstone River from Benson's Landing to the geyser basins and down the West Gallatin to

Bozeman. In the course of this work the party discovered a beautiful geyser with a large cone and many vents, in the woods about four miles south of Old Faithful. Assuming that they were its discoverers, they gave it the name Lone Star Geyser, and shortly after, they told photographer Frank J. Haynes of their find and he photographed it, selling views under that name until the original designation was displaced.[18] Actually, this was the geyser the Hayden Survey had named Solitary in 1871.

During the summer of 1882 a wagon road was built through the first canyon and into Paradise Valley, connecting the upper Yellowstone Valley with the site of the new town of Livingston. The road, which was known as the Blue Hill grade, was far from easy to negotiate and was the scene of a good many upsets. Legend has it that one of these accidents involved a wagon loaded with kegs of whiskey, which rolled down into the Yellowstone River. The kegs were too heavy to get back up the hill to the road, so the teamsters are said to have done the next best thing: they camped there until they had emptied the contents. Also that summer, the nondescript "ranch" that James C. McCartney had located at the mouth of the Gardner River in 1879, when he was put out of the Park by Superintendent Norris, became a scene of activity. A post office by the name of Gardiner had been established February 9, 1880,[19] and Surveyor Panton, who passed that way in March, 1882, says:

> We met Jim Gardiner at his settlement. He told us that he had located a homestead of 160 acres, including Mammoth Hot Springs, before the park was thought of, and had since been driven out of the park. But he was suing the government for return of his remarkable homestead and expected to win it.[20]

Despite that clear identification of "Jim Gardiner" with James C. McCartney, legend continues to associate the founding of the town with a person of whom no trace has ever been found in an extant record. The name of the town, like that of the river, had descended from Johnson Gardner (see page 44), while the habit of spelling the name with an *i* was begun by the Washburn party as a phonetic rendering of Jim Bridger's Virginian drawl (see Chapter 5, note 51). The mythical Jim Gardiner can be accounted for easily enough. Soon after James, or Jim, McCartney established himself at the mouth of the Gardner River, the practice of consigning mail and freight in his care was started. Thus, it became common procedure to mark merchandise, packages, and letters to be delivered to "Jim on the Gardiner," and time shortened that to just "Jim Gardiner."

Early in October the Northern Pacific surveyors received their orders to stake the park branch for construction, and ahead of them went Edwin Stone, of the railroad's land department, picking up such parcels of private land as might be needed. As Jim McCartney's holdings at Gardiner were definitely in that category, an agreement was concluded by which McCartney agreed to sell for $1,500.[21] However, the Northern Pacific Railroad never got the terminus they wanted for there was a complication. McCartney had previously leased most of his desert land claim, for such it was, to one Robert Eugene Cutler, better known as Buckskin Jim, and that bull-necked, bullet-headed, and very stubborn German refused to give up his lease; worse yet, he appears to have proceeded to sublet parcels of land in a manner that was construed as a sale.[22] While Stone was later able to legally dispose of "that perennial sagebrush blossom known as Buckskin Jim,"[23] he was unable to similarly dispose of the host of people who claimed to have purchased from him. Even worse, as the grading crews approached the Gardiner site, Jim came back for another round by throwing a placer claim across the right of way. The railroad was stymied and at last decided to develop a terminus a few miles down the valley on the property that had changed hands successively from the Hendersons to Clarence Stephens, and from him to George Huston and Joe Keeney early in 1883. A satisfactory site was readily purchased from Huston and Keeney, and on it arose the town of Cinnabar.[24]

The treaty with the Crow Indians, eliminating their title to that portion of the Park north of the forty-fifth degree of latitude and east of the Yellowstone River, was ratified by the Senate on April 11, 1882.[25] The ratification legitimized the mines on Clarks Fork, and mining speculators began to show new interest in them. Among those who took a close look at the settlement of "thirty to forty cabins and 150 inhabitants," which had gathered at the head of Soda Butte Creek, was Jay Cooke. His interest in the mines of that area was so great, and his promises so enticing (they included a railroad) that the residents saw fit to name their rude hamlet in his honor, and Cooke City it has been ever since.

General Sheridan returned from his 1882 trip through the Park convinced that affairs were not going well there. He appealed directly to eastern sportsmen, expressing the opinion that the Park was not nearly large enough, that it should be extended eastward about forty miles and that the southern boundary should be on the forty-fourth degree of latitude, which would increase its area by 3,344 square miles. His objective was primarily to create an additional game preserve in the mountainous and nearly uninhabited areas on the east and south of the Park. General Sheridan again suggested the use of troops for enforcement of rules and regulations and protection of wildlife of the Park, a proposal first advanced by Captain Ludlow in 1875. The effectiveness of his appeal is evident from the attention given it by *Forest and Stream*, which devoted three pages of its issue of January 11, 1883, to the park problem.

General Sheridan interested a senator from Missouri in taking up the Park's cause. Though an ex-confederate, Senator George Graham Vest, like Jack Baronett, had the complete confidence of General Sheridan and probably kept in close touch with him. His interest in Yellowstone Park began with two Senate resolutions which he sponsored in the Forty-seventh Congress; one, on December 7, sought information on the status of park concessions, while the other, on December 12, asked what was needed for the proper management of the Park. Thus, the editor of the *Bozeman Avant Courier* was correct in his speculation that the company of capitalists to whom Assistant Secretary Joslyn had granted exclusive privileges were "liable to have their franchises restricted, if not absolutely annulled, by a higher power—the Congress."[26]

Senator Vest and his committee used their information to draw up what was termed "an admirable bill." This effort to solve the Park's problems provided for the increased area General Sheridan had sought, and required the secretary of war to detail such troops to the Park as the secretary of the interior might require for its management. Most, but not all, of the fauna was given the protection of law under two provisions: park rules and regulations were given the force of law, and the Park was placed under the laws of Montana and the jurisdiction of Gallatin County, with penalties prescribed for violations. The latitude of the secretary of the interior in granting privileges within the Park was strictly limited; monopoly rights, and any restrictions of freedom of public access to the area were prohibited. Management of the Park was to be facilitated by appointment of a superintendent at a salary of $2,000 per annum and ten assistants at $900 per annum, all to carry the authority of deputy marshalls; further, the secretary of war was to detail an officer of the Corps of Engineers to make necessary surveys for roads and bridges.[27]

Although the legislation had the full support of Governor John Schuyler Crosby (of Montana Territory), of many scientific societies, and of the press generally, and despite the urgency created by events in the Park, it made no headway. According to an anonymous letter from Mammoth Hot Springs,

> The Park Improvement Company have a saw mill in operation at this place, getting out lumber for a 600 room hotel to be built here next spring, and I am creditably informed that Mr. E. Haupt, Superintendent of the N.P.I. Company, has let a contract for twenty thousand pounds of venison, at five cents per pound to supply his men. He has some eighty or a hundred now at work, and is going to feed them on elk, deer, mountain sheep, and bison, *killed in the park*, as it is *cheaper* than beef.
>
> It is a "Park Improvement Company" doing this, and I suppose they consider it an *improvement* to rid the park, as far as possible, of game. . . for the sake of a few dollars (very few) profit to themselves.[28]

Unable to get action on his legislation (S. 317 and its companion measure, H.R. 7439), Senator Vest took advantage of an opportunity offered by consideration of the Sundry Civil Appropriations Bill for the fiscal year 1884 to propose that the secretary of the interior be authorized to grant leases of limited areas for hotel use, but forbidding exclusive privileges or monopolies. According to L. C. Cramton,

> Mr. McCook, of New York, said the committee provision would improve the situation, but offered a substitute providing that the Secretary of the Interior be entirely prohibited from leasing any portions of the park; that all leases previously entered into should be of no force and effect; further that the Secretary of War be authorized and directed to make necessary detail of troops to prevent trespassers or intruders entering the park for any purpose prohibited by law. In this debate the report of General Sheridan had much weight. Mr. McCook's amendment was agreed to. When the sundry civil bill came up in the Senate, March 1, the appropriation was increased from $15,000 to $40,000. The Senate adopted an amendment of Senator Vest providing that $2,000 should be paid annually to the superintendent of the park, and $900 to each of ten assistants, etc. The McCook amendment as to leases was struck out and in lieu thereof a paragraph was inserted authorizing the Secretary of the Interior to lease small portions of the ground in the park not exceeding ten acres in extent for each tract, no such leased land to be within one-quarter of a mile of any of the geysers or of the Yellowstone Falls. Also the Senate inserted the provision that the Secretary of War, upon request of the Secretary of the Interior, was directed to make the necessary detail of troops to prevent trespassers, etc. As so amended, the provision became law.[29]

In that matter Senator Vest was handed an ace which was later used to great advantage in preserving Yellowstone National Park.

Certain events in the Park had transpired to make the senator's ace ultimately important. Although its agreement with Assistant Secretary Joslyn had never been formalized as a lease,[30] the Yellowstone Park Improvement Company entrenched itself in the Park with unseemly haste. During the fall and winter, lumber was cut from available stands of trees in the vicinity and, by February, a temporary boarding house and office, later to be a stable, was completed, and a start had been made at framing the hotel.[31] It was rough work which attracted rough men, and much of their leisure time was spent in gambling, drinking, and brawling.

St. Patrick's Day (March 17) was an occasion for a binge and James Armstrong, who was not a drinker, gathered up and hid all the firearms he could find, purely as a precautionary measure. A pistol owned by a young Iowan, David Kennedy, was hidden with the others, for he had a reputation for unreasoning violence when drunk; in fact, it was common knowledge that he had fled his home state after shooting his father while in such a condition. During the evening's revel Kennedy quarreled with another man as drunk as himself and went looking for his pistol to wipe out the fancied insult. When he couldn't find it he accused everybody of conspiring against him and threatened to kill the man who had stolen the gun. "Better ask Jim," someone suggested. With the other party to the quarrel out of the way, Jim accepted Kennedy's promise to behave and gave him back his pistol. That was a mistake, for Kennedy leveled on Jim and shot him down.

Assistant Superintendent Henderson was awakened in the middle of the night by a pounding on the door of the Norris blockhouse where he lived, followed by: "For God's sake, Henderson, hurry down to Hobart's boarding house and see if you can do anything for Jim Armstrong. One of the boys fired two shots into him and he may be dead before we get down there." Henderson dressed quickly and went to the construction camp at the mouth of Clematis Gulch. On entering the McCartney cabin, which served the contractor as a boarding house, he found a young teamster stretched out on the floor with two wounds: one in the left breast, just above the heart, and another in the pelvic region. Kennedy, sobered by the terrible thing he had done, stood nearby crying and asking for someone to help the man he had shot.

Henderson set to work binding up the wounds as best he could, for there was no doctor nearer than Livingston, and inquired into the cause of the shooting. After he had done what he could for Jim, he turned to Kennedy: "And what do you propose to do, you miserable scamp?"

"Anything and everything you order me to do, God knows that I would be only too glad to take Jim's place this moment," was the answer. It occurred to Henderson that there was a practical way Kennedy could make restitution: he drew up an agreement whereby the Iowan assigned all his overdue wages to Jim Armstrong and consented to act as his nurse until relieved by the death or recovery of the patient.

Meanwhile, some of the men were deliberating in a shadowy group on the Hymen Terrace not far away. Finally one went to the cabin, called for Henderson, and asked: "Is Jim dead?" and announced that the court of judge lynch had sentenced Kennedy to be hanged immediately, and he, as sheriff, was anxious to get on with his work. Henderson pointed out that they didn't quite have a murderer yet, and that Kennedy could be more useful through the agreement he had just signed. The result was a suspended sentence of a less deadly sort.

Jim Armstrong recovered and was up and about in six weeks, though still carrying the two bullets in his body. Kennedy fulfilled his obligations to the letter, and the "court" felt no necessity to use the gnarled old cedar tree that had been selected for a gallows. Soon thereafter David Kennedy left with the other "turbulent self-adjusting revolver regulators."[32]

This incident had a sequel of significance to the Park. In his annual report for the year 1883, Superintendent Conger said:

> I notified the Interior Office of one shooting that occurred last March near headquarters. I also gave notice of the commission of the crime to the Governor of Wyoming, who replied that he had placed my communication in the hands of the United States District Attorney, and requested me to furnish the names of the witnesses, which I promptly did. But in the meantime the culprit escaped, and, so far as I know, has not been apprehended or heard of since.[33]

Conger's action in taking the matter to the governor of Wyoming set in motion a train of events that led the Wyoming Legislative Assembly to pass "an act to render operative and effectual the laws of the Territory of Wyoming within that portion of the Yellowstone National Park lying within said Territory."[34] Among other things, the Wyoming law provided for "two justices of the peace and two constables for the said precinct of the Yellowstone National Park in said county of Uinta . . . " The Park was fairly launched upon a dubious experiment which ended most disgracefully, carrying down the early civilian administration of the area with it.

On March 9, 1883, the secretary of the interior gave the Yellowstone Park Improvement Company a ten-year lease that complied with the wishes of the Congress.[35] This at least legitimized the construction already rising from the white "formation" of an old terrace at Mammoth Hot Springs. It was a great hotel designed by a St. Paul architect, L. F. Buffington, to house 800 guests. However, as only 151 rooms were completed in the initial construction, the capacity was nearer 300 guests (or 500 guests when crowding tactics were used by the management). As built, the National Hotel was a three- to four-story frame building 414 feet long and 54 feet wide, with several wings behind. It had a tower and windows reminiscent of Queen Anne style, but the effect was spoiled by the great veranda that ran the full length of the front. The massive structure, painted green, with a red roof, was an entirely incongruous addition to a landscape dominated by grays and browns. As one guest remarked, it seemed to have an "air of discomfort."

The main entrance opened into a lobby 42 by 56 feet, from which ample hallways extended the length of the building. Both the lobby and the halls were heated by several large stoves, and an additional feature, which was considered "convenient and architectural," was a long line of vermilion spittoons precisely arrayed down the hall. To the left side of the entrance was a gentlemen's room, office and the newsstand where "everything costs four or five times what you pay in the east." To the right of the entrance was a ladies' waiting room, joined to a ladies' parlor, and then a general parlor and museum on opposite sides of the hallway. Behind the lobby a curtained doorway opened into a large dining hall which occupied one of the wings behind the hotel, and there were five staircases—one in the lobby and one at the end of each wing—to the guest rooms on the upper floors. Each room had an electric call bell, appropriately installed by a Mr. John C. Bell, and the public areas were lighted by twenty electric arc lights, installed by the United States Electric Light Company. Fixtures of this type, which created light by vaporization of carbon under alternating current, had been used successfully to illuminate the opening of New York's Brooklyn Bridge on May 24, 1883. The arc light was even then nearly obsolete, however, for the Edison lamp, invented October 21, 1879, soon proved superior.

The furnishings for the hotel represented an outlay of $60,000—one-third of the total investment. There was a Steinway pianoforte, beautiful silverware and china, and a kitchen range measuring 6 by 22 feet that could accommodate fifteen cooks, and feed 5,000 guests. Why such an oversized appliance was installed remains unexplained.

The National Hotel also featured a barber shop (with two barbers) and a bar, which was put out of business after the second season because of the problem with drunks.[36] In the lobby there was a stuffed mountain lion with a plaque in his mouth; the inscription read: "Meet me by moonlight alone!"

Even the bootblack seemed a bit rapacious to one guest. When he brought up the man's shined shoes, the guest said, "How much?"

"Quarter," responded the bootblack.

"Boy," said the guest, "The secretary of the interior says ten cents."

"The secktary ain't runnin' my part of this ranch," replied the bootblack. "Shell out yer quarter."[37]

The experiences of an English guest[38] give some picture of accommodations at the National Hotel. At the registration desk the Englishman was jostled by a man in a wet buffalo coat who smelled like a barnyard (probably a teamster); he had to walk to the fourth floor where he was lodged in an attic room (no reduction in price); then he had to go back down to the first floor washroom to clean up for dinner. In one way our Englishman was lucky—he didn't have to share his bed with a stranger. Not only was that common practice in the Park in those days, but often two couples would be put in the same room.

In the dining room, the din created by carpenters still working on the unfinished building competed successfully with dinner music from the Steinway. As for the cooking, he thought "the less said the better," which is surprising, since the two French chefs and the German baker received $3,000 each for the season, a princely wage in that day. At that meal the choice was between elk and bear steak, so he and his table companion decided they would trade some of their servings. The Briton said the result was like the opening of a Hans Christian Anderson fairy tale: "There were two little toy soldiers who were brothers, for they were made out of the same leaden spoon." It was just that way with the elk and the bear!

The cuisine probably improved later. A breakfast menu for August 2, 1885, has survived. (It was found in a pack rat's nest when the old hotel was torn down in 1935.) Manager E. C. Dyer, a professional hotel man who arrived in a silk top hat early in June of that year offered:

Oatmeal and Cream
Mountain Trout Fried
Soda Biscuit Corn Bread
Hot Cakes Plain Bread
Eggs
Fried Scrambled
Boiled
Fried Spring Chicken
Sirloin Steak Boiled Ham
Breakfast Bacon Venison Steak
French Fried Potatoe
Milk Toast Dry Toast
Chocolate
Coffee Tea

A newspaperman left us an interesting impression of the National Hotel in a bit of free verse titled, "John's Poetic Tribute To The Big Tavern":

Oh Mammoth structure,
Perched on a series of brevet stratifications
Composed of 40 percent of magnesia,
Five of sulphur, 5 of arsenic, 5 of iron,
Fifty-five of tourists cast off garments and
Yankee Jim's yellow dog which was
    poisoned by Jim McCartney, Esq. in
Winter of '71 and spring of '72,—
We hail thee as a lively affair and
Thy lofty colonnades and unutterable
Immensity in all its vasty vastness
Are exceeded only by the mortgage thereon.[39]

The mortgage is an everlasting theme in the story of the National Hotel. The season of 1883 was so short the operation didn't pay expenses, despite the high prices and a capacity house. The workmen, who had $9,000 coming in wages by February 1884, took possession of the hotel in a prolonged sit-in sustained by local elk meat, and the Yellowstone Park Improvement Company was bankrupt by March 21, 1884. A receiver operated the hotel at a loss of $4,587 that season, and it remained a loser to the end of its days.

The Yellowstone Park Improvement Company established facilities at other points in the Park. Three tent hotels were operated in 1883: at Norris Geyser Basin, at the Grand Canyon, and in the Upper Geyser Basin. The camp at Norris was located in a small grove of trees north of the geyser basin proper. Two large wall tents set end to end served as kitchen and dining room, while small wall tents, each provided with a double bed and floored with straw covered with carpeting, served for sleeping rooms.[40] Our English traveler left us a good description of the tent hotel at Norris. He says:

The tent hotel in the Upper Geyser Basin, 1884.

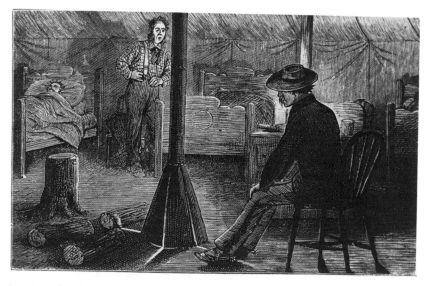

Interior of a sleeping tent at the Norris tent hotel, 1884. Both from sketches by
T.H. Thomas in *The Daily Graphic* (Aug. 11, 1888).

> Through forest green or forest burned we press on, and, emerging upon a dislocating piece of corduroy road, cross the stream and draw up at the row of tents which does duty for an hotel. A tent hotel, sometimes called a "krawl" is something fearful and wonderful; there appears to be a fixed price for every item—one dollar—and as man must have breakfast, dinner, "supper," and bed, it means a minimum of four dollars a day. The "nouriture," in park parlance, "grub pile," does not differ much at the different meals, and if the traveler wants to know what meal is set before him, consultation with the host or the watch is requisite. When we say a bed is necessary, perhaps we overstate the case, it would be more proper to say a moiety of a bed, for travelling in the National Park, like the poverty to which it leads, makes a man acquainted with strange bed-fellows.[41]

The English tourist pauses in his description and tells of eyeing carefully and suspiciously a newcomer, a dark visaged fellow arrayed in sombrero and leathers, whose fatigue from long riding gives him the air of revolving in his mind some crime of violence. Mr. Thomas' description continues:

> As for furniture, the tent is not so bad; an ingenious adaptation in iron of the earthen stove, used from time immemorial by Indians, keeps the frost out, a pine stump or two stick up conveniently out of the ground, beds of considerable capacity, well-furnished with blankets, and, of course a grass "whisk," which, in America is always with us. During the height of the season the principle upon which the beds are populated is said to be the addition of visitors so long as they may arrive, or until the occupants "go for their guns." The plan is simple, and relieves the authorities of responsibility.

Thomas thought that the arrangements for washing lacked something. As there was but one basin and pitcher, guests would stand around in the frosty dawn shivering and demanding their turn, often to decline, when it came, with the comment, "What! No soap?"

The tent camp at the Upper Geyser Basin stood between Castle and Old Faithful geysers, about where the west end of the hotel parking area is now. Upon seeing that canvas village, Owen Wister was led to comment that to sleep there "must have made you intimately acquainted with how your neighbors were passing the night."[42] Wister didn't stop there; he camped nearby; but one who did noted, "freezing, as usual, when I awoke . . . matters are very economically managed in the tent hotel here. In your canvas house you find no chairs, no mirror, a beer bottle candle stick, perhaps one towel, and other things to correspond; and for these luxuries, and your food, you pay the small sum of $5 (a guinea) a day."[43]

The tent camp at the Grand Canyon was at the head of a little rocky dell that slopes steeply down to the Yellowstone River above the Upper Falls; that is, it was very nearly on the site of the tourist cabin layout established there in the 1920s. It was described as "a double row of large canvas tents, capable of accommodating about 75 guests."[44] Dinner in a great tent, decorated with greenery, followed by a pleasant chat around a big fire under the starlit sky was all fine enough, but periods of storm, especially those sudden snow storms of early fall, made tent life unbearably frigid.

Arrangements for public transportation were worked out in the summer of 1883. George W. Wakefield and Charles W. Hoffman, both of Bozeman, entered into an agreement with the Yellowstone Park Improvement Company to haul passengers from the end-of-track on the park branch line to, and through, the Park, at twelve cents per mile for each passenger hauled. On July 20, they put on a daily coach to carry mail and passengers to the Mammoth Hot Springs, and as soon as the traffic required it, Concord coaches were put into service within the Park. Two stagecoaches took care of the business between Mammoth Hot Springs and the Lower Geyser Basin, two more were employed between the Falls of the Yellowstone and the Lower Geyser Basin and one was used between the Lower and Upper basins.[45] Wakefield and Hoffman were given permission to cut wild hay within the Park for the thirty to forty horses required, and they found it cheaper to stack hay and winter their horses in the Park than to take them out.

A newspaperman who reached Mammoth Hot Springs by stagecoach on August 6, 1883, describes the journey from the end-of-track, which was then eighteen miles from Mammoth Hot Springs. The train was late, and it was half past four in the afternoon before it reached the temporary terminus where two stagecoaches waited. Having been tipped off to sit beside the driver, our news hawk managed what he thought was a capital seat. He says:

> After awhile the horses were attached, the driver swung his long whip, and away we went. I shall not attempt to describe the roads; they are beyond me. I divided my time between holding myself on the seat with my left hand, and pressing my right against the driver in order that he might more effectively manage the brake. When the rain burst upon us I had a strange longing to get hold of Hare and slay him. [This was the companion who had encouraged him to ride outside.] My only satisfaction was in remembering that he was on the driver's seat on the coach ahead without a rubber coat or an umbrella.

About ten miles out the driver said it would be dangerous to proceed after dark and he would like to put up for the night at Keeney's ranch, just ahead.

"I drove Senator Conkling and party over ten days ago," he said, "And they stopped there. I told the Senator it was foolish to leave the cars that night, it was so late, but he insisted upon pushing on and we started. But he was glad enough to stop when we got to Keeney's."

I talked awhile to the jehu and made up my mind that he and Keeney had an understanding, and that the danger was mainly in his eye. However, upon arriving at the ranch we held a consultation. After discussing the situation, it was decided to go ahead. The house where the party was asked to stay was a low one story log and frame, about 20 feet long, and although we had the example of the illustrious New Yorker before us, we couldn't see it. So we went on.

We had got about half a mile from the ranch when we came to a bridge made out of round poles, like a corduroy road. The rain had made them slippery, and when the great lumbering wheels of the coach struck them the bridge began to roll up like a scroll. Then came the crack of the whip, and "You scoundrals! Go on!" Crack! Crack! Crack! "Whoa!" as the hind wheels of the coach dropped into the gully under the bridge. It usually takes some time to get out of one of these vehicles, as everybody knows who has gone out to the races in the Palmerhouse coach (a similar affair), but when I looked around last night every man was out, and Mac was standing several rods away with his hands in his pockets curiously surveying the wreck. . . . Taking the poles out of the bridge for levers, we inserted them under the wheels, and in less than fifteen minutes after the accident we were on the road again.

But our troubles had only begun. It grew darker and darker, and the road became more precipitous and dangerous. Some of the steep aclivities had become slippery by the rain, and in the middle of one a wheel horse went down, the coach groaned and stopped, and the driver, holding the brake with all his strength, called to us to get off and out as quickly as possible before the lumbering load dragged the team backward. Out we all jumped in the mud, and for half a mile struggled up through the sticky clay soil that clung to ones feet like pitch. Then we mounted again only to dismount a few minutes afterward, and so it went until finally it became so dark that from the driver's seat the horses in the lead could not be seen at all. The driver told us frankly that he was afraid. He could not see the road, and in some places a deviation of a foot from the track would send the coach tumbling down into a ravine. A lantern was procured and lighted, but the oil was low and it went out. Then two of the boys with white hats volunteered to go ahead, and slowly the driver followed them. At last he gave word that the dangerous places were past and we mounted again. In a little while we saw ahead of us a long row of lights, which we were glad to hear were from the hotel at the Park.[46]

Such was staging in the Park; if it wasn't rain and mud, it was heat and dust, and there was always plenty of opportunity to walk.

Many visitors preferred to hire rigs from local persons and either drive through the Park themselves or be driven through by someone who could serve as guide. However, notices posted in hotels and public places in mid-August by Superintendent Conger, bearing Secretary of the Interior Teller's name, forbade hiring any team or conveyance other than those provided by Wakefield and Hoffman.[47] This did not set well with local people who hoped to hire out their rigs or do a little independent guiding, and an incident was inevitable. The blow-up came during President Arthur's visit in the Park, in fact, while he was at Mammoth Hot Springs. A visitor who was preparing to make a tour of the Park had leased a proscribed rig from someone at the Springs, and Superintendent Conger proceeded to enforce the ruling by sending one of his assistants to serve the visitor with a copy of Secretary Teller's order. The visitor was naturally upset, and hearing that Senator Vest was in the area, he went to him and showed him the notice bearing Secretary Teller's name. The doughty senator from Missouri read it, handed it to President Arthur, and burst out, "There, I told you that _____, _____, _____ was in collusion with this Park Improvement Company!"[48] It is said that President Arthur merely laughed and handed the paper back; but Secretary Teller's order was immediately revoked.

Three great excursions climaxed the season of 1883 and turned the Park into a three-ring circus. During a three-week period in late August and early September, the Park was visited by President Chester A. Arthur's party, the Hatch excursion to celebrate the opening of the Yellowstone Park Improvement Company's facilities, and the Villard excursion incidental to the completion of the Northern Pacific Railroad and its park branch line. The Park was the scene of one great overlapping hubbub.

The president's party left their special train at Green River station on the Union Pacific line on the morning of August 6 for the 155-mile journey to Fort Washakie in the Wind River Valley. In addition to the president, the party included Robert T. Lincoln, secretary of war; Major General Anson Stager of Chicago; Senator George G. Vest of Missouri; Governor John S. Crosby of Montana Territory; Judge Rollins of Washington, D.C.; and Surgeon Major W. H. Forwood. The dignitaries rode in three spring wagons, escorted by a troop from the Fifth United States Cavalry, accompanied by a journalist representing the press, and Frank J. Haynes, official photographer of the Northern Pacific Railroad.

At Fort Washakie, they exchanged the spring wagons for saddle horses and obtained camp equipment, 40 days' rations, and 150 pack mules, many of them transporting the china, crystal, sterling, and linens carried on this outing. On August 10, the presidential party continued up the valley of the Wind River, moving slowly so that the president could enjoy the hunting and fishing. Senator Vest was the president's fishing competitor, while Governor Crosby remained in camp "consulting the mosquitoes and vetoing their bills." From the head of the Wind River the party crossed Togwotee Pass into Jackson Hole and entered Yellowstone Park from the south by way of the Sheridan trail. Instead of sightseeing as they traveled northward through the Park, the president's party pushed directly through to Mammoth Hot Springs, rested there a day, and then doubled back to the Upper Geyser Basin. There had been considerable speculation that the president's health was failing, and public anxiety was only heightened by the rigid censorship maintained throughout the journey. It was with considerable relief that he was seen to be in apparent good health, tanned, and affable. This feeling was mirrored in one of Frank Leslie's cartoons showing the president as he was expected to return to Washington—clad in buckskins and slouched hat, and lying in wait with Bowie knife and six-shooter for office seekers.[49]

While the presidential party was encamped at the Upper Geyser Basin, "Uncle" Rufus Hatch, the financial angel of the Yellowstone Park Improvement Company, who was also there with his party, dressed himself as a cowboy and staged a little comedy act that misfired; instead of pleasing President Arthur, it appears to have disgusted him because the wrong pose was inadvertently assumed.[50] The *Wood River Times*, a little newspaper at Hailey, Idaho, had just published details of a supposed plot to kidnap President Arthur while he was in the Park. According to the story, sixty-five cowboys (all former guerrillas) led by a Texas desperado with Shoshone and Bannock Indian guides, were to descend upon the presidential party, capture the chief executive, and spirit him off to the mountains where he was to be held for $500,000 ransom.[51] This crude sensationalism, for undoubtedly it was no more than that, was generally considered absurd and was written off with some such comment as, "the kidnappers will have to travel right quick or they will be a little too late for their game." But the military were sufficiently impressed to add another troop of cavalry to the president's escort, and the best that can be said for Hatch's cavorting was that it was in bad taste under those circumstances.

Jack Baronett was the president's guide through the Park, and after touring the sights, the party returned to Jack's cabin at the Baronett Bridge and rested there for several days. The stop was made not so much for the president's benefit, though he did appear much fatigued, but because General Sheridan was not well. The general's ill health was reflected in a petty dispute he had with Captain Hayes of the escort over whether the mules should be picketed at night or be loose-herded; the general became so angered he placed the captain under arrest.

From the Baronett Bridge the presidential party proceeded to Mammoth Hot Springs for their last night in Yellowstone Park. There, instead of stopping at the National Hotel, the party made camp on the prominent bench about one-half mile to the north. Rufus Hatch was very much chagrined, for he had planned to entertain the presidential party at his hotel; however, the most President Arthur would consent to was a private reception at the hotel that evening and a brief public appearance the next morning. An account of the evening reception as it appeared to a waiter at the National Hotel is fortunately available.

When Colonel Rufus Hatch heard of the arrival of the Presidential party, he gathered some of the notable men of his own party, and with them went to pay their respects to President Arthur.

The President and his party returned the visit to Colonel Hatch and his friends, and a reception was held in a private dining room of the hotel in which Colonel Hatch had arranged wines and cigars to be served for the evening entertainment. Only Colonel Michael Sheridan was missing. He, however, entered later, in a state of inebriation, and without an invitation . . . on account of his dislike for President Arthur, who had failed to give him a promotion.

As soon as President Arthur saw the intruder, he said: "please excuse me, gentlemen," then made a dignified departure from the room. As he passed Colonel Sheridan, the latter made a very uncomplimentary remark about the President. The party immediately broke up, leaving a dozen quarts of excellent champagne and two boxes of cigars which were hardly touched. These spoils were immediately confiscated by the waiters. We were having a merry time behind a locked door, when we were suprised by a hand on the door knob, and a loud demand: "Let me in there," was made in the voice of Colonel Sheridan.

We all kept very quiet; then we heard another voice outside the door coaxing Colonel Sheridan to go back to camp with him. Finally the Colonel said: "If you get a jug of whisky and order the ambulance I'll go back with you." Then they went away and left us in peace to enjoy the spoils at our leisure. It was good wine that had cost five dollars a quart at the hotel bar.[52]

The public reception the next morning was held on the second floor of the hotel around the lobby that was open to the roof. Rufus Hatch's foreign guests were particularly surprised by the democratic atmosphere and the approachability of the president.[53] The presidential party departed from Yellowstone Park by way of the just completed park branch line of the Northern Pacific Railroad, using the palatial private car, Edwin Forest, which had been held at the Cinnabar terminus for him.

The Hatch excursion, in the Park at the same time as the president's party, was a lavish, all-expense-paid tour arranged for a number of dignitaries from both sides of the Atlantic to show off the National Hotel and other facilities of the Yellowstone Park Improvement Company. Late in July, invitations had gone out to the "national elite of America, Great Britain, Germany, and France," and on August 23 the party of seventy-five guests in eight railway cars arrived at Livingston, Montana.[54] Edward Pierrepont, who had a speaking acquaintance with a good many of these "big bugs" (whom a local jokester described as "hatched out from both sides of the Atlantic"), thought that only the consummate tact and quiet diplomacy of Rufus Hatch could have kept them all in apparent good humor, considering the diversity of sexes, ages, nations, and tongues.[55]

The passenger list showed sixty-one names, among them those of lords, earls, counts, and barons—some in person, others represented by illustrious sons. One earl came with thirteen trunks; another had a retinue of servants; and there were enough monocles, tight pants, and effete manners to thoroughly amuse the natives. Also present were the editors of the Telegraph and the Morning Post of London; a writer for the Paris Figaro; a correspondent representing the Vienna Imperial Gazette and the Munich Allgemeine Zeitung; some solicitors, members of parliament, a few solid merchants, and a commoner who represented the king of Denmark.[56] The American contingent had been expected to include ex-President Grant and one or two stray members of the cabinet, an assortment of governors, and several congressmen. Most of these, however, including the ex-president, went with the Villard excursion instead. The only American name worth noting is Joseph Medill, publisher of the Chicago Tribune, who was later involved in the Payson incident. All of this led an editor to comment: "We of Livingston seem to live in the odor of greatness."[57]

Whatever that aroma was, it was soon wafted to the four corners of Yellowstone National Park, so that a plain, ordinary visitor was led to complain that "the park is full of notables and one cannot go ten rods in any direction without rubbing against a Lord, or a Duke, a

Senator, a government guide or some other gentleman of high degree."[58] Rufus Hatch had brought them to see the Park, and they saw it; they gagged on the dust raised by stagecoach wheels, they were awed over the geysers and properly horrified by the rude service in park hostels. An Englishman's group arrived at Norris camp to find all the beds taken, so "about twenty of us—ladies and gentlemen—had to lie on the ground in two rows, on opposite sides of the big dining tent, sleeping as best we could."[59]

That was no worse than the treatment visitors received at the hands of the black-coated waiters of the National Hotel, who were ill-trained transients under their professional garb. A correspondent of the *New York Tribune* observed the tyrannizing of an inoffensive Dutch merchant who had tired of waiting for his dishes to be removed and had set them beside his chair so he could finish his meal. The newsman, who was watching as the waiter came to the table, said:

> You ought to have seen the anger and disgust depicted in his face as he beheld the plates at his feet. The foreigners who saw him, I dare say, fully expected him then and there to draw a revolver from his pocket and avenge the indignity offered to his person in the blood of the poor Hollander, who was just then enjoying a quiet smoke, [however] the waiter contented himself by muttering in a snarling tone, loud enough for everybody within ten feet to hear, as he picked up the dishes, "If I was a Dutch prince, I'd have manners, d___d if I wouldn't; feel just like hitting him in the jaw with a plate.[60]

There were many complaints to the clerk at the hotel desk to the general effect that the language of the waiters was not quite as pure as the air in those parts, but Mr. Brownlow T. Gray was a western man with some idea of how hard it was to find waiters who would work for only a month or two at $35 and "found," so he tempered his remarks to the head waiter accordingly. "Will, can't you make your men do any better?" "It can't be helped Mister Gray," Will said, "if I complain the whole bunch will walk out on us. Then what?"[61]

Rufus Hatch engaged in some more pranks at Mammoth Hot Springs, but restricted them to members of his own party. Several young nobles had been boasting, enroute to the Park, of how well they could handle the "natives" of the wild west, and so "Uncle" Rufus connived with Lord Headley to put them to the test. The young men had been told of the delights of Bath Lake, some distance from the hotel, and were soon on their way to that famous swimming hole above the hot spring terraces. At the pool, they tied their horses, piled their clothes on the bank, and were luxuriating in the tepid water when four mounted men (actually stable boys) galloped up, whooping, and firing six-guns in the air. The "hold-up men" proceeded to appropriate the

Bathers in Bath Lake, Mammoth Hot Springs. From a sketch by T.H. Thomas in *The Daily Graphic* (Aug. 11, 1888).

Mock sermon from Pulpit Terrace, Mammoth Hot Springs (late 1870s or early 1880s). From H.B. Calfee's stereo-photo no. 20.

horses, clothing, weapons, jewelry, and money of the young Englishmen, leaving only enough raiment to barely cover one man. Thus, one of the swimmers was able to go back to the hotel for assistance which was ostentatiously furnished by a large party of armed men who were almost too eager to hear every little detail of their brave stand against hopeless odds. When the boasters were at last delivered safely to the hotel, their clothes and valuables were neatly piled on the veranda and a large crowd was standing around to hear about the "robbery." Realizing they had been put on, the young men "kicked up a lot of dust."[62]

The genteel folk also witnessed the end of a murder incident. On August 20, at about four o'clock in the afternoon, George Weber and John Zutavern got into a dispute in front of Charley's beer hall at Gardiner. They had made a trade involving some blankets and a razor and fell to arguing over the value, which did not exceed four dollars. Words led to blows and Zutavern hit Weber on the head with a rock, at which Weber drew his revolver and shot Zutavern in the left breast, then sat down on a nearby boulder and watched his victim die (a matter of less than five minutes). Weber then fled to the Yellowstone River, where it was supposed he dived into the water and either swam across or was drowned, but no one cared to follow him closely enough to make sure. Those who knew him thought he was much too cagey to throw his life away (Weber was a particularly hard case, a member of the Miles City gang which had been broken up by vigilante action somewhat earlier). The assistant superintendents in the Park and the soldiers serving as couriers for President Arthur's party were alerted to watch for him.

Actually, Weber had not entered the river but had slipped along the bank into the Park. That night, two professional hunters from the Little Missouri country were camped at Willow Park, and when they broke camp in the morning, they were surprised to see a man ahead of them on the road, walking rapidly. They overtook him and inquired as to why he was afoot and if he needed assistance. The man acted shy, said that he had lost his horse, yet declined help in finding it. Soon afterward, the hunters met one of the soldier-couriers and heard the details of the murder at Gardiner. They suspected that the man they had accosted earlier was the murderer and so decided to set a trap for him. Continuing rapidly down the road for a considerable distance, they made camp in a concealed place and took turns watching the road. At about 12:30 A.M. they heard footsteps, brought the man to a standstill with their guns, and placed him under arrest. Weber, relieved of his revolver and knife, admitted that he was the wanted man, though maintaining that he had killed Zutavern in self-defense.

The hunters, Bill Germayne and George W. Grow, took their prisoner back to the town of Gardiner where they contacted Judge D. H. Budlong, who had come up from Livingston to investigate the murder. The two captors agreed to accompany the judge and the prisoner to the train and were at Cinnabar when the Hatch excursionists arrived. "Uncle" Rufus soon heard the circumstances and decided he had a bonanza. He took Germayne and Grow through the cars introducing them to all, encouraging them to talk about their adventure. After that the hunters accompanied the Hatch party through the Park, entertaining the guests with trick shooting (Germayne's specialty). Lord Headley later hired them to guide him on a hunting trip into the mountains.

Weber was sentenced to twenty years in the Territorial Penitentiary at Deer Lodge, Montana, and John Zutavern became the second person to be buried in the cemetery that tops the prominent hill north of Mammoth Hot Springs.[63] In fact, when Judge Budlong arrived in Gardiner the day following the murder to hold an inquest, he found that Zutavern had already been buried, and, of course, asked that the body be exhumed so that he could satisfy the legal requirements of his office. This the people of Gardiner determinedly opposed, and it developed that a summary administration of Zutavern's estate was even then in progress. He had had a considerable amount of ready cash in his possession in addition to a horse, saddle, and other effects. The money had been divided up and the property was to be sold the next morning at public auction for the benefit of the community. Judge Budlong put a stop to those quasi-legal proceedings and saw justice done according to the letter of the law.[64]

The Hatch excursionists left the Park September 4, "loud in their praise of the treatment they had received," to which was added the remark that Uncle Rufus himself was too full of business to talk much.[65] It later developed that he had been struck dumb by the fact that the excursion had become somewhat of a financial catastrophe for him. The *Bismarck Tribune* spread his troubles on its pages in a style that could have had no other model than the King James version of the Bible. "Uncle Rufus' Recent Pilgrimage" begins this way:

1. Now it came to pass that there dwelt in the far east a high priest named Hatch whose surname was Rufus.
2. And he communed with himself, saying: Lo now I will guide me a caravan into the distant west.
3. I will summon hither the potentates of other climes and I will paralyze them with the grandeur of the national tree claim.

4. And steer them against my first class caravansary at the
usual rates. Strangers without baggage must pay in advance, and
meals sent to rooms charged extra.
5. And lifting up his voice he summoned his chief scribe unto
him and said:
6. "Go get thee hence and monkey with thy pens and parchment
that my chosen guests may journey hither for a royal picnic."
7. "Say unto them that the feast is ready, the fatted calf is
slain and that everything is lovely and the goose is suspended
at the elevation that seemeth meet and proper."
8. "And thou shalt sign each message, yours serenely and hope-
fully, Rufus Hatch."
9. And the scribe did even as his master bade him and the
message went forth upon the mighty deep.[66]

Two years later, in mentioning his Yellowstone Park excursion
of 1883, Rufus Hatch told a newspaper writer: "I had railroad passes
for every mother's son of my company, yet that picnic cost me $35,000
in cash. I didn't ask the boys to spend a penny, and you can gamble
that none of them pressed me to allow them to. Besides, while I was
gone, I got on the wrong side of the market, and went hopelessly lame
before I got back. I lost $460,000 on that trip."[67]

Anything the Hatch excursion accomplished was entirely in the
realm of advertising. It generated a great deal of newspaper copy
throughout the United States, some of it laudatory and some
positively jeering. In Europe the tone was probably better, and that
coverage undoubtedly contributed to an increase in the number of
European visitors to Yellowstone National Park.

The third and most impressive excursion of the summer of 1883
was organized by Henry Villard, president of the Northern Pacific
Railroad, to celebrate the completion of the line and its branch
connection with Yellowstone Park. Villard, who has gone down in
history as "the blind pool man," wrested control of the revitalized
Northern Pacific Railroad from Frederick Billings in 1881 and
pushed main line construction through to a finish late in the summer
of 1883. However, in order that the circumstance might be properly
commemorated, a section of the line was left open at the point where
the construction crews from east and west met (on Little Blackfoot
River about thirty-five miles west of Helena), and traffic was passed
around the gap during this time on temporary rails.[68] Invitations were
sent to capitalists, railroad officials, journalists, and other prominent
figures to attend the last-spike ceremony on September 10. Guests
were to enjoy a thirty-day excursion "at no personal expense."

The 300 guests were considered the "most remarkable aggrega-
tion of unadulterated greatness that we have ever seen—greatness
dependent upon intellect, wealth or title"; included were ex-President
Ulysses S. Grant, two cabinet members, five ministers to foreign
courts, U.S. Senators "in large numbers," members of Congress
"incomputable," generals "ad libitum," a "sprinkling" of governors
and mayors of great cities, a "fair showing" of eminent journalists,
railroad owners, and national and state figures and a good many
moneyed private citizens.[69]   The gathering of such an illustrious
group was considered to be an even greater achievement than the
completion of the Northern Pacific Railroad, particularly as Rufus
Hatch had tried to snare many of these same persons for his
excursion.

The special train left New York on August 29, carrying 365
guests in four sections traveling thirty minutes apart. Gala preparations had been made all along the line. Station agents and baggage
men were in uniform and the stations were decorated with flags and
bunting. The railroad company brought in two carloads of evergreens
for decorating the depot and the town of Livingston, which the
excursion reached on September 6. The east end of the station was
covered with a huge evergreen arch and on the front the German word
"wilkommen," or welcome, was spelled out in greenery. A gate on one
side of the station bore the motto "Livingston the gate to Wonderland," and beneath that was the information that population had
increased from 50 in December 1882 to 3,000 in August 1883.[70] The
ladies' waiting room had been provided with three oil paintings of
Yellowstone Park scenes, each 10 by 13 feet. All who gathered at the
station could hear the driving of the last spike at Gold Creek,
Montana Territory, by a telegraphic hookup in which a wire attached
to the silver maul closed the circuit at each blow.

The forty-four-car excursion train reached Gold Creek in this
order: Section A, special cars carrying President Villard and his
German friends; section B, special cars including the Northern Pacific
director's car, *Yellowstone*, carrying ex-President Grant; and sections C and D, Pullman sleepers and dining cars. At the ceremony,
there was music by the Fifth Infantry band and speeches by President
Villard, William M. Evarts (former secretary of state), Henry M.
Teller, secretary of the interior, and by former railroad president
Frederick Billings. Two hundred feet of roadbed had been prepared
with ballast and ties, and two gangs of workmen laid the rails from
east and west in competition before the assembled crowd. The eastern
construction gang were the winners.

At last, all was ready for driving the final spike. It was handed to President Villard by a Crow Indian named Iron Bull, whose remarks were of a more sombre nature.

> This is the last of it—this is the last thing for me to do. I am glad to see you here, and hope my people of the Crow Nation are glad to see you, too. There is a meaning in my part of the ceremony, and I understand it. The end of our lives is near at hand. The days of my people are almost numbered; already they are dropping off like the rays of sunlight in the western sky. Of our once powerful nation there are now few left—just a little handful, and we, too, will soon be gone.[71]

The last spike was then held aloft for all to see; it was rusty and battered, having been the first spike driven on the Northern Pacific line when construction began in February 1870. H. C. Davis, assistant general passenger agent, who had driven the first spike, now struck the first blow to drive it again, as the last spike. Others followed him, finally General Ulysses S. Grant, who with his blow completed the line.

A great task had been finished with a great celebration, but that was not quite the end of it. President Villard took his German friends back to Livingston for an anticlimactic celebration of the completion of the park branch line and a tour of Yellowstone National Park, thus helping to confound the confusion already existing within park boundaries. The entire junket,which cost the Northern Pacific Railroad about $500 per guest, or something in the neighborhood of a total $200,000 was, for Villard,

> a sort of Belshazzar's feast. While he and his companions filled themselves with wine and meat the Persians in Wall Street were diverting the golden Euphrates from his pockets and mounting the walls of his citadel. He awoke from his revel to find himself in the hands of his enemies. The writing on the wall, as interpreted by events, is that "Villard must go."[72]

Shortly thereafter, Villard resigned the presidency of the Northern Pacific Railroad, having lost the confidence of stockholders through the lavish expenditures by which he had completed the road.

The three extravaganzas of 1883 were costly affairs in other ways. It was soon reported that President Arthur's health was failing despite his vacation trips to Florida and Yellowstone, and it was at last admitted that the Yellowstone trip was "trying upon his strength."[73] From there on it was a downhill slide to his death at the age of fifty-six. Rufus Hatch, as his dividend on that season's activity, lost a sizeable personal fortune *and* the Yellowstone Park Improvement Company. Henry Villard lost his fortune and a great railroad. Between the two of them, they had publicized the Park in grand style.

With the completion of the park branch line to its Cinnabar terminus on September 3, 1883, Yellowstone Park had the railroad connection that its founders had expected ten years earlier. The fact that a good many people were not satisfied with what had been accomplished is evident from an editorial published at that time.

The National Park branch is a completed road, at least for the present. There are many who believe that Cinnabar is only a temporary terminus, and that within a very short time, perhaps twelve months, it will have been built within the borders of the Park itself to some point that will more fully accommodate tourist travel. The mines of the wonderfully productive area of the Clark's Fork region are also a lodestone which will attract to them a railroad sooner or later. Either the mainline or a spur of the National Park Branch will eventually pierce as far as possible into the mining districts of Cooke City. The Improvement Company want a railroad in the park and will ask Congress this winter for the privilege to build one. They profess the desire to control it themselves, subject only to the approval of the government, and to keep other rolling stock off the ground, would build an odd gauge road (four feet is mentioned), and by this means be entirely independent of other corporations. Whether this scheme can be consummated remains to be seen, but it may be safely concluded the Northern Pacific will not willingly permit any Company which it does not control, to build and operate a road within the Park. When the line of the Park Branch was located, the surveys were extended to within the Park, even to its southern border, and this alone would look as though the Northern Pacific officials were at that time considering the ultimate probability of extending the road far beyond its present terminus. The host of influential persons, great and small who have visited the Park this summer were not induced to come merely to advertise the Park. Other plans are in process of development, and a railway in the Park is one of them. Mr. Hobart, of the Improvement Company, in an after dinner speech to the Associated Press party, unfolded this, and when the time comes for its denouement, there will be plenty of advocates, both within the halls of Congress as well as throughout the country. It only remains to be seen whether the Park Company and the Northern Pacific will work in antagonism or whether they will agree on operations that will be mutually beneficial.[74]

Anyone reading between the lines of that account should have been able to foresee the future problem in the Park. If the purpose of the railroad interests had not already been evident, it was stated clearly enough there, and out of it would come the first Yellowstone war against monopoly interests.

But how about Superintendent Conger, alias Peterfunk's ghost; where was he and what was he up to during the great days of 1883? He spent his time mainly in fruitless bickering with officials of the improvement company and his own assistants. Conger quarreled personally with the Hobarts (Carroll T., manager of the improvement company, and Charles F., his contractor brother) over cutting of timber for the company sawmill and the killing of elk in the Park to feed the construction crews; the Hobarts retaliated by charging him with letting government horses out for hire. Conger seems to have been both arbitrary and petty in dealing with his assistants, taking it upon himself to judge whether they should be paid or not, and sometimes temporizing with men he should have fired. His course was particularly unwise, as many of the young men who formed his police force were politically well connected, particularly, George L. Henderson, whose brother, David B. Henderson, was speaker of the House of Representatives. Conger's difficulties with Assistant Henderson certainly did not help him when he was put on the defensive by Special Agent W. Scott Smith, whom the secretary of the interior sent out to determine conditions in the Park. Scott's report favored the removal of Superintendent Patrick H. Conger on the grounds of incompetency, though when at last Secretary Teller did ask for Conger's resignation, the local editor hazarded the opinion that "Hatch and his associates have all had a hand."[75] It was the further opinion of the editor that the superintendent had interfered with the monopolizing of the Park. He had not served his masters well.

CHAPTER 11

OF RABBIT CATCHERS

Bye, baby bunting
Daddy's gone a-hunting,
Gone to get a rabbit skin
To wrap the baby bunting in.
—Grammer Gurton's Garland, *1784*[1]

It could have been the nursery rhyme that inspired an editor to call the Park's first police force "those mighty nimrods and ramrods —'the rabbit catchers.' "[2] Regardless of its source, the term was apt, expressing very well the general contempt for the guardians of a nonexistent law. Individually, they were often ridiculous, and collectively they were mostly ineffective, and yet it was not entirely their fault that the Park reached the nadir of its fortune in their time.

The force of assistant superintendents came into being through a provision of the Sundry Civil Appropriation Act of March 3, 1883. An item contained in those amendments through which the Senate sought to correct the most troublesome deficiencies of the original Park act (see pages 268-69) allowed "not exceeding $900 annually to each of ten assistants, all of whom shall be appointed by the Secretary of the Interior, and reside continuously in the park and whose duty it shall be to protect the game, timber, and objects of interest therein."[3]

The first ten appointees were selected on the basis of their political connections, and all but George Henderson, who had been in the Park a year and was fifty-six years old, were inexperienced, brash young men. There were some hopeless misfits, but several turned out well after seasoning.[4]

The intention of the Congress was to create a Park police force, but neither the superintendent nor his assistants really understood that. It seems likely that Superintendent Conger thought of these assistants as interpreters, for when word was received that men were being selected by the secretary of the interior to fill the positions, a local editor referred to them as "the park guides, for such will be their duties," and that is the manner in which they were employed the first summer.[5] For their part, most of the assistants had an inflated idea of their employment. The first pair to reach Livingston signed the hotel register as "assistant commissioners of the national park," and it was duly noted that they already hailed from Mammoth Hot Springs, although as far as anyone knew they had not yet seen the Park.[6] In general, they were inclined to use stationery printed with the letterhead "Office of Assistant Superintendent" and were fond of loitering in the hotel lobbies; the impression they created was hardly the one they expected to make, however.

Local opinion of the assistant superintendents, after their first season in the Park, was well expressed by the editor of the *Livingston Enterprise.* When a soldier of President Arthur's escort was given a guardhouse sentence for prying pieces from the rim of Old Faithful Geyser with a pole, the editor suggested the assistant superintendents should be confined also—in a barrel—"until they learned the duties of their positions." The rumor that Superintendent Conger was likely to be replaced evoked the comment that he was "to be made the scapegoat for the sins of the lot of grossly incompetent and worse assistants who were saddled upon him last spring by government appointment."[7] Historian Hiram Chittenden has summed up their earned demerits thus: "The common verdict, as gathered from official reports and other sources, is that the body of police, styled assistants, were notoriously inefficient if not positively corrupt."[8] Such was their image; yet there were some extenuating circumstances.

Foremost among the influences working against the assistants was the state of lawlessness existing in and near the Park at that time. The completion of the park branch of the Northern Pacific Railroad (the last major construction on that line) left some of the riffraff that invariably followed the advance of western railroads stranded at the end-of-track. Many of these men had been driven out of Miles City, Livingston, or Bozeman, by vigilance committees. With every reason for not going back where they had come from, such undesirables tended to gravitate to Gardiner or Mammoth Hot Springs in the expectation of making an easy living at the expense of park visitors. Petty crime was their style (cheating at card games, pilfering luggage, and secreting visitors' horses in order to "find" them later for the reward), and there was occasional violence resulting in injury or death. They were not easy characters for greenhorns to cope with. Another rough lot were the hide-hunters who had drifted into the mountains around the Yellowstone Plateau prior to 1883, following destruction of the buffalo herds of the northern plains. Many of these had become determined poachers who would have given men of nerve and experience a bad time. The dishonest and disgruntled employees introduced by the Yellowstone Park Improvement Company added to the problems confronting the Park's first policemen. Even with adequate support, all this probably would have tried them severely; but support was just what they lacked.

Every criminal, poacher, and ruffian knew the park rules and regulations were toothless. The failure of Congress to provide penalties for their transgression and the lack of jurisdiction within which to try offenders left the Park's officers only one recourse, to expel "trespassers" from the area. Even that expedient was liable to be an idle exercise, with the culprit back in the Park as soon as the officer was out of sight. If that was frustrating, the ill-considered attempt to substitute the laws of Wyoming Territory for proper federal procedures added degradation. Such a makeshift arrangement forced the assistants to cooperate with territorial officials whose principal concern was their own aggrandizement; the situation eventually brought down wrath and disaster on all concerned.

The assistants might have done better, despite their handicaps, had they been adequately supervised; but they were not. In the report of Special Agent W. Scott Smith, who investigated affairs in the Park for the secretary of the interior late in the summer of 1883, is the statement, "Superintendent Conger does not possess the activity or energy necessary for a good officer," and Smith points out that the superintendent also failed to comprehend the duties of his position and intentionally disregarded instructions, flagrantly violating some and making no attempt to implement others.[9] Without a doubt Conger's laxity was reflected in the performance of his assistants. It is possible, however, that the assistant superintendents deserve a more lenient verdict than Chittenden gave in his appraisal.

George Henderson had come to the Park in 1882 as a replacement for Clarence M. Stephens; thus, he had seniority over the later assistants which should have made him Conger's right-hand man.

George L. Henderson, the dour Scot who rose from "rabbit catcher" to park concessioner. From Yellowstone Park Museum collection.

Mammoth Hot Springs settlement, early 1880s. The McCartney building at left was used by the Hendersons as post office and store. From a photograph by T.W. Ingersoll, St. Paul, Minn.

The indications are that his services were entirely satisfactory to the superintendent during the first summer season, and he certainly did as well during that difficult winter of 1882-83 (spent by the superintendent at his comfortable home in Waterloo, Iowa) as could be expected of one man with no specific authority. Upon Conger's return to the Park at the beginning of the summer of 1883, Henderson moved his family from the blockhouse into one of the abandoned McCartney buildings,[10] fitting it up at his own expense as a combined residence and post office (operated by his daughters, Jennie and Lillie).

To that point, the relationship between Superintendent Conger and his principal assistant was a satisfactory one, enriched beyond their official contacts by common literary inclinations. But the intense investigation of Conger's management put an end to their earlier cooperation. Although that sub rosa look into park affairs was part of the knavery of the Hobart-Hatch clique, the superintendent apparently thought Henderson, whose brother was speaker of the House of Representatives, had a hand in it. Conger therefore voiced his dissatisfaction with Henderson to Secretary of the Interior Henry M. Teller on his way through Livingston with the Villard excursion in September.[11] Nothing came of that attempt to scuttle Henderson, but Conger did manage to strip him of his former authority by issuing an order designating D.E. Sawyer "my sole representative while I am absent, and leave him in charge."[12]

Conger continued to move against Henderson. During July, two local men, David Dobson and William Ramsdell, who had permission to coat certain items in the mineral-laden waters for sale to visitors, approached Jennie Henderson with the proposition that she sell their handiwork at the post office on a commission basis. This she did after obtaining assurance that the arrangement had Conger's approval. Somewhat later, R. P. Miles and A. H. Wyatt, who were authorized to bring into the Park petrified wood, geodes, and crystals of amethyst and quartz for sale, asked Jennie to merchandise "specimens" for them. Thus, when the Hatch excursion reached Mammoth Hot Springs in August, Special Agent Smith saw a considerable line of curiosities on sale at the post office and presumed this traffic originated in the Park, contrary to the rules and regulations established by the secretary of the interior for its management. Without checking further into the matter, Smith made this apparent violation a pièce de résistance of his report.

The secretary of the interior wrote Superintendent Conger concerning a number of things that Smith considered unsatisfactory, among them, this matter of the sale of specimens at the post office.

The specimen-coating racks on the Mammoth Hot Springs terraces. From a W.H. Jackson photograph, 1883.

Instead of explaining that he had allowed specimens to be brought into the Park for sale there, Superintendent Conger's reply of November 4, 1883, was worded to keep himself clear of involvement. He admitted knowing that a large collection of specimens was being displayed for sale, but added, "Where or how obtained I am unable to ascertain."

Assistant Henderson was unaware of that false statement until the following January when he read it in a congressional document containing copies of correspondence relating to Yellowstone Park, as furnished by the secretary of the interior.[13] He was understandably put out and took pains to explain his side of the matter. The secretary was provided with statements explaining where the specimens were obtained (in Tom Miner Basin, well outside the Park) and how permission had been obtained before allowing their sale at the post office. This correspondence showed the superintendent to be a petty liar, and the question raised by R.P. Miles, "What is P.H.C. trying to get at anyway?" is answered indirectly by the superintendent's letter of January 5, 1884,[14] in which he informed the secretary of the interior,"In reference to Mr. Henderson, I know but little of what he does. . . . He has never reported to me in person nor in writing save once, in each case." Obviously, Conger intended to get rid of Assistant Henderson and he had no particular scruples as to how it was done.

Secretary Teller undoubtedly recognized the animus, but there was nothing he could do about it short of the removal of Superintendent Conger, and that step he was unwilling to take for political reasons; but he did have a remedy for the lack of communication between the superintendent and his assistants: he suggested that the assistants be required to make quarterly reports on their activities.[15] Such reporting was not instituted until the following summer, however, and then only after the secretary required it (weekly) in terms that could not be ignored. Assistant Henderson's response is interesting:

> In compliance with your request I shall report at the close of each week and will be glad to carry out any measure for the furtherance of the objects for which the Park was intended, which in your judgement may be deemed advisable and best.[16]

The animosity between Superintendent Conger and Assistant Henderson seems to have abated with the canny Scot's graceful acceptance of the reporting requirement; however, this incident is but one of many collisions that manifest Conger's inability to manage the assistants. In the all-important matter of paying his subordinates (upon which much of an organization's morale hangs) the superintendent's record was sorry indeed. In the discharge of his fiscal responsibilities, Conger often let his personal feelings precede the rights of his men. In several instances, assistants wrote him repeatedly for their pay and finally had to take the matter up with the secretary of the interior before they received their due.

In other ways, life was not easy for the assistants. James Dean, one of the two married men on the force, discovered, after a long journey from his Maryland home, that there were no government quarters available for his family in the Park. They managed to house themselves during July and August in one of the many shacks at Mammoth, but the thought of suffering through a Yellowstone winter in such a hovel induced Dean to ask for a leave of absence for the worst months. He was joined in this by Samuel Erret, whose family was in a similar fix. Their requested leave covered the period November 1, 1883, to March 1, 1884. Conger forwarded the request to Secretary Teller, who bluntly informed him,

> These gentlemen describe the severity of the winter and the lack of winter quarters as the reasons for asking such leave. You will please inform them that under the law but thirty days leave can be granted in one calendar year. If they cannot remain in their posts of duty during the winter, their resignations will be accepted.[17]

Neither man resigned; perhaps neither could afford to give up a salary of $900 per annum. On the other hand, they may have received some promise not obvious in the secretary's letter. In a later exchange of correspondence between the Park and Washington, D.C., Superintendent Conger was authorized to "construct a sufficient number of cabins, at such points as might be required for the use of the assistants." A plan for a building suitable for the Norris Geyser Basin (where Dean was to be assigned) was submitted November 3, 1883, with an estimate of $332.50 for its construction. This was approved by the secretary on April 18, 1884.[18]

Assistant Dean somehow managed to house his family during that difficult winter, and the following summer he selected a site for the station at Norris Geyser Basin.[19] William Douglas was soon at work with his crew of laborers, putting up a four-room frame house, using lumber supplied by the steam sawmill operated by the Corps of Engineers. The work progressed so rapidly that Dean was able, on August 14, to "respectfully report that my wife and self, with teamster and team loaded with our supplies and household effects, arrived here at 12.15 oclk on the morning of the 13th inst., and are now snugly fixed in the new quarters."[20]

Before long it was obvious to Dean that his family could not winter in such a rude building as had been provided at Norris; and so, with the first nip of fall in the air, he sought to justify a return to Mammoth Hot Springs by bringing these facts to the attention of the superintendent:

> The weather here is quite cold. For several nights past water has frozen in our room. Will you kindly order me on duty at the Springs for the winter? Order to take effect Oct. 1st or at your pleasure. I ask this only on account of this building not being plastered. Consequently not in condition to occupy during the winter. I am told that Mr. Clark and family intend leaving the park; if so can I have the use of the building they vacate? or the Geisinger cabin. Perhaps I might get the use of Mess. Wakefield & Hoffman's cabin.[21]

The Dean family did return to Mammoth for the winter of 1884-85, thus completing the first of those cyclic movements—out into the Park in spring and back to headquarters in the fall—so typical of ranger life at a later time.

Dean's problems at the Norris Geyser Basin stand out clearly in his reports for the summer of 1884. Of the daily routine at that station, he wrote:

> Each morning I look over the Geyser Basin, observe the action of tourists, remove all debris that may be thrown in the geysers, springs, pools, etc. I then proceed to Gibbon Meadows...giving my attention to campfires that may have been left burning. I always have a shovel with me for this purpose, returning to my quarters about noon. . . . Afternoon, I patrol towards Lake of the Woods and return. . .21 miles each day.[22]

Evidently, Dean's days were consumed in a singlehanded effort to undo the work of vandals and prevent serious consequences developing from the prevailing carelessness with fire.

The hopelessness of this after-the-fact approach at last became apparent to Dean, for he later noted that the tourists "continue to test the power of the geysers by throwing timber in them, this and the neglect of many campers to extinguish their fires gives me all I can do." Thus, the harrassed assistant was understandably irate when the escort of a Captain Snyder, from Fort Ellis, allowed three large campfires to burn into the forest. He angrily commented after many hours of grimy work controlling the blaze: "Let the military have charge of the park."[23] Regardless, Dean continued to do his job well, both at Norris and at other points in the Park, for he was a good man who eventually gravitated into the service of the Yellowstone Park Association and rose to the position of general manager.

The young man who went to the Upper Geyser Basin, the Kansan J.W. Weimer, was also a good man, though one would not think so from his early reports. He reached his station on June 20, 1884, to find only a few wandering "pilgrims" there, sheltering themselves in the dilapidated cabin that was to be his summer home and official station. His first report to Superintendent Conger consisted of two words: "mosquitoes intolerable." Conger thought that was rather too brief, and Weimer cleverly justified himself with the comment, "as to my last report, if it was not interesting it certainly has the merit of not being tedious."[24] Weimer, too, had trouble preventing visitors from throwing things into the geysers, but his greatest problem was how to check their tendency to gather specimens and break formations. Of this, Weimer said: "When I interfere I am met with the question 'why are the rules of the park not posted somewhere that people might know what they are'?" and he adds that he took the privilege of posting a notice reading, "Breaking or defacing formations and throwing things into the geysers are forbidden by order of the Sec. of the Interior. P.H. Conger Supt."[25]

In August, Weimer noted some improvement. He wrote:

> The basin has become quite lively with tourists. Saw less tendency to throw things into the geysers, but to carry off from the monarch of geysers (Old Faithful) a souvenir of some kind is a temptation *unabating* and *determined*. Wakefield and Hoffman should be notified that two of their drivers, the ones that were here on Friday last, are guilty of defacing formations and throwing stones into the geysers. They done so for the benefit of their passengers. Employees should be the last ones to need watching. We have enough to do to watch outsiders.[26]

Weimer decided that Old Faithful Geyser required special attention, and when Assistant William H. Terry was sent out to help him he arranged for one of them always to be in the vicinity of its cone during daylight hours. This was helpful so far as Old Faithful was concerned; the specimen collectors however merely shifted their operation to the Black Sand Basin, which soon began to suffer severely, particularly that marshy portion known then as Specimen Lake.

It was difficult for the assistants to protect the scattered formations in the geyser basins without mobility. James Dean had purchased a horse with his own money and so was able to patrol his district, but the men in the Firehole basins had not been so provident. Lorenzo D. Godfrey, who was stationed at the Lower Geyser Basin that summer, importuned the superintendent: "Can't you let me have a horse or mule to ride? The territory is so large I cannot walk over half of it. I would not ask you for a horse if I did not need one. The old horse that is here falls down every time I get on him."[27] If Godfrey accomplished little, it could be said in his defense that he had as little to work with; even the cabin at Nez Perce Creek, which was his station, was but a makeshift shelter without floor or door.

Edmund L. Fish, stationed at Soda Butte, was another of the better men. His reports show that the problems of that locality were entirely different from those of other stations. There, the Cooke City mining camp, and squatters along the freight road leading into the mining district, were filling their needs from the resources of the northeast corner of the Park. Miners and ranchmen alike considered themselves entitled to park game, the ranchmen even assuming a right to the wild hay of the meadows along Lamar River and its tributaries, Soda Butte and Slough creeks, by virtue of their residence there.

Assistant Fish lived at first in the old gamekeeper's cabin built for Harry Yount and later preempted by old Billy Jump. He had Weimer for company the first winter, which was fortunate as he was sick much of the time from what was roughly diagnosed as "indigestion and its complications." Weimer was quick to note the prevalence of illegal hunting in the area. On a trip to Yancey's, near the Baronett Bridge, in the fall of 1883, he saw "Uncle John" and his hired man come in with their pack horses loaded with fresh meat; and later he met Jack Rutherford with packhorse and rifle, who freely admitted that he was hunting. But it was a party of Cooke City miners who really stirred up Weimer. He met them as they came down from Cooke City with a Mr. Sanders, and they told him they were on their way out to Gardiner. Instead of going out, however, they stopped near Specimen Creek, killed many elk, and cached some of the meat before returning to Cooke City with all the meat their animals could carry. The story of how they had circumvented the assistant superintendent got around, to the great discomfiture of Weimer and Fish.[28] Later, after Fish saw a member of that hunting party camped near the Baronett Bridge, he commented, "Nothing can be done now but if we should be empowered to enforce the laws soon I should dearly love to snatch the *son of a bitch* bald headed."[29]

The two young assistants did get in a lick that winter when Fish found a tent about two miles above the mouth of Slough Creek containing nine quarters of elk meat and several pack saddles; in the vicinity were seven horses. The stock, equipment, and meat, which were said to belong to Tom Woody and "Horn" Miller (then hunting for Major Eaton of Cooke City), were confiscated, but not without some misgivings. As Fish said in his report on the matter: "Mr.

Weimer and myself feel anxious to do all in our power but unless we are invested with more authority this taking of other men's property under such circumstances seems to us to be dangerous business."[30] Though Fish evidently feared that his attempts to enforce the regulations might lead to a reprisal upon his person, the trouble which at last broke upon him took a different form.

The large trout taken in Fish Lake (now Trout Lake) were an important item in the diet of the Cooke City people, who had been accustomed to taking fish there with giant powder, spear, and seine. This practice was in violation of the secretary's regulations, which had been revised in 1883 to prohibit hunting and all methods of fishing except by hook and line.[31] In May 1884, Assistant Fish, with Cassius Conger, the superintendent's son, who had been hired as gamekeeper, were riding toward Fish Lake when they saw the Cooke City mail carrier, Frank Phiscater, ahead of them. Instead of waiting for them to come up, Frank turned his horse and galloped toward Trout Lake. Only one conclusion could be drawn from his peculiar action: that he was riding back to warn friends who were illegally fishing. Fish made the mistake of discussing his suspicions with Uncle John Yancey, who passed the information back to Frank Phiscater. As a result, Fish soon had to report that the mail carrier "refuses to carry my mail either way and even opened the bundle of mail for the Springs yesterday and took Cannon's and left mine. Now if you should be in a hurry to get word to me you would have to send a special messenger."[32] There were indications that the illegal fishing continued. On one occasion they found a man in the vicinity of the lake carrying a fish spear and they later heard that eighty pounds of fish were brought into Cooke City, which led Assistant Fish to remark, "What could I do if I caught them in the very act?" It was this frustration that caused him to write to the superintendent: "I am very anxious for power to act like a man and not like a sneak in Park matters and hope you can send good news from Congress soon."[33]

The squatters in the northeast corner of the Park were a considerable nuisance to the assistant superintendents. When questioned by the secretary of the interior concerning the presence of such persons Superintendent Conger answered as follows:

In the spring of 1882, Mr. Yancey made application to me for permission to build a cabin at a point in the Park about 18 miles from this place for the purpose of accommodating the stage which had recently been put on to the route to Cooke City. And also a Mr. Jackson made a like application to occupy a point about 12 miles further on towards Cooke City, and also a Mr. Jump to occupy another point some miles still further up the road, which would equip the route with the necessary stations. I considered these stopping places an indispensible necessity (for it was through an uninhabited wilderness), and therefore after careful inquiry as to the character of these men, and after each had pledged himself to me strictly to observe all the laws and rules governing (if any should come to their knowledge) of any trespassers in the park, I gave them my verbal consent.[34]

In that manner Uncle John Yancey became established at Pleasant Valley near the Baronett Bridge; George J. Jackson, whose partner was Buckskin Jim Cutler, gained lodgement at Rose Creek (where the Buffalo Ranch was later established); and William Jump took over the old gamekeeper's cabin near Soda Butte. These men were followed by other settlers who did not have even that improper authorization. Silley and Fitzgerald located at Soda Butte in connection with the staging operation; J. B. Tate and Winfield Scott located nearby in order to cut hay for the stage teams (though they were soon selling hay to Cooke City residents); and Yank Hodgson found himself a place near Rose Creek. The manner in which Yank Hodgson established himself is probably typical. In a letter to the superintendent, Assistant Fish says, "Yank Hodgson talks of putting a bridge across the east fork and has been waiting to see whether you would veto it but as you said nothing in your last he thinks it is alright."[35]

The real motive of many of these squatters was simply to be there and in control of a piece of ground if and when the Congress should pass a bill segregating a portion of the northern part of the Park, which would return that land to the public domain and open it for settlement. It was with such hopes that Charles Marston and Joseph Johnston located on Slough Creek, and Red Siwash established a saloon at Round Prairie. With these squatters came herds of cattle and bands of horses, mowing machines, buildings, corrals and fences, and, of course, a great deal of disregard for park rules and regulations.

The assistant superintendents stationed at Gardiner (William Chambers, Jr., and William H. Terry) also had problems, but theirs were largely of their own making; in fact, they seem to have measured up quite well to the popular image of a park officer. How these men were housed is not certain, though they probably occupied one of the cabins built illegally within the Park by Gardiner residents who hoped in that manner to establish a claim in the event that the Montana strip was returned to the public domain. There is no doubt that Chambers and Terry soon embraced some of the less virtuous ways of the neighboring townsmen. Word of their gambling and drinking reached Superintendent Conger, whose reprimand drew these replies: Chambers said, "I will acknowledge I played cards once or twice up there but come down to gambling it is something I know nothing about—I might have made the expression in a joking way that I was going to play them pretty high so that your informant could catch on as I wanted him to do. I guess I come pretty near knowing where it come from and if I was inclined to gamble I would have to have some money I think to gamble with."[36] As for Terry, he declared, "I will take an oath that I never gambled in my life or drank whisky to an excess. I never was drunk in my life but once and that was when I was about 12 years old. . . . I want to have a long talk with you about the reports that have been sent up to you."[37]

The most serious difficulty at Gardiner developed over the hauling of wood gathered in the Park. As fall turned to winter, the two assistant superintendents felt the need for a better wood supply than they were able to obtain by foraging among the sage bushes on the flat within the park boundary; so Terry made arrangements with a Cooke City freighter, H. D. Beaman, to haul wood in return for the privilege of taking his winter supply of fuel from the Park.[38] The result was predictable. Other townspeople considered that they, too, had a right to obtain their firewood in the Park, and the assistants began to levy upon this traffic. Chambers was soon able to report that they were getting all the wood they needed in that manner. He says: "The people here took a tumble when we told them we would report them. One man said we had no right to get wood that way. I asked him by what right he had to haul and he said nothing but took us a load over to the cabin."[39]

This irregular and high-handed procedure led to rumors that the assistants were selling wood, and a complaint finally reached the secretary of the interior. Superintendent Conger was told to put an end to the hauling of wood out of the Park and he passed that along. But Terry found it was not so easy to stop what he had started. He made the rounds of the town of Gardiner notifying the citizens not to haul any more wood, that he had orders from Superintendent Conger not to allow it; but Mr. Wannakee, the grocer, did not propose to stop, so that Terry had to inform the superintendent that "he said he did not care what you said, if he wanted a load of wood he would go and get a load, and I could report him."[40] Respect for park rules and regulations sank a little lower.

These troubles tended to generate attitudes that rendered even the good men ineffective. George Henderson, who had achieved some success in educating the park guides toward fair treatment of the parties they conducted through the Park and had gained their cooperation in properly extinguishing campfires, saw his efforts negated by a hostile attitude. One guide who was cautioned about leaving campfires said "if he did he would defy any of the ten assistants to take him." Henderson was forced to admit, "It is well understood that some lawless men know, or seem to know, that there is no legal authority to arrest and punish for any violation of park regulations."[41] Fortunately, not all guides were of that type. Henderson was able to speak highly of Elwood Hofer, both as guide and for his care in preventing the spread of fires. On one trip through the Park, Elwood and his guests suppressed six fires that had originated in the camp sites of other visitors.

Added to the hostility of park guides, most of whom lived immediately north of the Park, the assistant superintendents at Mammoth Hot Springs had their troubles with vandals and specimen collectors. A visitor of that day has left an interesting account of Assistant Samuel Erret's handling of such an incident. Our informant, a doctor from Butte, was walking about the terraces with a friend who was attracted by the beauty of some sulphur crystals and picked up a few. This happened in the presence of Assistant Erret, who did not take away the specimens but, instead, took out a copy of the park rules and regulations and read the pertinent passages to the offender, who, it is reported, "unconsciously dropped all his specimens."[42] Assistant Henderson has recorded a somewhat similar incident and his concern over it.

> A visitor came in carrying in his hand a small portion of a specimen detached from one of the terraces, which, he could not inform me as but few of them are named. On being informed that such mutilation was strictly prohibited he expressed his regret and confirmed his utter ignorance of having violated any law. Would you, in such cases, deprive parties of articles so found in their possession?[43]

If Superintendent Conger answered Henderson's question, the reply has not been found.

The most vexing of all problems for the assistants at Mammoth Hot Springs were generated by the Yellowstone Park Improvement Company. This company's attempt to establish a monopoly in the Park in 1882 was frustrated, it will be remembered, by Senator George Graham Vest backed by General P. H. Sheridan and *Forest and Stream*. As finally legitimized in 1883, the company was based upon a lease given by the secretary of the interior to Carroll T. Hobart and Henry F. Douglas, who took the New York capitalist, Rufus

Hatch, into partnership with them for financial backing. In return for financing the construction operations through the sale of $500,000 worth of bonds, Rufus Hatch was to have the presidency and 40 percent of the stock. Hatch failed to meet his commitment, with the result that the Yellowstone Park Improvement Company had financial difficulties almost from the beginning. Carroll Hobart, general manager, erected the National Hotel largely on credit by trading on Rufus Hatch's considerable reputation; he hoped that a profitable operation during the summer of 1883 would produce sufficient revenue to hold off creditors. Hobart attempted to economize by contracting with local hunters for wild meat to feed his workmen and, later, the guests of the National Hotel. The low bidders of course were hunters who intended to obtain meat from within the Park.

The presence of two of these hunters on Slough Creek, and the confiscation of their meat, equipment, and horses has already been noted; but the most serious case involved Ira Dodge, who had agreed to furnish meat at $5 per hundred weight and then proceeded to obtain it from the elk herd wintering on Swan Lake Flat and the slopes of Sepulcher Mountain. Superintendent Conger reported the incident:

> Three days ago two men were discovered in the mountains on snow shoes, having with them a dog. They were followed and watched by Messrs. Sawyer and Cannon for some three or four miles when their dog started an elk, ran it off the top of the mountain into the deep snow, when they caught and cut its throat and butchered it. They then cut the best parts of the meat off the animal, put it into bags they seemed to have with them for the purpose, shouldered the sacks and started for their house, here near the big hotel . . . I directed Sawyer and Cannon not to discover themselves to these men if they could avoid it, my object being to secure the legal proof beyond a doubt of the guilt of the parties. Therefore after the hunters had left for home Sawyer and Cannon explored the country round about there and were rewarded by discovering a hunters camp constructed of boughs and covered with snow, secreted in a deep and secluded gulch, in which they found three saddles, two bridles, and some ropes. They brought home one saddle and two bridles (all they could carry) and have returned today to secure the balance of the property, which I have seized as contraband. These saddles and bridles are supposed and doubtless did belong to the Park Improvement Company; they bear the company's brand. Indeed all, or nearly all, of the trouble I have had with hunters within the park has come through or by this hotel company. I am aware that they deny and will deny any complicity or knowledge of any illicit hunting in the park, but unfortunately for them circumstances which cànnot lie render it impossible for me to believe them. I have information which I think

trustworthy that this same hunter and contractor now has thirty elk carcasses hid in the snow near this place, watching his opportunity to deliver them on his contract, and they doubtless would have been delivered before this time had the company been in condition to receive and pay for them.[44]

A further search disclosed another hunting camp in which was found twenty quarters of elk meat and about one hundred pounds of dried meat, with a few camp utensils and some provisions, and in the vicinity were three caches of elk meat so frozen into the snow that the quantity could not be determined. All of this was traced to Ira Dodge, of whom Superintendent Conger says: "We were obliged to let him go for the want of the legal authority to detain him. He has left the park now."[45]

Carroll Hobart, who through his contracting was the instigator of this illegal meat hunting, was a difficult person to deal with in other matters. He cut timber for his sawmill without authorization and did it in such a way as to obstruct the Norris road (above the terraces) with tops, limbs, and other debris. This brought on an early conflict with Superintendent Conger and the two engaged in a running feud , thereafter, in which Conger accused Hobart of hunting in the vicinity of Mammoth Hot Springs (which he had done) and Hobart, in turn, accused Conger of renting government horses to visitors (of which there is no evidence). In the long run, Hobart's press relations, his connection with Assistant Secretary Joslyn, and his opportunity to influence Special Agent W. Scott Smith brought him a victory in the form of Superintendent Conger's dismissal.

The Yellowstone Park Improvement Company, to pursue its story to its demise, lost money during the summer of 1883 because of the short season. Far from being able to satisfy its many creditors, the concern was unable even to pay the workmen employed in finishing the National Hotel at Mammoth Hot Springs. The insolvency came to light quite by chance. Manager Hobart had employed a civil engineer by the name of Landon from Fargo, Dakota Territory, to subdivide the land at the Cinnabar townsite so that the company might sell the lots. Landon completed his work in September, but Hobart put off paying him for no good reason. Being a blunt sort of man, the engineer resorted to his six-shooter and forced Hobart to shell out $260, about half the amount due.[46] Word of this affair soon got around, and while it was not immediately believed that a corporation headed by Rufus Hatch could be in financial difficulties, the events of the following winter proved that to be the case.

By March the unpaid carpenters at the National Hotel were in desperate straits, many of them lacking adequate clothing to face a rigorous winter; Hobart finally had to mortgage lumber stacked at the Cinnabar mill to get $200 for their relief.[47] That was the tip-off the creditors needed. They swarmed in, placing liens on every movable thing, the stock of liquors and the piano included. The workmen then began the protracted sit-in mentioned in Chapter 10. To insure that they were not ousted by force, some of those desperate fellows prepared kindlings at places convenient for burning down the hotel and let it be known that if they were molested they would apply the torch.[48]

At this point, Rufus Hatch went before a United States court in New Jersey to complain that the company was insolvent; he sought the appointment of a receiver in the interest of creditors. In the absence of anything to the contrary, the petition was granted, and A.L. Love, a Livingston banker and old crony of Hatch, was appointed receiver on March 6.[49] Hobart and Douglas were taken by surprise, claiming Hatch had played them false—"a stockjobber's trick," they called it, which it undoubtedly was.

Receiver Love attempted to get control of the National Hotel, but was bluntly told to stay away or the workmen would put a bullet through him. And while he was busy trying to reason with the men through an intermediary, Hobart and Douglas were arranging to checkmate him. This they accomplished through the Wyoming courts, which appointed a receiver favorable to the Hobart-Douglas interests. This man, George B. Hulme, eventually won control of the company assets and its $38,000 indebtedness. (A curious fact of the accounting made then is that Rufus Hatch was shown to have paid $106,000 into the concern, while Douglas and Hobart together had contributed only $6,000.)[50]

Receiver Hulme was at first no more successful than Love had been in arriving at some settlement that would release the National Hotel from the control of the unpaid workmen. As the summer of 1884 approached, the Northern Pacific Railroad showed its concern by stating that unless the hotel strike was solved, the railroad would proceed to erect tents in the Park for the accommodation of its tourists. As Vice President Oakes put it, this was an important matter with the Northern Pacific.[51] The railroad did not have to go that far, as receiver Hulme was able to settle with the workmen. They received $10,000 in cash and sixteen passes east on the Northern Pacific Railroad, which allowed the National Hotel to open on July 10.[52]

The real winner in this skirmish over the Yellowstone Park Improvement Company was Carroll T. Hobart, for receiver Hulme kept him on as manager for the summer of 1884, which was another losing season. Based on that experience, Hulme leased the hotel to

Hobart for $1 in 1885, whereupon Hobart proceeded to clean up financially, proving he was not as incompetent as he had appeared. At that point, an end was put to the Yellowstone Park Improvement Company and its scheming stockholders, receivers, and manager through sale of the property to an agent of the Northern Pacific Railroad Company.

Superintendent Patrick H. Conger, who had displayed neither the wisdom nor the energy required by his official position, and who was yet too stubbornly honest to serve the park improvement company's interests, became a casualty on September 10, 1884, when he was replaced by Robert Emmett Carpenter. This appointment, which appears to have been decided on as early as the latter part of July,[53] must have delighted Mr. Hobart as much as Conger had disappointed him, for Carpenter was a politician of very simple views. As historian Hiram Chittenden has pointed out, the requirements of his office were quite clear to Mr. Carpenter: "In his opinion, the Park was created to be an instrument of profit to those who were shrewd enough to grasp the opportunity."[54] The new superintendent was probably in league with C. T. Hobart even before he reached the Park (subsequent events indicate as much), but his knavery was so crude and intolerable that he eliminated himself from the superintendency before he was of much service to the nearly defunct Yellowstone Park Improvement Company.

The assistant superintendents, whose image was blackened by Carroll Hobart more than even they deserved, have been seen as both good men and bad—average young men working under the disadvantages of poor leadership, inadequate housing, equipment, and experience, and unsupported by law, so that whatever enthusiasm they brought to their employment was finally drained away by constant frustration. More than that, they were often maligned. Recognizing as they did that their inabilities stemmed largely from the impotency of the park rules and regulations, these men welcomed the extension of Wyoming law into Yellowstone National Park in the summer of 1884. Had they been able to foresee the consequences of that law in operation, they would not have been so happy; it was Wyoming law that deprived them of their jobs and brought the Park to the verge of ruin.

In his annual report for 1881, Superintendent Norris had suggested that the Park should be placed in a county of Wyoming and that Wyoming law should be enforced within the area. As a result of the shooting of James Armstrong by David Kennedy on St. Patrick's Day in 1882, Superintendent Conger "gave notice of the commission of the crime to the governor of Wyoming,"[55] and while this did not bring the assailant to justice, it did acquaint Governor Hale with the state of lawlessness then existing in the Park. Subsequently, an effort was made to attach Yellowstone National Park to Montana for judicial purposes, and this immediately drew the ire of Wyoming.[56] Governor Hale asked the legislature at its next session to take steps to extend Wyoming law into the Park. Accordingly, the Eighth Legislative Assembly of the Territory of Wyoming passed an act "to render operative and effectual the laws of the Territory of Wyoming within that portion of the Yellowstone National Park lying within said Territory, and to protect and preserve the timber, game, fish, and natural objects and curiosities of the park, and to assist in preserving the rights of the United States therein."[57]

As approved March 6, 1884, the act provided that the portion of the Yellowstone National Park lying within the Territory of Wyoming should be considered a part of the county of Uinta and that it would constitute a voting precinct of that county. It required the governor to appoint two justices of the peace and two constables for the precinct and specified that all the laws of the Territory of Wyoming would be operative. In addition, the laws of the United States and the rules and regulations of the secretary of the interior for the government of the Park were given the same force and effect as the laws of the Territory of Wyoming, and the maximum penalty for a misdemeanor was set at not in excess of $100 or imprisonment for more than six months in a county jail. That section of the act specifically concerned with the protection of the animals, birds, and fish of the Park is identical to the order published by the secretary of the interior early in 1883. It was specified that one of the justices should have his office at Mammoth Hot Springs, and the other in the lower Firehole Basin, where provision was made for a jail. Money was appropriated for the establishment and operation of legal procedures, including an annual salary of $300 for each of the justices of the peace, and $400 annually, plus $100 for a horse and equipment, for each of the constables. In all specifics, and in its avowed purpose "to assist and aid the government of the United States in keeping and maintaining the said Park as a place of resort" there was nothing unusual or wrong. Section 17 of the act, however, was another matter. It provided "that one-half of all fines assessed against offenders under the provisions of this act shall be paid to the officer or other person who appears as the prosecuting witness or informer, and the residue shall be paid into the territorial treasury as is here and before provided." It was from that provision that trouble developed.

Assistant Superintendent Weimer's reaction to the passage of the act was jubilation. As he saw it, the Wyoming law "adds another object of interest to tourists in the shape of a club in my hands. The scheme works well as a bluff and when properly applied will work much good." A visitor admitted that the law "makes people more discreet about their thieving, and they seldom at present destroy the formations," but this same individual, after hearing the provisions of the law extolled by Assistant Cannon in the course of a ride toward Norris Geyser Basin, came to the conclusion that "not a thing that runs, walks, leaps, hops or crawls, but is covered, named and described by this awful law," and he thought it would probably be better to commit murder in the state of Connecticut than to be found guilty of killing an elk in the national park.[58]

Actually, he was not so far wrong, as events soon proved. The men selected by the governor of Wyoming Territory to fill the enforcement positions in the Park were almost unlettered products of the frontier, capable of meting out only the rudest justice, and certainly strangers to the fine points of law. Given the incentive of fee splitting, they were as industrious and uncritical as the vigilantes, from whom they were but one step removed. If this sounds harsh, we might look in at one of the first "trials" under Wyoming law. (The report is by an English tourist.) One of the party of Englishmen who had returned to Mammoth Hot Springs from the geyser basins had included with his baggage some fragments of geyserite which he was careless enough to display openly. This caused a constable to arrest the man and take him before the justice of the peace for trial.

> In an outbuilding a Court was hurriedly improvised, a Justice of the Peace of somewhat battered appearance presided, the general aspect of the Court and spectators seen by the light of two small lamps and through the cloud of cigar-smoke, might be described as rugose, and seemed to promise Justice neat, unsweetened by mercy. The accused was a blond gentleman, whose fairness was in touching contrast to the bronze of the members of the Vehmgericht. The presiding magistrate made a few remarks on the heinousness of the offense so impressively that we emptied our pockets of the geyserite fragments we had. . . After the observations of the Justice, the proceedings took a somewhat Pickwickian character; it was discovered that the Act was not yet quite sufficiently matured . . . and that the offender had been solely influenced by scientific considerations. The Court broke up and by detachments adjourned to the "saloon," to the discussion of the *cause celebre*. There we heard the decision of the court colloquialized—"Nary a fine, fer the Act only come down on the wires; and he weren't a goin' to sell the sp'c'm'ns, ner give 'em to gells fer toys."[59]

Another farce played out in that courtroom involved James Mc-Cartney's civil suit against George Henderson for rent on the cabin

George occupied, a building McCartney had erected on his claim before he was dispossessed. Justice Metcalf heard the arguments of counsel for both sides, deliberated for a time, and then decided he had no jurisdiction, and the case remained undecided.[60] These were the inauspicious beginnings of Wyoming law in the Park. While it was later made to serve reasonably well where poaching was concerned, its intemperate use against Park visitors finally generated serious trouble.

In the latter days of Superintendent Conger's regime, the secretary of the interior had requested that the unauthorized settlers in the northeast corner of the Park be removed, reciting the grounds for taking such action and suggesting the use of Wyoming law. Subsequently, the secretary had required compliance and Conger's failure to act was undoubtedly the immediate reason for his removal.[61] When this same request was made of Superintendent Carpenter, he was quick to act for such a course fitted neatly into his own plans. His letter of October 30 informed George J. Jackson, Jack Rutherford, and R.E. Cutler:

> Gentlemen: You and each of you are hereby notified that unless you shall have removed yourselves with all personal property to you belonging out of the boundaries of the Yellowstone National Park within thirty days (30 days) from the date of the service of this notice, you and each of you with your personal property will be removed from said park, through such means and by such measures, as, by the U.S. statutes and the rules and regulations of said park, are in such case made and provided. Given under my hand on the date first above written.[62]

The notice was duly served by Assistant Fish, who was given to understand that they would comply. But the stipulated time expired without their doing so and they were given eight additional days before Superintendent Carpenter acted.[63]

The superintendent then sent a party of assistants and constables under prosecutor D.H. Budlong (an official in the Park under Wyoming law). This force went first to the ranch of Tate and Scott, about five miles above Soda Butte, where, in the words of a local editor they "burned their buildings and their winter supply of bread and butter."[64] After that summary action the officers returned to Rose Creek with the intention of doing likewise there, but were opposed by Buckskin Jim Cutler. As they approached, Jim raised his gun and was on the point of firing on Constables Hale and Scott when Jack Rutherford prevented him. For his rashness, Jim was arrested, put in irons and taken to Evanston, Wyoming, where he stood trial on a charge of assaulting an officer. To the great disappointment of those who had arrested him and gone to such pains to bring him to the bar of justice, Jim received only a fine of $75 and costs. This action against the noncommissioned residents of the Park met with general disapproval, and the prevailing sentiment was probably accurately mirrored in the words of the same editor, who said: "It would seem that some better means of disposing of these law breakers (if such they are) could have been devised than the wanton destruction of property to the amount of several hundred dollars. At least those who are familiar with the facts in the case, judge Mr. Carpenter's action in the matter as altogether too hasty and utterly unjustifiable."

If Buckskin Jim Cutler appears to have come off better than he should have at his trial in Evanston, Wyoming, there was probably sound reasoning behind the leniency. The town had come off second-best in an earlier attempt to promote law and order in the Park and its citizens had no intention of repeating that mistake. The May 9, 1885 issue of the *Livingston Enterprise* notes that "James Nelson, sometimes familiarly called 'Big Jim,' 'Buckskin,' and other dime-novel names, attempted to gain lodgings at the Riepan Hotel on last Monday night by brandishing a six-shooter under the nose of the landlord and boarders and warning them that he was a 'b-a-d m-a-n.'" Of course, he was corralled and lodged in jail, which was exactly what he wanted. The editor continues, "Jim's first appearance in Evanston was last winter, when he was brought here from the Yellowstone National Park to serve a sentence in our county jail for petty larceny. Since his release from jail his conduct has not been such as to inspire public opinion in his favor. It has been hoped for some time that he would return to grace society in the park; but failing to thus accommodate himself to public sentiment our officers have been compelled to 'gather him in.'" Like the bowery bum who, when he was down and out, could always get a bed in a warm jail cell by tossing a brick through a store window, Jim had also learned a trick or two about survival.

The adverse reaction that followed Superintendent Carpenter's ouster of settlers in the northeast corner of the Park was nothing compared to the furor that was soon raised against him. The winter session of Congress found the superintendent in the national capital for the purpose of lobbying (probably in the interests of the Northern Pacific Railroad Company) for the segregation of the lands that the Yellowstone Park Improvement Company wanted cut off from Yellowstone Park in order to build a railroad from Cinnabar to Cooke City along the Yellowstone and Lamar rivers. Carpenter was a key man in a scheme that would enable certain persons to profit from the expected withdrawal of lands from the Park. Carpenter was to telegraph news of the successful passage of the segregation bill to a confederate at Livingston (apparently his son), who was to pass the word along to interested persons at Gardiner by means of the new telephone. The information thus obtained would allow those in the know to rush out and claim certain coal deposits and other valuable lands lying within the area detached from the Park. It was a neat scheme, theoretically.

Events in Washington, D.C., had matured so far by Friday, February 20, that Carpenter thought there was no reason to doubt swift passage of the segregation measure; so he telegraphed his man at Livingston.

Attempts to relay the message to Gardiner were not successful. A code had been agreed upon, the wording "secure that horse at once" was to be used to initiate the land grab. But the message did not come in clearly at the Gardiner end of the line, and the ensuing shouting soon put all the loafers in Hall's store on the qui vive. An attempt to use an alternative signal ("no wind in Livingston") was, as the editor of the *Livingston Enterprise* pointed out,"so manifestly mysterious and doubtful in its probability that it aroused suspicion outside the circle for whose benefit it was particularly intended."[65]

The chosen ones prepared for an early start the next morning, but so many others had smelled a rat that when the conspirators left town in the predawn hours they were tagged by forty or fifty persons who straggled along to find out what was going on. According to our informant, the stampede over mountains and valleys that bitter night resulted in almost every man at Gardiner and Mammoth Hot Springs securing "a horse." Among the names that appeared on location notices attached to claim posts were those of C.T. Hobart and R.E. Carpenter, and the latter soon had reason to regret the kindness of his friends.

Actually, the segregation bill failed to pass the Senate and the land grab was premature. The only result of this awkwardly engineered affair was to make the plan public knowledge. Locally, there was much disapproval, and surprisingly most of it came from the town of Cooke City. A dispatch originating there said:

> The action of certain park officials in locating valuable property when it was reported that a part of the park was segregated is criticised here. They pounced upon Soda Butte springs and other properties and went so far as to have their location notices posted in advance and changed from day to day. This they did while professing great commiseration for the squatters who were summarily ejected from their homes on the park borders in the dead of last winter.[66]

But the fat was really in the fire when word of such happenings reached the East. The editor of the New York weekly *Forest and Stream* lashed out with an article calling on Secretary of the Interior L.Q.C. Lamar to remove Superintendent Carpenter. He was charged with neglect of duty, working in the interests of the Yellowstone Park Improvement Company, placing obstacles in the way of law enforcement, and with "having laid claim to a portion of the national park."[67] At that stage of developments, the secretary's response was predictable. He was quoted as follows:

> Charges were filed against Carpenter before I came into this office. I believe they were withdrawn by the persons who made them. The matter will be investigated. Generally, it is not wise to act upon newspaper charges, for there is seldom anyone accountable and responsible for them. In the matter of so much importance as the preservation of a national park, we cannot overlook charges of this kind.[68]

While the secretary's slow-moving investigation was getting under way, Superintendent Carpenter had his opportunity to defend himself publicly in the press and he began,

> I have every reason to believe that this false and cowardly attack upon me originated in the park and is written by one who has been inimical to me ever since I assumed the duties of my office. The charges are all susceptible of refutation and most of them are so transparently gauzy that they do not need to be disproved in this vicinity where the facts are known.

From there he went on to deny a number of charges dealing with issues other than the segregation of park lands His defense in that matter was:

> The charges that I am interested in various schemes with the Hobarts is, as I have said, false in every particular. While I was in Washington I was called before the House Committee of Military Affairs to give my views regarding the proposed reduction of the park, and was also frequently approached by Congressmen on the same subject. On such occasions, I stated the fact that the portion proposed to be segregated contained no objects of interest and expressed my opinion that to cut off enough of that region of the park to allow a railroad to the mines outside its borders was much better than to have a freighting thoroughfare through the park, as is now the case. But I had no interest whatever in seeing the reduction made from other than my opinion of what was best for the park, and for the country as a whole. I was in communication with no one outside of Washington directly or indirectly regarding the progress of the Vest bill. I asked no one to give me a share in the lands to be segregated and no such share had been offered me. The use of my name in locating those coal lands was without my knowledge, consent

or expectation. When I heard that Mr. Hoppe had done so I was very sorry, as I knew it was not in accordance with my official position and might lead to a false inference, which has been the case.

Superintendent Carpenter concluded with a correct assessment of his future when he added: "I do not expect to hold the office very long, but I should like to retain the position through one tourist season only to show that I am competent, as I claim to be, and to refute this cowardly publication against me."[69]

In this great farce, there is one more note of comedy. At the time the news of the supposed passage of the segregation bill reached Livingston, a rider was dispatched to carry the message to Gardiner as a hedge against failure of the telephone; and so Dave Roberts mounted his horse at 5 P.M. that fateful Friday and galloped off up the valley through sixty miles of snow and cold, bearing the details of what had presumedly transpired at the capital. It was later remarked that his ride would live in history with such famous events as the ride from Ghent to Aix, Paul Revere's ride, Sheridan's famous ride to Winchester, or "any other ride." Dave's unappreciative friends christened him "fly-by-night."

As a direct result of his dereliction, and in spite of a vigorous defense by Assistant Secretary M.A. Joslyn (who thought the charges were "frivolous and unworthy of consideration"[70]), Robert D. Carpenter was removed from the position of superintendent of Yellowstone National Park on June 20, 1885, and replaced by David W. Wear, a stern and unbending Missourian, whose misfortune was mainly that he arrived too late upon the scene.

Ten days before Superintendent Carpenter's removal, his relationship with the Yellowstone Park Improvement Company was made public, and that summer he served as the manager of a hotel erected at the Upper Geyser Basin.[71] The first hotel at Old Faithful was built by Charles F. Hobart, the contractor brother of the park improvement company's manager. The building (considered "a shack and a disgrace to the park") was flimsily constructed with a foundation of small posts set shallowly in the loose soil, sills and joists of small pine poles, a floor of slabs with the sawn side up, and sides of the same. The inner walls were lined with very thin muslin to cover the rough side of the slabs, and the entire structure was so poorly braced it was immediately classed as dangerous.[72] Assistant Weimer also found that shortly after Carpenter took charge of the building a privy for the hotel had been built in the grove of trees halfway between the building and the cone of Old

The "Shack" hotel in the Upper Geyser Basin, 1889 (on site of present Old Faithful Inn). Such round-format pictures were taken by the first box cameras marketed by George Eastman. Yellowstone Park Museum collection.

In 1885 he developed a practicable "dry" photographic emulsion on a flexible base and followed that up by offering the new medium to the public in a small, hand-held camera. Such "Kodaks" – his trade name – were loaded at the factory, where they had to be returned for film processing and reloading after 100 exposures were made. The initial cost for the loaded camera was $25.00, and each processing and reloading was $10.00 (amounting to ten cents for each printed picture returned with the camera). This system of snap-shot photography was continued until 1896.

Faithful geyser, and that the ground in front of the hotel was littered with construction and occupational debris. His comment: "Such unsightlyness on the part of the landlord is utterly intolerable."[73] Weimer was so disgusted that he informed his superior, "I only want five minutes time to remove both houses."[74]

Despite Assistant Weimer's temptation to apply the torch to the Hobart-Carpenter hotel, it remained a blight upon the landscape for nine years until its accidental destruction by fire in November 1894. But the summer of 1885 was a total loss as far as Carpenter was concerned. His makeshift hotel was barely in operation when contractor C.F. Hobart seized the building because manager C.T. Hobart had not paid him for his work. The resulting squabble kept the hotel closed for the remainder of the season, and with that Robert E. Carpenter disappeared from the scene.

Superintendent Wear proceeded to make good use of the force of assistant superintendents; or rather, of those he considered worth retaining. He soon replaced the defectives with good western men such as Collins Jack Baronett and Edward Wilson. Under his strict supervision the revitalized force began to perform quite credibly.

This was particularly true in regard to the poachers who were operating in the Park. The first of these to feel the effect of vigorous law enforcement was a Gardiner resident by the name of George Reeder, who had vexed the assistants stationed in the northern part of the Park from the very beginning. Of this event, which marked such an important change in the management of the Park, the *Livingston Enterprise* noted

> George Reeder and John Ferguson were arrested at the falls by Ed Wilson with four hind quarters of elk and eight beaver skins in their possession. They were taken before justice Metcalf on the charge of hunting and trapping in the park. Ferguson was fined $75 and costs and Reeder got the full penalty provided by the statutes—$100 fine, costs and 6 months imprisonment in the Uinta County jail. Deputy sheriff Hale has started overland for Evanston with his prisoner. Both men paid their fines and costs which aggregated $40.65.[75]

Of this sudden show of toothiness on the part of the local law, former Assistant Henderson gloated, "the old hunters are coming to grief in the National Park. Reeder has killed his last elk and trapped his last beaver and it will take six months to awaken him to glory again. Shooting game in the park didn't pay at $100 per shot and six months for meditation."[76] Proof that this new regime was not at all partial came in the trial of Steven A. Alpine, a member of the Hague party of the United States Geological Survey. The "learned geologist" had killed a buffalo in the vicinity of the Upper Geyser Basin, was found guilty and fined, but that did not satisfy the Park's stern superintendent: he preferred charges against the scientist with the intention of getting him dismissed from the government service.[77]

That episode was followed by the apprehension of five poachers in the northwest corner of the Park. Assistant Weimer and Ed Wilson caught the party with an elk and five deer killed within the Park, arrested them, and brought them to Mammoth Hot Springs for trial. The poachers were Box Miller, J.M. Pearson, David Gard, R.W. White, and Jno. F. Hoskins, all of whom were found guilty by Justice Metcalf. Gard and White, who plead guilty, were fined only $25 each and costs, while the others were fined twice as much. All their guns were confiscated. Following this success, the local newspaper said: "The officers of the Park are vigilant and energetic in the discharge of their duties and ever on the alert to catch all trespassers and while it gives the superintendent or his assistants no pleasure to punish anyone they have a sworn duty to perform, and will do and are doing it fearlessly."[78]

This good work promised to restore public confidence in the management of Yellowstone Park, and it would have except for an unfortunate occurrence in the summer of 1885. Superintendent Wear had also embarked upon a policy of deliberate toughness toward campers who left their fires unextinguished, intending to make it "cheaper to extinguish them." Thereafter, the justices of the peace under Wyoming law in the Park enjoyed much profitable business— their customers including such well-known individuals as Livingston merchants Babcock and Miles, and the Bozeman superintendent of schools, Mr. W.W. Wylie. The fine assessed for the offense was an appalling $50, which caused the editor of the *Livingston Enterprise* to comment: "Wear, it would appear, is a shoulder striker from away back."[79] The objective was commendable and the result would probably have been as satisfactory as that obtained by the prosecution of poachers, if all the fuctionaries of law enforcement under Wyoming law had been good men, or at least honest men. But some were not.

The constable at the Lower Geyser Basin was Joe Keeney, a one-time hotel keeper at Cinnabar who had been involved in a series of discreditable happenings in and around the Park. Joe, being the kind of cat who always lands on his feet, managed a commission as constable under Wyoming law at the Lower Geyser Basin. The justice of the peace at that place (Judge Hall) is not so well known; in fact, he is described only as a "former wood cutter," which would hint that his politics were superior to his legal training. Anyhow, these two came to the conclusion that the more cases they handled, the more fees there would be to split between them. For their purpose, Superintendent Wear's passion for enforcement of the rule requiring the thorough extinguishment of campfires was made to order.

Joe Keeney was satisfied with a live coal or two left amid dampened down ashes, or even with a little warm ground, as evidence that a campfire had not been entirely extinguished. Upon just such flimsy evidence he apprehended a wagon party of eleven persons, among whom was Judge Lewis E. Payson, a congressman from Illinois, and Joseph Medill, the editor of the *Chicago Tribune*. Their driver was A.L. Brown of Livingston, who also served as cook in the fashion of that day, and he had built a campfire on a patch of bare sand for preparing breakfast; afterward he extinguished it by sprinkling a large pail of water carefully over the embers. As they were loading up to leave for the Upper Geyser Basin, they saw a little steam or smoke arising from the hearth; so it was covered completely with sand as a further precaution. The party then went on their way and were later served with a warrant for their arrest and ordered to appear before Judge Hall. At the hearing there was a delay while the justice consulted with Joe Keeney as to what the fine should be. During the "trial," evidence was presented to the effect that the campfire had been built in a reasonably safe place where its spread into inflammable materials was impossible, and that reasonable care had been taken to extinguish it; nevertheless, they were found guilty, and a fine of $60.00 with costs of $12.80 was imposed. Judge Payson then gave notice of his intention to appeal the verdict and offered a $1,000 bond. This was a quandary quite beyond Judge Hall, who offered to reduce the fine. A compromise was finally reached by which $1 and costs was accepted in full settlement,[80] and that ridiculous outcome was made even worse when the justice asked Judge Payson for legal advice.[81] At that point, Joseph Medill, who had been standing by, delivered a lecture directed toward Judge Hall, in the course of which he called him a "d_____d old Dogberry." The editor of the *Livingston Enterprise* gleefully reports the incident:

> It is also told that Justice Hall was heard to inquire diligently of his friends as to the meaning of the strange term "Dogberry" and, not gaining any satisfactory information, demanded a dictionary of his assistant— doubtless with the intention of fastening a charge of malicious slander or abusive language on Mr. Medill. If Mr. Hall has not yet laid the foundation of his case we commend him to a story called "Much Ado About Nothing" by a writer of some repute named William Shakespeare, since

deceased, for an explanation of the offensive epithet as well as for a very faithful mirror of the administraton of justice at Norris Basin.[82]

Justice Hall and Constable Keeney could hardly have done the Park more damage if they had tried. Mr. Medill, who was a former mayor of Chicago and head of the Republican party, wired an account of the incident to his paper, the *Chicago Tribune*. In it, he stated that "in a national park the national laws and regulations should be enforced by a national tribunal." Supported, as it soon was, by the adverse report of W. Hallet Phillips, special agent of the Department of the Interior, this attack on the use of Wyoming law in Yellowstone Park proved to be the death knell of that misguided legislation. The act was repealed by the Territory of Wyoming on March 10, 1886—a mere two years and four days from its inception.

Oddly, the majority report of the Holman Select Committee (of the House of Representatives), which was in the Park at the same time as the Payson-Medill party, came to the opposite conclusion—an approval of the use of Wyoming law—and looked forward to the day when the Park could be turned over to a state of Wyoming (an outcome that might have terminated the national park movement at that early date, had it materialized).[83] A statement of policy enunciated by the committee has proven of more lasting value. According to their view,

> The park should so far as possible be spared the vandalism of improvement. Its great and only charms are in the display of wonderful forces of nature, the ever varying beauty of the rugged landscape, and the sublimity of the scenery. Art cannot embellish them.[84]

The Holman Select Committee consisted of Judge W. S. Holman of Indiana, Joseph G. Cannon of Illinois, Thomas Ryan of Kansas, and two clerks. Chairman Holman, who was known as "the Great Objector," was a believer in strict economy in all aspects of government. He practiced this virtue on the journey to the Park by refusing to put his travel account to the expense of Pullman accommodations; so they sat up in a coach, day and night, until Cannon and Ryan finally rebelled. "Uncle Joe" Cannon, whose reputation as a protector of the public purse was quite formidable, made no headway with Holman and finally remarked: "Well, Ryan, I'll be d____d if I don't pay my own bills from this time out and report the same to Congress. I am not going to travel for the government like a d____d backwoodsman."[85]

The damage done to Yellowstone Park through the Payson incident and the two investigations (both of which aided its foes) was soon apparent. The Sundry Civil Appropriation bill for the 1887 fiscal year (beginning July 1, 1886) contained the usual item of $40,000 for the Park; but the House deleted the $20,000 intended to pay the superintendent and his ten assistants. On July 24, the Senate restored the disputed item, and conferees representing the two branches of Congress were unable to work out a compromise. Ordinarily, such an impasse would doom a bill, but an overdue appropriation measure was another matter.

Debate in the two houses showed a great diversity of opinion regarding the Park. In the House, David B. Henderson was for turning the area over to the military. He ridiculed Superintendent Wear and his efforts, supporting his view with charges appropriate to the regimes of Conger and Carpenter, but not at all true when applied to Wear's effective administration; nevertheless, his arguments were harmful. Representative John A. Reagan of Texas sought the repeal of the law that had established the Park, expressing his belief that the government ought not engage in "show business." William S. Holman, who had chaired the select committee the previous summer, wanted to follow the precedent of Yosemite and Mackinac Island by turning the Park over to Wyoming Territory. Finally, the House insisted on an end to civilian administration in the Park.

The debate on the floor of the Senate showed equally adverse sentiments. Senator Preston B. Plumb of Kansas argued for a return of the Park to the public domain, and he was supported by Henry M. Teller (the former secretary of the interior, whose anti-park activities had always been fronted by Assistant Secretary Joslyn). However, the Park's staunch supporter, Senator Vest, was able to hold the Senate to his viewpoint, which favored a civilian administration of the area. The contested bill was sent into conference a second time, but on August 4, with the end of that session only two days off, the Senate conferees decided to accept the House version of the Yellowstone Park provision in order that passage of the whole appropriation bill would not be further delayed.

Senator Vest was disappointed with the outcome, though it was probably better than the result a prolongation of the struggle would have brought; the anti-park forces in the House were even then organizing the "railroad gang" that would have been satisfied with nothing less than total destruction of the Park. The leader of that determined group was none other than Judge Lewis E. Payson, who was thereafter an arch foe of the Park.

The failure of the Congress to provide funds for the administration of Yellowstone National Park in 1886 put an end to Superintendent Wear's efficient administration. Left without means for the management of the Park, the secretary of the interior had no alternative but to fall back upon the provision of the Sundry Civil Act of 1883 that authorized him to call upon the secretary of war for assistance. By the wise provision that Senator George Graham Vest had the foresight to make, the way was open for a timely rescue by the military.

Several incidents that occurred during the period of the assistant superintendents are worth mentioning. The cemetery established in 1883 on Sepulcher Hill (north of Mammoth Hot Springs) continued to grow. By 1886 five more persons had been buried: two suicides, two drowning victims, and one who suffocated in a snowslide. The suicides were Mrs. Emily Moore, who took an overdose of morphine for a neuralgia attack;[86] and Mr. Bassett, who ended his life with poison at Cinnabar in May 1884.[87] The drowned men were Thomas P. Parker and John Fogarty, who attempted to ford the Yellowstone River at its outlet in August 1883. A year later, a relative of one of them had the bodies removed from their temporary burial places at present Fishing Bridge and reburied them in the graveyard at Mammoth Hot Springs.[88] The snowslide victim was one of Oscar Swanson's workmen, a Finlander by the name of Jacob Hess, who had been to Gardiner with a sleigh load of men bent on relaxation. On the return they were in no condition to manage the team and succeeded in triggering a slide on the snow-burdened slopes above the Gardner River. Four men got out immediately and two more were saved by those who came down from Mammoth Hot Springs to help dig; but Hess was dead when found.[89]

During 1885, Mammoth Hot Springs acquired its third hotel, the Cottage, built by the Cottage Hotel Association, a Henderson family concern, on land leased to Walter J. and Helen L. Henderson (son and daughter of Assistant Superintendent George L. Henderson). The Cottage competed with the National Hotel, providing lower cost lodging, until 1889 when it was sold to the Yellowstone Park Association. The facilities in the geyser basins were also increased when George W. Marshall received a lease early in 1884 for a site near the mouth of Nez Perce Creek. There he built the Marshall House, which he operated briefly in partnership with G. G. Henderson (no relation to the Hendersons at Mammoth Hot Springs). Also in this period, Frank J. Haynes established a photographic business that was to continue nearly to the present.[90]

With the end of the era of early civilian administration, the force of assistant superintendents was disbanded and replaced by those "boys-in-blue" who would be the Park's protectors for thirty-two years. One of the assistants, "Yellowstone Jack" Baronett, stayed on for a time as a scout for the soldiers—the first of the almost legendary mountaineers who served as the army's "eyes" in the wilderness back country.

John H. Baronett, aka Collins Jack Baronett and "Yellowstone Jack." Photograph by Finn, Livingston, Mont.

NOTES

NOTES

CHAPTER 1

1. Peter Pond notes that a French deserter from the fort on the Illinois River

> toock his Boate up the Miseura among the Indians and Spent Maney years among them. He Learnt Maney Langwedgeis and from Steap to Steap he Got among the Mondons whare he found Sum french traders who Belonged to the french traders of Cannaday. These people toock Pinneshon to the factorey with them and the Consarn toock him into thare Sarvis til the Hole cuntrey was Given up to the English.

From "Adventures in American Northwest," *Journal of American History* 1, no. 2 (1907), pp. 362-63. Elliot Coues, ed., provides some information on early trading expeditions to the Mandan towns in *The Manuscript Journals of Alexander Henry . . . and of David Thompson, 1799-1814,* 3 vols. (New York: Francis P. Harper, 1879), 1: 302.

2. Ernest Staples Osgood, ed., *The Field Notes of Captain William Clark, 1803-1805* (New Haven, Conn.: Yale University Press, 1964), p. 165n. The "Old Menard" of the American explorers is the "Manoah" of David Thompson; see Richard Glover, ed., *David Thompson's Narrative, 1784-1812* (Toronto: Champlain Society, 1962), pp. 170, 174.

3. Wilson O. Clough, "Wyoming's Earliest Place Names?" *Annals of Wyoming* 37, no. 2 (October 1965), p. 214.

4. In the *Narrative,* p. 160, Thompson says: "Our guide and interpreter, who has resided eight years in their villages was a Monsr Rene Jussomme who fluently spoke the Mandane Language . . ." Though illiterate, he was an adequate intermediary, providing Thompson with information that allowed him to place the source of the Yellowstone River with an error of only 21 miles; see Hiram M. Chittenden, *The Yellowstone National Park* (Cincinnati: Robert Clarke Co., 1895), pp. 1-2, hereafter cited as *Yellowstone.*

5. Chittenden, *Yellowstone,* pp. 5-7.

6. Ibid., p. 3. According to the editor of the *Livingston* (Mont.) *Enterprise,* Oct. 23, 1883, the Crow Indian name should be *Encheda-cahchi-ichi.* Both are forms of the same Crow Indian expression.

7. Clarence E. Carter, ed., "The Territories of Louisiana-Missouri, 1803-1806," in *The Territorial Papers of the United States,* vol. 13 (1948), p. 243. Multivolume series (Washington D.C.: Govt. Printing Office, 1934–), hereafter cited as "Territories."

8. On September 8, 1805, Wilkinson had written to the secretary of war stating,

> I have equipt a perogue . . . to ascend the missouri and enter the River Piere jaune, or yellow Stone, called by the natives, Unicorn River, the same by which Capt. Lewis I since find expects to return and which my informants tell me is filled with wonders, this party will not get back before the summer of 1807.

Carter, "Territories," p. 199.

9. "Yellowstone Expedition of 1819 a Miserable Failure," *Box Elder Valley* (Mont.) *Press,* June 2, 1922.

10. Pike wrote:

> Our citizens. . .will, through necessity be constrained to limit their extent to the west to the borders of the Missouri and Mississippi, while they leave the prairies incapable of cultivation to the wandering and uncivilized aborigines of the country,

a view which Long materially encouraged. See *Scribner's Dictionary of American History,* vol. 2 (1940), p. 140.

11. "Steamboats Coming to Fort Benton Had Varied and Interesting Stories," *Fort Benton* (Mont.) *River Press,* Aug. 21, 1946.

12. George Catlin, *Letters and Notes on the Manners, Customs, and Conditions of the North American Indians,* 2 vols. (New York, 1841), 1:261-62.

13. Yellowstone Lake was described by Daniel T. Potts in his letter of July 8, 1827 (published anonymously) in the *Philadelphia Gazette and Daily Advertiser,* Sept. 27, 1827, and reprinted in *Niles Register,* Oct. 6, 1827. Warren Angus Ferris, a clerk of the American Fur Company, referred to Yellow Stone Lake in 1831. See *Life in the Rocky Mountains,* Paul C. Phillips, ed. (Denver: Old West Publishing Co., 1940), p. 83.

14. The Raynolds map was drawn from data obtained in 1859-60. The Yellowstone details were contributed by Jim Bridger, who guided Raynolds' party in its near approach to that terra incognita.

15. "The Valley of the Upper Yellowstone," *Western Monthly Magazine* 4 (Chicago, July 1870), pp. 60-67.

16. Hiram M. Chittenden, "The 'National Park Range' of Mountains; What is its Rightful Name?" manuscript, n.d., p. 2, Yellowstone National Park Reference Library.

17. Henry Gannett, *Boundaries of the United States,* 3d ed. (Washington, D.C.: Govt. Printing Office, 1904), p. 131.

18. U.S., *Statutes at Large,* vol. 17, sec. 2474, 32.

19. N.P. Langford to Columbus Delano, May 20, 1872, Letter received—Interior—Referring to Yellowstone National Park, Record Group 48, National Archives, Washington, D.C.

20. Frank B. Harper, *Fort Union and Its Neighbors On the Upper Missouri* (Great Northern Railway Company, n.d.), p. 34.

21. *Bozeman* (Mont.) *Avant Courier,* Dec. 31, 1875 and Mar. 17, 1876.

22. E.S. Topping, *The Chronicles of the Yellowstone* (St. Paul: Pioneer Press Co., 1883), pp. 30-32.

23. Captain L.A. Smith, Navy Department, to author, July 19, 1967.

24. "Railroad Racket," *Bozeman Avant Courier,* Feb. 9, 1882, p. 2.

25. Freeman Tilden, *Following the Frontier* (New York: Alfred A. Knopf, 1964), pp. 3-18.

26. Notes from the records of the Northern Pacific Mechanical Division, St. Paul, Minn., February 15, 1967. The file is incomplete and it is likely that additional use of the name Yellowstone was made during the years 1885 to 1898.

CHAPTER 2

1. From the symposium "Early Man in the Western American Arctic" (1962), published in *Anthropological Papers of the University of Alaska*

10, no. 2 (1963), and reviewed by Dr. Frederica de Laguna in *American Anthropologist* 66 (4): 950.

2. The most favorable conditions existed about 40,000 and 18,500 years ago, when the sea level was, respectively, 465 and 400 feet lower than at present. (See James R. Moriarity's graph of "Late Quaternary fluctuations of sea level. . .," *Science,* February 3, 1967, p. 554.) However, a land bridge undoubtedly existed throughout the period 21,600 B.C. to 8200 B.C., when the sea level was more than 25 fathoms (150 feet) below its present mean.

3. For convenience in speaking of the prehistory of this region, three eras are recognized here: the Early Prehistoric, peopled by Early Hunters (prior to 6000 B.C.); the Middle Prehistoric, peopled by Foragers (6000 B.C. to 2500 B.C.), and the Late Prehistoric, peopled by Late Hunters (2500 B.C. to A.D. 1700, when the historic period begins). The foregoing do not indicate ethnic relationships other than common cultural traits.

4. The Clovis point of the mammoth hunters is considered to belong to the period 9500 B.C. to 9000 B.C., while the Folsom point of the bison hunters falls in the period 9000 B.C. to 8000 B.C. C. Vance Haynes, Jr., "Fluted Projectile Points: Their Age and Dispersion," *Science,* September 25, 1964, pp. 1408-13. Some other projectile points used by the Early Hunters, to which there will be occasion to refer, are: Hell Gap (9000 B.C. to 8000 B.C.), Agate Basin (8000 B.C. to 7350 B.C.), and Eden Valley (7000 B.C. to 6000 B.C.).

5. Joe Ben Wheat to Otho Mack, June 24, 1962, and Marie H. Wormington to Otho Mack, January 1963.

6. The prevalence of heel portions of projectile points at camp sites is generally explained by assuming the hunter would recover his spear or arrow shaft, when possible, for it required considerable effort to make a good one; when the point was found to be damaged, it was probably replaced later, at the camping place, where the detached heel was usually thrown aside. Fortunately, these heels are the diagnostic portion of most projectile points.

7. Information provided by lookout Richard Klukas, by Jack MacDonald, then caretaker at the Silver Tip Ranch, and by Verne Waples, Montana state game warden in that area, is recorded in two reports: Aubrey L. Haines, "A Preliminary Report on High-Altitude Indian Occupation Sites Near the North Boundary of Yellowstone National Park," December 1963, manuscript, 16 pp.; and a supplementary report on the same subject, January 6, 1965, manuscript, 40 pp. Both reports were submitted to the superintendent, Yellowstone National Park, and are in Yellowstone National Park Reference Library.

8. This point, catalogued as No. 6642 in the Yellowstone museum study collection, has been identified by Dr. Dee C. Taylor, Montana State University, Missoula. See his "Preliminary Archaeological Investigations in Yellowstone National Park," a report submitted in fulfillment of Contract No. 14-10-232-320 between the National Park Service and Montana State University, 1964, pp. 102-4.

9. It is the opinion of Mr. Kenneth Pierce that the lake level was 110 feet higher at the crest of the Pinedale glaciation (13,000 to 10,000 B.C.), with ice filling all the lake except the arms; by 6000 B.C. the level was between 45 and 60 feet above its present stage.

10. Earl H. Swanson, Jr., "Cultural Relations Between Two Plains," *Archaeology in Montana* 7, no. 2 (April-June 1966), pp. 1-2.

11. Carling Malouf, "Preliminary Report, Yellowstone National Park Archeological Survey, Summer 1958," mimeographed, Montana State University, Missoula, January 5, 1959, p. 7.

12. Aubrey L. Haines, "Preliminary Report on the Rigler Bluffs Prehistoric Indian Site, 24 PA 401," November 26, 1962, manuscript, 8 pp. and addenda, Yellowstone National Park Reference Library.

13. Robert Stuart says, "Some of the best warriors shoot an arrow with such force as to send it thro' an elk or buffalo at the distance of 12 to 15 paces & they seldom shoot at anything farther than 30 yards." See *The Discovery of the Oregon Trail,* Phillip Ashton Rollins, ed. (New York: Charles Scribner's Sons, 1935), p. 253. Rudolph Kurz makes a similar observation, noting, "At 20 feet they hit small objects with great accuracy.... At 100 feet they fly the arrows with great skill but cannot be sure." See *Journal of Rudolph Friederich Kurz,* Myrtis Jarrell, trans., J.N.B. Hewitt, ed. (Smithsonian Institution, Bureau of American Ethnology, Bull. 115, 1937), p. 55.

14. Louis C. Steege and Warren W. Welch, *Stone Projectile Points* (Colorado Springs: Northwestern Plains Publishing Co., 1961), pp. 94-102.

15. Carling Malouf, "Historic Tribes and Archaeology," *Archeology in Montana* 8, no. 1 (January-March 1967), pp. 5, 13.

16. This loose confederacy included the Piegans, Northern Blackfoot, Bloods, and another group of Algonkian linguistic stock—the Atsina. The latter group became allied with the Blackfoot, proper, after their earlier close relationship with the Arapahos was broken.

17. Mark H. Brown, *The Plainsmen of the Yellowstone* (New York: G.P. Putnam's Sons, 1961), p. 41.

18. There has been a tendency to substitute fancy for fact in the early literature dealing with these people. The romanticizing about them varies from the well-intended surmise of P.W. Norris that they were a "Pigmy tribe... remnant of some former race" (see *Annual Report of the Superintendent of the Yellowstone National Park,* November 30, 1880, p. 35) to the ridiculous, Hiawatha-like images conjured up by Charles R. Sunderlee, "A Thrilling Event on the Yellowstone," *Helena* (Mont.) *Herald,* May 18, 1870; and William A. Allen, *The Sheep Eaters* (New York, 1913).

19. *Annals of Wyoming* 33, no. 1 (April 1961), pp. 19-41.

20. Ibid., pp. 34-35.

21. Phillip Martindale, "An Additional Note on the Wickiups," *Yellowstone Nature Notes* 4, no. 5 (May 31, 1927), p. 4. Dr. Carling Malouf's opinion appears in the report cited in note 11; see p. 7 of that report.

22. Albert J. Partoll, "The Flathead Indian Name in Montana Nomenclature," *Montana Magazine of History* 1 (January 1951), pp. 37-47.

23. Alvin M. Josephy, Jr., *The Nez Perce Indians and the Opening of the West* (New Haven: Yale University Press, 1965), p. 14.

24. Osborne Russell, *Journal of a Trapper,* A.L. Haines, ed. (Portland: Oregon Historical Society, 1955), pp. 26-27.

25. Francis Fuller Victor, *The River of the West* (Hartford, Conn.: R.W. Bliss & Co., 1870), pp. 75-76.

26. W.T. Hamilton, *My Sixty Years on the Plains* (Columbus, Ohio: Long's College Book Co., 1951), p. 95.

27. Frederick Webb Hodge, *Handbook of the American Indians*, Part 2 (Smithsonian Institution, Bureau of American Ethnology, Bull. 30, 1910), p. 378. The thesis of Raymond E. Borton, "Irrigation on the Crow Reservation..." (Bozeman: Montana State College, 1964) discusses the Crow Indian treaties, pp. 12-13 and 25-28.

28. This route is discussed in greater detail in Aubrey L. Haines, "The Bannock Indian Trails of Yellowstone National Park," *Archaeology in Montana* 4, no. 1 (March 1962), pp. 1-8.

29. P.H. Sheridan et al., *Report of an Exploration of Parts of Wyoming, Idaho and Montana in August and September, 1882* (Washington, D.C.: Govt. Printing Office, 1882), p. 12. R.P. Haas, superintendent of the Wind River Indian Reservation (Fort Washakie), in a letter of August 12, 1929, adds: "These Indians [Sheepeaters] came to the Shoshone reservation about the year 1871. There are some of their descendents on the Reservation at this time."

30. In his book *Chronicles of the Yellowstone*, E.S. Topping has recorded many of the brutal incidents that occurred in the Yellowstone Valley below the Gate-of-the-Mountains, above which the Sioux were reluctant to come.

31. This date is on the Julian calendar.

32. Henry Gannett, *Boundaries of the United States*, 3d ed. (Washington, D.C.: Govt. Printing Office, 1904), p. 39. This source has been used extensively here.

33. Lord Dunraven has this to say of our acquisition of the Oregon country:

> There is a legend current... to the effect that the cession of Oregon was not strongly opposed at home because some plenipotentiary sent out to examine into the matter reported that it was a useless and disgusting country, for the salmon in the Columbia would not take the fly. I am afraid that this myth is too good to be true, and that the Colonial Office has no such valid excuse to offer....We abandoned Oregon very easily.

See *The Great Divide* (London: Chatto and Windus, 1876), p. 330.

CHAPTER 3

1. Henry M. Brackenridge, *Views of Louisiana Together with a Journal of a Voyage Up the Missouri River in 1811* (Pittsburgh: Cramer, Spear, and Eichbaum, Franklin head office, 1814), p. 91.

2. About 1809, Clark prepared a map showing the track of the Lewis and Clark Expedition across the continent, adding to it information he had recently obtained from John Colter. The map was forwarded to Nicholas Biddle at Philadelphia in 1810, and an engraving prepared from it by Samuel Lewis was published in Biddle's *History of the Expedition Under the Command of Captains Lewis and Clark*, 2 vols., Paul Allen, ed. (Philadelphia: Bradford and Inskeep, 1814), vol. 2. The original of this map is in Record Group 77, U.S. 529, National Archives, Washington, D.C.

3. M.O. Skarsten, "George Drouillard," in *The Mountain Men and the Fur Trade of the Far West*, vol. 4, LeRoy R. Hafen, ed. (Glendale, Calif.: Arthur A. Clark Co., 1966), p. 70.

4. *Three Years Among the Mexicans and Indians*, W.B. Douglas, ed. (St. Louis: Missouri Historical Society, 1916), p. 58.

5. Merrill J. Mattes, "Behind the Legend of Colter's Hell: The Early Exploration of the Yellowstone National Park," *Mississippi Valley Historical Review* 36, no. 2 (September 1949), pp. 253-54.

6. Quoted by H.M. Chittenden in *The American Fur Trade of the Far West*, vol. 2 (New York: Francis P. Harper, 1902), p. 715, hereafter cited as *American Fur Trade;* in 1880, P.W. Norris suggested such an alternative routing in his *Fifth Annual Report of the Superintendent of the Yellowstone National Park* (Washington, D.C.: Govt. Printing Office, 1881), pp. 38-40.

7. See the Clark-Drouillard manuscript map (1808) in the collection of the Missouri Historical Society, St. Louis. This important map is reproduced by Burton Harris in *John Colter: His Years in the Rockies* (New York: Charles Scribner's Sons, 1952), p. 80f.

8. *The Fur Hunters of the Far West: A Narrative of Adventures in the Oregon and Rocky Mountains,* 2 vols. (London: Smith, Elder and Co., 1855), 1:267.

9. Norris, *Fifth Annual Report,* pp. 40-41; H.M. Chittenden, *The Yellowstone National Park* (Cincinnati: Robert Clarke Co., 1895), p. 35, hereafter cited as *Yellowstone.*

10. Agnes C. Laut, *Conquest of the Great Northwest* (New York: G.H. Doran & Co., 1908), pp. 255-57.

11. Norris, *Annual Report of the Superintendent of the Yellowstone National Park to the Secretary of the Interior ,1880* (Washington, D.C.: Govt. Printing Office, 1881), p. 29.

12. E.S. Topping, *The Chronicles of the Yellowstone* (St. Paul: Pioneer Press, 1883), p. 14.

13. Merrill J. Mattes, *Colter's Hell and Jackson's Hole* (Yellowstone Park: Yellowstone Library and Museum Assoc., 1962), pp. 33-34.

14. Reprinted in *Niles Register,* Oct. 6, 1827, from which fact it has attained some historical prominence as "the *Niles Register* letter."

15. See "Early Yellowstone and Western Experiences," in *Yellowstone Nature Notes* 21, no. 5 (September-October 1947), pp. 49-56.

16. Mrs. Francis Fuller Victor, *The River of the West* (Hartford, Conn.: R.W. Bliss & Co., 1870), p. 75.

17. Chittenden, *Yellowstone,* p. 43.

18. Chittenden, *American Fur Trade,* pp. 941-45.

19. Aubrey L. Haines, "Johnson Gardner" in *The Mountain Men,* vol. 2, pp. 157-59.

20. Warren A. Ferris, *Life in the Rocky Mountains, 1830-1835,* P.C. Phillips, ed. (Denver: Old West Publishing Co., 1940), pp. 257-58, hereafter cited as *Rocky Mountains.*

21. Ferris was misled by the whiteness of the deposited siliceous sinter; the underlying rock is volcanic in origin, rather than sedimentary.

22. Ferris, *Rocky Mountains,* pp. 257-60. Other thermal features near the outlet of Lake Yellowstone are described from information provided by trappers who had seen them (pp. 260-61). See also "Rocky Mountain Geysers," *Western Literary Messenger* 2, no. 2 (July 13, 1842), pp. 12-13. This material was reprinted as "Life in the Rocky Mountains," in vol. 3, no. 25 (January 6, 1844), p. 196, and it was the latter, slightly different, version that Dr. Phillips used in his work, cited here and in note 20.

23. Ibid., p. 261.

24. Osborne Russell, *Journal of a Trapper,* Aubrey L. Haines, ed. (Portland: Oregon Historical Society, 1955), p. 46, hereafter cited as *Journal.* Some

punctuation has been added in this and subsequent quotations as a reading aid.

25. Ibid., p. 27.

26. Ibid., p. 43.

27. Ibid., pp. 63-64.

28. Ibid., p. 98.

29. Ibid., p. 105.

30. W.T. Hamilton, *My Sixty Years on the Plains* (Columbus, Ohio: Long's College Book Co., 1951), pp. 94-95.

31. As will be seen later, Bridger served as Captain Raynolds' guide on his Yellowstone expedition of 1859-60; Gunnison said of him:

> With a buffalo skin and a piece of charcoal he will map out any portion of this immense region, and delineate mountains, streams, and the circular valleys, called *holes*, with wonderful accuracy.

Quoted by Chittenden in *Yellowstone*, 4th ed., 1903, pp. 54-55. A manuscript map that Jim Bridger prepared for DeSmet is with DeSmet's papers at St. Louis University.

32. Nathaniel P. Langford, *Diary of the Washburn Expedition to the Yellowstone and Firehole Rivers in the Year 1870* (St. Paul: F.J. Haynes Co., 1905), p. viii.

33. Russell, *Journal*, p. 45.

34. *James Bridger, Trapper, Frontiersman, Scout and Guide* (Columbus, Ohio: Long's College Book Co., 1951), p. 588.

35. George Frederic Ruxton, *Life in the Far West*, LeRoy R. Hafen, ed. (Norman: University of Oklahoma Press, 1959), pp. 7-9. Ruxton picked up the story in Colorado in 1847, but reference to "the year it rained fire"—1833, according to Hafen—indicates this version may have been around for some time; however, it is different from the tale he told earlier (note 34). See also, Chittenden, *Yellowstone* (1903), pp. 50-51.

36. *The Report of Brevet Brigadier General W.F. Raynolds on the Exploration of the Yellowstone and the Country Drained by that River,* U.S., 40th Cong., 1st sess., Senate Ex. Doc. 77, July 17, 1868, p. 77.

37. *A Few Memories of a Long Life* (privately printed, 1900), pp. 57-61. A similar story appears in the *Bozeman Avant Courier,* Apr. 28, 1875, where the editor, in commenting upon the purported finding of petrified birds' eggs in a petrified tree in Utah, says:

> This is almost equal to Ed Hibbard's yarn about having seen a petrified bird sitting on a petrified limb of a petrified tree, with a petrified song sticking out of its mouth ten or fifteen feet.

38. P. 56. Chittenden fails to cite an authority for this version, which appears to be his own creation.

39. *Personal Recollections and Observations of General Nelson A. Miles* (Chicago: Werner Co., 1897), p. 137.

40. Merrill D. Beal, *The Story of Man in Yellowstone* (Yellowstone Park: Yellowstone Library and Museum Assoc., 1960), p. 113. He has managed to turn Chittenden's version into a quotation that has Bridger saying, "Yes, Siree, thar's miles o' peetrefied hills, covered with layers o' peetrefied trees, and on 'em trees air peetrefied birds a singin' peetrefied songs!"

41. Raynolds, *Report*, p. 77 (the stream-heated-by-friction tale); and Captain Eugene Fitch Ware, *The Indian War of 1864* (New York: St. Martin's

Press, 1960), pp. 204-6, 214-15, 250. The only one of Ware's collection that deals specifically with the Yellowstone region is the Hell-close-below tale, pp. 205-6.

42. James Stevenson, United States Geological Survey, Washington, D.C., to Prof. J.D. Butler, February 28, 1886.

CHAPTER 4

1. Excerpt from a popular song inscribed on the flyleaf of the personal diary of William Emory Atchison (1864). See "An Epic of the Middle West," edited by Charles H. Ramsdell and mimeographed by J.E. Haynes, St. Paul, Minn., February 1, 1933. There is a copy in the Yellowstone National Park Reference Library.

2. Henry Gannett, *Boundaries of the United States,* 3d ed., Bull. no. 226, Series F, Geography, United States Geological Survey (Washington, D.C.: Govt. Printing Office, 1904), p. 131.

3. William S. Greever, *The Bonanza West* (Norman: University of Oklahoma Press, 1963), *passim.*

4. For a biographical sketch of Walter Washington deLacy, see Olin D. Wheeler, "Walter Washington deLacy," in *Contributions to the Historical Society of Montana,* vol. 2 (Helena: State Publishing Co., 1896), pp. 241-51.

5. Walter W. deLacy, "A Trip up the South Snake River in 1863," *Contributions to the Historical Society of Montana,* vol. 1 (Helena: Rocky Mountain Publishing Co., 1876), p. 128.

6. P.W. Norris, who saw no likelihood of a restoration of deLacy's name to the lake, "as a small token of deserved justice, named the stream and park crossed by our trail above the Shoshone Lake after their discoverer." *Fifth Annual Report of the Superintendent of the Yellowstone National Park* (Washington, D.C.: Govt. Printing Office, 1881), p. 44.

7. In 1864, the first Territorial Legislature of Montana commissioned deLacy to prepare an official map to be used in establishing county boundaries. The published map was periodically improved during the twenty-four years it was in print, and its many editions circulated widely—particularly among prospectors. Information available to Montana prospectors prior to the year 1865 was noted by Granville Stuart in his book *Montana As It Is* (New York: C.S. Westcott & Co., Printers, 1865), p. 91.

> This plateau [Yellowstone] lies at a great elevation, probably over six thousand feet, and it almost obliterates the Rocky mountain chain in that region. Some spurs and isolated peaks, however, stand around its edges. It is swampy in many places, and it is said that some of those swamps furnish water to both oceans—in other parts are craters still hot and smoking, and old mountaineers tell many strange stories of "fire holes," "beds of hot ashes," "boiling swamp," "stinking tar and sulphur springs," and of many strange and startling sights and sounds seen and heard in this volcanic region.
> It is a singular fact that less is known of this particular locality of about two hundred miles square, than of any other part of the Rocky mountains north or south of it—in fact it is almost as much of a "terra incognita" at this time as Central Africa. But it will not be long now until it will be thoroughly explored by miners in search of that particular ramification of "the root of all evil," yclept "gold dust," which is supposed to abound "over there."

Stuart also had some rather accurate information concerning the Yellowstone Lake, which he described as "about sixty miles long and from fifteen to twenty wide . . . very irregular in shape." He knew that it lay at the eastern edge of the plateau, upon the source of the Yellowstone River.

8. F.V. Hayden, *Sixth Annual Report of the United States Geological Survey of the Territories* (Washington, D.C.: Govt. Printing Office, 1873), p. 244.

9. Letter, May 9, 1874. A copy is in the collection of the Montana Historical Society, Helena.

10. F.V. Hayden, *Twelfth Annual Report of the United States Geological and Geographical Survey of the Territories,* part 2 (Washington, D.C.: Govt. Printing Office, 1883), p. 249.

11. Carl I. Wheat, *Mapping the Trans-Mississippi West,* vol. 5 (San Francisco: Institute of Historical Cartography, 1963), p. 153.

12. Hiram M. Chittenden, *The Yellowstone National Park* (Cincinnati: Robert Clarke Co., 1895), p. 69.

13. Rossiter W. Raymond, *Mineral Resources of the States and Territories* (Washington, D.C.: Govt. Printing Office, 1869), p. 142, quotes from one of deLacy's letters as follows: "At the head of the South Snake, and also on the south fork of the Madison, there are hundreds of hot springs, many of which are 'geysers.' "

14. See article in *Progressive Men of the State of Montana* (Chicago: A.W. Bowen & Co., 1902), pp. 202-3.

15. The Fisk train of more than fifty wagons and a military escort originated at Fort Abercrombie, on the west bank of the Red River of the North in present North Dakota, where a Minnesota contingent joined it. Because the Missouri and Platte river routes were thought to be endangered by Confederate sympathizers, the train pioneered a northern route toward the gold fields of present Idaho. However, when word was received that the Salmon River diggings had played out, the train was diverted, first to Gold Creek, and then to Bannack.

16. N.P. Langford to S.T. Hauser, May 8, 1865. The original letter was not destroyed, but was retained with Hauser's papers, which are now in the collection of the Montana Historical Society, Helena. From other passages in this interesting letter, it is obvious that Langford and Hauser were speculating with money obtained by Langford in his official capacity as collector of internal revenue for Montana Territory; hence, he had a very cogent reason for asking that the missive be destroyed.

17. Norris, *Fifth Annual Report,* pp. 41, 44.

18. The Davis account appeared under the title "Yellowstone Park," *Louisville* (Ky.) *Courier Journal,* Apr. 18, 1884, p. 12.

19. This is the pass over which Sacajawea guided Captain William Clark and ten men, from the Gallatin Valley to the Yellowstone River, in 1806.

20. These designations are no longer used. The first canyon is now sometimes unofficially called The Gateway. The second canyon is the present Yankee Jim Canyon.

21. From the personal diary of William Emory Atchison (see note 1), p. 10.

22. E.S. Topping, *The Chronicles of the Yellowstone* (St. Paul: Pioneer Press Co., 1883), p. 28, hereafter cited as *Chronicles.*

23. The town that soon sprang up at Alder Gulch was named Varina by southern sympathizers, as a compliment to the charming wife of President

Jefferson Davis, but a frontier judge with northern leanings (G.G. Bissell) changed it to Virginia City. Since there already was a Virginia City in Nevada, the miners humorously compounded the problem by establishing the town of Nevada at the lower end of Alder Gulch.

24. Topping, *Chronicles,* p. 24, calls him Austin, but he was George A. Huston. The adventuring of these prospectors is more adequately presented by Norris, *Fifth Annual Report,* p. 44.

25. Topping, *Chronicles,* p. 25.

26. The fur trappers made such a deposit by digging a pit in which furs, equipment, or supplies were placed and covered over in a manner to disguise their presence. The name comes from a French Canadian expression, *en cache.*

27. N.C. Abbott, *Montana in the Making* (Billings, Mont.: Gazette Printing Co., 1931), p. 411. Topping, *Chronicles,* p. 25, indicates that Elliot Rouse made the original location there in July 1864.

28. Norris, *Fifth Annual Report,* p. 45.

29. Information supplied by Jefferson Jones in December 1953, from the file of "Territorial Post Offices and Their Dates of Establishment," U.S. Post Office Department, Washington, D.C.

30. Original letters in the "Langford Papers, 1707-1942," in the manuscript collection of the Minnesota Historical Society, St. Paul.

31. Mark H. Brown, *The Plainsmen of the Yellowstone* (New York: G.P. Putnam's Sons, 1961), p. 178.

32. Among these was Collins Jack Baronett, probably born John H. Baronett, who will appear prominently in the Yellowstone story.

33. Entries on pp. 59-61 and 76 of Henderson's "Journal of the Yellowstone Expedition of 1866 Under Captain Jeff Standifer" (copy in the Wyoming Historical Society Library, Cheyenne) indicate that he and other members of the expedition were recruited for service in Mexico. The background of this little-known episode is explained in an article by Lately Thomas, "The Operator and the Emperors," *American Heritage* 15, no. 3 (April 1964), pp. 4-8, 83.

34. Horses stolen in one territory could be sold across the mountain barrier in the other without being recognized. Two routes were utilized: one ran southward through the present Park to Jackson Hole and then into Idaho; the other, diagonally across the Park to the Yellowstone River and then onto the Snake River plains.

35. Topping, *Chronicles,* pp. 44-45.

36. Topping states that Freeman "wrote an account of the country, which was printed in the *Omaha Herald"* (see note 35), but a check of that source has not supported him. But Freeman did contribute Yellowstone information, and misinformation, to three issues of the *Frontier Index:* "The Greatest Bear Story Yet," in the issue of Mar. 6, 1868, published at Fort Sanders, D.T.; some incidental comments in a story on California, in the issue of May 5, 1868, published at Laramie City, D.T.; and "The Great Shoshone Falls" in the issue of Aug. 21, 1868, published at Green River City, D.T.

37. Both forts were abandoned when the Volunteers were withdrawn in July; however, the regular army may have reused the Fort Elizabeth Meagher site when Fort Ellis was established August 27, 1867.

38. Topping, *Chronicles,* p. 76.

39. Ibid., pp. 62-63.

40. The portions of Henderson's "Journal" that cover his Yellowstone experiences have been reproduced in *The Yellowstone Interpreter,* vol. 2 (1964), as follows: Part 1, "Narrative of a Prospecting Trip in the Summer of 1867," pp. 8-14; Part 2, "Narrative of a Prospecting Expedition to the East Fork & Clarks Fork of Yellowstone—1870," pp. 20-26; and Part 3, "Journal of Various Prospecting Trips, Stampedes, etc., during the Years 1871 & 1872 (and 1873)," pp. 33-40. The original is in the Coe Collection, Beinecke Library, Yale University.

41. "The Very Latest," *Virginia City Montana Post,* May 11, 1867.

42. See "Gone With Provisions," May 25, 1867, and "From Bozeman," June 1, 1867; both in the *Virginia City Montana Post.*

43. General William T. Sherman first proposed to build this post at Yellowstone Lake in order to restrain the Sioux. A sarcastic editorial appeared in the *Virginia City Montana Post,* May 18, 1867.

> By the way, that is where Sherman proposes to send his regulars, going up there to build a fort at the lake, probably to keep the trout from catching the blue-tailed flies. There has not been a Sioux on the headwaters of the Yellowstone for 30 years, that Bridger affirms he knows from personal observation, and that none of the living Sioux have ever been there.

44. Letters bearing his signature indicate Sawtell did not use the terminal "e" so often attached to his name. The peak overlooking Henrys Lake, Idaho, which is his lasting memorial, is misspelled on current maps.

45. H.R. Horr, J.C. McCartney, and J. Shaffer to Hon. Columbus Delano, secretary of the interior, March 28, 1872. Record Group 57, microfilm 62, reel 1, National Archives, Washington, D.C.

46. The Bottler ranch was two miles south of the present town of Emigrant, on Sections 6, 7, and 12, T. 6 S., R. 7 E., and T. 6 S., R. 8 E., Montana Meridian. Frederick had earlier decided on land near Strickland Creek, but found the Crow Indians on the reservation across the Yellowstone River too threatening.

47. Topping, *Chronicles,* pp. 76-77. Miller has added to the story in a reminiscence in which he says he was later riding across the Crow Indian Reservation and spied an Indian wearing a "plug hat" he knew to be Dougherty's. The sight gave Miller an itchy trigger finger, but he didn't dare shoot the Indian on the reservation. See Memorandum, District Ranger Hugh Ebert to the Chief Ranger, Yellowstone National Park, April 12, 1944, pp. 2-3.

48. From the *Helena Herald,* Dec. 26, 1867.

49. Freeman's "Greatest Bear Story Yet," *Frontier Index* (Fort Sanders, D.T.), March 6, 1868, is a queer mixture of distorted fact and deliberate whopper-telling, while Sunderlee's "A Thrilling Event on the Yellowstone," *Helena Herald,* May 18, 1870, is a gross falsification presented in the romantic manner best termed a Hiawatha treatment. It seems likely that Sunderlee created his news item out of the same Crow Indian legend that appears as "Defiance at Yellowstone Falls," in *Indian Legends from the Northern Rockies,* Ella E. Clark, comp. (Norman: University of Oklahoma Press, 1966), pp. 323-24.

CHAPTER 5

1. *The Mormans, or Latter-Day Saints* (Philadelphia: Lippincott, Grambo & Co., 1852), pp. 51-52.

2. Manuscript map at St. Louis University, Missouri. Jesuits, Missouri Province, Archives IX: DeSmetiana, C-B: Atlas, no. 5.

3. Current geological studies indicate the improbability of relatively recent volcanic activity. However, the observed presence, here and there, of fumaroles charged with burnable gases tended to create an impression of barely latent volcanism. One such "burning spring" in the Calcite Springs group near Tower Fall, which was observed by the Folsom party in 1869, has repeatedly set fire to adjacent forest materials in recent years—apparently through the spontaneous ignition of very hot gases vented into the air.

4. *The Report of Brevet Brigadier General W.F. Raynolds on the Exploration of the Yellowstone and the Country Drained by that River*, U.S., 40th Cong., 1st sess., Senate Ex. Doc. 77, July 17, 1868, p. 11, hereafter cited as *Report.*

5. Ibid., p. 86.

6. Evidently, Bridger thought they had crossed Togwotee Pass and were descending onto the Buffalo Fork, from which he could have ascended Pacific Creek to Two Ocean Pass, thus reaching the upper Yellowstone River by the fur-trapper's route he had often used in earlier times. Raynolds remarked that the effort "was of course useless, as it turned out, and resulted from a mistake of Bridger's. These little errors in matters of detail, upon his part, are not remarkable, as it is 15 years since he last visited this region, and they fade into insignificance compared with his accurate general knowledge of the country." Raynolds, *Report*, p. 91.

7. Ibid., p. 99. It should be noted that the Burnt Hole of the fur trappers is not synonymous with the geyser basins of the Firehole River. W.A. Ferris, in *Life in the Rocky Mountains, 1830-1835*, P.C. Phillips, ed. (Denver: Old West Publishing Co., 1940), pp. 85-86, says: "The Burnt Hole is a district on the north side of the Piney Woods [Madison Plateau] which was observed to be wrapped in flames a few years since. The conflagration that occasioned this name must have been of great extent, and large forests of half-consumed pines still evidence the ravages." Trapper Osborne Russell in *Journal of a Trapper* (Portland: Oregon Historical Society, 1955), p. 100, also clearly identifies the Burnt Hole with the present Madison Valley.

8. Francis X. Kuppens, "On the Origin of the Yellowstone National Park," reprinted from *The Woodstock Letters* (1897), in *The Jesuit Bulletin*, vol. 41, no. 4 (October 1962), p. 6, hereafter cited as "Origin."

9. "An Account of a Trip to Fort Benton in October, 1865, with Acting Governor Thomas F. Meagher to Treat with the Blackfeet Indians," *Rocky Mountain Magazine* 1, no. 3 (November 1900), p. 155. See also Lyman E. Munson, "Pioneer Life in Montana," in *Contributions to the Historical Society of Montana*, vol. 5 (Helena: Independent Publishing Co., 1904), pp. 214-16.

10. Kuppens, "Origin," p. 7. The Canadian was Francois "Crazy" Viele, mentioned in the John Healy Papers, Montana State Historical Society, Helena.

11. Under the heading of "The Upper Yellowstone," in *Virginia City Montana Post*, Aug. 24, 1867, a person identified only as "B.G." presents information attributed to Dunlevy. E.S. Topping mentions the expedition in *Chronicles of the Yellowstone* (St. Paul: Pioneer Press, 1883), p. 66.

12. Quoted in *Helena* (Mont.) *Herald*, Dec. 12, 1867.

13. Charles W. Cook, David E. Folsom, and William Peterson, *The Valley of the Upper Yellowstone*, Aubrey L. Haines, ed. (Norman: University of

Oklahoma Press, 1965), p. 7, hereafter cited as *Valley of Yellowstone*. This reconstructed account is the source of information on the Cook-Folsom-Peterson party, unless otherwise noted.

14. Despite Folsom's sarcastic opinion that no Indian would have the temerity to attack Fort Ellis because it was so near a town, horses were occasionally stolen from its immediate vicinity, and much worse would have happened without the restraining influence of the two troops of the Second United States Cavalry then composing the garrison.

15. The post office of Hayden was established there, June 21, 1876 (Mrs. Ferrell, postmistress).

16. Franklin Frederick Fridley took up a homestead there in February 1876. In 1884, he platted the town of Fridley (now Emigrant) on his land.

17. West of Strickland Creek (see Chapter 4, note 46). Because it was situated about halfway to Mammoth Hot Springs (thirty-nine miles from Bozeman), the ranch was an important stopover in pre-railroad days.

18. For a prospector by that name. The earlier name referred to an Indian trailway used by trappers as early as 1835. See Osborne Russell, *Journal of a Trapper*, A.L. Haines, ed. (Portland: Oregon Historical Society, 1955), p. 29.

19. The name Cinnabar was given the mountain because some prospector thought the iron-oxide exposed in the Devils Slide was the blood-colored ore of mercury.

20. At present Big Creek.

21. They camped on the small flat midway through Yankee Jim Canyon, where Sphinx Station now stands.

22. From the dark coloration of its rocks. The Indian trail by which this third obstacle to a direct ascent of the Yellowstone River was bypassed later became the Turkey Pen Road, used by early freighters to the mines on Clarks Fork (present Cooke City, Mont.).

23. See Chapter 3.

24. Cook et. al., *Valley of Yellowstone*, p. 22. The Grand Canyon of the Yellowstone *is* impassable through much of its fifteen-mile length, but either rim can be negotiated.

25. Their figure was 360 feet for a drop that has since been determined to be 308 feet, an error of just under 17 percent. (At the Upper Fall their percentage error was only one-third as great.)

26. Folsom thought the lake had an extent of thirty miles, a considerable improvement on the Bridger-inspired estimates of sixty miles, which appeared in earlier descriptions.

27. The stone left at that campsite on September 25, 1869, has not been recovered.

28. Their usage is evidence that the translocation of the name Burnt Hole from the Madison Valley into the Firehole River drainage was an outgrowth of the mining era (see note 7), while the alternative Death Valley is reminiscent of David B. Weaver's description of a thermal area visited by prospectors in 1867. See "The Upper Yellowstone," *Virginia City Montana Post*, Aug. 31, 1867.

29. Before it ceased its activity in 1888, this giant among the great geysers displayed an awe-inspiring energy. It is credited with eruptions to a height of 300 feet, during which siliceous debris was thrown out and the level of the Firehole River was raised appreciably. The crater continues to discharge 6 cubic feet of hot water per second.

30. Nathaniel P. Langford, *Diary of the Washburn Expedition to the Yellowstone and Firehole Rivers in the year 1870* (St. Paul: F.J. Haynes, 1905), p. xi, hereafter cited as *Diary*.

31. Cook is vague about which magazine it was.

32. William Turrentine Jackson, "The Early Exploration and Founding of Yellowstone National Park" (doctoral dissertation, University of Texas, 1940), p. 139.

33. Langford, Diary, p. xx. (*Continued on p. 367.*)

34. From "Remarks of C.W. Cook, Last Survivor of the Original Explorers of the Yellowstone Park Region, on the Occasion of His Second Visit to the Park in 53 years, During the Celebration of the Park's Golden Anniversary," official transcript, July 14, 1922, in Yellowstone National Park Reference Library.

35. Philetus W. Norris, "Meanderings of a Mountaineer, or, the Journals and Musings (or Storys) of a Rambler over Prairie (or Mountain) and Plain," manuscript prepared from newspaper clippings (1870-1875), and annotated by Norris about 1885 (original in Huntington Library, San Marino, Calif.), p. 16, hereafter cited as "Meanderings."

36. Henry, or Hank, Bottler was a half-brother whose real surname was Henselbecker.

37. How Norris thought they could be first where so many white men had already gone, and from whence the Folsom party had returned the previous fall, is beyond explanation; but it is typical of the naivete of all the explorers of 1870.

38. Norris, "Meanderings," p. 23.

39. Langford's visit at "Ogontz" is recorded in his personal diary for the years 1870 and 1871, now held with the "Langford Papers, 1707-1942," in the manuscript collection, Minnesota Historical Society, St. Paul.

40. Langford, *Diary,* p. xii. This is the diary cited in notes 30 and 33, not the "personal diary" referred to in note 39, above.

41. Langford, *Diary,* p. xiii. A photocopy of Stuart's letter is presented on pp. xiv and xv.

42. Original in collection of Montana Historical Society, Helena.

43. "Diary of Samuel T. Hauser, August 17 to September 4, 1870," Coe Collection, manuscript no. 249, Yale University Library; hereafter cited as "Diary of Hauser."

44. Aug. 18, 1870; "Departure of the Expedition."

45. It was in that unlimited game of twenty-one that Jake, as banker, doled out beans at ten cents each, then went broke when Hauser's attempt to cash in his winnings uncovered the fact that the "bank's" resources of a mere $5 were somewhat overextended. Langford later used this incident to Jake's discredit (*Diary,* pp. 18-19), but the personal diaries of Hedges and Gillette indicate that the bean incident occurred the evening of August 21.

46. "Diary of Warren Caleb Gillette (1870)," original in the collection of the Montana Historical Society, Helena. See the entry for August 22. It is appropriate to note here that Jake Smith was a person with a sharp wit and a great dislike for "stuffed shirts," which is doubtless how he classified the dignified Langford. That oversensitive individual resented Jake's unmerciful humor and later took his revenge through those "pen pricks" that illuminate

Langford's *Diary* (a diary in form only; it is really an account prepared more than thirty years later from his own notes and those of others; Langford's contribution cannot now be assessed because of the disappearance of the personal record he drew upon in 1905. The absence of that one segment of personal diary from the papers of a man who was a dedicated stringsaver leads one to suspect that the absence may be the result of a purpose rather than chance).

47. Compare Langford's *Diary*, pp. 9-10, with *The Report of Lieut. Gustavus C. Doane Upon the So-Called Yellowstone Expedition of 1870 to the Secretary of War,* as reprinted in Louis C. Cramton, *Early History of Yellowstone National Park and Its Relation to National Park Policies* (Washington, D.C.: Govt. Printing Office, 1932), p. 114, hereafter cited as *Early History.*

48. "Diary of Hauser," p. 5.

49. Walter Trumbull, "Yellowstone Papers—No. 2," *Helena Rocky Mountain Daily Gazette,* Oct. 19, 1870. Probably a bit of camp humor.

50. "Diary of Cornelius Hedges, July 6, 1870, to January 29, 1871," p. 15, original in collection of Montana Historical Society, Helena, hereafter cited as "Diary of Hedges." Doane and Langford also comment on this trailway.

51. As previously noted, this second oldest place name of the Yellowstone Park area immortalizes Johnson Gardner, an American free-trapper who took beaver on its headwaters early in the 1830s. However, that name disappeared from use following the fur-trade era, and the prospectors of the 1860s knew the stream as Warm Spring Creek. The Washburn party's reversion to the earlier usage can be traced to Jim Bridger, who gave Langford much information on the Yellowstone region while connected with the latter's wagon road enterprise in 1866; indeed, the spelling of the name as Gardiner, which originated with this party, would appear to be only a phonetic rendering of Bridger's Virginian drawl. More will be said subsequently about the attachment of this name to the town that grew up at the mouth of the river.

52. Langford noted for the twenty-fifth: "From the top of the mountain back of our camp we can see tonight a smoke rising from another peak, which some of our party think is a signal from one band of the Indians to another, conveying intelligence of our progress" (*Diary,* p. 14). More likely it was smoke from a fire set upon the heights by lightning during the storm of the twenty-third and twenty-fourth.

53. "Diary of Hauser," p. 6.

54. The Tower Fall area was the first point at which the Folsom party (1869) had encountered thermal activity, and their observations had given it a somewhat exaggerated importance.

55. See Cramton, *Early History,* p. 119.

56. Ibid., p. 120; also Langford, *Diary,* p. 22, and "Diary of Hauser," p. 7.

57. "Diary of Hauser," p. 6. His figure is considerably less than the 132 feet that is now the accepted height. Hedges describes another measurement of the fall by the packer, Elwyn Bean, who "went to the water edge at top of falls & lowered a cord with stone to ascertain the height . . . 105 feet." ("Diary of Hedges," p. 19)

58. Langford's comments on the gambling (*Diary,* pp. 18-19) should be taken with a grain of salt since his unvarying purpose was the discomfiture of

Jake Smith. As mentioned in note 45, the basis for Langford's "story" was an incident that occurred at Fort Ellis on August 21.

59. Walter Trumbull, "The Washburn Yellowstone Expedition—No. 1," *Overland Monthly* 6 (May 1871), pp. 433-34. Langford elaborates this joke in the *Diary*, pp. 21-22.

60. Cramton, *Early History*, p. 120.

61. It is a strange coincidence that the mean of the four values obtained is only 18 feet over the mountain's accepted elevation of 10,243 feet.

62. Oct. 19, 1870.

63. "Diary of Hedges," p. 22.

64. Hedges' impressions were presented to the readers of the *Helena* (Mont.) *Daily Herald* under the title of "The Great Falls of the Yellowstone," Oct. 15, 1870.

65. Langford, *Diary*, pp. 33 and 36.

66. "Diary of Hauser," p. 9; Langford, *Diary*, p. 37.

67. "Diary of Hedges," p. 24.

68. Langford, *Diary*, p. 38. Considerable confusion later developed over this name. The Folsom party had described a similar stream on the Mirror Plateau, and it was subsequently identified (wrongly) with a stream entering the Yellowstone River from the east. The dilemma of having two Alum Creeks with their mouths only a few hundred yards apart was solved when the Barlow party renamed the stream east of Yellowstone River as Sour Creek. The basis for further confusion was laid in 1871 when the Hayden Survey carelessly designated two more streams as Alum Creek: one northeast of Yellowstone Lake, commonly known even then as Pelican Creek, and one on the east shore since renamed Alluvium Creek.

69. Langford, *Diary*, pp. 40-41. See also Doane's statement in Cramton, *Early History*, p. 126.)

70. This feature has also been called Devil's Den, Devil's Workshop, Grotto, and Green Gable Grotto.

71. Langford, *Diary*, p. 47.

72. Ibid., p. 51. In his report, Doane has this to say concerning the necessity for that crude operation: "My hand was enormously swelled, and even ice water ceased to relieve the pain. I could scarcely walk at all, from excessive weakness. The most powerful opiates had ceased to have any effect." (See Cramton, *Early History*, p. 130.)

73. Dr. Merrill G. Burlingame had this information from Mrs. Doane, and a comparison of the lieutenant's handwriting before and after the operation does support that conclusion.

74. Walter Trumbull, "Yellowstone Papers," in *Rocky Mountain Weekly Gazette* (Helena, Mont.), Oct. 24, 1870. Bart Henderson had brought back some of these remarkably formed objects picked up on the lake shore in the course of his prospecting junket across the Yellowstone Plateau in the fall of 1867 (see Chapter 4). Of course, the prospectors considered they had found relics of the Aztec civilization.

75. From Doane's report; See Cramton, *Early History*, p. 131.

76. Ibid., p. 133.

77. On August 21, 1963, the author accompanied South District Naturalist Bob Johnsson and Seasonal Ranger Naturalist Lowell Biddulph in a retracement of the route by which Langford and Doane made this ascent. Through-

out, Langford's description was found to be quite accurate, except that his "granite" is dacite, a volcanic rock of similar appearance. The snowbank that occupied a shallow cirque on the east side of the saddle to a depth of thirty feet in 1870 was not permanent as Langford had supposed; we found only scattered remnants—none more than a foot or two in depth.

78. The name of that body of water survives from fur-trade times. It was shown as Bridger's Lake on the manuscript map drawn by Father DeSmet in 1851, and it appeared in the same form on the 1870 edition of W.W. deLacy's *Map of the Territory of Montana.* Thereafter it was a feature of most maps, though Dr. F.V. Hayden seems to have entertained such an antipathy for the name that he was willing to refute what his eyes had seen, stating: "The lake which had been placed on the maps as Bridgers Lake has no real existence." See his *Preliminary Report of the United States Geological Survey of Montana and Portions of Adjacent Territories. . .*(Washington, D.C.: Govt. Printing Office, 1872), p. 133.

79. That ford, which is still an important crossing place, was probably well marked by the constant passage of wild animals.

80. In a lengthy footnote to his *Diary* (p. 66), N.P. Langford mentioned the transferring of his name as follows:

> Dr. Hayden, the geologist . . . made his first visit to this region the following year (1871), and on the map which he issued in connection with his 1871 report, the name "Mount Langford" was given to another mountain far to the northeast.

Though Langford was under the impression that his name was later moved again, to the southeast, it never was, and both his and Doane's remain misplaced, just where Hayden put them in 1871.

81. "Diary of Hedges," p. 30. See also Hedges' description of this ascent in his article, "Mount Everts," *Helena Daily Herald,* Oct. 8, 1870.

82. "Diary of Hedges," p. 31.

83. Truman C. Everts, "Thirty-seven Days of Peril," *Scribner's Monthly* 3, no. 1 (November 1871), pp. 1-17, hereafter cited as "Thirty-seven Days." For a modern recapitulation, see Aubrey L. Haines, "Lost in the Yellowstone," *Montana* 22, no. 3 (Summer 1972), pp. 31-41.

84. Lieutenant Doane refers to this prominent summit as the Yellow Mountain, alluding also to the coloration of its volcanic rocks. Though Everts claims General Washburn named it for him (see "Thirty-seven Days," p. 4), the Washburn map drawn subsequent to the expedition's return attached Everts' name to a mountain in the north of the present Park; only the General Land Office map prepared by Blaine (1871) supports Everts' claim.

85. Everts, "Thirty-seven Days," p. 6.

86. Of course they were looking at Shoshone Lake, the Snake Lake of the early fur trappers that was also known for a time as deLacy's Lake from the fact that Walter Washington deLacy was first to show, on a published map, its relation to the Snake River. Following the death of General Washburn, Cornelius Hedges delivered a eulogistic address at the Methodist-Episcopal Church in Helena, Mont., January 29, 1871, in which he attempted to engraft Washburn's name upon that body of water with these words: "Between the Yellowstone Lake and the Great Geyser basin of the Madison, is also a beautiful sheet of pure, clear trout haunted water named Washburn Lake by Messrs. Folsom and Cook." (They had *not* so-named those waters, which were

barren of fish; but it sounded good.) Fortunately, little notice was taken of Hedges' attempt to further immortalize his friend, and the problem of a suitable name for those waters was not solved until 1872, when Professor Frank H. Bradley gave them the name Shoshone—thus returning in spirit to the nomenclature of the trappers, even though not exactly in their usage.

87. Doane says: "This valley is known in the wretched nomenclature of this region as the Firehole, and contains phenomena of thermal springs unparalleled upon the surface of the globe." (Cramton, *Early History*, p. 138)

88. This pond, which was midway between Old Faithful and Castle Geysers, was drained after 1921. Much of the flat to the north was a marsh, in which Lieutenant Doane noted "fresh signs of buffalo, driven out by the noise of our hasty intrusion." (Cramton, *Early History*, p. 138)

89. Trumbull, "The Washburn Yellowstone Expedition—No. 2," *Overland Monthly* 6, (June 1871), p. 493.

90. Lieutenant Doane, in Cramton, *Early History*, p. 142.

91. Langford, *Diary*, pp. 117-18.

92. "Diary of Hedges," p. 39.

93. In its issue of Sept. 23, 1870, the *Helena Herald* noted "Yellowstone Party Heard From: We are in receipt, this afternoon, of a dispatch from Virginia City, dated 23d, announcing the arrival there of N.P. Langford, of the Yellowstone expedition, who brings the sad intelligence of the loss of Truman C. Everts."

94. "Arrival of Warren C. Gillette, of the Yellowstone Expedition," Oct. 3, 1870.

95. "The Lost Man—$600 Reward Offered," *Helena Herald*, Oct. 6, 1870. Pritchett is sometimes called Pritchard.

96. For some unknown reason, he preferred to refer to himself as Jack Baronett—from Collins Jack Baronett (note that there is no terminal "e" as he signed his name); yet, his real name probably was John H. Baronett. See "Capt. Baronette," *Livingston Enterprise*, Apr. 20, 1901.

97. Theodore Gerrish, *Life in the World's Wonderland* (Biddleford, Me.; n.p., 1887), p. 238. Quoted from an interview with Baronett in the summer of 1886. The interview ended with the statement, "The mountain which bears his name is six miles from the place where I found him" (p. 240), a fact which H.M. Chittenden confirmed in a letter to Capt. George Anderson, March 28, 1895, as follows: "By the way I got an interesting item from Baronett lately. It was he, you know, who found Everts. I was surprised to learn that he found him over near the 'Devil's Cut' (or 'Gut') and not on Mt. Everts at all. He says he piled up a mound of stones where he found him. I find this statement confirmed by Norris who visited the spot when he was Supt."

98. The Turkey Pen Cabin was occupied by three old-timers—George Huston, John Evans, and one Groves. According to legend, Huston was putting up the wall logs for this building in 1867 when he was visited by several of his rough friends. The conversation went this way: "What you doin', George?" "Puttin' up a cabin." The interrogator took a long look at the unchinked poles and replied, "Huh, looks like a turkey pen!"

99. "Harry Horr's Hot Spring Claim," *Bozeman Avant Courier*, Jan. 11, 1883.

100. While many people thought Everts' mind was unbalanced by this suffering, it appears he only experienced the hallucinations that often

accompany extreme mental and physical exhaustion. Young Indians under-
going the privation and exposure of the "vision quest" were similarly affected.
    101. "The Yellowstone Expedition," *Helena Herald,* Oct. 26, 1870.
    102. "Correspondence," *Helena Herald,* Nov. 11, 1870. The same issue
carries Everts' acceptance.
    103. "The Yellowstone Banquet," *Helena Herald,* Nov. 14, 1870. For those
interested in frontier gormandizing, here is the Bill of Fare:

> Soup–Oyster
> Oysters–Raw and roasted
> Fish–Mountain Trout
> Boiled Meats–Leg of mutton with Capers, Tongue [with] Egg sauce, Ham, Chicken
> Roast Meats–Beef, Chicken, Mutton, Breast of Lamb with green peas, Breast of Veal
> [with] White sauce
> Entries–Spring Chicken, *vol a vout,* Breaded Veal and Mushrooms, Sweet Breads,
> Oyster Patties
> Vegetables–Sweet Potatoes, Green Corn, Tomatoes, Asparagus, String Beans, Collia
> Flower
> Relishes–Celery, Horseradish, Picalily Pickles, Beats
> Pastry–(Pies) Green Pear, Peach, Cranberry, Gooseberry
> (Puddings) Peach Marangue, Straberry, Custard
> Desert–Fruit Cake, Pound Cake, Jelly Cake, Citron Cake, Jelly Roll, Jelly Tarts,
> Rustar Tart Cream, Strawberry Cream, Puff Paste, Nuts, Raisens, confections
> Coffee–Mocha
> Wines–Champaigne, Imperial

He who would question the sophistication of Helena, Montana, might note the
standing advertisement of the Kan-Kan Restaurant: "All the Delicacies of the
Season are now 'en route' from New York for the Celebrated Kan-Kan,"
where, incidentally, they served Kan-Kan Kocktails.
    104. They were: "Mount Everts" (Oct. 8); "The Great Falls of the Yellow-
stone" (Oct. 15); "Hell Broth Springs" (Oct. 19); "Pictures of the Yellowstone"
(Oct. 24); "Sulphur Mountain and Mud Volcano" (Oct. 27); and "Yellowstone
Lake" (Nov. 9). An unpublished manuscript found with Hedges' personal
papers indicates he also prepared a sketch of the Upper Geyser Basin.
    105. From Cramton, *Early History,* p. 107.
    106. See "The Yellowstone Expedition," *Helena Herald,* Oct. 26, 1870.
Washburn's article, which ran in the *Herald* under the overworked heading of
"The Yellowstone Expedition," appears in the issues of Sept. 27 and 28 and
in its entirety in the issue of Sept. 30, 1870.
    107. See "Yellowstone Expedition" (Oct. 3, 1870) and "Yellowstone
Papers" (Oct. 18, 19, 24, and 31, 1870).
    108. "The Washburn Yellowstone Expedition" (June 1871), p. 496.
    109. Letter to Cornelius Hedges, February 26, 1905. This diary was kept
separately (his regular diary, now in the collection of the Minnesota Historical
Society, was left blank for the period the Washburn party was in the Yellowstone country). Such a separate and detailed record hints strongly at a special
purpose to be served, for in Langford's remaining diaries he habitually made
only the briefest entries of a mnemonic character.
    110. "Notes of Lectures given by N.P. Langford During the Winter of 1870-
71" (this title appears to have been added later), 185 pp., carefully hand-
written in ink in a ledger, using only the right-hand pages. Original now in
Yellowstone National Park Reference Library.
    111. "A Grand Lecture," *Helena Herald,* Nov. 17, 1870.

112. E.P. Oberholtzer, *Jay Cooke, Financier of the Civil War,* vol. 2 (Philadelphia: George W. Jacobs & Co., 1907), pp. 235-36.

113. "Yellowstone River," *Daily Morning Chronicle* (Washington, D.C.), Jan. 20, 1871.

114. H.M. Chittenden, *The Yellowstone National Park* (Cincinnati: Robert Clarke Co., 1895), p. 95.

115. Ibid., p. 92.

116. Langford's lecture was also covered by the *New York Herald,* Jan. 22: "Science and Art; 'Wonders of Montana—The Boiling Wells of the Yellowstone'—Discourse by Mr. N.P. Langford," and the *New York Times,* Jan. 22: "Travels in Montana." The *World* did not mention the lecture.

117. Albert Matthews, "The Word Park in the United States," *Publications of the Colonial Society of Massachusetts* 8 (April 1904), pp. 378-81.

118. Ibid., p. 380.

119. C. Frank Brockman, *Recreational Use of Wild Lands* (New York: McGraw-Hill Book Co., 1959), p. 56n. Henry James visited Niagara Falls in 1871, and his vivid impressions leave no doubt as to how bad the situation was. He said,

> There is every appearance that the spectacle you have come so far to see is to be choked in the horribly vulgar shops and booths and catchpenny artifices which have pushed and elbowed to within the very spray of the Falls, and ply their importunities in shrill competition with its thunder. You see a multitude of hotels and taverns and stores, glaring with white paint, bedizined with placards and advertisements, and decorated by groups of those gentlemen who flourish most rankly on the soil of New York and in the vicinage of hotels. . . . A side glimpse of the Falls, however, calls out your philosophy; you reflect that this may be regarded as one of those sordid foregrounds which Turner liked to use, and which may be effective as a foil; you hurry to where the roar grows louder, and I was going to say, you escape from the village. In fact, however, you don't escape from it; it is constantly at your elbow, just to the right or left of the line of contemplation. . . . You wonder, as you stroll about, whether it is altogether an unrighteous dream that with the slow progress of taste and the possible or impossible growth of some larger comprehension of beauty and fitness, the public conscience may not tend to confer upon such sovereign places of nature something of the inviolability and privacy which we are slow to bestow. From *Encyclopedia of American Facts and Dates,* 2d ed., Gorton Carruth, ed. (New York: Thomas Y. Crowell Co., 1959), p. 295.

120. In a letter of March 27, 1871, to Montana's territorial governor, J.M. Ashley, who had already lectured $500 worth on the circuit, the railroad's position was stated by Frederick Billings as follows: "Even if it were the policy of the Dept. to stimulate emigration by general lecturing there seems to be no call for any additional work in that respect just now."

121. Personal letter in the possession of James Taylor Dunn, librarian of the Minnesota Historical Society. "Tan" was the pet name by which others of the family referred to Nathaniel. Periods of illness seem to have followed each serious reverse in Langford's personal fortunes, and one biographer has suggested this might have been a neurotic response to adversity (A.W. Orton, "Some Scattered Thoughts on the Early Life of N.P. Langford," unpublished manuscript).

122. From Cramton, *Early History,* p. 18.

123. Ibid., pp. 32, 35.

124. Hayden's excellent public relations had gained him an order, signed by Secretary of War Belknap, upon all posts in the West "for such assistance as could be afforded without detriment to the service." F.V. Hayden, *Preliminary Report of the United States Geological Survey of Montana and Portions of Adjacent Territories* . . . (Washington, D.C.: Govt. Printing Office, 1872), p. 6, hereafter cited as Hayden, *Fifth Report.*

125. Cramton, *Early History,* p. 21.

126. "The Yellowstone Scientific Expedition," *Helena Daily Herald,* July 11, 1871. This finds confirmation in a letter from the files of the Geological Survey. On June 7, 1871, A.B. Nettleton wrote to Hayden on stationery of Jay Cooke & Co., Bankers, Financial Agents Northern Pacific Railroad Company seeking permission for Thomas Moran to accompany the expedition and offering to pay his expenses.

127. The details of this Barlow-Heap expedition are taken from *Report of a Reconnaissance of the Basin of the Upper Yellowstone in 1871,* U.S., 42d Cong., 2d sess., Senate Ex. Doc. 66, 1872, pp. 3-43, hereafter cited as Barlow, *Report.*

128. The name came from the stream of hot spring water that flows underground from the terraces above and appears on the margin of Gardner River in a feature called Hot River. The original name of Gardner River (see Chapter 3) was lost in the twenty-year hiatus between the end of the fur trade and the coming of the prospectors, and its fortunate renaissance is due solely to the fact that the Washburn party of 1870 had the benefit of Jim Bridger's geographical knowledge. The hot spring terraces had also been known as the White Hot Springs, White Mountain Hot Springs, Great Springs, and Sulphur Mountain, and were then about to receive the name of Mammoth Hot Springs, by which they have ever since been known.

129. A Bozeman party that arrived there a few days prior to the two expeditions described the place this way:

> About 3 o'clock we hove in sight of the camp on Warm Spring Creek, and met with a hearty reception from the denizens of that impromptu village—Chestnutville. Colonel Chestnut [of Bozeman], the founder of this embryo city, 'called us,' We 'saw him,' went in and partook of a luscious feast of any amount of elk, trout, calf, side dishes. . . .
>
> At dusk we gathered around a huge camp fire, fill our pipes, and stretching ourselves on the ground listen to the wonderful description of the country beyond, of curiosities and sights, many of which the Washburn party are ignorant of, but all these did not astonish us as much as some sights now before us. To explain, one of the party, Mr. Ben Green, of Bozeman, who had been an invalid for years, was in the circle, talking and laughing with great gusto, apparently in the full enjoyment of health.
>
> "Why man the springs did it. There is nothing like them. I am going to winter here."

From "The Mineral Springs of the Yellowstone—Wonderful Health Restoring Qualities," *Helena* (Mont.) *Rocky Mountain Weekly Gazette,* July 24, 1871.

130. H.R. Horr to Superintendent D.W. Wear, July 6, 1885; Doc. 1049, Yellowstone National Park Archives. Names that the Hayden Survey applied to features at Mammoth Hot Springs at that time are: Liberty Cap, for the pillar-like cone of an extinct hot spring at the foot of the terraces; and Blue and Main springs upon the principal terrace (see map opposite p. 64 in Hayden, *Fifth Report*).

131. For the story of this first bridge to span the Yellowstone River at any point, see Aubrey L. Haines, "The Bridge That Jack Built," *Yellowstone Nature Notes* 21, no. 1 (1947), pp. 1-4.

132. The earlier name (an unimaginative relic of the era of the prospectors) was replaced in 1885 by one honoring L.Q.C. Lamar, a Mississippian who was secretary of the interior from March 6, 1885, to January 16, 1888.

133. The mountain was named by P.W. Norris in 1880 from the marked resemblance to a riding saddle when viewed from the Lamar Valley. Seen from the shore of Yellowstone Lake between Gull and Rock points, the effect is that of a huge, prone figure, which has raised the fanciful image of a sleeping giant.

134. Barlow, *Report,* p. 14.

135. Lord Dunraven gave Hayden Valley its name in 1874, over the protest of Dr. Hayden, according to S.P. Panton. See "Early Days in Yellowstone Recalled by N.P. Surveyor," *Wolf Point* (Mont.) *News,* Nov. 23, 1939.

136. The name of this first boat to sail the waters of Yellowstone Lake is used here as it appears in Hayden's *Fifth Report,* p. 96. However, a woodcut opposite page 2 in his *Twelfth Report* (1878) shows the name as *Annie,* which can only be an engraver's error.

137. Barlow, *Report,* p. 26. Due to an error in identification, the original Comet is now called Daisy Geyser, and a nearby feature has the name Comet.

138. Hayden, *Fifth Report,* p. 116.

139. The present form of the lake's name comes from Captain Barlow's *Report,* p. 33; however H.M. Chittenden believes it should be Hart Lake, for Hart Hunney, a fur trapper who is supposed to have frequented the area prior to 1852. Truman C. Everts, the unfortunate member of the Washburn party who camped among the hot springs on the shore of this lake while lost, called it Bessie Lake for his grown daughter (see note 83).

140. This ungenerous aspect of Hayden's nature occasionally appeared where place names were concerned. Perhaps his earlier association with Jim Bridger led to an antipathy for the old scout.

141. In 1878 the Hayden Survey renamed this feature Turret Mountain, transferring the early name to a peak on the summit of the range, four miles to the north.

142. See p. 124 and note 80.

143. Hayden, *Fifth Report,* p. 139.

144. Even that small remnant seems to have disappeared during the intervening years, leaving no basis for evaluating his work.

145. "Around Montana," *Helena Daily Herald,* July 10, 1871.

146. Letter in Record Group 57, National Archives, Washington, D.C. *Records of the Department of the Interior,* Geological Survey, Letters received by F.V. Hayden, 1871. A.B. Nettleton was Jay Cooke's office manager at Philadelphia. The Judge Kelley to whom Nettleton credited the suggestion was William Darrah Kelley, a Philadelphia jurist who was a Republican representative from Pennsylvania in all the Congresses from March 4, 1861, until his death on January 9, 1890. Judge Kelley was a supporter of the transcontinental railroad idea from 1845, when he joined Asa Whitney in an attempt to further that dreamer's proposal to span the continent with iron rails. The judge was influential in the affairs of Jay Cooke & Co. because of previous services to the firm. He was always a broad-visioned man.

CHAPTER 6

1. From the issue of March 7, 1872 (vol. 14, no. 349), p. 153.

2. Hiram M. Chittenden was first to call attention to the national park idea by devoting a chapter of his book, *The Yellowstone National Park* (Cincinnati: Robert Clarke Co., 1895), pp. 87-97, to a discussion of its origin and realization.

3. Hans Huth, "Yosemite: The Story of an Idea," *Sierra Club Bulletin* 33, no. 3 (Mar. 1948), p. 47, hereafter cited as "Yosemite." It should be noted that Chittenden was unaware of the extent to which the American people had been prepared for an acceptance of the national park idea; thus, he oversimplified his conclusions. This is particularly true of his identification of the origin of the idea with the creation of Yellowstone National Park.

4. Ralph Waldo Emerson, "Nature" (1844) in *Harvard Classics,* vol. 5 (New York: P.F. Collier & Son, 1910), p. 236.

5. *The Standard History of the World,* vol. 1 (Cincinnati: Standard Historical Society, 1931), pp. 251, 253, 268.

6. Wilhelmina Jashemski, "Pompeii" in *Natural History* 73, no. 10 (December 1964), p. 39.

7. James Fisher, "The Idea of Wilderness," *The Listener* (London) 67, no. 1726 (April 26, 1962), p. 722.

8. *The Encyclopedia Britannica,* vol. 6 (1929), pp. 124-28.

9. Huth, "Yosemite," pp. 61-62.

10. Roderick Nash, "The American Wilderness in Historical Perspective," *Forest History* 6, no. 4 (Winter 1963), p. 3.

11. Genesis 1:28.

12. A listing of such conservation measures is omitted because it adds nothing to the park story. Information on early conservation measures is contained in the series of articles by various authors in *American Forests* 41, no. 9 (September 1935), pp. 416-539.

13. Donald Culross Peattie, *Green Laurels* (New York: Literary Guild, 1936), p. 271.

14. Huth, "Yosemite," pp. 48-59.

15. Harold D. Hampton has provided a good analysis of the content of Transcendentalism, which he calls

a mixture of faith, philosophy, mysticism and religion. Its origins have been traced to the revolutionary thought of Rousseau, the idealism of Kant, the literary romanticism of Coleridge, Wordsworth, and Carlyle, and to the mysticism of Oriental writers. Its theological base was that of Unitarianism; for its psychological base it drew from the various elements of Yankee shrewdness, self-reliance and conscience.

From "Conservation and Cavalry: A Study of the Role of the United States Army in the Development of a National Park System, 1886-1917" (doctoral dissertation, University of Colorado, 1965), p. 6, hereafter cited as *"Conservation and Cavalry."* This thesis has recently been revised and published as *How the U.S. Cavalry Saved our National Parks* (Bloomington: Indiana University Press, 1971), 246 pp.

16. Henry David Thoreau, "Walking," in *Harvard Classics,* vol. 28, p. 407.

17. These excerpts have been drawn from the essays "Walking" and "Nature" cited in notes 4 and 16.

18. Walter J. Black, *The Best of Ralph Waldo Emerson* (New York: Walter J. Black, 1941), p. xvii.

19. Huth, "Yosemite," pp. 51-55.

20. Suzanne T. Cooper, "Summertime Revisited," *American Heritage* 14, no. 4 (June 1963), pp. 36-37.

21. Huth, "Yosemite," p. 60.

22. This suggestion is said to have appeared first in the *New York Daily Commercial Advertiser* in 1833, but the text quoted is from the book, *Letters and Notes on the Manners, Customs, and Conditions of the North American Indians*, vol. 1 (New York, 1843), p. 262.

23. From "Chesuncook," *Atlantic Monthly* 2 (August 1858), p. 134.

24. Huth, "Yosemite," p. 62. Bryant was not only a New England transcendentalist, but also the author of "Thanatopsis," "The Burial," "A Forest Hymn," and "An Indian at the Burial Place of His Father," so that his rationale paralleled the scenic cemetery movement if it did not stem from it.

25. The Central Park project was not considered finished in accordance with the original plan of Olmsted and Calvert Vaux until 1876. See *The Encyclopedia of American Facts and Dates*, Gorton Carruth, ed. (New York: Thomas Y. Crowell Co., 1959), p. 309.

26. Act of June 30, 1864 (U.S., *Statutes at Large*, vol. 13, p. 325).

27. Hampton, "Conservation and Cavalry," p. 27.

28. Cited in note 26 above. See also Aubrey L. Haines, *Yellowstone National Park: Its Exploration and Establishment* (Washington, D.C.: Govt. Printing Office, 1974), p. 111, hereafter cited as *Yellowstone*.

29. A note from the *Helena Herald*, reprinted in the *Bozeman Avant Courier*, Nov. 9, 1871, p. 2, c. 3. From an entry in Langford's personal diary, it is evident that he left Helena on November 2, just five days after Hayden received the letter from Nettleton. Governor William R. Marshall, the husband of Langford's sister Abigail, was a promoter of the Northern Pacific Railroad, as well as a principal source of Langford's political influence.

30. For example, the written notes for the lectures conclude with, "What, then, is the one thing wanting to render this remarkable region of natural wonders accessible? I answer, the very improvement now in process of construction, the N.P.R.R., by means of which, the traveller . . . will be enabled to reach this region from the Atlantic seaboard within 3 days, and can see all the wonders I have described." (From "Notes of Lectures given by N.P. Langford During the Winter of 1870-71," pp. 184-85, original manuscript in Yellowstone National Park Reference Library. The magazine article ends somewhat similarly with "By means of the Northern Pacific Railroad, which will doubtless be completed within the next three years, the traveler will be able to make the trip to Montana from the Atlantic seaboard in three days . . . in order to behold with their own eyes the wonders here described." From "The Wonders of the Yellowstone," *Scribner's Monthly*, June 1871, p. 128.

31. This reply to an inquiry not now available is among the boxed but unclassified records stored in the Como warehouse of the Northern Pacific Railroad.

32. William H. Goetzmann, *Exploration and Empire* (New York: Alfred A. Knopf, 1966), p. 508.

33. Hampton, "Conservation and Cavalry," pp. 46-47.

34. Albert Matthews, "The Word Park in the United States," *Publications of the Colonial Society of Massachusetts* 8 (April 1904), pp. 380-81. According to Clagett, "In December, 1871, Mr. Langford came to Washington and remained there for some time, and we two counseled together about the park project." See N.P. Langford, *Diary of the Washburn Expedition to the Yellowstone and Firehole Rivers in the Year 1870* (St. Paul: F.J. Haynes, 1905), p. xxi, hereafter cited as *Diary*.

35. Louis C. Cramton, *Early History of Yellowstone National Park and Its Relation to National Park Policies* (Washington, D.C.: Govt. Printing Office, 1932), p. 31, hereafter cited as *Early History*.

36. "The Cataracts and Geysers of the Upper Yellowstone—Why They Should be Given in Perpetuity to Montana," *Bozeman Avant Courier*, Dec. 7, 1871.

37. Hampton, "Conservation and Cavalry," p. 45.

38. In a letter of July 14, 1894, to William R. Marshall, then secretary of the Minnesota Historical Society, Clagett wrote:

> Since the passage of this bill there have been so many men who have claimed the exclusive credit for its passage, that I have lived for twenty years, suffering from a chronic feeling of disgust whenever the subject was mentioned. So far as my personal knowledge goes, the first idea of making it a public park occurred to myself; but from information received from Langford and others, it has always been my opinion that Hedges, Langford, and myself formed the same idea, about the same time, and we all three acted together in Montana.

Published in Langford, *Diary*, p. xxii. The foregoing statement is groundless, and it must be added that other statements made by Delegate Clagett on the subject of the Yellowstone Act have been shown to be faulty. See Cramton, *Early History*, pp. 28-31.

39. Ibid., p. 30.

40. See U.S., *Congressional Globe*, 42d Cong., 2d sess., December 18, 1871, part 1, pp. 159 and 199. The introduction of these bills is discussed by the author in *Yellowstone*, pp. 113-14.

41. Langford, *Diary*, p. xxii.

42. "Geyser Land," *Deer Lodge* (Mont.) *New North-West*, Dec. 28, 1871, p. 2.

43. Quoted by *Helena Herald*, Jan. 16, 1872, from *Virginia City* (Nev.) *Territorial Enterprise*, Jan. 7, 1872.

44. See "A Natural Wonder," quoted from *Santa Cruz* (Cal.) *Sentinel* in *Bozeman Avant Courier*, Jan. 25, 1872, p. 1, c. 3.

45. Cramton, *Early History*, p. 25.

46. U.S., *Congressional Globe*, 42d Cong., 2d sess., January 30, 1872, part 1, p. 697.

47. Cramton, *Early History*, p. 29. This was probably a result of his preoccupation with legislation to accomplish removal of the Flathead Indians from the Bitterroot Valley and with several railroad bills vital to Samuel Hauser's business schemes.

48. Ibid., pp. 25-26. Hayden resorted to the same arguments used to promote the Yosemite legislation, that is, "The entire area comprised within the limits of the reservation contemplated in this bill is not susceptible of cultivation with any degree of certainty, and the winters would be too severe for stock-raising." Also, he did not think the area contained "any mines or minerals of any value." See Hampton, "Conservation and Cavalry," p. 52.

49. "A National Park," in *Helena Herald,* Jan. 31, 1872, p. 1, c. 1.

50. See *Scribner's Monthly,* February 1872, p. 396.

51. Cramton, *Early History,* p. 25.

52. Ibid., pp. 26, 54.

53. U.S., *Congressional Globe,* 42d Cong., 2d sess., February 27, 1872, part 2, p. 1243.

54. Cramton, *Early History,* p. 37.

55. "Our National Park," February 28, 1872, p. 1, c. 2. This article gave the Yellowstone its sobriquet of "Wonderland" (from the story "Alice's Adventures Underground" written by Charles Ludwidge Dodgson in July 1862 for the amusement of a small companion while on an outing on an English river. The Oxford University Press published the story in 1866 as *Alice's Adventures in Wonderland,* and that title gave the new park a nickname before it had a formal designation). It is good to be able to add that the little girl Dodgson wrote his story for visited Yellowstone National Park as a grown-up and seemed almost as thrilled as if she had really gotten into that peculiar place through the rabbit hole.

56. Cramton, *Early History,* p. 28.

CHAPTER 7

1. *Helena* (Mont.) *Rocky Mountain Gazette,* quoted in the *Helena Daily Herald,* Mar. 1, 1872. The *Gazette* file is incomplete.

2. "The Park Again," Mar. 9, 1872, p. 2.

3. Quoted in *Deer Lodge* (Mont.) *New North-West,* Mar. 16, 1872.

4. Editorial comment, May 1872, p. 120.

5. Louis C. Cramton, *Early History of Yellowstone National Park and Its Relationship to National Park Policies* (Washington, D.C.: Govt. Printing Office, 1932), p. 37, hereafter cited as *Early History.*

6. Earl of Dunraven, *The Great Divide* (London: Chatto and Windus, 1876), p. 13, hereafter cited as *Great Divide.*

7. H.R. Horr, J.C. McCartney, and J. Shaffer to Hon. Columbus Delano, secretary of the interior, March 28, 1872. Record Group 57, microfilm 62, reel 1, National Archives, Washington, D.C.

8. Cramton, *Early History,* pp. 37-38.

9. N.P. Langford, *Annual Report of the Superintendent of the Yellowstone National Park for the year 1872,* U.S., 42d Cong., 3d sess., Senate Ex. Doc. 35, February 4, 1873, pp. 1-2, hereafter cited as *Annual Report [year].*

10. Cramton, *Early History,* p. 38.

11. Manuscript notebook marked "A.C. Peale U.S.G.S. 2," covering the period July 21 to October 24, 1872, p. 165.

12. Ibid., pp. 163-64.

13. From *Deer Lodge New North-West,* June 15, 1872.

14. Langford to Columbus Delano, secretary of the interior, July 27, 1872. Record Group 48, microfilm 62, reel 1, National Archives, Washington, D.C.

15. Hiram M. Chittenden made a particular study of this matter and arrived at the conclusion that the Stevenson-Langford ascent of 1872 *did* reach the summit of the Grand Teton. Those who are interested will find a lucid exposition of his reasoning in "The Ascent of the Grand Teton," a letter to the editor of *Forest and Stream,* February 14, 1899.

16. The official height of the Grand Teton was taken as 13,858 feet, which was computed from gradienter observations by Rudolf Hering. See F.V.

Hayden, *Sixth Annual Report of the United States Geological Survey of the Territories. . . 1872* (Washington, D.C.: Govt. Printing Office, 1873), p. 222, hereafter cited as *Sixth Annual Report.* However, Langford's value of 13,762 feet is only 4 feet below the present accepted elevation. See "The Ascent of Mount Hayden," *Scribner's Monthly* 6, no. 2 (June 1873), p. 148. Other values given by members of the Hayden Survey for the elevation of the Grand Teton were James Stevenson's aneroid reading of 13,400 feet and A.C. Peale's value of 13,600 feet, for which no method is given.

17. The two best accounts of this meeting are Langford's, in "The Ascent of Mount Hayden," pp. 151-52; and an article written by Joseph Savage, "The Wonders of the Yellowstone," in *Western Home Journal* (Lawrence, Kan.), Sept. 19, 1872, hereafter cited as "Wonders."

18. Savage, "Wonders." A photograph taken by W.H. Jackson on this occasion shows 61 men, 35 of whom are identified by name. This was probably the only occasion on which so many of the men of the Hayden Survey were gathered in one place.

19. Though frequently referred to as Lord Blackmore, he was not of the nobility, and the title is improper. See Herbert O. Brayer, "Exploring the Yellowstone with Hayden, 1872," *Annals of Wyoming* 14, no. 4 (October 1942), pp. 253-98.

20. Hayden, *Sixth Annual Report,* p. 121. A later survey raised the elevation of this peak to 11,111 feet, but recent measurements have shown that Gannett's determination was correct. See the U.S.G.S. Quadrangle Sheet, *Miner, Mont.-Wyo.* (N5400-W11045/15), edition of 1955.

21. William Blackmore, personal diary no. 7, p. 104, photocopy in Yellowstone National Park Reference Library.

22. Ibid., p. 88.

23. "Botanicus" [Robert Adams, Jr.], "The Geological Survey," *Philadelphia Inquirer,* Sept. 19, 1872, p. 7.

24. From the diaries of A. Bart Henderson, 1866-72, p. 107, transcript in Yellowstone National Park Reference Library, hereafter cited as Henderson diaries.

25. *Bozeman Avant Courier,* Sept. 13, 1871.

26. Ibid., Oct. 26, 1871.

27. Ibid., Nov. 2, 1871.

28. Henderson diaries, entry for October 7, 1872, p. 110.

29. *Bozeman Avant Courier,* July 11, 1873.

30. Hayden, *Sixth Annual Report,* p. 230.

31. Hayden says, "We have named this stream in honor of General [Colonel] John Gibbon, United States Army, who has been in military command of Montana for some years, and has, on many occasions, rendered the survey most important services." See *Sixth Annual Report,* p. 55. Colonel Gibbon's experiences in the Yellowstone region appear in "The Wonders of the Yellowstone," *Journal of the American Geographical Society of New York* 5 (1874), pp. 112-37, hereafter cited as "Wonders."

32. From "W.H. Holmes, Artist to the Survey of the Territories," consisting of notes abstracted by him from the 1872 diary, June 25, 1928, p. 14, copy in Yellowstone National Park Reference Library.

33. An item in the *Bozeman Avant Courier,* Aug. 22, 1872.

34. See Hayden, *Sixth Annual Report,* pp. 243-44. Thus, they were at last

able to correct the erroneous impression gained by members of the Hayden
Survey of 1871, when it was thought that Shoshone Lake was at the head of
Firehole River; instead they found, as Captain W.W. deLacy had, that it
drained to Lewis Lake which in turn fed into Snake River and thus was tributary to westward-flowing waters of Jackson Hole.

35. See *Bozeman Avant Courier*, Oct. 17 and Nov. 28, 1872.

36. Hayden, *Sixth Annual Report*, p. 92.

37. *Annual Report*, 1872, p. 3.

38. "From the Far West," *Western Home Journal*, July 2, 1872 (date-line).

39. Ibid.

40. From "James A. Garfield's Diary of a trip to Montana in 1872" in
Hakola's *Frontier Omnibus* (Helena, Mont.: Historical Society of Montana,
1962), p. 355.

41. Joseph Savage, "From the Yellowstone Expedition," *Western Home
Journal*, Aug. 1, 1872.

42. Personal diary for 1872, pp. 154-57.

43. Dunraven, *Great Divide*, p. 43.

44. Item in the *Bozeman Avant Courier*, Oct. 3, 1873.

45. "For the Mammoth Hot Springs," in *Bozeman Avant Courier*, July 10,
1874.

46. Harry J. Norton, *Wonderland Illustrated; or, Horseback Rides Through
the Yellowstone National Park* (Virginia City, Mont.: Harry J. Norton, 1873),
p. 73.

47. Edwin J. Stanley, *Rambles in Wonderland; or, Up the Yellowstone and
Among the Geysers and Other Curiosities of the National Park* (New York:
D. Appleton and Co., 1878), pp. 60-61, hereafter cited as *Rambles*.

48. Hayden, *Twelfth Annual Report of the United States Geological and
Geographical Survey of the Territories*, part 2 (Washington, D.C.: Govt.
Printing Office, 1883), p. 488.

49. Dunraven, *Great Divide*, p. 194.

50. Gibbon, "Wonders," p. 118.

51. "Sudden Death," *Bozeman Avant Courier*, Sept. 18, 1874.

52. "To Wonderland," *Bozeman Avant Courier*, Dec. 20, 1872. Jessup's
departure from Bozeman is recorded in the issue of Mar. 21, 1873.

53. See *Bozeman Avant Courier*, Sept. 12, 1873.

54. William Ludlow, *Report of a Reconnaissance from Carroll, Montana
Territory, on the Upper Missouri to the Yellowstone National Park, and
Return, Made in the Summer of 1875* (Washington, D.C.: Govt. Printing Office,
1876), p. 26, hereafter cited as *Report*.

55. "Killing Bear by Wholesale," *Bozeman Avant Courier*, Sept. 26, 1873.

56. T.E.S., "Across the Continent II—The National Park," *Woodstock
Letters*, vol. 11 (Maryland: Woodstock College, 1882), pp. 29-30.

57. From *Bozeman Avant Courier*, Sept. 26, 1873.

58. William A. Jones, *Report Upon the Reconnaissance of Northwestern
Wyoming, Including Yellowstone National Park, Made in the Summer of
1873* (Washington, D.C.: Govt. Printing Office, 1875), 331 pp.

59. Ibid., p. 20. As previously noted, both the trappers and the prospectors
had crossed these mountains frequently.

60. From the unpublished "Autobiography of Paul LeHardy," p. 99. The
Yellowstone National Park Reference Library has a copy of the portion
covering his Yellowstone experiences.

61. Issue of Aug. 15, 1873.

62. Hiram M. Chittenden, "Improvement of Yellowstone National Park, Including the Construction, Repair and Maintenance of Roads and Bridges," Appendix KKK, in *Annual Report of the Chief of Engineers for 1903* (Washington, D.C.: Govt. Printing Office, 1903), p. 2937.

63. One result of the field work is worth noting: Ludlow's *very* accurate determination of the heights of the two falls of the Yellowstone River. He found the Upper to be 110 feet and the Lower 310 feet—high by one and two feet, respectively.

64. Ludlow, *Report,* p. 38.

65. *The Yellowstone National Park* (Cincinnati: Robert Clarke Co., 1895), p. 105.

66. *Bozeman Avant Courier,* Aug. 20, 1875.

67. "Important Cut-off," *Bozeman Avant Courier,* Aug. 7, 1874.

68. P.W. Norris, "Meanderings of a Mountaineer, or, The Journals and Musings (*or* Storys) of a Rambler Over Prarie (*or* Mountain) and Plain," p. 33, an unpublished manuscript of Norris' adventures, probably prepared in 1885; original in the Huntington Library, San Marino, Calif., hereafter cited as "Meanderings."

69. Stanley, *Rambles,* 5th ed. (Nashville, Tenn.: Publishing House of the Methodist Episcopal Church, South, 1898), p. 91.

70. Norris, "Meanderings," pp. 35-36.

71. W.E. Strong, *A Trip to the Yellowstone National Park in July, August, and September, 1875* (Washington, D.C., 1876), p. 80. Secretary Balknap's public image was so damaged by his involvement in the post-trader scandal of the Grant administration that this attempt to honor him came to nothing. Frank Island retained the name given it in 1871 by Henry Elliot, artist of the Hayden Survey, for his brother.

72. Ibid., pp. 92-93. Also, reprint edited by Richard A. Bartlett (Norman: University of Oklahoma Press, 1968), vol. 39 in "Western Frontier Library" series, pp. 104-6.

73. The Yellowstone adventure occupies pp. 193-347 in the first edition (London: Chatto and Windus).

74. Gannett says: "This I have named Dunraven Peak, in honor of the Earl of Dunraven, whose travels and writings have done so much towards making this region known to our cousins across the water." Hayden, *Twelfth Annual Report,* p. 478.

75. Details are from Doane's diary; typescript available in Yellowstone National Park Reference Library as "Expedition of Lt. G.C. Doane, 1876-77," 44 pp. Also published under the same title in *Campfire Tales of Jackson Hole,* Merlin K. Potts, ed. (Moose, Wyo.: Grand Teton Natural History Association, 1960), pp. 20-37. Orrin H. and Lorraine Bonney present this expedition in considerable detail in *Battle Drums and Geysers* (Chicago: Swallow Press, 1970), pp. 439-587. A typescript of Sergeant Fred E. Server's diary, "Diary of a Trip through Yellowstone Park, down the Snake River to Fort Hall and back to Fort Ellis, 1876-77," 27 pp., was provided by Montana State University Library, Bozeman.

76. Affidavit of Matthew McGuirk, May 18, 1891. See Doc. 1149, Yellowstone National Park Archives; also, "McGuirk's Medicinal Springs," *Yellowstone Nature Notes* 21, no. 2 (1947), pp. 22-23.

77. N.P. Langford to secretary of interior, September 7, 1874. Record Group 48, microfilm 62, reel 1, item 42, National Archives, Washington, D.C.

78. Langford, *Annual Report*, 1872, p. 3.

79. B.F. Potts to Hon. N.P. Langford, November 27, 1873. Record Group 48, microfilm 62, reel 1, item 20, National Archives, Washington, D.C.

80. As reported in *Bozeman Avant Courier*, Dec. 12, 1873.

81. Gilman Sawtell to George G. Boutwell, January 5, 1874 (forwarded to the secretary of the interior). Record Group 48, microfilm 62, reel 1, item 25, National Archives, Washington, D.C.

82. H.R. Horr to secretary of the interior, May 25, 1874. Record Group 48, microfilm 62, reel 1, item 37, National Archives, Washington, D.C.

CHAPTER 8

1. P.W. Norris to J.C. McCartney, April 19, 1877. Record Group 79, National Archives, Washington, D.C.

2. John S. Gray, "Last Rites for Lonesome Charley Reynolds," in *Montana* 13, no. 3 (Summer 1963), p. 43.

3. P.H. Sheridan and W.T. Sherman, *Reports of Inspections Made in the Summer of 1877* (Washington, D.C.: Govt. Printing Office, 1878), p. 32, hereafter cited as Sherman Reports.

4. P.W. Norris, *Report Upon the Yellowstone National Park, to the Secretary of the Interior, for the Year 1877* (Washington, D.C.: Govt. Printing Office, 1877), p. 837.

5. Letter to the secretary of war, from Fort Ellis, August 19, 1877, in Sherman Reports, p. 35.

6. "T.E.S." [Thomas Ewing Sherman], "Across The Continent, II—The National Park," *Woodstock Letters* 11 (1882), pp. 27-28.

7. Sherman's letter of August 19, 1877, in Sherman Reports, p. 37.

8. Unless otherwise noted, the details used for the reconstruction of subsequent events within the Park are taken from the following sources: Frank Carpenter, *The Wonders of Geyser Land,* as reprinted by Guie and McWhorter under the title *Adventures in Geyser Land* (Caldwell, Idaho: Caxton Printers, 1935), 319 pp. (hereafter cited as *Adventures*), including accounts by Yellow Wolf, John Shively, Mrs. Cowan, Duncan McDonald, and notes by Colonel J.W. Redington; "Life with the Nez Perce—The Capture and Adventures of [Shively]," *Deer Lodge* (Mont.) *New North-West*, Sept. 14, 1877, p. 2, c. 4; Andrew J. Weikert, "Journal of the Tour Through the Yellowstone National Park, in August and September 1877," *Contributions to the Historical Society of Montana*, vol. 3 (Helena, 1900), pp. 154-74, hereafter cited as Weikert, "Journal"; S.G. Fisher, "Journal of S.G. Fisher," *Contributions*, vol. 2, pp. 269-82, hereafter cited as Fisher, "Journal"; "Wonderland, Scenes of Bloodshed," interview with Ben Stone, *Bozeman Avant Courier*, Sept. 6, 1877, p. 3, c. 4, and Sept. 13, 1877, p. 2, c. 3; "Stewart's Story, interview with Jack Stewart," *Bozeman Avant Courier*, Sept. 27, 1877, p. 3, c. 3.

9. George F. Cowan was a veteran of the Civil War, in which he served as a sergeant in Company B, 4th Wisconsin Cavalry. That service and his training as a lawyer undoubtedly contributed to his bluntness. At the time of this incident, he was thirty-five years old.

10. Poker Joe was a Nez Perce-French half-breed who had gained his nickname in the Bitterroot Valley because of his love of gambling. His people knew him as Chief *Ho-ho-to,* or Lean Elk, and he had added his band of six lodges to the hostile array as it passed through western Montana. He commanded the retreat after the Battle of Big Hole, where Chief Looking Glass lost face through failure to anticipate General Gibbon's dawn attack on the village.

11. Weikert, "Journal," p. 159.

12. Fisher, "Journal," p. 272.

13. Dietrich was a Helena music teacher and probably the least rugged individual of his party.

14. Carpenter, *Adventures,* p. 86.

15. Oliver O. Howard, *Nez Perce Joseph* (Boston: Lee and Shepherd, 1881), pp. 239-40.

16. Weikert, "Journal," p. 174.

17. Item in *Bozeman Avant Courier,* Oct. 25, 1877, p. 3.

18. Item in *Bozeman Avant Courier,* Nov. 1, 1877, p. 3.

19. Issue of October 18, 1877, pp. 233-34.

20. Diary of W.H. Holmes, copy in Yellowstone National Park Reference Library. See entry for August 27, p. 25.

21. S. Weir Mitchell, "Through the Yellowstone Park to Fort Custer," *Lippincott's Magazine* 26 (July 1880), p. 38.

CHAPTER 9

1. Hiram M. Chittenden, *The Yellowstone National Park* (Cincinnati: Robert Clarke Co., 1895), p. 304, hereafter cited as *Yellowstone.*

2. P.W. Norris, *Report upon the Yellowstone National Park, to the Secretary of the Interior, for the Year 1878* (Washington, D.C.: Govt. Printing Office, 1879), pp. 979-80, hereafter cited as *Report for [year].*

3. "The Cunning Fox Caught at Last," *Bozeman Avant Courier,* Mar. 20, 1879.

4. Norris, *Report for 1878,* p. 981. See also Aubrey L. Haines, "The Bridge That Jack Built," *Yellowstone Nature Notes* 21, no. 1 (1947), pp. 1-4.

5. Norris, *Report for 1880,* p. 7.

6. Chittenden, *Yellowstone,* p. 131.

7. Norris, *Report for 1879,* p. 5. An elaborate description of the "Norris blockhouse" can be found on pages 23-25 of P.W. Norris, *Fifth Annual Report of the Superintendent of the Yellowstone National Park* (Washington, D.C.: Govt. Printing Office, 1881), hereafter cited as *Fifth Annual Report.* A floor plan is included.

8. Norris, *Report for 1879,* pp. 6, 9.

9. Norris, *Fifth Annual Report,* p. 69.

10. Norris, *Report for 1880,* pp. 6-8. Included are a number of sketches of features in the Hoodoo Basin.

11. "A newsy and Interesting Letter from the Yellowstone," *Bozeman Avant Courier,* Aug. 19, 1880.

12. "The Yellowstone Park—its management," *Bozeman Avent Courier,* Sept. 30, 1880.

13. "Another 'Faber-Pusher' after Col. Norris," *Bozeman Avant Courier,* Sept. 9, 1880.

14. Norris, *Report for 1881,* p. 7.

15. P.W. Norris, "Prehistoric Remains in Montana, between Fort Ellis and the Yellowstone River," in *Annual Report of the Board of Regents of the Smithsonian Institution . . . 1875* (Washington, D.C.: Govt. Printing Office, 1880), pp. 327-28.

16. Norris, *Report for 1878*, p. 985.

17. Norris, *Report for 1881*, p. 27.

18. Norris, *Report for 1877*, p. 843.

19. "Report of Gamekeeper," included in Norris, *Report for 1881*, pp. 62-63.

20. *15,000 Miles by Stage*, 2d ed. (New York: G.P. Putnam's Sons, 1915), p. 259.

21. Biographical statement by G.W. Marshall in about the year 1887, from a manuscript in the Bancroft Library, Berkeley, California.

22. Ibid., pp. 3-4.

23. Statement of J.C. McCartney, May 15, 1891. Filed as Doc. 1137, Yellowstone National Park Archives.

24. "Eastern Montana Boom," *Bozeman Avant Courier*, Feb. 26, 1880.

25. Norris, *Report for 1880*, p. 4.

26. *Bozeman Avant Courier*, Aug. 5, 1880.

27. Ibid., Aug. 12, 1880.

28. Ibid., Aug. 19, 1880.

29. Letters Received, Department of the Interior, Appointments Division, Record Group 48, National Archives, Washington, D.C.

30. *Report of Lieut. General P.H. Sheridan, of his expedition through the Big Horn Mountains, Yellowstone National Park, etc.*, dated September 20, 1881 (Washington, D.C.: Govt. Printing Office, 1882), p. 21.

31. *Bozeman Avant Courier*, Sept. 30, 1880.

32. Ibid., Dec. 23, 1880.

33. Ibid., Mar. 3, 1881.

34. Ibid., Aug. 25, 1881.

35. Ibid., Jan. 26, 1882.

36. Ibid., Feb. 2, 1882.

37. Ibid., Feb. 9, 1882.

38. Ibid., Feb. 16, 1882.

39. Excerpts from this article in *Bozeman Avant Courier*, May 4, 1882.

CHAPTER 10

1. *Bozeman Avant Courier*, June 8, 1882.

2. Hiram M. Chittenden, *The Yellowstone National Park* (Cincinnati: Robert Clarke Co., 1895), pp. 131-32.

3. Stephens to secretary of interior, May 18, 1882. Doc. 13, Yellowstone National Park Archives.

4. Secretary of interior to Conger, June 2, 1882. Doc. 12, Yellowstone National Park Archives.

5. P.H. Conger, *Annual Report of the Superintendent of the Yellowstone National Park, to the Secretary of the Interior, for the Year 1882* (Washington, D.C.: Govt. Printing Office, 1882), p. 3, hereafter cited as *Annual Report for [year]*. Stephens remained several days, filling in the new superintendent on affairs in the Park and turning the property over to him; then he retired to the ranch he had purchased from the Hendersons (the present game ranch on Stephens Creek, north of Gardiner, Mont.).

6. *Bozeman Avant Courier,* June 1, 1882.

7. "Thoughts of Old," *Livingston* (Mont.) *Post,* Jan. 11, 1900.

8. Entry in the Cottage Hotel Register for December 7, 1885, p. 255. Item 141, Yellowstone National Park Archives.

9. *Bozeman Avant Courier,* Sept. 28, 1882.

10. Ibid., Dec. 14, 1882.

11. P.H. Sheridan, Jas. F. Gregory, and W.H. Forwood, *Report of an Exploration of Parts of Wyoming, Idaho and Montana, in August and September, 1882* (Washington, D.C.: Govt. Printing Office, 1882), pp. 17-18.

12. *Bozeman Avant Courier,* Sept. 7, 1882.

13. Ibid., Dec. 14, 1882.

14. Ibid., Oct. 5, 1882.

15. "The Park Grab," *Forest and Stream,* January 4, 1883, p. 441.

16. "Newsy letter from upper Yellowstone," *Bozeman Avant Courier,* Apr. 6, 1882.

17. E.V. Smalley, comp., *Northern Pacific Railroad; Book of Reference, for the use of the directors and officers of the company* (New York: E. Wells, Sacket & Rankin, 1883), p. 435. The name change is also mentioned in the *Bozeman Avant Courier,* Oct. 19, 1882.

18. S.P. Panton, "Early Days in Yellowstone recalled by N.P. Surveyor," *Wolf Point* (Mont.) *News,* Nov. 23, 1939, hereafter cited as "Early Days."

19. From the data on territorial post offices supplied by Jefferson Jones to Jack Ellis Haynes, December 1952.

20. Panton, "Early Days."

21. *Bozeman Avant Courier,* Oct. 19, 1882.

22. Ibid., May 17, 1883.

23. Ibid., May 24, 1883.

24. C.M. Stephens' sale of his ranch to George Huston and Joe Keeney is noted in the *Bozeman Avant Courier,* Apr. 19, 1883; notice of their transfer of the property to C.T. Hobart appears in the *Livingston* (Mont.) *Enterprise,* Dec. 1, 1883.

25. Frederick Webb Hodge, *Handbook of American Indians,* part 2 (Washington, D.C.: Govt. Printing Office, 1910), p. 378.

26. The issue of Dec. 21, 1882. The extent of Bozeman's pique at being short-circuited as an outfitting point for park tours by the Northern Pacific Railroad's selection of the Yellowstone River Valley for its park branch line, rather than the West Gallatin, is evident in the editor's comment that "Congressional light on the subject may reveal a somewhat gigantic scheme to enrich a few persons at the expense of the government and travelling public."

27. "The Senate Bill," *Forest and Stream,* January 11, 1883., p. 462.

28. *Bozeman Avant Courier,* Dec. 28, 1882.

29. *Early History of Yellowstone National Park and its Relation to National Park Policies* (Washington, D.C.: Govt. Printing Office, 1932), p. 42.

30. *Bozeman Avant Courier,* Feb. 22, 1883.

31. Ibid., Feb. 15, 1883.

32. The foregoing account is from G.L. Henderson, "Thoughts of Old," in *Livingston Post,* Jan. 11, 1900; with supplemental information from *Bozeman Avant Courier,* Apr. 12, 1883.

33. *Annual Report for 1883,* p. 7.

34. Eighth Legislative Assembly, Territory of Wyoming, 1884. *Laws,*

chapter 103, Yellowstone National Park (approved March 6, 1884).

35. *Bozeman Avant Courier,* Mar. 22, 1883.

36. The sale of liquor at the hotel was prohibited by the Department of the Interior on November 15, 1884. See *Livingston Enterprise,* Nov. 15, 1884.

37. "In Yellowstone Park," *Chicago Weekly News,* Aug. 23, 1883.

38. From Thomas Henry Thomas, "Yellowstone Park Illustrated," *The Graphic,* Aug. 11, 1888, p. 158, hereafter cited as "Yellowstone." Mr. Thomas visited Yellowstone Park during September and October of 1884.

39. From *Livingston Enterprise,* July 18, 1885.

40. George Thomas, "My recollections of the Yellowstone Park," an account of events in the spring and summer of 1883. Manuscript in the Yellowstone National Park Reference Library, p. 7, hereafter cited as "Recollections."

41. T.H. Thomas, "Yellowstone," p. 190.

42. "Old Yellowstone Days," *Harper's Monthly Magazine,* March 1936, p. 474.

43. Charles T. Whitmell, "The American Wonderland, the Yellowstone National Park," *Report and Transactions of the Cardiff Naturalists Society,* vol. 17 (Cardiff, Wales: South Wales Printing Works, 1886), p. 93, hereafter cited as "American Wonderland."

44. W.H. Dudley, *The National Park From the Hurricane Deck of a Cayuse, or the Liederkranz Expedition to Geyserland* (Butte City, Mont.: Frederick Loeber, 1886), p. 102.

45. Ibid., p. 98. The Concord was a type of stagecoach designed by the Abbott-Downing Co. of Concord, Vermont; the vehicle was slung on thorough-brace-leather straps that acted like springs.

46. "In Yellowstone Park," *Chicago Weekly News,* Aug. 23, 1883.

47. *Livingston Enterprise,* Aug. 17, 1883.

48. Ibid., Aug. 23, 1883.

49. Ibid., Aug. 23, 1883.

50. Ibid., Aug. 31, 1883.

51. Ibid., Aug. 27, 1883.

52. George Thomas, "Recollections," p. 19.

53. Information received from Mrs. Julia S. Brackett during an interview at the Park Hotel, Livingston, Montana, November 9, 1950.

54. *Livingston Enterprise,* Aug. 23, 1883.

55. *Fifth Avenue to Alaska* (New York: G.P. Putnam's Sons, 1884), p. 246.

56. *Livingston Enterprise,* Aug. 11, 1883.

57. Ibid., Aug. 13, 1883.

58. Ibid., Sept. 1, 1883.

59. Whitmell, "American Wonderland," p. 95.

60. "About Hotel Waiters," *Livingston Enterprise,* Oct. 3, 1883.

61. George Thomas, "Recollections," p. 22.

62. See the interview with Mrs. Brackett (note 53) and also George Thomas, "Recollections," pp. 16-18.

63. The first burial in this cemetery was that of Mary J. Foster, who died June 10, 1883, at the age of thirty-three years. Though her grave remains the best marked of the fourteen burials known to have been made there, nothing has ever come to light concerning the circumstances of her death, and the best guess is that she was a waitress or domestic employed at the National Hotel at the time of its opening. Considerable information is available concerning six

of the burials and it is evident that the cemetery was something between a boothill and a potter's field. (Data from personal notes.)

64. Details of the killing of John Zutavern and the capture of his murderer have been taken from the *Livingston Enterprise,* Aug. 23, 24, and 25, 1883.

65. Ibid., Sept. 4, 1883.

66. Reprinted from *Bismarck Tribune,* by the *Livingston Enterprise,* Nov. 22, 1883.

67. *Livingston Enterprise,* Sept. 5, 1885.

68. Ibid., Aug. 23, 1883.

69. Ibid., Aug. 29, 1883.

70. Ibid., Sept. 6, 1883.

71. "The Redman's Welcome to Villard," *Livingston Enterprise,* Mar. 28, 1884.

72. *Livingston Enterprise,* Dec. 29, 1883.

73. Ibid., Jan. 8, 1884.

74. Ibid., Sept. 3, 1883.

75. "Major Conger asked to resign," *Livingston Enterprise,* July 19, 1884. There is considerable additional information in the issue of July 21.

CHAPTER 11

1. Bergan Evans, comp., *Dictionary of Quotations* (New York: Delacorte Press, 1968), p. 42.

2. *Livingston Enterprise,* July 18, 1885.

3. U.S., *Statutes at Large,* vol. 22, p. 626.

4. The *St. Paul* (Minn.) *Pioneer Press* for June 2, 1883, announced eight appointments made that day: William C. Cannon of Montgomery, Indiana; William Chambers, Jr., of Adair County, Iowa; James H. Dean of Frederick, Maryland; Edmund L. Fish of Fish's Eddy, New York; George L. Henderson of Iowa; a man named McGowan who did not accept; Daniel E. Sawyer of Pine Island, Minnesota, and J.W. Weimer of Topeka, Kansas. Three men added later to complete the force were Samuel S. Erret of Santa Fe, New Mexico, Samuel D. Leech of New York, and William Houghton Terry of Danville, Illinois.

5. *Livingston Enterprise,* June 6, 1883. Persons returning from the Park later complained that "the salaried government guides sent here a few weeks ago are levying taxes upon tourists for acting as guides." See issue of August 31.

6. *Livingston Enterprise,* June 29, 1883.

7. Issues of Sept. 20 and Dec. 20, 1883.

8. Hiram Martin Chittenden, *The Yellowstone National Park* (Cincinnati: Robert Clarke Co., 1895), p. 135, hereafter cited as *Yellowstone.*

9. "Report on the National Park," *Livingston Enterprise,* Feb. 4, 1884.

10. This structure stood on the site of the present coffee shop operated by Hamilton Stores, Inc.

11. U.S., 48th Cong., 1st sess., Senate Ex. Doc. 207, July 5, 1884, p. 5, item no. 3.

12. Doc. 1555, Yellowstone National Park Archives. This order is undated but its issuance in the fall of 1883 is supported by Sawyer's assumption of the administrative responsibilities when Conger retired to his Iowa home to pass the winter of 1883-84.

13. U.S., 48th Cong., 1st sess., Senate Ex. Doc. 47, January 9, 1884.

14. Ex. Doc. 207 (cited in note 11); pp. 7-9, enclosures no. 1-3 and item no. 11. This document includes the letter of January 5, 1884. The two statements of R.P. Miles included with the foregoing are most enlightening in regard to Conger's character.

15. Secretary of the interior to Supt. Conger, January 18, 1884. Doc. 78, Yellowstone National Park Archives.

16. G.L. Henderson to Supt. Conger, June 11, 1884. Doc. 1454, Yellowstone National Park Archives.

17. Secretary of the interior to Supt. Conger, September 22, 1884. Doc. 132, Yellowstone National Park Archives.

18. Doc. 30, Yellowstone National Park Archives.

19. Report of Assistant James H. Dean, July 14, 1884. Doc. 1359, Yellowstone National Park Archives.

20. Doc. 1356, Yellowstone National Park Archives.

21. Report of Assistant James H. Dean, September 3, 1884. Doc. 1354, Yellowstone National Park Archives.

22. Report of Assistant James H. Dean, August 14, 1884. Doc. 1356, Yellowstone National Park Archives.

23. Report of Assistant James H. Dean, August 26, 1884. Doc. 1355, Yellowstone National Park Archives.

24. Report of Assistant J.W. Weimer, July 20, 1884. Doc. 1590, Yellowstone National Park Archives.

25. Report of Assistant J.W. Weimer, July 27, 1884. Doc. 1588, Yellowstone National Park Archives.

26. Report of Assistant J.W. Weimer, August 10, 1884. Doc. 1586, Yellowstone National Park Archives.

27. Report of Assistant Lorenzo D. Godfrey, August 15, 1884. Doc. 1437, Yellowstone National Park Archives.

28. Report of Assistant J.W. Weimer, December 27, 1883. Doc. 1424, Yellowstone National Park Archives.

29. Report of Assistant Edmund I. Fish, May 12, 1884. Doc. 1420 Yellowstone National Park Archives.

30. Report of Assistant Edmund I. Fish, November 11, 1884. Doc. 1431, Yellowstone National Park Archives.

31. *Bozeman* (Mont.) *Avant Courier*, Feb. 22, 1883. The essential text of the regulation, as published locally, follows:

> Washington, Jan. 15, 1883. *To the Superintendent of the Yellowstone National Park:* Sir . . . the regulations . . . are amended so as to prohibit absolutely the killing, wounding or capturing [of] buffalo, bison, moose, elk, black tailed or white tailed deer, mountain sheep, Rocky Mountain goat, antelope, beaver, otter, martin, fisher, grouse, prairie chicken, pheasant, fool hen, partridge, quail, wild goose, duck, robin, meadow lark, thrush, gold finch, flicker or yellow hammer, black bird, oriel, jay, snow bird, or any of the small birds commonly known as singing birds . . . in regard to fishing [they are] amended so as to prohibit the taking of fish by means of seines, nets, traps, or by the use of drugs, or any explosive substances or compounds, or in any other way than hook and line . . . all cutting of timber . . . except upon special permission . . . is prohibited. II. N. Teller, Secretary.

32. Report of Assistant Edmund I. Fish, May 18, 1884. Doc. 1417, Yellowstone National Park Archives.

33. Report of Assistant Edmund I. Fish, June 4, 1884. Doc. 1418, Yellowstone National Park Archives.

34. Supt. Conger to the secretary of the interior, January 5, 1884; included in the secretary's reply to the Senate resolution of May 28, 1884, 48th Cong., 1st sess., Senate Ex. Doc. 207.

35. Report of Assistant Edmund I. Fish, April 29, 1884. Doc. 1421, Yellowstone National Park Archives.

36. Report of Assistant William Chambers, November 14, 1883. Doc. 1346, Yellowstone National Park Archives.

37. Report of Assistant William H. Terry, December 15, 1883. Doc. 1569, Yellowstone National Park Archives.

38. Report of Assistant William H. Terry, November 26, 1883. Doc. 1571, Yellowstone National Park Archives.

39. Report of Assistant William Chambers, December 6, 1883. Doc. 1343, Yellowstone National Park Archives.

40. Report of Assistant William H. Terry, December 11, 1883, Doc. 1517, Yellowstone National Park Archives.

41. Report of Assistant G.L. Henderson, June 28, 1884. Doc. 1453, Yellowstone National Park Archives.

42. W.H. Dudley, *The National Park from the Hurricane Dick of a Cayuse, or the Liederkranz Expedition to Geyserland* (Butte City, Mont.: Frederick Loeber, 1886), p. 41, hereafter cited as *National Park.*

43. See note 41.

44. Supt. Conger to the secretary of the interior, March 28, 1884; included in the secretary's reply to the Senate resolution of May 28, 1884, 48th Cong., 1st sess., Senate Ex. Doc. 207, p. 11.

45. Conger to secretary of interior, April 13, 1884; ibid., p. 13.

46. *Livingston Enterprise,* Sept. 19, 1883.

47. Ibid., Mar. 11, 1884.

48. Ibid., Mar. 12 and Mar. 21, 1884.

49. Ibid., Mar. 21, 1884.

50. Ibid., May 8 and May 12, 1884.

51. Ibid., June 12, 1884.

52. "Settled at last," *Livingston Enterprise,* July 5, 1884.

53. *Livingston Enterprise,* July 26, 1884.

54. Chittenden, *Yellowstone,* p. 136.

55. *Annual Report of the Superintendent of the Yellowstone National Park to the Secretary of the Interior, for the Year 1883* (Washington, D.C.: Govt. Printing Office, 1883), p. 7.

56. *Livingston Enterprise,* Aug. 29, 1883.

57. *Laws Appertaining to the Yellowstone National Park* (Cheyenne, Wyo.: Leader Printing Co., 1884), pp. 8-16.

58. Dudley, *National Park,* p. 46.

59. Thomas Henry Thomas, "Yellowstone Park Illustrated," *Graphic,* August 11, 1888.

60. *Livingston Enterprise,* Aug. 8, 1885.

61. Secretary of the interior to Supt. Conger, August 16, 1884. Doc. 158, Yellowstone National Park Archives.

62. Doc. 1411, Yellowstone National Park Archives.

63. "The Park Arrests," *Livingston Enterprise*, Dec. 20, 1884.

64. "Trouble in the Park," *Livingston Enterprise*, Dec. 13, 1884. Tate and Scott were not included in the notice previously given because they had been specifically refused the use of park lands and could not argue that they had been permitted to settle there, as did Jackson, Cutler, and Rutherford. See Docs. 117 and 118, Yellowstone National Park Archives.

65. "That Horse," *Livingston Enterprise*, Feb. 21, 1885.

66. "News from the Mountains," *Livingston Enterprise*, March 14, 1885.

67. "Superintendent Carpenter's Resignation Asked For," *Livingston Enterprise*, Apr. 18, 1885.

68. "The Charges Against Carpenter," *Livingston Enterprise*, Aprl 18, 1885.

69. "The Other Side of the Story," *Livingston Enterprise*, Apr. 18, 1885.

70. Harold Duane Hampton, "Conservation and Cavalry: A Study of the Role of the United States Army in the Development of a National Park System, 1886-1917" (doctoral dissertation, University of Colorado, 1965), p. 132, hereafter cited as "Conservation and Cavalry." The editor of the *Livingston Enterprise* mentioned his satisfaction with the certainty that Joslyn, who had "always been the tool of the Park Improvement Company," would be swept away when the Democrats took over the administration on March 4, 1885.

71. *Livingston Enterprise*, June 20, 1885.

72. Report of Assistant J.W. Weimer, November 7, 1885. Doc. 1580, Yellowstone National Park Archives.

73. Report of Assistant J.W. Weimer, July 18, 1885. Doc. 1584, Yellowstone National Park Archives.

74. Report of Assistant J.W. Weimer, August 29, 1885. Doc. 1581, *Yellowstone* National Park Archives.

75. "Rounding Up Offenders," Aug. 15, 1885.

76. *Livingston Enterprise*, Aug. 22, 1885.

77. Ibid., Nov. 14, 1885.

78. Ibid., Nov. 7, 1885.

79. Aug. 22, 1885.

80. "An Unextinguished Camp Fire," *Livingston Enterprise*, Aug. 20, 1885.

81. Louis C. Cramton, *Early History of Yellowstone National Park and its Relation to National Park Policy* (Washington, D.C.: Govt. Printing Office, 1932), p. 44.

82. Aug. 29, 1885. The locale is incorrectly given; the event occurred at the Lower Geyser Basin.

83. Hampton, "Conservation and Cavalry," p. 136.

84. Ibid., p. 135.

85. *Livingston Enterprise*, Aug. 15, 1885.

86. Ibid., Jan. 29, 1884. At that time morphine was sold without any restriction whatever, and as it often varied in concentration, fatalities from its use were not uncommon.

87. *Livingston Enterprise*, May 4, 1884.

88. Report of Assistant Supt. Henderson, August 10, 1884. Doc. 1448, Yellowstone National Park Archives. See also numerous items in *Livingston Enterprise*, Aug. 28 to Sept. 22, 1883.

89. *Livingston Enterprise*, Feb. 23 and 26, 1884.

90. The Haynes Picture Shops, established by Frank J. Haynes in 1884, were operated by him until January 1, 1916, when their management passed

to Jack Ellis Haynes. After Jack Haynes' death on May 12, 1962, the operation was continued by Mrs. J.E. Haynes until the fall of 1967, when the business in the Park was sold to Hamilton Stores, Inc.

---

33. (*Continued from p. 342.*) The information furnished General Washburn by David E. Folsom (then employed in Washburn's General Land Office at Helena, Mont.) is entered in ink on the first nine pages of the pocket diary Washburn carried through the Yellowstone wilderness August 17 to September 24, 1870. This information consists of a verbatim transcript of David E. Folsom's 1869 diary (Sept. 9 through Oct. 4 – five pages) and a set of travel instructions for following the route of the 1869 expedition – four pages. Washburn's own diary entries are all in pencil, adding another twenty-six pages to the text.

INDEX

ABOUT THE AUTHOR

Aubrey L. Haines was born in Portland, Oregon. After graduating from the University of Washington in 1938, he was employed as a park ranger in Yellowstone National Park. Following four years of service with the U.S. Army Corps of Engineers during World War II, he returned to Yellowstone and in 1946 was appointed assistant park engineer. Additional schooling in 1949–1950 at the University of Montana led to a degree of Master of Science, and in 1959 he was promoted to the newly created position of park historian, remaining in that post until retirement in 1969. Since that time, Mr. Haines has served as a consultant on historical research for the National Park Service and the Bureau of Outdoor Recreation and has continued writing on historical subjects.

His other books include *Mountain Fever: Historic Conquests of Rainier* (Oregon Historical Society), *Historic Sites Along the Oregon Trail* (The Patrice Press), *An Elusive Victory: The Battle of the Big Hole* (Glacier Natural History Association), and *Yellowstone Place Names: Mirrors of History* (University Press of Colorado). He also is the editor of Osborne Russell's Journal of a Trapper (University of Nebraska Press).

Mr. Haines lives with his wife in Tucson, Arizona.

PUBLISHER'S NOTE

The Yellowstone Story continues in Volume II, in chapters as follows: ORDER OUT OF CHAOS—the army takes over. THE RAILROAD BOGEY—railroad monopoly attempts to penetrate the Park. THE YELLOWSTONE CRUSADE—the military undertakes wildlife management. ON THE GRAND TOUR—the "carriage trade" and "sagebrushers" patronize park hotels and tent camps. FORT YELLOWSTONE IDYLL—management by officers and soldiers proves effective. THE WORK OF THE CORPS—the Army Corps of Engineers, notably Captain H.M. Chittenden, develops roads and landmarks. THE COMING OF THE AUTO—the Park is democratized with advent of the motor car. ENTER THE RANGERS—under the National Park Service, the ranger force is created for protection and interpretation. GREATER YELLOWSTONE—efforts to enlarge the Park result in forest reserves and the Grand Teton National Park. WORDS OVER WATER—commercial uses of water and power are successfully banned from the Park in the 1930s. ASPHALT AND CABINS—visitor facilities and roads are improved prior to World War II. THROUGH A GLASS, DARKLY—after revitalization through Mission 66, there remains the need to protect park values by controlled visitation.

See Volume II, also, for a complete appendix of biographical, legislative, and statistical information, and for sources used.